# THE GREAT NAVIGATORS OF THE EIGHTEENTH CENTURY

Hoisting the signals for triangulation.

CELEBRATED TRAVELS AND TRAVELLERS

# THE GREAT NAVIGATORS

## OF THE

# EIGHTEENTH CENTURY

## BY JULES VERNE

WITH 96 ILLUSTRATIONS BY PHILIPPOTEAUX, BENETT, AND MATTHIS,
AND 20 MAPS BY MATTHIS AND MORIEU.

*TRANSLATED FROM THE FRENCH.*

New Hanover County Public Library
201 Chestnut Street
Wilmington, NC 28401

This edition published in 2001 by
Gerald Duckworth & Co. Ltd.
61 Frith Street, London W1D 3JL
Tel: 020 7434 4242
Fax: 020 7434 4420
Email: enquiries@duckworth-publishers.co.uk
www.ducknet.co.uk

First published in 1880 by
Sampson, Low, Marston, Searle & Rivington

A catalogue record for this book is available
from the British Library

ISBN 0 7156 3086 5

Typeset by Derek Doyle & Associates, Liverpool
Printed in Great Britain by
Bookcraft (Bath) Limited, Midsomer Norton, Somerset

# PUBLISHERS' NOTE.

This volume forms the second of three volumes under the *general title* of CELEBRATED TRAVELS AND TRAVELLERS. The first volume, already published, is entitled The EXPLORATION OF THE WORLD, and covers a period in the World's History extending from B.C. 505, to the close of the xviith century. The present volume extends over the xviiith century, and the third volume will give an account of the GREAT EXPLORERS AND TRAVELLERS OF THE XIXTH CENTURY.

1880

# THE
# GREAT NAVIGATORS OF THE 18TH CENTURY

## LIST OF MAPS AND ILLUSTRATIONS

REPRODUCED IN FACSIMILE FROM THE ORIGINAL DOCUMENTS,
GIVING THE SOURCES WHENCE THEY ARE DERIVED.

### PART THE FIRST

PART THE SECOND

# LIST OF WORKS CONSULTED

ANSON (Geo., Lord). "Voyage round the World in 1740-44."

BARROW (Sir John). "Travels into the Interior of Southern Africa." London, 1806.

BOUGAINVILLE (Com. de). "Voyage round the World, 1766-69." Paris, 1771.

BRUCE (James). "Travels in Abyssinia between 1768-73." Edin. 1813.

COOK (Captain James). "Second Voyage to the South Pole and Round the World, 1772-75." London, 1777.

COOK and KING (Captain James). "Third Voyage to the Pacific Ocean, 1776-80." London, 1784.

GROSIER (L'Abbé). "China, General Description of the Empire." Paris, 1735.

HAWKESWORTH (Dr. J.) "Account of the Voyages of Discovery in the Southern Hemisphere by Commodore Byron, and Captains Wallis, Carteret, and Cook." London, 1773.

KENNEDY. "New Zealand." London, 1873.

LABILLARDIÈRE (T.). "Voyage in Search of La Pérouse, 1791-93." Paris, 1801.

MASON. "Costumes of China." London, 1800.

PARK (Mungo). "Travels in Africa." London, 1815-16.

PARKINSON (S.). "Voyage to the South Seas." London, 1784.

PÉRON (F.) and FREYCINET (Louis d'), "Voyage to Australasia, 1800-4." Paris, 1808.

PÉROUSE (J. Fr. G. de la). "Voyage round the World, 1785-88." Paris, 1798.

"TRANSACTIONS of the French Academy of Sciences," Vol. 7. Paris.

VAILLANT (Fr. le). "Travels in the Interior of Africa." Paris, 1790.

VANCOUVER (Capt. G.). "Voyage of Discovery to the North Pacific Ocean, and round the World, from 1790-95." London, 1798.

# TABLE OF CONTENTS

## FIRST PART

### CHAPTER I.

### CHAPTER II.
### CAPTAIN COOK'S PREDECESSORS.

## CHAPTER III.

### CAPTAIN COOK'S FIRST VOYAGE.

## CHAPTER IV.

### CAPTAIN COOK'S SECOND VOYAGE.

## CHAPTER V.
### CAPTAIN COOK'S THIRD VOYAGE.

# SECOND PART.

## CHAPTER I.
### FRENCH NAVIGATORS.

## CHAPTER II.

CHAPTER III.

CHAPTER IV.

# PART I.

# CHAPTER I.

## I.

### ASTRONOMERS AND CARTOGRAPHERS.

Cassini, Picard and La Hire – The arc of the Meridian and the Map of France – G. Delisle and D'Anville – The Shape of the Earth – Maupertuis in Lapland – Cond.mine at the Equator.

Before we enter upon a recital of the great expeditions of the eighteenth century, we shall do well to chronicle the immense progress made during that period by the sciences. They rectified a crowd of prejudices and established a solid basis for the labours of astronomers and geographers. If we refer them solely to the matter before us, they radically modified cartography, and ensured for navigation a security hitherto unknown.

Although Galileo had observed the eclipses of Jupiter's satellites as early as 1610, his important discovery had been rendered useless by the indifference of Governments, the inadequacy of instruments, and the mistakes committed by his followers.

In 1660 Jean Dominique Cassini published his "Tables of the Satellites of Jupiter", which induced Colbert to send for him the following year, and which obtained for him the superintendence of the Paris Observatory.

In the month of July, 1671, Philippe de La Hire went to Uraniborg in the Island of Huen, to take observations for the situation of Tycho Brahe's Observatory. In that spot he calculated with the assistance of Cassini's Tables, and with an exactitude never before obtained, the difference between the longitudes of Paris and Uraniborg.

The Academy of Sciences sent the astronomer Jean Richter the same year to Cayenne, to study the parallaxes of the sun and moon, and to determine the distance of Mars and Venus from the earth. This voyage, which was entirely successful, was attended with unforeseen consequences, and resulted in inquiries shortly after entered into as to the shape of the earth.

Richter noticed that the pendulum lost two minutes, twenty-eight seconds at Cayenne, which proved that the momentum was less at this place than at Paris. From this fact, Newton and Huyghens deduced the flatness of the Globe at the Poles. Shortly afterwards, however, the computation of a terrestrial degree given by Abbé Picard, and the determination off the Meridional arc, arrived at by the Cassinis, father and son, led scientific men to an entirely different result, and induced them to consider the earth an elliptical figure, elongated towards the polar regions. Passionate discussions arose from this decision, and in them originated immense undertakings, from which astronomical and mathematical geography profited.

Picard undertook to estimate the space contained between the parallels of Amiens and Malvoisine, which comprises a degree and a third. The Academy, however, decided that a more exact result could be obtained by the calculation of a greater distance, and determined to portion out the entire length of France, from north to south, in degrees. For this purpose, they selected the meridian line which passes the Paris Observatory. This gigantic trigonometrical undertaking was commenced twenty years before the end of the seventeenth century, was interrupted, and recommenced, and finally finished towards 1720.

At the same time Louis XIV., urged by Colbert, gave orders for the preparation of a map of France. Men of science undertook voyages from 1679 to 1682, and by astronomical observations found the position of the coasts on the Ocean and Mediterranean. But even these undertakings, Picard's computation of the Meridional arc, the calculations which determined the latitude and longitude of certain large cities in France, and a map which gave the environs of Paris in detail with geometrical exactitude, were still insufficient data for a map of France.

As in the measurement of the Meridional arc, the only course to adopt was to cover the whole extent of the country with a network of triangles. Such was the basis of the large map of France which justly bears the name of Cassini.

The result of the earlier observations of Cassini and La Hire was to restrict France within much narrower limits than had hitherto been assigned to her.

Desborough Cooley in his "History of Voyages", says, "They deprived her (France) of several degrees of longitude in the length of her western coast, from Brittany to the Bay of Biscay. And in the same way retrenched about half a degree from Languedoc and La Provence. These alterations gave rise to a "bon-mot". Louis the

XIV., in complimenting the Academicians upon their return, remarked, 'I am sorry to see, gentlemen, that your journey has cost me a good part of my kingdom!".

So far, however, cartographers had ignored the corrections made by astronomers. In the middle of the seventeenth century, Peiresc and Gassendi had corrected upon the maps of the Mediterranean a difference of "five hundred" miles of distance between Marseilles and Alexandria. This important rectification was set aside as nonexistent until the hydrographer, Jean Matthieu de Chazelles, who had assisted Cassini in his labours, was sent to the Levant to draw up a coast-chart for the Mediterranean.

"It was sufficiently clear", say the Memoirs of the Academy of Sciences, that the maps unduly extended the Continents of Europe, Africa, and America, and narrowed the Pacific Ocean between Asia and Europe. These errors had caused singular mistakes. During M. de Chaumont's voyage, when he went as Louis XIV.'s ambassador to Siam, the pilots, trusting to their charts, were mistaken in their calculations, and both in going and in returning went a good deal further than they imagined. In proceeding from the Cape of Good Hope to the island of Java they imagined themselves a long way from the Strait of Sunda, when in reality they were more than sixty leagues beyond it. And they were forced to put back for two days with a favourable wind to enter it. In the same way upon their return voyage from the Cape of Good Hope to France, they found themselves at the island of Flores, the most western of the Azores, when they conceived themselves to be at least a hundred and fifty leagues eastward of it. They were obliged to navigate for twelve days in an easterly direction in order to reach the French coast. As we have already said, the corrections made in the map of France were considerable. It was recognized that Perpignan and Collioures more especially were far more to the east than had been supposed. To gain a fair idea of the alteration, one has only to glance at the map of France published in the first part of the seventh volume of the memoirs of the Academy of Sciences. All the astronomical observations to which we have called attention are noted in it, and the original outline of the map, published by Sanson in 1679, makes the modification apparent.

Cassini was right in saying that cartography was no longer at its height as a science. In reality Sanson had blindly followed the longitudes of Ptolemy, without taking any note of astronomical observations. His sons and grandsons had simply re-edited his maps as they were completed, and other geographers followed the same course.

William Delisle was the first to construct new maps, and to make use of modern discoveries. He arbitrarily rejected all that had been done before his time. His enthusiasm was so great that he had entirely carried out his project at the age of twenty-five. His brother, Joseph Nicolas, who taught astronomy in Russia, sent William materials for his maps. At the same time his younger brother, Delisle de la Ceyére, visited the coast of the Arctic Ocean, and astronomically fixed the position of the most important points. He embarked on board De Behring's vessel and died at Kamtchatka. That was the work of the three Delisles, but to William belongs the glory of having revolutionized geography.

"He succeeded," says Cooley, "in reconciling ancient and modern computations, and in collecting an immense mass of documents. Instead of limiting his corrections to any one quarter of the earth, he directed them to the entire globe. By this means he earned the right to be considered the founder of modern geography.

Peter the Great, on his way to Paris, paid a tribute to his merit by visiting him, and placing at his disposal all the information he himself possessed of the geography of Russia.

Could there be a more conclusive testimony to his worth than this from a stranger? and if French geographers are excelled in these days by those of Germany and England, is it not consolatory and encouraging to them to know, that they have excelled in a science, in which they are now struggling to regain their former superiority?

Delisle lived to witness the success of his pupil, J.B. d'Anville. If the latter is inferior to Adrian Valois in the matter of historical science, he deserved his high fame for the relative improvement of his outlines, and for the clear and artistic appearance of his maps.

"It is difficult," says M.E. Desjardins, in his *Géographie de la Gaule Romaine*, "to understand the slight importance which has been attributed to his works as a geographer, mathematician, and draughtsman." The latter more especially do justice to his great merit. D'Anville was the first to construct a map by scientific methods, and that of itself is sufficient glory. In the department of historical geography, d'Anville exhibited unusual good sense in discussion, and a marvellous topographical instinct for identifications, but it is well to remember that he was neither a man of science, nor even well versed in classic authorities. His most beautiful work is his map of Italy, the dimensions of which, hitherto exaggerated, extended from the east to the west in accordance with the ideas of the ancients.

In 1735, Philip Buache, whose name as a geographer is justly celebrated, inaugurated a new method in his chart of the depths of the English Channel, by using contour levels to represent the variations of the soil.

Ten years later d'Après De Mannevillette published his *Neptune Oriental*, in which he rectified the charts of the African, Chinese, and Indian coasts. He added to it a nautical guide, which was the more precious at this period, as it was the first of the kind. Up to the close of his life he amended his manual, which served as a guide for all French naval officers during the latter part of the eighteenth century.

Of English astronomers and physicists, Halley was the chief. He published a theory of "Magnetic Variations," and a History of the Monsoons, which gained for him the command of a vessel, that he might put his theory into practice.

That which d'Après achieved for the French, Alexander Dalrymple accomplished for the English. His views, however, bordered on the hypothetical, and he believed in the existence of an Antarctic Continent.

He was succeeded by Horsburgh, whose name is justly dear to navigators.

We must now speak of two important expeditions, which ought to have settled the animated discussion as to the shape of the earth. The Academy of Sciences had despatched a mission to America, to compute the arc of the meridian at the Equator. It was composed of Godin, Bouguer, and La Condamine.

It was decided to entrust a similar expedition to the North to Maupertuis.

"If," said this scientific man, "the flatness of the earth be not greater than Huyghens supposed, the margin between the degrees of the meridian measured in France, and the first degrees of the meridian near the Equator, would not be too considerable to be attributed to possible errors of the observers, or to the imperfection of instruments. But, if the observation can be made at the Pole, the difference between the first degree of the meridian nearest the equatorial line, and, for example, the sixty-sixth degree, which crosses the polar circle, will be great enough, even by Huyghens' hypothesis, to show itself irresistibly, and beyond the possibility of miscalculation, because the difference would be repeated just as many times as there are intermediate degrees.

The problem thus neatly propounded ought to have obtained a ready solution both at the Pole and the Equator – a solution which would have settled the discussion, by proving Huyghens and Newton to be right.

The expedition embarked in a vessel equipped at Dunkerque. In addition to Maupertuis, it comprised De Clairaut, Camus, and Lemonnier, Academicians, Albey Outhier, canon of Bayeux, a secretary named Sommereux, a draughtsman, Herbelot, and the scientific Swedish astronomer, Celsius.

When the King of Sweden received the members of the mission at Stockholm, he said to them, "I have been in many bloody battles, but I should prefer finding myself in the midst of the most sanguinary, rather than join your expedition".

Certainly, it was not likely to prove a party of pleasure. The learned adventurers were to be tested by difficulties of every kind, by continued privation, by excessive cold. But what comparison can be made between their sufferings, and the agonies, the trials and the dangers which were to be encountered by the Arctic explorers, Ross, Parry, Hall, Payer, and many others.

Damiron in his Eulogy of Maupertuis, says, "The houses at Tornea, north of the Gulf of Bothnia, almost in the Arctic Circle, are hidden under the snow. When one goes out, the air seems to pierce the lungs, the increasing degrees of frost are proclaimed by the incessant crackling of the wood, of which most of the houses are built. From the solitude which reigns in the streets, one might fancy that the inhabitants of the town were dead. At every step one meets mutilated figures, people who have lost arms or legs from the terrible severity of the temperature. And yet, the travellers did not intend pausing at Tornea."

Now-a-days these portions of the globe are better known, and the region of the Arctic climate thoroughly appreciated, which makes it easier to estimate the difficulties the inquirers encountered.

They commenced their operations in July, 1736. Beyond Tornea they found only uninhabited regions. They were obliged to rely upon their own resources for scaling the mountains, where they placed the signals intended to form the uninterrupted series of triangles.

Divided into two parties in order thus to obtain two measurements instead of one, and thereby also to diminish the chance of mistakes, the adventurous savants, after inconceivable hairbreadth

Pierre Louis Moreau de Maupertuis.

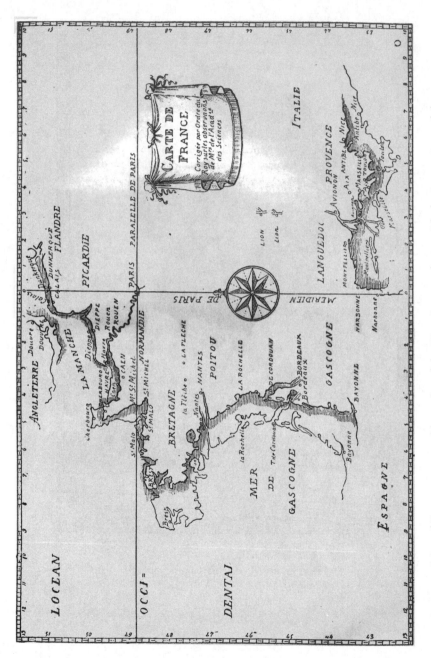

Map of France, corrected by order of the King, in accordance with the instructions of the Members of the Academy of Sciences. (Facsimile of early engraving)

escapes, of which an account can be found in the Memoirs of the Academy of Sciences for 1737, and after incredible efforts, decided that the length of the meridian circle, comprised between the parallels of Tornea and Kittis was 55,023 fathoms and a half. Thus below the Polar circle, the meridian degree comprised a thousand fathoms more than Cassini had imagined, and the terrestrial degree exceeded by 377 fathoms the length which Picard has reckoned it between Paris and Amiens.

The result, therefore, of this discovery (a result long repudiated by the Cassinis, both father and son), was that the earth was considerably flattened at the poles.

Voltaire somewhat maliciously said of it, –

> Courrier de la physique, argonaute nouveau,
> Qui, franchissant les monts, qui, traversant les eaux,
> Ramenez des climats soumis aux trois couronnes,
> Vos perches, vos secteurs et surtout deux Laponnes.
> Vous avez confirmé dans ces lieux pleins d'ennui
> Ce que Newton connut sans sortir de lui.

In much the same vein he alludes to the two sisters, who accompanied Maupertuis upon his return, the attractions of one of whom proved irresistible, –

> Cette erreur est trop ordinaire
> Et c'est la seule que l'on fit
> En allant au cercle polaire.

M.A. Maury in his *History of the Academy of Sciences*, remarks, –

"At the same time, the importance of the instruments and methods employed by the astronomers sent to the North, afforded a support to the defenders of the theory of the flattening of the globes, which was hardly theirs by right, and in the following century the Swedish astronomer, Svanburg, rectified their involuntary exaggerations, in a fine work published by him in the French language."

Meantime the mission despatched by the Academy to Peru proceeded with analogous operations. It consisted of La Condamine, Bouguer, and Godin, three Academicians, Joseph de Jussieu,

Governor of the Medical College, who undertook the botanical branch, Seniergues, a surgeon, Godin des Odonais, a clock-maker, and a draughtsman. They started from La Rochelle, on the 16th of May, 1635.

Upon reaching St. Domingo, they took several astronomical observations, and continued by way of Porto Bello, and Carthagena. Crossing the Isthmus of Panama, they disembarked at Manta in Peru, upon the 9th of March, 1736.

Arrived there, Bouguer and Condamine parted from their companions, studied the rapidity of the pendulum, and finally reached Quito by different routes. Condamine pursued his way along the coast, as far as Rio de las Esmeraldas, and drew the map of the entire country, which he traversed with such infinite toil. Bouguer went southwards towards Guayaquil, passing through marshy forests, and reaching Caracol at the foot of the Cordillera range of the Andes, which he was a week in crossing. This route had been previously taken by Alvarado, when seventy of his followers perished; amongst them, the three Spaniards who had attempted to penetrate to the interior. Bouguer reached Quito on the 10th of June. At that time this city contained between thirty and forty thousand inhabitants, and boasted of an episcopal president of the Assembly, and numbers of religious communities, besides two colleges.

Living there was cheap, with the exception of foreign merchandises, which realized exorbitant prices, so much so indeed, that a glass goblet fetched from eighteen to twenty francs.

The adventurers scaled the Pichincha, a mountain near Quito, the eruptions from which had more than once been fatal to the inhabitants, but they were not slow in discovering that they could not succeed in carrying their implements to the summit of the mountains, and that they must be satisfied with placing the signals upon the hills.

"An extraordinary phenomena may be witnessed almost every day upon the summit of these mountains," said Bouguer in the account he read before the Academy of Sciences, "which is probably as old as the world itself, but what it appeared was never witnessed by anyone before us. We first remarked it when we were altogether upon a mountain called Pamba Marca. A cloud in which we had been enveloped, and which dispersed, allowed us a view of the rising sun, which was very brilliant. The cloud passed on, it was scarcely removed thirty paces when each of us distinguished his own shadow reflected above him, and saw only his own, because the cloud presented a broken surface.

"The short distance allowed us fully to recognize each part of the shadow; we distinguished the arms, the legs, the head, but we were most amazed at finding that the latter was surrounded by a glory, or aureole formed of two or three small concentric crowns of a very bright colour, containing the same variety of hues as the rainbow, red being the outer one. The spaces between the circles were equal, the last circle the weakest, and in the far distance, we perceived one large white one, which surrounded the whole. It produced the effect of a transfiguration upon the spectator."

The instruments employed by these scholars were not as accurate as more modern ones, and varied with changes of temperature, in consequence of which, they were forced to proceed most carefully and with most minute accuracy, lest small errors accumulating should end by leading to greater ones. Thus, in their trigonometrical surveys Bouguer and his associates never calculated the third angle by the observation of the two first, but always observed all three.

Having calculated the number of fathoms contained in the extent of country surveyed, the next point was to discover what part this was of the earth's circumference, which could only be ascertained by means of astronomical observations.

After numerous obstacles, which it is impossible to give in detail, after curious discoveries, as for example the attraction exercised on the pendulum by mountains, the French inquirers arrived at conclusions which fully confirmed the result of the expedition to Lapland. They did not all return to France at the same time.

Jussieu continued his search after facts in natural history, and La Condamine decided to return by way of the Amazon River, making an important voyage, to which we shall have occasion to refer later.


## II.


### VOYAGES IN THE EIGHTEENTH CENTURY.

The war of the Spanish succession was at its height, when some privateers of Bristol determined to fit out ships to attack the Spanish vessels, in the Pacific Ocean, and to devastate the coasts of South America. The two vessels chosen, the *Duke* and *Duchess*, under Captains Rogers and Courtenay, were carefully equipped, and stocked with everything necessary for so long a voyage, the famous Dampier, who had acquired a great reputation by his daring adventures and piracies, did not disdain to accept the title of chief pilot, and although this trip was richer in material results than in geographical discoveries, the account of it contains a few curious particulars worthy of preservation.

The *Duke* and *Duchess* set sail from the Royal Port of Bristol on the 2nd April, 1708. To begin with, we may note one interesting fact. Throughout the voyage a register was at the service of the crew, in which all the incidents of the voyage were to be noted, so that the slightest errors, and the most insignificant oversights could be rectified before the facts of the case faded from memory.

Nothing of note occurred on this voyage till the 22nd December, when the Falkland Islands, previously noticed by few navigators, were discovered. Rogers did not land on them, but contented himself with observing that the coast, although less precipitous, resembled that of Portland.

"All the hills," he added, "with their well-wooded and gradually sloping sides, appeared fertile, and the shore is not wanting in good harbours."

Now these islands do not possess a single tree, and the good harbours, as we shall presently see, are anything but numerous, so we can judge of the exactitude of the observations made by Rogers. Navigators have done well not to trust to them.

After passing this archipelago the two vessels steered due south, and penetrated as far as south lat. 60° 58'. Here, there was no night, the cold was intense, and the sea so rough that the *Duchess* sustained a few injuries. The chief officers of the two vessels assembled in council, agreed that it would be better not to attempt to go further south, and the course was changed for the west. On the 15th January, 1709, Cape Horn is said to have been doubled, and the southern ocean entered.

Up to this date the position of the island of Juan Fernandez, was differently given on nearly all maps, and Wood Rogers, who intended to harbour there, take in water, and get a little fresh meat, came upon it almost unawares.

On the 1st February, he embarked in a little boat to try and find an anchorage. Whilst his people were awaiting his return, a large fire was noticed on shore. Had some Spanish or French vessels cast anchor here? Would it be necessary to fight for the water and food required? Every preparation was made during the night, but in the

morning no ship was in sight. Conjectures were already being haz-
arded as to whether the enemy had retired, when the end was put to
all surmises by the return of the boat, bringing in it a man clad in
goatskins, whose personal appearance was yet more savage than his
garments.

It was a Scotch mariner, Alexander Selkirk by name, who in consequence of a quarrel with the captain of his ship, had been left on
this desert island four years and a half before. The fire which had
attracted notice had been lighted by him.

During his stay on the island of Juan Fernandez, Selkirk had seen
many vessels pass, but only two, both Spanish, had cast anchor.
Discovered by the sailors, Selkirk had been fired upon, and only
escaped death by the agility with which he managed to climb into a
tree and hide.

He told how he had been put ashore with his clothes, his bed, a
pound of powder, some bullets, a little tobacco, a hatchet, a knife,
a kettle, a Bible, with a few other devotional books, his nautical
instruments and books.

Poor Selkirk provided for his wants as best he could, but
during the first few months he had great difficulty in conquering
the sadness and mastering the horror consequent upon his terrible loneliness. He built two huts of willow, which he covered
with a sort of rush, and lined with the skins of the goats he killed
to satisfy his hunger, so long as his ammunition lasted. When it
was likely to fail, he managed to strike a light by rubbing two
pieces of pimento wood together. When he had quite exhausted
his ammunition, he caught the goats, as they ran, his agility had
become so great by dint of constant exercise, that he scoured the
woods, rocks, and hills, with a perfectly incredible speed. We
had sufficient proof of his skill, when he went hunting with us.
He outran and exhausted our best hunters, and an excellent dog
which we had on board; he easily caught the goats, and brought
them to us on his back. He himself related to us, that one day he
chased his prey so eagerly to the edge of a precipice, which was
concealed by bushes, that they rolled over and over together,
until they reached the bottom. He lost consciousness through
that fall, and upon discovering that the goat lay under him quite
dead, after remaining where he was for twenty-four hours, he
with the utmost difficulty succeeded in crawling to his cabin,
which was about a mile distant; and he was unable to walk again
for six days.

Selkirk falling over the precipice with his prey.

This deserted wretch managed to season his food with the turnips sown by the crew of a ship, with cabbages, capsicums, and allspice. When his clothes and shoes were worn out, a process which occupied but a short time, he ingeniously constructed new ones of goatskin, sewing them together with a nail, which served him as a needle. When his knife was useless, he constructed a new one from the cask-hoops he found on the shore. He had so far lost the use of speech, that he could only make himself understood by an effort. Rogers took him on board, and appointed him boatswain's mate.

Selkirk was not the first sailor abandoned upon the island of Juan Fernandez. It may be remembered that Dampier had already rescued an unfortunate Mosquito man, who was abandoned from 1681 to 1684. Sharp and other buccaneers have related that the sole survivor of a crew of a vessel wrecked on this coast, lived there for five years, until he was rescued by another ship. Saintine, in his recent novel, *Alone*, has detailed Selkirk's adventures.

Upon the 14th of February, the *Duke* and *Duchess* left Juan Fernandez, and commenced their operations against the Spaniards. Rogers seized Guayaquil, for which he obtained a large ransom, and captured several vessels, which, however, provided him with more prisoners than money.

This part of his voyage concerns us but little, and a few particulars only are interesting, as, for instance, his mention of a monkey in the Gorgus Island, who was so lazy, that he was nicknamed the Sluggard, and of the inhabitants of Tecamez, who repulsed the new-comers with poisoned arrows, and guns. He also speaks of the Galapagos Islands, situated two degrees of northern latitude. According to Rogers, this cluster of islands was numerous, but out of them all one only provided fresh water. Turtle-doves existed there in great quantities, and tortoises, and sea-turtles, of an extraordinary size abounded, thence the name given by the Spaniards to this group.

Sea-dogs also were common, one of them had the temerity to attack Rogers. "I was walking along the shore," he says, "when it left the water, his jaws gaping, as quickly and ferociously as a dog escaping from his chain. Three times he attacked me, I plunged my pike into his breast, and each time I inflicted such a wound that he fled howling horribly. Finally, turning towards me, he stopped to growl and show his fangs. Scarcely twenty-four hours earlier, one of my crew had narrowly escaped being devoured by a monster of the same family."

"I plunged my pike into his breast."

In December, Rogers repaired to Puerto Seguro, upon the Californian coast, with a Manilla galleon, which he had seized. Many of his men penetrated to the interior; he found large, forest trees, but not the slightest appearance of culture, although smoke indicated the existence of inhabitants.

The inhabitants, according to Albey Presort's *History of Voyages*, were straight built and powerful, blacker than any Indian tribe hitherto met with in the Pacific Ocean Seas. They had long black hair plaited, which reached below the waist. All the men went about naked, but the women wore a garment, either composed of leaves or of stuff made from them, and sometimes the skins of beasts and birds. Occasionally they wore necklaces and bracelets made of bits of wood or shells. Others adorned their necks with small red berries and pearls. Evidently they did not know how to pierce holes in them, for they notched them and joined them by a thread. They valued these ornaments so highly, that they refused to change them for English necklaces of glass. Their chief anxiety was to obtain knives and useful implements.

The *Duke* and *Duchess* left Porto Seguro on the 12th January, 1710, and reached the island of Guaham, of the Mariannes, in the course of two months. Here they revictualled, and passing by the Straits of Boutan and Saleyer, reached Batavia. After a necessary delay at the latter place, and at the Cape of Good Hope, Rogers cast anchor in the Downs upon the 1st of October.

In spite of Rogers' reticence with regard to the immense riches he brought with him, a good idea of their extent may be gathered from the account of ingots, vessels of silver and gold, and pearls, with which he delighted the shipowners.

We now come to our account of Admiral Anson's voyage, which almost belongs to the category of naval warfare, but with it we may close the list of piratical expeditions, which dishonoured the victors without ruining the vanquished. And if he brought no new acquisition to geography, his account teams with judicious observations, and interesting remarks about a country then little known.

The merit of them, however, if we are to believe Nichols' literary anecdotes, rests rather with Benjamin Robins, than, as the title would appear to indicate, with the chaplain of the expedition, Richard Walter.

George Anson was born in Staffordshire in 1697. A sailor from his childhood, he early brought himself into notice.

He was already well known as a clever and fortunate captain, when in 1739 he was offered the command of a squadron. It consisted of the *Centurion*, 60 guns, the *Gloucester* and *Severe*, each 50 guns, the *Pearl*, 40 guns, the *Wager*, 28 guns. To it were attached also the sloop *Trial*, and two transports carrying food and ammunition. In addition to the crew of 1,460, a reinforcement of 470 marines was added to the fleet.

Leaving England on the 18th September, 1740, the expedition proceeded by way of Madeira, past the island of St. Catharine, along the Brazilian coast, by St. Julian Harbour, and finally crossed the Strait of Lemaire.

"Terrible," said the narrative, "as the aspect of Tierra del Fuego may be, that of Staten Island is more horrible still. It consists of a series of inaccessible rocks, crowned with sharp points. Prodigiously high, they are covered with eternal snow, and edged with precipices. In short it is impossible to conceive anything more deserted, or more wild than this region."

Scarcely had the last vessels of the squadron filed through the strait, than a series of heavy gales, squalls, and storms, caused the oldest sailors to vow that all they had hitherto known of tempests were nothing in comparison.

This fearful experience lasted seven weeks without intermission. It is needless to state that the vessels sustained great damage, that many men were swept away by the waves, numbers destroyed by illnesses occasioned by the exposure to constant damp, and want of sufficient nourishment.

Two of the vessels, the *Severe* and the *Pearl*, were engulfed, and four others were lost sight of. Anson was unable to reach Valdivia, the rendezvous he had selected in case of separation; carried far to the north, he could only arrest his course at Juan Fernandez, which he reached upon the 9th of June.

The *Centurion* had the greatest need of rest. She had lost eighty of her crew, her supply of water had failed, and the sailors were so weakened by scurvy, that ten only of the remaining number were available for the watch. The other vessels, in an equally bad plight, were not long in regaining her.

The first care was to restore the exhausted crews, and to repair the worst injuries sustained by the vessels. Anson sent the sick on shore and installed them in a sheltered hospital in the open then putting himself at the head of the most enterprising sailors, he scoured the entire island, and thoroughly examined its roads and shores. The best anchorage, according to his report, was in Cumberland Bay. The south-eastern portion of Juan Fernandez, a little island scarcely five leagues by two in extent, is dry, rocky, treeless; the ground lies low, and is level in comparison with the northern portion. It produces water-cresses, purslain, sorrels, turnips, and Sicilian radishes in abundance, as well as oats and clover. Anson sowed carrots and lettuces, and planted plums, apricots, and peaches. He soon discovered that the number of goats, left by the buccaneers, and which had multiplied marvellously, had since decreased.

The Spaniards, eager to deprive their enemies of this valuable resource, had let loose a quantity of famished dogs upon the island, who chased the goats, and devoured so many of them, that, at the time of Anson's visit, scarcely two hundred remained. The Commodore, for so Anson is always called in the narrative of this voyage, reconnoitered the Island of Mas a Fuero, which is only twenty-five leagues west of Juan Fernandez. Smaller than the latter, it is more wooded, better watered, and possessed more goats.

At the beginning of December, the crews were sufficiently recovered for Anson to put into execution his projected attack upon the Spaniards. He commenced by seizing several ships laden with precious merchandise and ingots, and then set fire to the city of Paita. Upon this occasion the Spaniards estimated their loss at one and a half million piastres.

Anson then proceeded to Quibo Bay, near Panama, to lie in wait for the galleon which, every year, transported the treasures of the Philippine Islands to Acapulco. There, although the English met with no inhabitants in the miserable huts, they found heaps of shells and beautiful mother of pearl left there during the summer months by the fishermen of Panama. In mentioning the resources of this place, we must not omit the immense turtles, which usually weighed two hundred pounds, and which were caught in a singular manner. When a shoal of them were seen floating asleep upon the surface of the ocean, a good swimmer would plunge in a few fathoms deep, and rising, seize the turtle towards the tail, and endeavour to force it down. Upon awakening, the creature's struggles to free itself suffice to support both the man and his prey, until the arrival of a boat to receive them both.

After a fruitless cruise, Anson determined to burn three of the Spanish vessels which he had seized and equipped. Distributing the crews and cargo upon the *Centurion* and the *Gloucester*, the only two vessels remaining to him, he decided upon the 6th of May, 1742, to make for China, where he hoped to find reinforcements and supplies.

But this voyage, which he expected to accomplish in sixty days, took him fully four months. After a violent gale, the *Gloucester*, having all but floundered, and her crew being too reduced to work her, was burnt. Her cargo of silver, and her supplies were transshipped to the *Centurion*, which alone remained of all that magnificent fleet which two years earlier had set sail from England!

Thrown out of his course, far to the north, Anson discovered on the 26th of August, the Isles of Atanacan and Serigan, and the following day those of Saypan, Tinian, and Agnigan, which form a part of the Marianne Archipelago.

A Spaniard, a sergeant, whom he captured in a small bark in these seas, told him that the island of Tinian was inhabited, and abounded with cattle, fowls, and excellent fruits, such as oranges, lemons, limes, bread fruit, &c. Nowhere could the *Centurion* have found a more welcome port for her exhausted crew, now numbering only seventy-one men, worn out by privation and illness, the only survivors of the 2,000 sailors who had manned the fleet at its departure.

"The soil of this island," says the narrative, "is dry and somewhat sandy, which makes the verdure of the meadows and woods more delicate and more uniform than is usually the case in tropical climates.

"The ground rises gently from the English encampment to the centre of the isle, but before its greatest height is reached, one meets with sloping glade, covered with fine clover, and many brilliant flowers, and bordered by beautiful fruit-trees.

"The animals, who, for the greater part of the year, are the only lords of this beautiful retreat, add to its romantic charm, and contribute not a little to its marvellous appearance. Thousands of cattle may be seen grazing together in a vast meadow, and the sight is the more singular as the animals are all of a milk white colour, with the exception of their ears, which are generally black. Although it is a desert-island, the sight and sound of such a number of domestic animals, rushing in crowds through the woods, suggest the idea of farmhouses and villages."

Truly an enchanting description! But has not the author rather drawn upon his imagination for the charming details of his description?

After so long a voyage, after so many storms, it is little to be wondered at, if the verdant woods, the exuberant vegetation, and the abundance of animal life, profoundly impressed the minds of Anson's companions. Well! we shall soon learn whether his successors at Tinian found it as wonderful as he did.

Meanwhile Anson was not altogether free from anxiety. It was true that his ships were repaired, but many of his men remained on land to recover their strength, and but a small number of able-bodied seamen remained on board with him. The roadstead being lined with coral, great precautions were necessary to save the cables from being cut, but in spite of them, at new moon, a sudden tempest arose and broke the ship loose. The anchors held well, but the hawsers gave way, and the *Centurion* was carried out to sea. The thunder growled ceaselessly, and the rain fell with such violence, that the signals of distress which were given by the crew were not even heard. Anson, most of his officers, and a large part of the crew, numbering one hundred and thirteen persons, remained on land and found themselves deprived of the only means they possessed of leaving Tinian. Their despair was great, their consternation inexpressible. But Anson, with his energy and endless resources, soon roused his companions from their despair! One vessel, that which they had captured from the Spaniards, still remained to them, and it occurred to them to lengthen it, until it could contain them all with the necessary provisions for a voyage to China. However, after nineteen days, the *Centurion* returned, and the English, embarking in her upon the 21st of October, were not long in reaching Macao, putting into a friendly and civilized port for the first time since their departure from England, two years before.

"Macao," says Anson, "formerly rich, well populated, and capable of self-defence against the Chinese Government, is greatly shorn of its ancient splendour! Although still inhabited by the Portuguese and ruled by a Governor, nominated by the King of Portugal, it is at the mercy of the Chinese, who can starve the inhabitants, or take possession of it, for which reasons the Portuguese Governor is very careful not to offend them."

Anson was forced to write an imperious letter to the Chinese Governor, before he could obtain permission to buy, even at high prices, the provisions and stores he required. He then publicly announced his intention of leaving for Batavia and set sail on the 19th of April, 1743. But, instead of steering for the Dutch possession, he directed his course towards the Philippine Islands, where, for several days, he awaited the arrival of the galleon returning from Acapulco, laden with the proceeds of the sale of her rich cargo. These vessels usually carried forty-four guns, and were manned by a crew of over 500 men. Anson had only 200 sailors, of whom thirty were but lads; but this disproportion did not deter him, for he had the expectation of rich booty, and the cupidity of his men was sufficient to guarantee of their courage.

"Why," asked Anson one day of his steward, "why do you no longer give us mutton for dinner? Have we eaten all the sheep we bought in China?"

"Pray excuse me, Commodore," replied the steward, "but I am reserving the only two which remain for the Captain of the galleon."

No one, not even the steward, doubted of success! Anson well understood how to secure it, and the efficiency of his men compensated for their reduced numbers. The struggle was hot, the straw mats which filled the rigging of the galleon took fire and the flames rose as high as the mizen mast. The Spaniards found the double enemies too much! After a sharp contest of two hours, during which sixty-seven of their men were killed and eighty-four wounded, they surrendered.

It was a rich prize, 1,313,842 "pieces of eight",[1] and 35,682 ounces of ingot silver, with other merchandise of little value in comparison with the money. This booty, added to others, amounted to nearly 400,000*l*, without taking into account the vessels, goods, &c., of the Spaniards which the English squadron had burnt or destroyed, and which could not be reckoned at less than 600,000*l*.

Anson convoyed his prize to the Canton River, where he sold it much below its value, for 6,000 piastres. He left on the 10th of December, and reached Spithead on the 15th of June, 1744, after an absence of three years and nine months. He made a triumphal entry into London. The half-million of money, which was the result of his numerous prizes, was conveyed through the city in thirty-two chariots, to the sound of trumpets and beating of drums and amidst the shouts of the people.

The money was divided between himself, his officers, and men; the king himself could not claim a share.

Anson was created rear-admiral shortly after his return, and received important commands.

In 1747, he captured the Marquis of La Jonquière Taffanel, after an heroic struggle. For this exploit, he was made First Lord of the Admiralty and Admiral.

In 1758, he covered the attempted descent of the English near St. Malo, and died in London a short time after his return.

---

[1] A Spanish coin, so called, because it represents the eighth of a doubloon; it is worth about nine shillings English money.

Fight between the *Centurion* and a Spanish galleon.
(Facsimile of early engraving.)

# CHAPTER II.

## CAPTAIN COOK'S PREDECESSORS.

### I.

Roggewein – The little that is known of him – The uncertainty of his discoveries – Easter Island – The Pernicious Islands – The Bahamas – New Britain – Arrival in Batavia – Byron – Stay at Rio Janeiro and Port Desire – Entrance into Straits of Magellan – Falkland Islands and Port Egmont – The Fuegians – Masafuero – Disappointment Islands – Danger Islands – Tinian – Return to Europe.

As early as 1669, Roggewein the elder had petitioned the Dutch West India Company for three armed vessels, in order to prosecute his discoveries in the Pacific Ocean. His project was favourably received, but a coolness in the relations between Spain and Holland forced the Batavian government to relinquish the expedition for a time. Upon his death-bed Roggewein forced from his son Jacob a promise to carry the plan he had conceived into execution.

Circumstances, over which he had no control, for a long time hindered the fulfilment of his promise. It was only after several voyages in the Indian seas, after having even been judge in the Batavian Justice Court, that at length Jacob Roggewein was in a position to take the necessary steps with the West India Company. We have no means of finding out Roggewein's age in 1721, or of ascertaining what were his claims to the command of an expedition of discovery. Most biographical dictionaries honour him with but a slight mention, perhaps of a couple of lines, and Fleurieu, in his learned and exhaustive account of the Dutch navigator, was unable to find out anything certain about him.

Moreover, the narrative of the voyage was written not by Roggewein, but by a German named Behrens. We may, therefore, with some justice, attribute the obscurities and contradictions of the particulars given, and their general want of accuracy, rather to the narrator than to the navigator. It even appears sometimes (and this is far from improbable), that Roggewein was ignorant of the voyages and discoveries of his predecessors and contemporaries.

Upon the 21st of August, 1721, three vessels set sail from Texel, under his command. They were, the *Eagle* of 36 guns, and with a crew of 111 men, the *Tienhoven* of 28 guns and 100 men, Captain James Bauman, and the galley *African* of 14 guns and a crew of 60 men, Captain Henry Rosenthal. Their voyage across the Atlantic afforded no particulars of interest. Touching at Rio, Roggewein went in search of an island which he named Auke's Magdeland, and which would appear to be the same as the Land of the Virgin, Hawkins' Virginia, and the Archipelago of the Falkland, or Malouine Islands, unless indeed it was Southern Georgia. Although these islands were then well known, it would appear that the Dutch knew little of their whereabouts, as after vainly seeking the Falkland Isles, they set to work to look for the island St. Louis, belonging to the French, apparently quite unaware that they belonged to the same group.

There are few lands indeed which have borne so many different names as Pepys Isles, Conti Isles, and many which we need not mention. It would be easy to count up a dozen.

After discovering, or rather noticing an island below the parallel of the Straits of Magellan, about twenty-four leagues from the American continent, of two hundred leagues in circumference, which he named South Belgium, Roggewein passed through the Straits of Lemaire, or possibly was carried by the current to 62½° of southern latitude. Finally, he regained the coast of Chili; and cast anchor opposite the island of Mocha, which he found deserted. He afterwards reached Juan Fernandez, where he met with the *Tienhoven*, from which he had been separated since the 21st of December.

The vessels left this harbour before the end of March, and steered to the west-north-west, in search of the land discovered by Davis, between 27° and 28° south.

After a search of several days, Roggewein sighted an island upon the 6th of April, 1722, which he named Easter Island.

We will not stop to enumerate the exaggerated dimensions claimed for this island by the Dutch navigator, nor to notice his observations of the manners and customs of the inhabitants. We shall have occasion to refer to them in dealing with the more detailed and reliable accounts of Cook and La Perouse. "But," said Fleurieu, "we shall vainly look in this narrative for any sign of learning on the part of Roggewein's sergeant-major." After describing the Banana, of which the leaves are six or eight feet high, and two or three wide, he adds that this was the leaf with which our first parents covered their nakedness after the Fall; and to make it clearer, further remarks that those who accept this view, do so on account of this leaf being the largest of all the plants growing either in eastern or western countries, thereby plainly indicating his notion of the proportions of Adam and Eve.

A native came on board the *Eagle*. He delighted every one by his good humour, gaiety, and friendly demonstrations.

In the morning Roggewein distinguished an eager multitude upon the shore, which was adorned with high statues, who awaited the arrival of the strangers with impatient curiosity. For no discoverable purpose a gun was fired, one of the natives was killed and the multitude fled in every direction, soon, however, to return in greater haste. Roggewein, at the head of 150 men, fired a volley, stretching a number of victims on the ground. Overcome with terror, the natives hastened to appease their terrible visitors by offering them all they possessed.

Fleurieu is of opinion that Easter Island and Davis Land are not identical; but in spite of the reasons with which he supports his opinions, and the differences which he points out in the situation and description of the two islands, it is impossible to avoid the conclusion, that Roggewein and Davis's discoveries are one and the same. No other island answering to the description is to be found in these latitudes, which are now thoroughly well known.

A violent storm of wind drove Roggewein from his anchorage on the eastern side of the island, and obliged him to make for the west-north-west. He traversed the sea called Mauvaise by Schouten, and having sailed eight hundred leagues from Easter island, fell in with what he took to be the Isle of Dogs, so called by Schouten. Roggewein named it Carlshoff, a name which it still retains.

The squadron passed this island in the night, without touching at it, and was fored in the following night, by the wind and adverse currents, to the midst of a group of low islands, which were quite unexpectedly encountered. The *African* was dashed against a coral rock, and the two consorts narrowly escaped the same fate. Only after five days of unceasing effort, of danger and anxiety, the crew succeeded in extricating the vessels and in regaining the open sea.

The natives of this group were tall, with long and flowing hair. They painted their bodies in various colours. It is generally agreed now to recognize in Roggewein's description of the Pernicious Islands, the group to which Cook gave the name of Palliser Isles.

On the morning succeeding the day in which he had so narrowly escaped the dangers of the Pernicious Islands, Roggewein discovered an island to which he gave the name of Aurora. Lying low, it was scarcely visible above the water, and had the sun not shone out, the *Tienhoven* would have been lost upon it.

As night approached, new land was perceived, to which the name of Vesper was given, and it is difficult to decide whether or no it belonged to the Palliser group.

Roggewein continued to sail between the 15th and 16th degrees, and was not long in finding himself "all of a sudden" in the midst of islands which were half submerged.

"As we approached them," says Behrens, "we saw an immense number of canoes navigating the coasts, and we concluded that the islands were well populated. Upon nearing the land we discovered that it consisted of a mass of different islands, situated close the one to the other, and we were insensibly drawn in amongst them. We began to fear that we should be unable to extricate ourselves. The admiral sent one of the pilots up to the look-out to ascertain bow we could get free of them."

"We owed our safety to the calm that prevailed. The slightest movement of the water would have run our ships upon the rocks, without the possibility of assistance reaching us. As it was, we got away without any accident worth mentioning. These islands are six in number, all very pleasant, and taken together may extend some thirty leagues. They are situated twenty-five leagues westward of the Pernicious Islands. We named them the Labyrinth, because we could only leave them by a circuitous route."

Many authors identify this group with Byron's Prince of Wales Islands. Fleurieu holds a different opinion. Dumont d'Urville thinks them identical with the group of Vliegen, already seen by Schouten and Lemaire.

After navigating for three days in a westerly direction, the Dutch caught sight of a beautiful island. Cocoa-nuts, palm-trees, and luxuriant verdure testified to its fertility. But finding it impossible to anchor there, the officers and crews were obliged to visit it in well-armed detachments.

Once more the Dutch needlessly shed the blood of an inoffensive population which had awaited them upon the shore, and whose only fault consisted in their numbers.

After this execution, worthy rather of barbarians than of civilized men, they endeavoured to persuade the natives to return, by offering presents to the chiefs, and by deceitful protestations of friendship. But they were not to be deceived by the latter, and having enticed the sailors into the interior, the inhabitants rushed upon them and attacked them with stones. Although a volley of bullets stretched a number upon the ground, they still bravely persisted in attacking the strangers, and forced them to re-embark, carrying with them their dead and wounded.

Of course the Dutch cried treason, not knowing how to find epithets strong enough for the treachery and disloyalty of their adversaries. But, who struck the first blow? Who was the aggressor? Even admitting that a few thefts were committed, which is probable enough, was it necessary to visit them with so severe a punishment, to revenge upon an entire population the wrong-doing of a few individuals, who after all can have had no very strict notions of honesty?

In spite of their losses, the Dutch called this island, in memory of the refreshment they had enjoyed there, Recreation Island. Roggewein gives its situation as below the sixth parallel, but his longitude is so incorrect, that it is impossible to depend upon it.

The question now arises, whether the captain should prosecute his search for the Island Espirito Santo de Quiros in the west, or whether, on the contrary, he should sail northward and reach the East Indies during the favourable season?

The counsel of war, which Roggewein called to the consideration of this question, chose the latter alternative.

The third day after this decision, three islands were simultaneously discovered. They received the name of Bauman, after the captain of the *Tienhoven*, who was the first to catch sight of them. The natives came round the vessels to traffic, whilst an immense crowd of the inhabitants lined the shore, armed with bows and spears. They were white skinned, and only differed from Europeans in appearance, when very much tanned by the sun. Their bodies were not painted. A strip of stuff, artistically arranged and fringed, covered them from the waist to the heels. Hats of the same material protected their heads and neck-laces of sweet-smelling flowers, adorned their necks.

"It must be confessed," says Behrens, "that this is the most civilized nation, as well as the most honest, which we have met with in the southern seas. Charmed with our arrival, they received us like

The counsel chose the latter alternative.

gods, and when we showed our intention of leaving, they testified most lively regrets."

From the description, these would appear to have been the inhabitants of the Navigators Islands.

After having encountered the islands which Roggewein believed to be Cocoa and Traitor Islands, already visited by Schouten and Lemaire, and which Fleurieu, imagining them to be a Dutch discovery, named Roggewein Islands; after having caught sight of Tienhoven and Groningue Islands, which were believed bv Pingré to be identical with Santa Cruz of Mendana, the expedition finally reached the coast of New Ireland. Here the discoverers perpetrated new massacres. From thence they went to the shores of New Guinea, and after crossing the Moluccas, cast anchor at Batavia.

There their fellow-countrymen, less humane than many of the tribes they had visited, confiscated the two vessels, imprisoned the officers and sailors indiscriminately, and sent them to Europe to take their trial. They had committed the unpardonable crime of having entered countries belonging to the East India Company, whilst they themselves were in the employ of the West India Company.

The result was a trial, and the East India Company was compelled to restore all that it had appropriated, and to pay heavy damages.

We lose all sight of Roggewein after his arrival at Texel upon the 11th July, 1723, and no details are to be obtained of the last years of his life. Grateful thanks are due to Fleurieu for having unravelled this "chaotic" narrative, and for having thrown some light upon an expedition which deserves to be better known.

Upon the 17th of June, 1764, Commodore Byron received instructions signed by the Lord of the Admiralty. They were to the following effect, – "As nothing contributes more to the glory of this nation, in its character of a maritime power, to the dignity of the British crown, and to the progress of its national commerce and navigation, than the discovery of new regions; and as there is every reason for believing in the existence of lands and islands in great numbers, between the Cape of Good Hope and the Straits of Magellan, which have been hitherto unknown to the European powers, and which are situated in latitudes suitable for navigation, and in climates productive of different marketable commodities; and as moreover, his Majesty's islands, called Pepys and Falkland Islands, situated as will be described, have not been sufficiently examined for a just appreciation of their shores and productions, although they were discovered by English navigators; his Majesty, taking all these considerations into account, and conceiving the existing state of profound peace now enjoyed by his subjects especially suitable for such an undertaking, has decided to put it into execution."

Upon what seaman would the choice of the English Government fall?

Commodore John Byron, born on the 8th of November, 1723, was the man selected. From his earliest years, he had shown an enthusiastic love of sea-faring life, and at the age of seventeen had offered his services upon one of the vessels that formed Admiral Anson's squadron, when it was sent out for the destruction of Spanish settlements upon the Pacific coast.

We have have already given an account of the troubles which befell this expedition before the incredible fortune which was to distinguish its last voyage.

The vessel upon which Byron embarked was the *Wager*. It was wrecked in passing through the Straits of Magellan, and the crew being taken prisoners by the Spaniards, were sent to Chili. After a captivity which lasted at least three years, Byron effected his escape, and was rescued by a vessel from St. Malo, which took him to Europe. He returned at once to service, and distinguished himself in various encounters during the war with France. Doubtless it was the recollection of his first voyage round the world, so disastrously interrupted, which procured for him the distinction conferred upon him by the Admiralty.

The vessels entrusted to him were carefully armed. The *Dauphin* was a sixth-rate man-of-war, and carried 24 guns, 150 sailors, 3 lieutenants, and 37 petty officers. The *Tamar* was a sloop of 16 guns, and 90 sailors, 3 lieutenants, 27 petty officers, commanded by Captain Mouat.

The start was not fortunate. The expedition left the Downs upon the 21st of June, but the *Dauphin* grounded before leaving the Thames, and was obliged to put into Plymouth for repairs.

Upon the 3rd of July, anchor was finally weighed, and ten days later, Byron put in at Funchal in the Island of Madeira for refreshments. He was forced to halt again at Cape Verd Islands, to take in water, that with which he was supplied having become rapidly wasted.

Nothing further occurred to interrupt the voyage, until the two English vessels sighted Cape Frio.

Byron remarked a singular fact, since fully verified, that the copper sheathing of his vessels appeared to disperse the fish, which he expected to meet with in large quantities.

The tropical heat, and constant rains, had struck down a large proportion of the crew, hence the urgent need of rest and of fresh victuals which they experienced.

These they hoped to find at Rio de Janeiro, where they arrived on the 12th December. Byron was warmly welcomed by the viceroy, and thus describes his first interview.

"When I made my visit, I was received in the greatest state, about sixty officers were drawn up by the palace. The guard was under arms. They were fine, well-drilled men. His Excellency accompanied by the nobility received me on the staircase. Fifteen salutes from the neighbouring fort honoured my arrival. We then entered the audience-chamber, and after a conversation of a quarter of an hour, I took my leave, and was conducted back with the same ceremonies."

We shall see a little later how slightly the reception given to Captain Cook some years afterwards resembled that just related.

The Commodore obtained ready permission to disembark his sick, and found every facility for revictualling. His sole cause of complaint was the repeated endeavour of the Portuguese to tempt his sailors to desert.

The insupportable heat experienced by the crew shortened their stay at Rio. Upon the 16th of October, anchor was weighed, but it was five days before a land breeze allowed the vessels to gain the open sea.

Up to this moment, the destination of the expedition had been kept secret. Byron now summoned the captain of the *Tamar* on board, and in the presence of the assembled sailors, read his instructions.

These enjoined him not to proceed to the East Indias, as had been supposed, but to prosecute discoveries, which might prove of great importance to England in the southern seas. With this object the Lords of the Admiralty promised double pay to the crew, with future advancement and enjoyments, if they were pleased with their services. The second part of this short harangue was the most acceptable to the sailors and was received by them with joyous demonstrations.

Until the 29th of October no incident occurred in their passage. Upon that date sudden and violent squalls succeeded each other, and culminated in a fearful tempest, the violence of which was so great that the Commodore ordered four guns to be thrown overboard, to avoid foundering. In the morning the weather moderated somewhat, but it was as cold as in England at the same time of year, although in this quarter of the globe the month of November answers to the month of May. As the wind continued to drive the vessel eastward, Byron began to think that he should experience great difficulty in avoiding the east of Patagonia.

Suddenly, upon the 12th of November, although no land was marked on the chart in this position, a repeated cry of "Land! land ahead!" arose. Clouds at this moment obscured almost the entire horizon, and it thundered and lightened without intermission.

"It seemed to me," says Byron, "that what had at first appeared to be an island, was really two steep mountains, but, upon looking windward, it was apparent that the land which belonged to these mountains stretched far to the south-east." Consequently, he steered south-west. I sent some officers to the masthead to watch the wind, and to verify the discovery. They unanimously asserted that they saw a great extent of country. We then went E.S.E. The land appeared to present entirely the same appearance. The mountains looked blue, as is often the case in dark and rainy weather, when one is near them. Shortly afterwards, several of our number fancied they could distinguish waves breaking upon a sandy shore, but after steering with the utmost caution for an hour, that which we had taken for land disappeared suddenly, and we were convinced to our amazement that it had been only a land of fog! I have passed all my life at sea," continues Byron, "since I was twenty-seven, but I never could have conceived so complete and sustained an illusion.

"There is no doubt, that had the weather not cleared so suddenly as it did, we should one and all on board have declared that we had discovered land in this latitude. We were then in latitude 43° 46' S. and longitude 60° 5' W."

The next morning a terrible gale of wind arose, heralded by the piercing cries of many hundred birds flying before it. It lasted only twenty minutes – sufficiently long, however, to throw the vessel on its beam end before it was possible to let go the halliards. At the same moment a blow from the sheet of the mainsail overthrew the first lieutenant, and sent him rolling to a distance, while the mizenmast, which was not entirely lowered, was torn to pieces.

The following days were not much more favourable. Moreover,

the ship had sunk so little, that she drifted away as the wind freshened. After such a troublesome voyage, we may guess how gladly Byron reached Penguin Island and Port Desire on the 24th of November. But the delights of this station did not by any means equal the anticipations of the crew.

The English sailors landed and upon advancing into the interior, met only with a desert country, and sandy hills, without a single tree. They found no game, but they saw a few guanacos too far off for a shot; they were, however, able to catch some large hares, which were not difficult to secure. The seals and sea birds, however, furnished food for an entire fleet.

Badly situated and badly sheltered, Port Desire offered the further inconvenience that only brackish water could be procured there. Not a trace of inhabitants was to be found! A long stay in this place being useless and dangerous, Byron started in search of Pepys Island on the 25th.

The position of this island was most uncertain. Halley placed it 80° east of the continent. Cowley, the only person who asserted that he had seen it, declared it was about 47° latitude, S., but did not fix its longitude. Here then was an interesting problem to solve.

After having explored to the N., to the S., and to the E., Byron, satisfied that this island was imaginary, set sail for the Sebaldines, in haste to reach the first possible port where he could obtain food and water, of which he had pressing need. A storm overtook him, during which the waves were so terrific, that Byron declared he had never seen them equalled, even when he doubled Cape Horn with Admiral Anson. This danger surmounted, he recognized Cape Virgin, which forms the northern entrance to the Straits of Magellan.

As soon as the vessels neared the shore, the sailors distinguished a crowd of men on horseback, who set up a white tent, and signed to them to land. Curious to see these Patagonians, about whom preceding navigators had so disagreed, Byron landed with a strong detachment of armed soldiers.

He found nearly 500 men, most of them on horseback, of gigantic stature, and looking like monsters in human shape. Their bodies were painted in the most hideous manner, their faces traced with various coloured lines, their eyes encircled with blue, black, or red, so that they had the appearance of wearing enormous spectacles. Almost all were naked, with the exception of a skin thrown over their shoulders – the wool inside, and a few of them wore boots. Truly, a singular costume! primitive and not expensive!

Most of them on horseback.

With them were numbers of dogs and of very small horses, excessively ugly, but not the less extremely swift.

The women rode on horseback like the men without stirrups, and all galloped on the shore, although it was covered with immense stones and very slippery.

The interview was friendly. Byron distributed numbers of toys, ribbons, glass trinkets, and tobacco, to the crowd of giants.

As soon as he had brought the *Dauphin* to the wind. Byron entered the Straits of Magellan with the tide. It was not his intention to cross it, but merely to find a safe and commodious harbour, where he might secure wood and water before starting in his search for the Falkland Islands.

On leaving the second outlet, he met with St. Elizabeth, St. Bartholomew, and St. George Islands, and Sandy Point. Near the last he found a delicious country, springs, woods, fields covered with flowers, which shed an exquisite perfume in the air. The country was swarming with hundreds of birds, of which one species received the name of the "Painted Goose", from the exceeding brilliancy of its plumage. But nowhere could a spot be found where the ship's boat could approach without extreme danger. The water was shallow everywhere, and the breakers were heavy. Fish of many kinds – more especially mullets, – geese, snipe, teal, and other birds of excellent flavour, were caught and killed by the crew.

Byron was obliged to continue his voyage to Port Famine, which he reached on the 27th of December.

"We were sheltered from all winds," he says, "with the exception of the south-east, which rarely blows, and no damage could accrue to vessels which might be driven on shore in the bay, because of the profound calm that prevails. Wood enough floated near the shore to stock a thousand vessels, so we had no need to go and cut it in the forest.

"The River Sedger ran at the bottom of the bay, the water of which is excellent. Its banks are planted with large and beautiful trees, excellent for masts; parrots, and birds of brilliant plumage thronged the branches." Abundance reigned in Famine Port during Byron's stay.

As soon as his crew were completely recovered from their fatigue and the ships well provisioned, the Commodore, on the 5th of January, 1765, resumed his search for the Falkland Islands. Seven days later, he discovered a land in which he fancied he recognized the Islands of Sebald de Wert, but upon nearing them he found that what he had taken for three islands, was, in reality, but one, which extended far south. He had no remaining doubt that he had found the group marked upon the charts of the time as New Ireland, 51° south latitude, and 63° 32' west longitude.

First of all, Byron steered clear of them, fearing to be thrown upon a coast with which he was unacquainted, and after this summary bearing, a detachment was selected to skirt the coast as closely as possible, and look for a safe and commodious harbour – which was soon met with. It received the name of Port Egmont, in honour of Earl Egmont, First Lord of the Admiralty.

"I did not expect," says Byron, "that it would be possible to find so good a harbour. The depth was excellent, the supply of water easy; all the ships of England might be anchored there in shelter from winds.

"Geese, ducks, and teal abounded to such an extent, that the sailors were tired of eating them. Want of wood was general, with the exception of some trunks of trees which floated by the shore, and which were apparently brought here from the Strait of Magellan.

"The wild sorel and celery, both excellent anti-scorbutics, were to be found in abundance. Sea-calves and seals, as well as penguins, were so numerous that it was impossible to walk upon the strand without seeing them rush away in herds. Animals resembling wolves, but more like foxes in shape, with the exception of their height and tails, several times attacked the sailors, who had great difficulty in defending themselves. It would be no easy task to guess how they came here, distant as the country is from any other continent, – by at least a hundred leagues; or to imagine where they found shelter, in a country barren of vegetation, producing only rushes, sword-grass, and not a single tree."

The account of this portion of Byron's voyage, in Didot's biography, is a tissue of errors.

"The flotilla," says M. Alfred de Lacaze, "became entangled in the Straits of Magellan, and was forced to put into a bay near Port Famine, which was named Port Egmont." A singular mistake, which proves how lightly the articles of this important collection were sometimes written.

Byron took possession of Port Egmont and the adjacent isles, called Falkland, in the name of the King of England. Cowley had named them Pepys Islands, but in all probability the first discoverer was Captain Davis in 1592. Two years later Sir Richard Hawkins

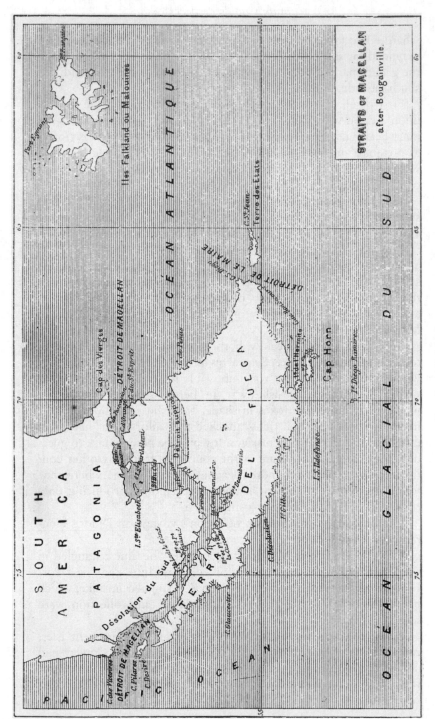

STRAITS OF MAGELLAN
after Bougainville.

Gravé par E. Morieu.

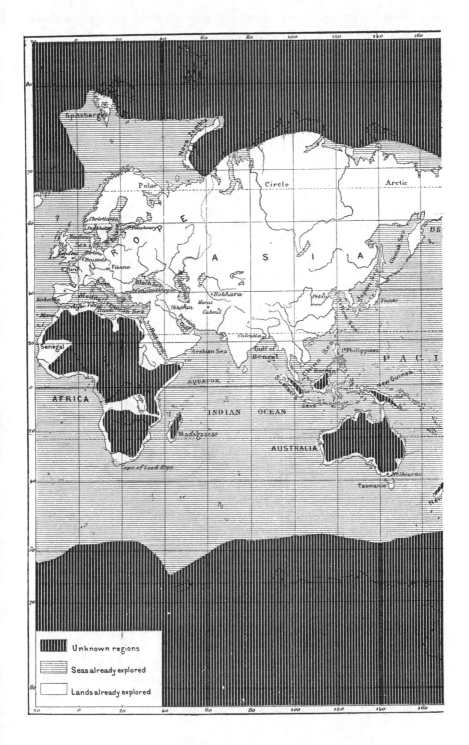

Engraved by E. Morieu 23.r.de Brea Paris.

found land which was thought to be the same, and named it Virginia, in honour of his queen Elizabeth. Lastly, vessels from St. Malo, visited this group, and no doubt it was owing to this fact that Prezier called them the Malounies Islands.

After having named a number of rocks, islets, and capes, Byron left Port Egmont on the 27th of January, and set sail for Port Desire, which he reached nine days later. There he found the *Florida* – a transport vessel, which had brought from England the provisions and necessary appliances for his long voyage.

But this anchorage was too dangerous. The *Florida* and the *Tamar* were in too bad a condition to be equal to the long operation of transhipment. Byron therefore sent one of his petty officers, who had a thorough knowledge of the Straits of Magellan, on board the *Florida*, and with his two consorts set sail for Port Famine. He met with a French ship so many times in the straits, that it appeared as if she were bent upon the same course as himself. Upon returning to England, he ascertained that she was the *Aigle*, Captain M. de Bougainville, who was coasting Patagonia in search of the wood needed by the French colony in the Falkland Islands.

During the various excursions in the straits, the English expedition received several visits from the inhabitants of Tierra del Fuego.

"I have never seen such wretched beings," says Byron; "they were entirely naked, with the exception of a skin thrown across the shoulders. They offered me the bows and arrows with which they were armed in exchange for beads, necklaces, and other trifles. Their arrows, which were two feet long, were made of cane, and pointed with greenish stone; the bows were three feet long and were furnished with catgut for strings.

"Their nourishment consisted of certain fruits, mussels, and the remains of putrid fish thrown upon the beach during the storms. Pigs only could have relished their food. It consisted of large pieces of whale, already putrified, the odour of which impregnated the air for some distance. One of them tore the carrion in pieces with his teeth, and handed the bits to his companions, who devoured them with the voracity of wild beasts.

"Several of these miserable beings decided to come on board. Wishing to give them a pleasant reception, one of my petty officers played the violin and the sailors danced. This delighted them. Anxious to show their appreciation, one of their number hastened to his pirogue (small boat) and returned with a little bag of wolf-skin, containing a red ointment, with which he rubbed the face of

One of them tore the carrion with his teeth.

the violinist. He was anxious to pay me the same attention, but I drew back. He then tried every means of overcoming my delicacy, and I had great difficulty in avoiding the mark of esteem he was so anxious to give me."

It will not be out of place here to record the opinion held by Byron, an experienced seaman, upon the advantages and disadvantages offered to the passage through the Straits of Magellan. He does not agree with the majority of navigators who have visited these latitudes. He says, –

"Our account of the difficulties and dangers we encountered may lead to the idea that it is not prudent to attempt this passage, and that ships leaving Europe for the southern seas, should prefer to double Cape Horn. I am by no means of this opinion, although I have twice doubled Cape Horn. There is one season in the year when not only one ship, but an entire fleet, might safely cross the straits, and to profit by this season one should enter them in the month of December. One inestimable advantage which should weigh with all navigators is that celery, scurvy-grass, fruits, and other anti-scorbutic vegetables abound. Such obstacles as we encountered, and which delayed us from the 17th of February till the 8th of April in the straits, were mainly due to the equinoctial season, a season which is invariably stormy, and which, more than once, tried our patience."

Until the 26th of April, the day upon which they found Mas-a-Fuero, belonging to the Juan Fernandez group, Byron had sailed to the N.W. He hastened to disembark several sailors, who after obtaining water and wood, chased wild goats, which they found better flavoured than venison in England.

During their stay in this port, a singular fact occurred. A violent surf broke over the shore, and prevented the shore-boats from reaching the strand. Although he was provided with a lifebelt, one of the sailors, who could not swim, refused to jump into the sea to reach the boat. Threatened with being left alone on the island, he still persistently refused to venture, when one of his companions cleverly encircled his waist with a cord, in which he had made a running knot, and one end of which was made fast to the boat. When he reached the vessel, Hawksworth's narrative relates, that the unfortunate fellow had swallowed so much water that he appeared lifeless. He was accordingly hung up by the heels, whereupon he soon regained his senses, and the next day was completely restored. But in spite of this truly wonderful recovery, we can hardly venture to recommend this course of treatment to humane rescue societies.

Leaving Mas-a-Fuero, Byron changed his route, with the intention of seeking Davis Land, now known as Easter Island, which was placed by geographers in 27° 30', a hundred leagues westward of the American coast. Eight days were devoted to this search.

Having found nothing after this cruise, which he was unable to prolong, Byron, following his intention of visiting the Solomon group, steered for the north-west. Upon the 22nd of May scurvy broke out on board the vessels, and quickly made alarming havoc.

Fortunately land was perceived from the look-out on the 7th of June in 14° 58' west longitude.

Next day, the fleet neared two islands, which presented an attractive appearance.

Large bushy trees, shrubs and groves were seen, and a number of natives who hastened to the shore and lighted fires.

Byron sent a boat in search of anchorage. It returned without having found the requisite depth at a cable's length from shore.

The unfortunate victims of scurvy who had crawled on to the forecastle, cast looks of sorrowful longing at the fertile islands, which held the remedy for their sufferings and which Nature placed beyond their reach!

The narrative says, –

"They saw the cocoa-trees in abundance, laden with fruit, the milk of which is probably the most powerful anti-scorbutic in the world. They had reason for supposing that limes, bananas, and other tropical fruits abounded, and to add to their torments they saw the shells of tortoises floating on the shore."

All these delights, which would have restored them to vigour, were no more attainable than if they had been separated by half the globe, but the sight of them increased the misery of their privations.

Byron was anxious to curtail the tantalizing misery of his unfortunate crew, and giving the name of Disappointment Islands to the group, he set sail once more on the 8th of June.

The very next day he found a new land, long, flat, covered with cocoa-nut trees. In its midst was a lake with a little islet. This feature alone was indicative of the madreporic formation of the soil, simple deposit, which was not yet, but which in time would become, an island. The boat sent to sound met in every direction with a coast as steep as a wall.

Meanwhile the natives made hostile demonstrations. Two men

entered the boat. One stole a sailor's waistcoat, another put out his hand for the quarter-master's cocked hat, but not knowing how to deal with it, pulled it towards him, instead of lifting it up, which gave the quarter-master an opportunity of interfering with his intention. Two large pirogues, each manned by thirty paddlers, showed an intention of attacking the vessels, but the latter immediately chased them. Just as they were running ashore a struggle ensued, and the English, all but overwhelmed by numbers, were forced to use their arms. Three or four natives were killed.

Next day, the sailors and such of the sick as could leave their hammocks landed.

The natives, intimidated by the lesson they had received in the evening, remained in concealment, whilst the English picked cocoanuts, and gathered anti-scorbutic plants. These timely refreshments were so useful that in a few days there was not a sick man on board.

Parrots, rarely beautiful, and tame doves, and several kinds of unknown birds composed the fauna of the island, which received the name of King George – that which was discovered afterwards was called Prince of Wales' Island. All these lands belonged to the Pomotou group, which is also known as the Low Islands, a very suitable name for this archipelago.

On the 21st again a new chain of islands surrounded by breakers was sighted. Byron did not attempt a thorough investigation of these, as to do so he would have incurred risks out of proportion to the benefit to be gained. He called them the Dangerous Islands.

Six days later, Duke of York Island was discovered. The English found no inhabitants, but carried off two hundred cocoa-nuts, which appeared to them of inestimable value.

A little farther, in latitude 1° 18' south, longitude 173° 46' west, a desert island received the name of Byron; it was situated eastward of the Gilbert group.

The heat was overwhelming, and the sailors, weakened, by their long voyage and want of proper food, in addition to the putrid water they had been forced to drink, were almost all attacked by dysentery.

At length, on the 28th of July, Byron joyfully recognized Saypan and Tinian Islands, which form part of the Marianne or Ladrone Islands, and he prepared to anchor in the very spot where Lord Anson had cast anchor with the *Centurion*. Tents were immediately prepared for the sufferers from scurvy. Almost all the sailors had been attacked by this terrible disease, many even had been at the point of death. The captain undertook to explore the dense wood which extended to the very edge of the shore, in search of the lovely country so enthusiastically described in the account written by Lord Anson's chaplain. How far were these enchanting descriptions from the truth! Impenetrable forests met him on every side, overgrown plants, briars, and tangled shrubs, at every step caught and tore his clothes. At the same time the explorers were attacked and stung by clouds of mosquitoes. Game was scarce and wild, the water detestable, the roadstead was never more dangerous than at this season.

The halt was made, therefore, under unfortunate auspices. Still, in the end limes, bitter oranges, cocoa-nuts, bread-fruits, guavas, and others were found. But although these productions were beneficial to the invalids, who were shortly restored to vigour, the malarious atmosphere caused such violent fever that two sailors succumbed to it. In addition, the rain fell unceasingly and the heat was overpowering. Byron says that he never experienced such terrific heat, even in his visits to the coast of Guinea, the East Indies, or St. Thomas Island, which is immediately below the equator.

Fowls and wild pigs which weighed about 2 cwt. each, were easily procurable, but had to be eaten immediately, as in less than a hour decomposition took place. Lastly, the fish caught upon this shore was so unwholesome, that even those who ate it in moderation became dangerously ill, and risked their lives.

After a stay of nine weeks, the two ships, amply provisioned, left the port of Tinian. Byron continued his route to the north, after having passed Anatacan Island, already discovered by Anson. He hoped to meet the N.E. monsoon before reaching the Bashees, which form the extreme north of the Philippines. Upon the 22nd he perceived Grafton Island, the most northerly of this group, and upon the 3rd of November he arrived at Timoan, which had been mentioned by Dampier as a favourable place for procuring provisions. The natives, however, who are of Malay descent, refused the offer of hatchets, knives, and iron instruments in exchange for fowls – they demanded rupees. Finally they accepted some handkerchiefs in payment of a dozen fowls, a goat and its kid. Fortunately fish was abundant, as it would have been impossible to procure fresh victuals.

Byron set sail once more on the 7th November, passed Poulo Condor at a distance, stopped at Poulo Taya, where he encountered a vessel bearing Dutch colours, but which was manned entirely by Malays. Reaching Sumatra, he explored the coast and cast anchor at Batavia, the principal seat of Dutch power in the East Indies, on the 20th November.

At this time there were more than one hundred ships, large and small, in this roadstead, so flourishing was the trade of the East India Company at this epoch. The town was at the height of its prosperity. Its large and open thoroughfares, its admirable canals, bordered by pine-trees, its regular buildings, singularly recalled the cities of the Netherlands.

Portuguese, Chinese, English, Dutch, Persians, Moors, and Malays, mixed in the streets, and transacted business. Fêtes, receptions, gaieties of every kind impressed new comers with a high idea of the prosperity of the town, and contributed to make their stay a pleasant one. The sole drawback, and it was a serious one to crews after so long a voyage, was the unhealthiness of the locality, where endemic fevers abound. Byron being aware of this, hurried the embarkation of his provisions, and set sail, after an interval of twelve days.

Short as their stay had been, it had been too long. The fleet had scarcely reached the strait of the sound, before a malignant fever broke out among the crew, disabling half their number, and ending in the death of three sailors.

After forty-eight days' navigation, Byron perceived the coast of Africa, and cast anchor three days later in Table Bay.

Cape Town furnished all that he could require. Provisions, water, medicines, were all shipped with a rapidity which sufficiently indicated their anxiety to return, and once more the prow of the vessel was directed homewards.

Two incidents occurred on the passage across the Atlantic, thus described by Byron.

"Off St. Helena, in fine weather, and with a favourable wind, the vessel, then at a considerable distance from land, received a shock which was as severe as if she had struck on a rock. Its violence so alarmed us that we all ran to the bridge. Our fears were dissipated when we saw the sea tinged with blood to a great distance. We concluded that we had come in contact with a whale or a grampus, and that our ship had apparently received no damage, which was true."

A few days later, however, the *Tamar* was found to be in such a dilapidated state, such grave injuries were discovered in her rudder, that it was necessary to invent something to replace it, and to enable her to reach the Antilles, it being too great a risk to allow her to continue her voyage.

Upon the 9th of May, 1766, the *Dauphin* anchored in the Downs, after a voyage round the world which had lasted for twenty-three months.

This was the most fortunate of all the circumnavigation voyages undertaken by the English. Up to this date, no purely scientific voyage had been attempted. If it was less fruitful of results than had been anticipated, the fault lay not so much with the captain as with the Lords of the Admiralty. They were not sufficiently accurate in their instructions, and had not taken the trouble (as was done in later voyages) of sending special professors of the various branches of science with the expedition.

Full justice, however, was paid to Byron. The title of Admiral was conferred on him, and an important command in the East Indies was entrusted to him. But we have no interest in the latter part of his life, which ended in 1786, and to that, therefore, we need not allude.

## II.

Wallis and Carteret – Preparations for the Expedition – Difficult navigation of the Strait of Magellan – Separation of the *Dauphin* and the *Swallow* – Whitsunday Island – Queen Charlotte's Island – Cumberland, Henry Islands, &c. – Tahiti – Howe, Boscawen, and Keppel Islands – Wallis Island – Batavia – The Cape – The Downs – Discovery of Pitcairn, Osnaburgh, and Gloucester Islands by Carteret – Santa Cruz Archipelago – Solomon Islands – St. George's canal and New Ireland, Portland and Admiralty Islands – Batavia and Macassar – Meeting with Bougainville in the Atlantic.

The impulse once given, England inaugurated the series of scientific expeditions which were to prove so fruitful of results, and to raise her naval reputation to such a height.

Admirable indeed is the training acquired in these voyages round the world. In them the crew, the officers, and sailors, are constantly brought face to face with unforeseen difficulties and dangers, which call forth the best qualities of the sailor, the soldier, and the man!

If France succumbed to the naval superiority of Great Britain during the revolutionary and imperial wars, was it not fully as much owing to this stern training of the British seaman, as to the internal dissensions which deprived France of the services of the greater part of her naval staff?

Be this as it may, the English Admiralty, shortly after Byron's return, organized a new expedition. Their preparations appear to have been far too hasty. The *Dauphin* only anchored in the Downs at the beginning of May, and six weeks later, on the 19th of June, Captain Samuel Wallis received the command.

This officer, after attaining the highest rank in the military marine service, had been entrusted with an important command in Canada, and had assisted in the capture of Louisburgh. We cannot tell what qualities commended him to the Admiralty in preference to his companions in arms, but in any case, the noble lords had no reason to regret their decision. Wallis hastened the needful preparations on board the *Dauphin*, and on the 21st of August (less than a month after receiving his Commission), he joined the sloop *Swallow* and the *Prince Frederick* in Plymouth Harbour.

The latter was in charge of Lieutenant Brine, the former was commanded by Philip Carteret. Both were most distinguished officers who had just returned from a voyage round the world with Commodore Byron, and whose reputation was destined to be increased by their second voyage.

The *Swallow*, unfortunately, appears to have been quite unfit for the service demanded of her. Having already been thirty years in service, the sheathing was very much worn, and her keel was not studded with nails, which might have served instead of sheathing to protect her from parasites. Again the provisions and marketable commodities were so unequally divided, that the *Swallow* received much less than the *Dauphin*. Carteret begged in vain for a rope yarn, a forge, and various things which his experience told him would be indispensable.

This rebuff confirmed Carteret in his notion that he should not get further than the Falkland Isles, but none the less he took every precaution which his experience dictated to him.

As soon as the equipment was complete, on the 22nd of April 1766, the vessels set sail. It did not take Wallis long to find out that the *Swallow* was a bad sailer, and that he might anticipate much trouble during his voyage. However, no accident happened during the voyage to Madeira, where the vessels put in to revictual.

Upon leaving the port, the commander supplied Carteret with a copy of his instructions, and selected Port Famine, in the Strait of Magellan, as a rendezvous, in case of separation.

Their stay at Port Praya, in the Island of Santiago, was shortened on account of the ravages committed there by the smallpox, and Wallis would not even allow his crew to land. Shortly after leaving the Equator, the *Prince Frederick* gave signs of distress, and it was necessary to send the carpenter on board to stop up a leak on the larboard side. This vessel, which was provided with inferior provisions, counted already a number of sick among her crew.

Towards eight o'clock in the evening of the 19th of November, the crews perceived in the N.E. a meteor of extraordinary appearance, moving in a straight line towards the S.W. with marvellous rapidity. It was visible for almost a minute, and left behind a trail of light, so bright that the deck was illuminated as if it were midday.

On the 8th of December, the coast of Patagonia was at last visible. Wallis skirted it until he reached Cape Virgin, where he landed with the armed detachments of the *Swallow* and *Prince Frederick*. A crowd of natives awaited them upon the shore, and received with apparent satisfaction the knives, scissors, and other trifles which it was usual to distribute upon such occasions, but they would not part with guanacos, ostriches, or any other game which were seen in their possession for any consideration. Wallis says, –

"We took the measure of the largest of them, one was six feet six inches in height, several were five feet five inches, but the average was five foot six, or six feet."

It must be remembered that these were English feet, which are only 305 millemetres.

If these natives were not quite so tall as the giants mentioned by previous navigators, they were very little less striking.

"Each one," continues the narrative, "carried a strange kind of weapon, it consisted of two round stones, covered with copper, each, of which weighed about a pound, and they were attached at both ends to a cord about eight feet long. They used them like slings, holding one of the stones in the hand, and whirling the other round the head until it attained sufficient velocity, when they threw it towards the object they wished to strike. They managed this weapon so adroitly that they could strike a butt no larger than a shilling with both stones, at a distance of fifteen roods. They did not, however, employ it in chasing guanacos or ostriches."

Wallis conducted eight of these Patagonians on board. They did not appear surprised, as one would have expected, at the number of new and extraordinary things they met with. They advanced, retired, made a thousand grimaces before the mirrors, shouted with laughter, and conversed animatedly among themselves. Their attention was attracted by the pigs for a moment, but they were immensely amused, with the guinea fowls and turkeys. It was difficulty to persuade them to leave the vessel. At last they returned to the shore, singing and making signs of delight to their countrymen who awaited them on the bank.

On the 17th of December, Wallis signalled the *Swallow* to head the squadron for the passage of the Straits of Magellan.

At Port Famine the commander had two tents erected on shore for the sick, the wood-cutters, and the sailors. Fish in sufficient quantities for each day's meal, abundance of celery, and acid fruits similar to cranberries and barberries, were to be found in this harbour, and in the course of about a fortnight these remedies completely restored the numerous sufferers from scurvy. The vessels were repaired and partially calked, the sails were mended, the rigging, which had been a good deal strained, was overhauled and repaired, and all was soon ready for sea again.

But Wallis first ordered a large quantity of wood to be cut and conveyed on board the *Prince Frederick*, for transport to the Falkland Isles, where it is not obtainable. At the same time he had hundreds of young trees carefully dug up, and the roots covered in their native soil to facilitate their transplantation in Port Egmont, that in taking root – as there was reason to hope they would, they might supply the barren archipelago with this precious commodity.

Lastly, the provisions were divided between the *Dauphin* and the *Swallow*. The former taking sufficient for a year, the latter for ten months.

We will not enlarge upon the different incidents which befell the two ships in the Straits of Magellan, such as sudden gales, tempests and snowstorms, irregular and rapid currents, heavy seas and fogs, which more than once brought the vessels within an inch of destruction. The *Swallow* especially, was in such a dilapidated condition, that Carteret besought Wallis to consider his vessel no longer of any use in the expedition, and to tell him what course should best be pursued for the public good.

Wallis replied, "The orders of the Admiralty are concise, and you must conform to them, and accompany the *Dauphin* as long as possible. I am aware that the *Swallow* is a bad sailer; I will accommodate myself to her speed, and follow her movements, for it is most important that in case of accident to one of the ships, the

They made a thousand grimaces.

other should be within reach, to give all the assistance in her power."

Carteret had nothing to urge in reply, but he augured badly for the result of the expedition.

As the ships approached the opening of the straits on the Pacific side, the weather became abominable. A thick fog, falls of snow and rain, currents which sent the vessels on to the breakers, a chopping sea, contributed to detain the navigators in the straits until the 10th of April. On that day, the *Dauphin* and *Swallow* were separated off Cape Pilar, and could not find each other, Wallis not having fixed a rendezvous in case of separation.

Before we follow Wallis on his voyage across the Pacific, we will give a short account of the wretched natives of Tierra del Fuego, and of the general appearance of their country. These wretches, who were as miserable and debased as possible, subsisted upon the raw flesh of seals and penguins.

"One of our men," says Wallis, "who fished with a line, bestowed a live fish, which he had just caught, and which was about the size of a herring, upon one of these Americans. He took it with the eagerness of a dog snatching a bone. He commenced operations by killing the fish with a bite near the gills, and proceeded to devour it, beginning at the head and finishing at the tail, without rejecting the bones, fins, scales, or entrails. In fact, these people swallowed everything that was offered to them, cooked or uncooked, fresh or salt, but they refused all drink but water. Their sole covering was a miserable seal-skin reaching to the knees. Their weapons were javelins tipped with a fish-bone. They all suffered from bad eyes, which the English attributed to their custom of living in smoke to protect themselves from mosquitos. Lastly, they emitted a most offensive smell, only to be likened to that of foxes, which doubtless arose from their excessively filthy habits."

Although certainly not inviting, this picture is graphic, as all navigators testify. It would appear that progress is not possible to these savages, so nearly allied to brutes. Civilization is a dead letter to them, and they still vegetate like their forefathers, with no wish to improve, and with no ambition to attain a more comfortable existence. Wallis continues, –

"Thus we quitted this savage and uninhabitable region, where for four months we had been in constant danger of shipwreck, where in the height of summer the weather is foggy, cold, and stormy, where almost all the valleys are without verdure, and the mountains without woods, in short where the land which one can see rather resembles the ruins of a world, than the abode of living creatures."

Wallis was scarcely free of the strait, when he set sail westward in spite of dense fogs, and with high wind and such a heavy sea, that for weeks together there was not a dry corner in the ship.

The constant exposure to damp engendered cold and severe fevers, to which scurvy shortly succeeded. Upon reaching 32° south latitude, and 100° west longitude, the navigator steered due north.

Upon the 6th of June, two islands were discovered amidst general rejoicings.

The ships' boats, well armed and equipped, reached the shore under command of Lieutenant Furneaux. A quantity of cocoa-nuts and anti-scorbutic plants were obtained, but although the English found huts and sheds, they did not meet with a single inhabitant. This island was discovered on the eve of Whitsunday and hence received the name Whitsunday Island.

It is situated in 19° 26' south latitude, and 137° 56' west longitude. Like the following islands, it belongs to the Pomotou group.

Next day, the English endeavoured to make overtures to the inhabitants of another island, but the natives appeared so ill-disposed and the coast was so steep, that it was impossible to land. After tacking about all night, Wallis despatched the boats, with orders not to use violence to the inhabitants if they could avoid it, or unless absolutely obliged.

As Lieutenant Furneaux approached the land, he was astonished by the sight of two large pirogues with double masts, in which the natives were on the eve of embarking.

As soon as they had done so, the English landed, and searched the island thoroughly. They discovered several pits full of good water. The soil was firm, sandy, covered with trees, more especially cocoanut-trees, palm-trees, and sprinkled with anti-scorbutic plants. The narrative says, –

"The natives of this island were of moderate stature. Their skin was brown, and they had long black hair, straggling over the shoulders. The men were finely formed, and the women were beautiful. Some coarse material formed their garment, which was tied round the waist, and appeared to be intended to be raised round the shoulders. In the afternoon, Wallis sent the lieutenant to procure water and to take possession of the island in the name of King George III. It was called Queen Charlotte's Island, in honour of the English queen."

After reconnoitring personally; Wallis determined to remain in this region for a week, in order to profit by the facilities it afforded for provisioning.

In their walks the English met with working implements made of shells, and sharpened stones shaped like axes, scissors, and awls. They also noticed boats in course of construction, made of boards joined together. But they were most of all astonished at meeting with tombs upon which the dead bodies were exposed under a sort of awning, and where they putrified in the open air.

When they quitted the island, they left hatchets, nails, bottles, and other things as reparation for any damage they might have committed.

The 17th century teamed with philanthropic aspirations! And from the accounts of all navigators one is led to believe that the theory so much advocated was put into practice upon most occasions. Humanity had made great strides. Difference of colour no longer presented an insuperable barrier to a man's being treated as a brother, and the convention which at the close of the century ordered the freedom of the black, set a seal to the convictions of numbers.

The *Dauphin* discovered new land, the same day that she left Queen Charlotte's Island. It lay to the westward, but after cruising along the coast, the vessel was unable to find anchorage. Lying low, it was covered with trees, neither cocoa-nuts nor inhabitants were to be found, and it evidently was merely a rendezvous for the hunters and fishers of the neighbouring islands. Wallis therefore decided not to stop. It received the name of Egmont, in honour of Earl Egmont, then chief Lord of the Admiralty. The following days brought new discoveries. Gloucester, Cumberland, William, Henry, and Osnaburgh Islands, were sighted in succession. Lieutenant Furneaux was able to procure provisions without landing at the last named.

Observing several large pirogues on the beach, he drew the conclusion that other and perhaps larger islands would be found at no great distance, where they would probably find abundant provisions, and to which access might be less difficult. His prevision was right. As the sun rose upon the 19th, the English sailors were astonished at finding themselves surrounded by pirogues of all sizes, having on board no less than eight hundred natives. After having consulted together at some distance, a few of the natives approached, holding in their hands banana branches. They were on the point of climbing up the vessels, when an absurd accident interrupted these cordial relations.

The natives waving palm-leaves as a sign of welcome.

One of them had climbed into the gangway when a goat ran at him. Turning he perceived the strange animal upon its hind legs preparing to attack him again. Overcome with terror he jumped back into the sea, an example quickly followed by the others. It recalled the incident of the sheep of Panurge.

Recovering from this alarm, they again climbed into the ship, and brought all their cunning to bear upon petty thefts. However, only one officer had his hat stolen. The vessel all the time was following the coast in search of a fitting harbour, whilst the boats coasted the shore for soundings.

The English had never found a more picturesque and attractive country in any of their voyages. On the shore, the huts of the natives were sheltered by shady woods, in which flourished graceful clusters of cocoanut-trees. Graduated chains of hills, with wooded summits, and the silver sheen of rivers glistening amid the verdure as they found their way to the sea, added to the beauty of the interior.

The boats sent to take soundings were suddenly surrounded at the entrance of a large bay by a crowd of pirogues. Wallis, to avoid a collision, gave the order for the discharge from the swivel gun above the natives' heads, but although the noise terrified them, they still continued their approach.

The captain accordingly ordered his boats to make for the shore, and the natives finding themselves disregarded, threw some sharp stones which wounded a few sailors. But the captains of the boats replied to this attack by a volley of bullets, which injured one of them, and was followed by the flight of the rest.

The *Dauphin* anchored next day at the mouth of a large river in twenty fathoms of water. The sailors rejoiced universally. The natives immediately surrounded them with pirogues, bringing pigs, fowls, and various fruits, which were quickly exchanged for hardware and nails. One of the boats employed in taking soundings, however, was attacked by blows from paddles and sticks, and the sailors were forced to use their weapons. One native was killed, a second severely wounded, and the rest jumped into the water. Seeing that they were not pursued, and conscious that they themselves had been the aggressors, they returned to traffic with the *Dauphin* as if nothing had happened. Upon returning on board, the officers reported that the natives had invited them to land, more especially the women, with unequivocal gestures, and that moreover, there was excellent anchorage near the shore within reach of water.

The only inconvenience arose from a considerable swell. The

*Dauphin* accordingly weighed anchor and proceeded into the open sea to run with the wind, when all at once Wallis perceived a bay seven or eight miles distant, which he determined to reach. The captain was soon to experience the truth of the proverb which asserts that one had better leave well alone.

Although soundings were taken by the boats as they advanced, the *Dauphin* struck on a rock and damaged her forepart. The usual measures in such a case were taken immediately, but outside the chain of madreporic rocks no depth could be sounded. It was consequently impossible to cast anchor, or to use the capstan. What course had best be pursued in this critical situation? The vessel beat violently against the rocks, and a host of pirogues waited in expectation of a shipwreck, eager to clutch their prey. Fortunately at the end of an hour a favourable breeze rising, disengaged the *Dauphin*, and wafted her into good anchorage. The damage done was not serious, and was as easily repaired as forgotten.

Wallis, rendered prudent by the constant efforts of the natives, divided his men into four parties, one of which was always to be armed. And he ordered guns to be fired. But after one or two rounds the number of pirogues increased, and no longer laden with poultry, they appeared to be filled with stones. The crews of the larger vessels also were augmented.

All at once upon a given signal a storm of pebbles fell upon the ship. Wallis ordered a general discharge, and had two guns loaded with fine shot. The natives, after some slight hesitation and disorder, returned to the attack with great bravery; and the captain, noticing the constantly increasing numbers of the assailants, was not without anxiety as to the result, when an unexpected event put an end to the contest.

Among the pirogues which attacked the *Dauphin* most energetically, was one which appeared to contain a chief, as from it the signal of attack was given. A well-directed shot cut this double pirogue in two.

This was enough to decide the natives upon retreat. They set about it so precipitately that in less than half an hour not a single boat remained in sight. The vessel was then towed into port, and so placed as to protect the disembarkation. Lieutenant Furneaux landed at the head of a strong detachment of sailors and marines, and planting the English flag, took possession of the island in the name of the King of England, in whose honour it was named George the Third. The natives called it Tahiti.

# POLYNESIA

Gravé par E. Morieu.

After prostrating themselves, and offering various marks of repentance, the natives appeared anxious to commence friendly and honest business with the English, but fortunately Wallis, who was detained on board by severe illness, perceived preparations for a simultaneous attack by land and sea upon the men sent to find water. The shorter the struggle the less the loss! Acting upon which principle, directly the natives came within gunshot range, a few discharges dispersed their fleet.

To put a stop to these attempts, it was necessary to make an example. Wallis decided with regret that it was so. He accordingly sent a detachment on shore at once with his carpenters, ordering them to destroy every pirogue which was hauled up on the beach. More than fifty, many of them sixty feet long, were hacked to pieces. Upon this the Tahitians decided to give in. They brought pigs, clogs, stuffs, and fruits to the shore, placed them, there, and then withdrew. The English left in exchange hatchets and toys which were carried off to the forest with many delighted gestures.

Peace was established, and from the morrow a regular and abundant traffic commenced, which supplied the ships with the fresh provisions needed by the crews. There was ground for hope that these amicable relations would continue during their stay in the island, now that the natives had once realized the power and effect of the strangers' weapons. Wallis, therefore, ordered a tent to be prepared near the water supply, and disembarked all the sufferers from scurvy, whilst the healthy members of his company were engaged in repairing the rigging, mending the sails, and calking and repainting the vessel, putting her, in short, in a condition fitted for the long journey which was to take her to England.

At this juncture Wallis's illness assumed an alarming character. The first lieutenant was in hardly better health. All the responsibility of the expedition fell upon Furneaux, who was quite equal to the task. After a rest of fifteen days, during which the peace had not been disturbed, Wallis found all his invalids restored to health.

Provisions, however, became less plentiful. The natives, spoilt by the abundance of nails and hatchets, became more exacting.

Upon the 15th of July, a tall woman, apparently some forty-five years of age, of majestic appearance, and who seemed to be much respected by the natives, came on board the *Dauphin*. Wallis at once perceived by the dignity of her deportment, and the freedom of her manner, peculiar to persons habituated to command, that she was of high station. He presented her with a blue mantle, a looking-glass, and other gewgaws, which she received with an expression of profound contentment. Upon leaving the vessel she invited the captain to land, and to pay her a visit. Wallis, although still very weak, did not fail to comply with this request next day. He was conducted to a large hut, which covered about 327 feet in length, and 42 in width. The roof was constructed of palm leaves and was supported by fifty-three pillars.

A considerable crowd, collected together by the event, lined the approach, and received him respectfully. The visit was enlivened by a comical incident. The surgeon of the vessel, who perspired greatly from the effects of the walk, to relieve himself took off his wig. A sudden exclamation from one of the Indians at this sight, drew general attention to the prodigy, and all fixed their eyes upon it. The whole assemblage remained perfectly still for some moments, in the silence of astonishment, which could not have been greater if they had seen one of our company decapitated.

Next day, a messenger, sent to convey a present to Queen Oberoa, in acknowledgment of her gracious reception, found her giving a feast to several hundred persons.

Her servants carried the dishes to her already prepared, the meat in cocoa-nut shells, and the shell fish in a sort of wooden trough, similar to those used by our butchers. She herself distributed them with her own hands to each of her guests, who were sitting and standing all round the house. When this was over, she seated herself upon a sort of raised dais, and two women beside her gave her her food. They offered the viands to her in their fingers; and she had only to take the trouble to open her mouth.

The consequences of this exchange of civilities were speedily felt. The market was once more fully supplied with provisions, although no longer at the same low price as upon the first arrival of the English.

Lieutenant Furneaux reconnoitred, the length of the coast westward, to gain an idea of the island, and to see what it was possible to obtain from it. The English were everywhere well received. They found a pleasant country, densely populated, whose inhabitants appeared in no hurry to sell their commodities. All their working implements were either of stone or of bone, which led Lieutenant Furneaux to infer that the Tahitians possess no metals.

As they had no earthenware vessels, they had no idea that water could be heated. They discovered it one day when the queen dined on board. One of the principal members of her suite, having seen the surgeon pour water from the boiler into the teapot, turned the tap and received the scalding liquor upon his hand. Finding himself burnt, he uttered most frightful screams, and ran round the cabin making most extravagant gestures. His companions, unable to imagine what had happened to him, stared at him with mingled astonishment and fear. The surgeon hastened to interfere, but for a long time the poor Tahitian refused to be comforted.

Some days later, Wallis discovered that his sailors stole nails to give them to the native women. They even went so far as to raise the planks of the ship to obtain screws, nails, bolts, and all the bits of iron which united them to the timbers. Wallis countered the offence rigorously, but nothing availed, and in spite of the precaution he took, of allowing no one to leave the vessel without being searched, these robberies constantly occurred.

An expedition, undertaken into the interior, discovered a large valley watered by a beautiful river. Everywhere the soil was carefully cultivated, and arrangements had been made for watering the gardens and the fruit plantations. Farther penetrations into the interior proved the capacious windings of the river; the valley narrowed, the hills were succeeded by mountains, at every step the way became more difficult. A peak, distant about six miles from the place of landing, was climbed, in the hope of thus discovering the entire island, even to its smallest recesses. But the view was intercepted by yet higher mountains. On the side towards the sea, however, nothing interfered with the magnificent view which stretched before their gaze, everywhere hills, covered with magnificent woods, upon whose verdant slopes the huts of the natives stood out clearly, and in the valleys with their numberless cabins, and gardens surrounded by hedges, the scenes were still more enchanting. The sugar cane, ginger plant, tamarind and tree ferns, with cocoanut-trees, furnished the principal resources of this fertile country.

Wallis, wishing to enrich it still more with the productions of our own climate, caused peach, cherry, and plum stones to be planted, as well as lemon, orange and lime pips, and sowed quantities of vegetable seeds. At the same time he gave the queen a present of a cat about to kitten, of two cocks, fowls, geese, and other domestic animals, which he hoped might breed well.

However, time pressed, and Wallis decided to leave. When he announced his intention to the queen, she threw herself upon a seat and cried for a long time, with so much grief that it was impossible to comfort her. She remained upon the vessel up to the last

moment, and as it set sail "embraced us," says Wallis, "in the ten-
derest way, weeping, plenteously, and our friends the Tahitians bade
us farewell, with so much sorrow, and in so touching a manner, that
I felt heavy-hearted, and my eyes filled with tears." The uncour-
teous reception of the English, and the repeated attempts made by
the natives to seize the vessel, would hardly have led to the idea of
a painful separation! However, as the proverb has it, All's well that
ends well!

Of Wallis' observations of the manners and customs of the
island, we shall only enumerate the few following as we shall have
occasion to return to them again in relating the voyages undertaken
by Bougainville and Cook.

Tall, well built, active, slightly dark in complexion, the natives
were clothed in a species of white stuff made from the bark of trees.
Two pieces of stuff completed their costume, one was square and
looked like a blanket. The head was thrust through a hole in the
centre, and it recalled the "zarapo" of the Mexicans, and the
"poncho" of the South American Indian. The second piece was
rolled round the body, without being tightened. Almost all, men
and women, tattoo their bodies with black lines close together, representing different figures. The operation was thus performed: the
pattern was pricked in the skin, and the holes filled with a sort of
paste composed of oil and grease, which left an indelible mark.

Civilization has little advanced. We have already stated that the
Tahitians did not understand earthenware vessels. Wallis, therefore,
presented the queen with a saucepan, which everybody flocked to
inspect with extreme curiosity.

As to, religion, the captain found no trace of that! He only
noticed that upon entering certain places, which he took to be
cemeteries, they maintained a respectful appearance, and wore
mourning apparel.

One of the natives, more disposed than his companions to adopt
English manners, was presented with a complete suit of clothes,
which became him very well. Jonathan – so they had named him,
was quite proud of his new outfit. To put the finishing touch to his
manners, he desired to learn the use of a fork. But habit was too
strong for him! his hands always went to his mouth! and the bit of
meat at the end of the fork, found its way to his ear.

It was the 27th of July, when Wallis left the George III. Island.
After coasting Duke of York Island, he discovered several islands or
islets in succession, upon which he did not touch. For example,

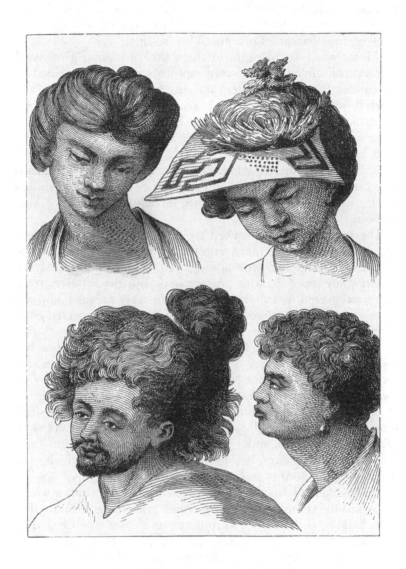

Head-dresses of natives of Tahiti.
(Facsimile of early engraving).

Charles Saunders, Lord Howe, Scilly, Boscawen, and Keppel Islands, where the hostile character of the natives, and the difficulty of disembarkation prevented his landing.

Winter was now to begin in the southern region. The vessel leaked in all directions, the stern especially was much strained by the rudder. Was it wise, under such circumstances, to sail for Cape Horn or the Straits of Magellan? Would it not be running the risk of certain shipwreck? Would it not be better to reach Tinian or Batavia, where repairs were possible, and to return to Europe by the Cape of Good Hope?

Wallis decided upon the latter course. He steered for the northwest, and upon the 19th of September, after a voyage which was too fortunate to supply any incidents, he cast anchor in the Tinian harbour.

The incidents which marked Byron's stay in this place were repeated with far too much regularity. Wallis could not rejoice over its facilities for provisioning, or the temperature of the country, any more than his predecessors. But the sufferers from scurvy recovered in a short time, the sails were mended, and the vessel calked and repaired, and the crew had the unexpected good fortune of catching no fever.

On the 16th October, 1769, the *Dauphin* returned to sea, but this time, she encountered a succession of frightful storms, which tore the sails reopened the leakage, broke the rudder, and carried away the poop with all that was to be found on the forecastle.

However, the Bashees were rounded, and Formosa Strait crossed, Sandy Isle, Small Key, Long Island, and New Island were recognized, as also, Condor, Timor, Aros, and Pisang, Pulo-Taya, Pulo-Toté, and Sumatra, before the arrival at Batavia, which took place upon the 30th of November.

We have already had occasion to mention the localities which witnessed the completion of the voyage. It is enough to state that from Batavia, where the crews took the fever, Wallis proceeded by the Cape, thence to St. Helena, and finally arrived in the Downs, on the 20th of May, 1768, after six hundred and thirty-seven days' voyage.

It is to be regretted that Hawkesworth has not reproduced the instructions Wallis received from the Admiralty. Without knowing what they were, we cannot decide whether this brave sailor carried out the orders he had received *au pied de la lettre*. We have seen that he followed with little variation the route traced by his predecessors, in the Pacific Ocean. In fact, nearly all had approached by the dangerous archipelago, leaving unexplored that portion of Oceania, where islands are most numerous, and where Cook was later to make such important discoveries.

Clever as a navigator, Wallis understood how to obtain from a hasty and incomplete equipment unexpected resources, which enabled him to bring an adventurous enterprise to a successful close. He is equally to be honoured for his humanity and the efforts he made to collect reliable information of the countries he visited. Had he only been accompanied by special men of science, there is no doubt that their scientific harvest would have been abundant.

The fault lay with the Admiralty.

We have related how, on the 10th of April, 1767, as the *Dauphin* and the *Swallow* entered the Pacific, the former, carried away by a strong breeze, had lost sight of the latter, and had been unable to follow her. This separation was most unfortunate for Captain Carteret. He knew better than any of his crew the dilapidated condition of his vessel and the insufficiency of his provisions. In short, he was well aware that he could only hope to meet the *Dauphin* in England, as no plan of operation had been arranged, and no rendezvous had been named – a grave omission on Wallis' part, who was aware of the condition of his consort.

Nevertheless, Carteret allowed none of his apprehensions to come to the knowledge of the crew. At first the detestable weather experienced by the *Swallow* upon the Pacific Ocean (most misleading name), allowed no time for reflection. The dangers of the passing moment, in which there was every prospect of their being engulfed, hid from them the perils of the future.

Carteret steered for the north, by the coast of Chili. Upon investigating the quantity of soft water which he had on board he found it quite insufficient for the voyage he had undertaken. He determined therefore, before setting sail for the west, to take in water at Juan Fernandez, or at Mas-a-Fuero.

The weather continued wretched. Upon the evening of the 27th a sudden squall was followed by a rising wind, which carried the vessel straight to the Cape. The violence of the storm failed to carry away the masts or to founder the ship. The tempest continued in all its fury, and the sails being extremely wet, clung round the masts and rigging so closely, that it was impossible to work them. Next day a sudden wave broke the mizen-mast, just where there was a flaw in the sail, and submerged the vessels for a few moments. The storm only abated sufficiently to allow the crew of the *Swallow* time to recover a little, and to repair the worst damage; then recommenced, and continued with violent squalls until the 7th of May. The wind then became favourable, and three days later Juan Fernandez was reached.

Carteret was not aware that the Spaniards had fortified this island. He was, therefore, extremely surprised at seeing a large number of men upon the shore, and at perceiving a battery of four pieces on the beach, and a fort, pierced with twenty embrasures and surmounted by the Spanish flag, upon a hill.

The rising wind prevented an entrance into Cumberland Bay, and after cruising about for an entire day, Carteret was obliged to content himself with reaching Mas-a-Fuero. But he met the same obstacles, and the surge which broke upon the shore interfered with his operations, and it was only with the utmost difficulty that he succeeded in shipping a few casks of water. Some of the crew, who had been forced by the state of the sea to remain on land, killed guinea fowls enough to feed the entire crew. These, with the exception of some seals and plenty of fish, were the sole result of a stay, marked by a succession of squalls and storms, which constantly placed the ship in danger.

Carteret, who, owing to unfavourable winds, had had several opportunities of noticing Mas-a-Fuero, corrected many of the errors in the account of Lord Anson's voyage, and furnished many details of inestimable use to navigators.

On leaving Mas-a-Fuero, Carteret steered northward in the hope of meeting the south-eastern trade wind. Carried farther than he had counted upon, he determined to seek St. Ambrose, and St. Felix Island, or the island of St. Paul. Now that the Spaniards had taken possession of and fortified Juan Fernandez, those islands might be of great value to the English in the event of war.

But Mr. Green's charts and the "Elements of Navigation" by Robertson did not tally as to their situation. Carteret, having most confidence in the latter work, sought for them in the north, and failed to find them. In re-reading the description given by Waser, Davis' surgeon, he thought these two islands were identical with the land met with by that filibuster, in his route to the south of the Galapagos Islands, and that Davis' Land did not exist. This caused a double error, that of identifying St. Felix Island with Davis' Land, and of denying the existence of the latter, which is in reality Easter Island.

"At this parallel," says Carteret, that is in 18° west from his point of departure, "we had fresh breezes, and a strong northerly current, and other reasons for conjecturing that we were near Davis' Land, which we were seeking so carefully. But a stiff breeze rising again, we steered quarter S.W. and reached 28½° southern latitude, from which it follows that if this land or anything answering to it exists, I must infallibly have fallen in with it, or at least have seen it. I afterwards remained in 28° south latitude, and 40° west of my point of departure, and as far as I can conjecture 121° west London.

All the navigators combined in insisting upon the existence of a southern continent. Carteret could not conceive that Davis' Land was but a small island, a spot lost in the immensity of the ocean. As he found no continent, he decided upon the nonexistence of Davis' Land. It was precisely in this way that he was misled.

Carteret continued his search until the 7th of June. He was in 28° south latitude and 112° west longitude, that is to say, he was in the immediate neighbourhood of Easter Island. It was still the depth of winter. The sea ran continually high, violent and variable winds, dull, foggy, and cold weather was accompanied by thunder, rain, and snow. No doubt it was owing to the great darkness. and to the thick fog, which hid the sun for several days, that Carteret failed to perceive Easter Island, for many signs, such as the number of birds, floating seaweeds, &c., announced the neighbourhood of land.

These atmospheric troubles again retarded the voyage, in addition to which the *Swallow* was as bad a sailer as possible, and one may guess at the weariness, the preoccupation, even the mental suffering of the captain, who saw his crew on the point of starvation. But in spite of all, the voyage was continued by day and night in a westerly direction until the 2nd of July. Upon this day land was discovered to the north, and on the morrow, Carteret was sufficiently close to recognize it. It was only a great rock five miles in circumference, covered with trees, which appeared uninhabited, but the swell, so prevalent at this time of year, prevented the vessel coming alongside. It was named Pitcairn, after the first discoverer. In these latitudes, the sailors, previously in good health, felt the first attacks of scurvy.

Upon the 11th, a new land was seen in 22° southern latitude, and 145° 34' longitude. It received the name of Osnaburgh in honour of the king's second son.

Next day Carteret sent an expedition to two more islands, where neither eatables nor water were found. The sailors caught many birds in their hands, as they were so tame that they did not fly at the approach of man.

All these islands belonged to the Dangerous group, a long chain of low islands, clusters of which were the despair of all navigators, for the few resources they offered. Carteret thought he recognized Quiros in the land discovered, but this place, which is called by the natives Tahiti, is situated more to the north.

Sickness, however, increased daily. The adverse winds, but especially the damage the ship had sustained, made her progress very slow. Carteret thought it necessary to follow the route upon which he was most likely to obtain provisions and the needful rapairs.

"My intention in the event of my ship being repaired," says Cartaret, "was to continue my voyage to the south upon the return of a favourable season, with a view to new discoveries in that quarter of the world. In fact, I had settled in my own mind, if I could find a continent where sufficient provisions were procurable, to remain near its coast until the sun had passed the Equator, then to gain a distant southern latitude and to proceed westward towards the Cape of Good Hope, and to return eastward after touching at the Falkland Islands, should it be necessary, and thence to proceed quickly to Europe."

These laudable intentions show Carteret to have been a true explorer, rather stimulated than intimidated by danger, but it proved impossible to carry them into execution.

The trade wind was only met on the 16th, and the weather remained detestable. Above all, although Carteret navigated in the neighbourhood of Danger Island, discovered in 1765 by Byron, and by others, he saw no land.

"We probably were close by land," he says, "which the fog prevented our seeing, for in these waters numbers of birds constantly flew round the ship. Commodore Byron in his last voyage had passed the northern limits of this portion of the ocean, in which the Solomon Islands are said to be situated, and as I have been myself beyond the southern limit without seeing them, I have good reasons for thinking, that if these islands exist they have been badly marked on all the charts."

This last supposition is correct, but the Solomon Islands do exist, and Carteret stopped there a few days later without recognizing them. The victuals were now all but consumed or tainted, the rigging and the sails torn by the tempest, half the crew on the sick list, when a fresh alarm for the captain arose. A leak was reported, just below the load water-line; it was impossible to stop it, as long as they were in the open sea. By unexpected good fortune land was seen on the morrow. Needless to say what cries of delight, what acclamations followed this discovery. To use Carteret's own comparison, the feelings of surprise and comfort experienced by the crew can only be likened to those of a criminal, who at the last moment on the scaffold receives a reprieve! It was Nitendit Island, already discovered by Mendana.

No sooner was the anchor cast than landing was hurried, in search of water supply. The natives were black, with woolly hair, and perfectly naked. They appeared upon the shore, but fled again before the boat could come up with them.

The leader of the landing-party described the country as wild, bristling with mountains and impenetrable forests of trees and shrubs reaching to the shore itself, through which ran a fine current of fresh water.

The following day, the master was sent in search of an easier landing-place, with orders to propitiate the natives, if possible, by presents. He was expressly enjoined not to expose himself to danger, to return if several pirogues advanced against him, not to leave the boat himself, and not to allow more than two men to land at once, whilst the remainder held themselves on the defensive.

Carteret, at the same time, sent his ship's boat on shore for water. Some natives attacked it with arrows, which fortunately hit no one.

Meantime, the sloop regained the *Swallow*, the master had three arrows in his body, and half his crew were so dangerously wounded that three sailors and he himself died a few days later.

This is what had happened. Landing the fifth in succession, in a spot where he had noticed huts, he entered into friendly traffic with the natives. The latter soon increased in numbers, and several large pirogues advanced towards his sloop, and he was unable to rejoin it until the very moment when the attack commenced. Pursued by the arrows of the natives, who waded up to their shoulders into the water, chased by pirogues, he only succeeded in escaping after having killed several natives and foundered one of their boats.

This effort to find a more favourable spot where he might run the *Swallow* ashore, having ended so unfortunately, Carteret heaved his ship down where he was, and efforts were made to stop the leak. If the carpenter, the only healthy man on board, did not succeed in perfectly stopping it, he at least considerably diminished it.

Whilst a fresh landing for water was sought, the fire of the guns was directed upon the woods as well as volleys of musketry from the sloop. Still the sailors worked for a quarter of an hour, when they were attacked by a shower of arrows which grievously wounded one or two in the breast. The same measures were necessary each time they fetched water.

At this juncture, thirty of the crew became incapable of performing their duty. The master died of his wounds. Lieutenant Gower was very ill. Carteret, himself, attacked by a bilious and inflammatory illness, was forced to keep his bed.

These three were the only officers capable of navigating the *Swallow* to England, and they were on the point of succumbing.

To stay the ravages of disease, it was necessary to procure provisions at all costs, and this was utterly impossible in this spot. Carteret weighed anchor on the 17th of August, after calling the island Egmont, in honour of the Lord of the Admiralty, and the bay where he had anchored, *Swallow*. Although convinced that it was identical with the land named Santa Cruz by the Spaniards, the navigator nevertheless followed the prevailing mania of giving new appellations to all the places he visited. He then coasted the shore for a short distance, and ascertained that the population was large. He had many a crow to pick with the natives. These obstacles, and moreover the impossibility of procuring provisions, prevented Carteret's reconnoitring the other islands of this group, upon which he bestowed the name of Queen Charlotte.

"The inhabitants of Egmont Isle," he says, "are extremely agile, active, and vigorous. They appear to live as well in water as on land, for they are continually jumping from their pirogues into the sea. One of the arrows which they sent passed through the planks of the boat, and dangerously wounded the officer at the poop in the thigh."

Their arrows are tipped with stone, and we saw no metal of any kind in their possession. The country in general is covered with woods and mountains and interspersed with a great number of valleys.

Pursued by the arrows of the natives.

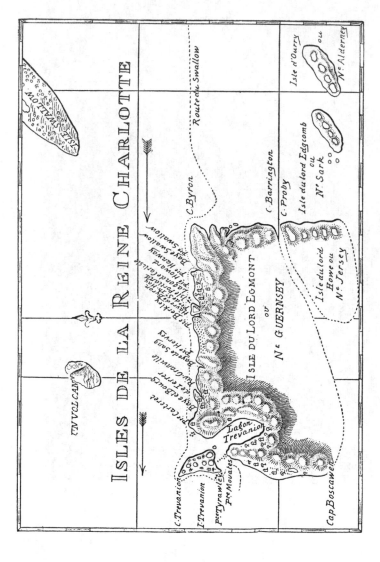

Map of Queen Charlotte Islands.
(Facsimile of early engraving.)

On the 18th of August, 1767, Carteret left this group with the intention of regaining Great Britain. They fully expected to meet with an island on his passage, where he might be more fortunate. And on the 20th, he actually did so, discovering a little low island, which he named Gower, where cocoa-nuts were procurable. Next day he encountered Simpson and Carteret Islands, and a group of new islands which he took to be the Ohang Java, discovered by Tasman; then successively, Sir Charles Hardy and Winchelsea Islands, which he did not consider as belonging to the Solomon Archipelago, the Island of St. John, so-called by Schouten, and finally that of New Britain, which he gained on the 28th of August.

Carteret coasted this island, in search of a safe and convenient port, and stopped in various bays, where he obtained water, wood, cocoa, nutmegs, aloes, sugar-canes, bamboos, and palm-cabbages.

"This cabbage," he says, "is white, crisp, of a substance filled with sugar. Eaten raw, the flavour resembles that of a chestnut, and boiled it is superior to the best parsnip. We cut it into small strips, and boiled it in the broth made from our cakes, and this broth, afterwards thickened with oatmeal furnished us with a good meal."

The wood was all alive with pigeons, turtle-doves, parroquets, and other unknown birds. The English visited several deserted huts.

If an idea of the civilization of a people can be drawn from their dwellings, these islanders were on the lowest rung of the social ladder, for their huts were the most miserable Carteret had ever seen.

The commander profited by his stay in this place, by once more overhauling the *Swallow*, and attending to the leak, which the carpenters doctored as well as they could. The sheathing was greatly worn, and the keel quite gnawed away by worms; they coated it with pitch and warm tar mixed together.

On the 7th of September, Carteret accomplished the ridiculous ceremony of taking possession of the country in the name of George III., he then despatched one of his boats upon a reconnoitring expedition, which returned with a quantity of cocoa and palm-cabbages, most precious provision for the sick on board.

In spite of the fact that the monsoon would soon blow from the east for a long time, Carteret, alive to the dilapidated condition of his ship, determined to start for Batavia, where he hoped to make up his crew, and to repair the *Swallow*.

Upon the 9th September, therefore, he left Carteret harbour, the best which he had met with since leaving the Straits of Magellan.

He soon penetrated to a gulf to which Dampier had given the name of St. George Bay, and was not long in reconnoitring for a strait which separated New Britain and New Ireland. This passage he found and named St. George. He describes it in his narrative with a care which should certainly have earned for him the thanks of all his contemporary navigators. He then followed the coast of New Ireland to its southern extremity. Near a little island, which he named Sandwich, Carteret had some dealings with the natives.

"These natives," he says "are black, and have woolly hair like negroes, but they have not flat noses or large lips. We imagine them to be of the same race as the inhabitants of Egmont Island. Like them they are entirely naked, if we except some ornaments of shells which they attach to their arms and legs. At the same time, they have adopted a fashion, without which our fashionable men and women are not supposed to be perfectly dressed. They powder their hair or rather the wool on their heads white, from which it follows that the fashion of wearing powder is probably of greater antiquity and of more extended fashion than we would have generally supposed. They are armed with spears and large sticks in the shape of clubs, but we perceived neither bows nor arrows."

At the south-western extremity of New Ireland Carteret found another land, to which he gave the name of New Hanover, and shortly afterwards the group of the Duke of Portland.

Although all this portion of the narrative of his voyage, in countries unknown before his time, abounds in precious details, Carteret, a far more able and zealous navigator than his predecessors Byron and Wallis, makes excuses for not having collected more facts.

"The description of the country," he says, "and of its productions and inhabitants, would have been far more complete and detailed had I not been so weakened and overcome by the illness to which I had succumbed through the duties which devolved upon me from want of officers. When I could scarcely drag myself along, I was obliged to take watch after watch and to share in other labours with my lieutenant, who was also in a bad state of health."

After leaving St. George's Strait, the route was westward. Carteret discovered several other islands, but illness for several days prevented his coming on deck, and therefore he could not determine their position. He named them Admiralty Islands, and after two attacks, found himself forced to employ fire-arms to repulse the natives.

He afterwards reconnoitred Durour and Matty Islands and the Cuedes, whose inhabitants were quite delighted at receiving bits of an iron hoop. Carteret affirms, that be might have bought all the productions of this country for a few iron instruments. Although they are the neighbours of New Guinea, and of the groups they had just explored, these natives were not black, but copper coloured. They had very long black hair, regular features, and brilliantly white teeth. Of medium height, strong and active, they were cheerful and friendly, and came on board fearlessly. One of them even asked permission to accompany Carteret upon his voyage, and in spite of all the representations of his countrymen and even of the captain, he refused to leave the *Swallow*. Carteret, meeting with so decided a will, consented, but the poor Indian, who had received the name of Joseph Freewill, soon faded away and died at Celebes.

On the 29th October, the English reached the north-eastern portion of Mindanao. Always on the look-out for fresh water and provisions, Carteret in vain looked for the bay which Dampier had spoken of as abounding in game. A little farther off he found a watering-place, but the hostile demonstrations of the inhabitants forced him to re-embark.

After leaving Mindanao, the captain sailed for the Straits of Macassar, between the islands of Borneo and Celebes. They entered it on the 14th of November. The vessel then proceeded with so much difficulty that she only accomplished twenty-eight leagues in fifteen days.

"Ill," he says, "weakened, dying, tortured by the sight of lands which we could not reach, exposed to tempests which we found it impossible to overcome, we were attacked by a pirate!"

The latter, hoping to find the English crew asleep, attacked the *Swallow* in the middle of the night. But far from allowing themselves to be cowed by this new danger, the sailors defended themselves with so much courage and skill, that they succeeded in foundering the Malay prah.

On the 12th of December Carteret sorrowfully perceived that the western monsoon had commenced. The *Swallow* was in no condition to struggle against this wind and current to reach Batavia by the west. He must then content himself with gaining Macassar, then the principal colony of the Dutch in the Celebes Islands.

A struggle between the *Swallow* and a Malay prah.

When the English arrived, it was thirty-five weeks since they left the Straits of Magellan.

Anchor was scarcely cast, when a Dutchman, sent by the governor, came on board the *Swallow*. He appeared much alarmed on finding that the vessel belonged to the English marine service. In the morning, therefore, when Carteret sent his lieutenant, Mr. Gower, to ask for access to the port in order to secure provisions for his dying crew, and to repair his dilapidated ship, and await the return of the monsoon, not only could he not obtain permission to land, but the Dutch hastened to collect their forces and arm their vessels. Finally, after five hours, the governor's reply was brought on board. It was a refusal couched in terms as little polite as they were equivocal. The English were simultaneously forbidden to land at any port under Dutch government.

All Carteret's representations, his remarks upon the inhumanity of the refusal, even his hostile demonstrations, had no other result than the sale of a few provisions, and permission to proceed to a small neighbouring bay.

He would find there, he was told, certain shelter from the monsoon, and might set up a hospital for his sick, that indeed he could procure more plentiful provisions there than in Macassar, from whence they would send him all that he could need. Fearing death by starvation and foundering, it was necessary to overlook these exactions, and Carteret proceeded to the roadstead of Bonthain.

There the sick, installed in a house, found themselves prohibited from going more than thirty roods from their hospital.

They were kept under guard, and could not communicate with the natives. Lastly they were forbidden to buy anything excepting through the agency of the Dutch soldiers, who strangely abused their power, often making more than a thousand per cent profit. All the complaints of the English were useless. They were forced to submit during their stay, to a surveillance to the last degree humiliating. It was only on the 22nd of May, 1768, on the return of the monsoon, that Captain Carteret was able to leave Bonthain, after a long series of annoyances, vexations, and alarms, which it is impossible to give in detail and which had sorely tried his patience.

"Celebes," he says, "is the key to the Moluccas, or Spice Islands, which are necessarily under the power of the people who are masters of this island. The town of Macassar is built upon a promontory, and is watered by one or two rivers which cross it or flow in its vicinity. The ground is even and beautiful in appearance. There are many plantations and cocoa-nut woods, interspersed with houses, which convey the idea that it is well populated.

"At Bonthain the beef is excellent, but it is difficult to procure enough of it to feed a fleet. Fowls, and as much rice and fruits as can be wished, are procurable. The woods abound with wild pigs, which are to be had cheap, because the natives, being Mohamedans, do not eat them."

These details, however incomplete, had great interest at the time they were collected, and we go so far as to believe, that even now, some hundred years since they were first written, they yet contain a certain amount of truth. No incident marked the voyage to Batavia. After several delays, caused by the desire of the Dutch Company to make Carteret give them a testimonial as to the treatment he had met with from the government of Macassar, and which he steadily refused, Carteret at last obtained permission to repair his vessel.

On the 15th of September, the *Swallow*, partially refitted, set sail. She was reinforced with a supplementary number of English sailors, without which it would have been impossible to regain Europe. Eighty of her original crew were dead, and eighty more were so reduced that seven of their number died before they reached the Cape.

After a stay in this port, a most salutary one for the crew, which lasted until the 6th of January, 1769, Carteret set out once more, and a little beyond Ascension Island, at which he had touched, he met a French vessel. It was the frigate, *La Boudeuse*, with which Bougainville had just been round the world.

On the 20th of March the *Swallow* anchored in Spithead roadstead, after thirty-one months of a voyage as painful as it had been dangerous.

All Carteret's nautical ability, all his *sang-froid*, all his enthusiasm were needed to save so inefficient a vessel from destruction, and to make important discoveries, under such conditions. If the perils of the voyage, add lustre to his renown, the shame of such a miserable equipment falls upon the English Admiralty, who, despising the representations of an able captain, risked his life and the lives of his crew upon so long a voyage.

## III.

Bougainville – A notary's son metamorphosed – Colonization of the Malouine Islands, Buenos Ayres, and Rio Janeiro – The Malouines relinquished to the Spaniards – Hydrography of the Strait of Magellan – The Pecherais – The Quatre Facardius – Tahiti – Incidents of the stay there – Productions of the country and manners of the inhabitants – Samoa Islands – The Land of the Holy Spirit, or the New Hebrides. The Louisiade – The Anchorite Isles – New Guinea – Boeton – From Batavia to St. Malo.

Whilst Wallis completed his voyage round the world, and Carteret continued his long and hazardous circumnavigation, a fresh expedition was organized for the purpose of prosecuting new discoveries in the Southern Seas.

Under the old régime, when all was arbitrary, titles, rank, and places were obtained by interest. It was therefore not surprising that a military officer, who left the army scarcely four years before with the rank of colonel, to enter the navy as a captain, should obtain this important command.

Strangely enough, this singular measure was amply justified, thanks to the talents possessed by the favoured recipient.

Louis Antoine de Bougainville was born at Paris, on the 13th of November, 1729. The son of a notary, he was destined for the bar, and was already an advocate. But having no taste for his father's profession, he devoted himself to the sciences, and published a Treatise on the Integral Calculus, whilst he obtained a commission in the Black Musqueteers.

Of the three careers he thus entered upon, he entirely abandoned the two first, slightly neglected the third, for the sake of a fourth – diplomacy, and finally left it entirely for a fifth – the naval service. He was destined to die a member of the senate after a sixth metamorphosis.

First aide-de-camp to Chevret, then Secretary of the Embassy in London, where he was made a member of the Royal Society, he left Brest in 1756, with the rank of captain of Dragoons, to rejoin Montcalm in Canada. Becoming aide-de-camp to this general, he distinguished himself on various occasions, and obtained the confidence of his chief, who sent him to France to ask for reinforcements.

Portrait of Bougainville.
(Facsimile of early engraving.)

That unhappy country was just then overwhelmed with reverses in Europe, and had need of all her resources. Therefore, when young Bougainville entered, upon the object of his mission to M. de Choiseul, the minister answered brusquely, –

"When the house is on fire, one does not worry oneself about the stables!"

"At least," replied Bougainville, "no one can say that you speak like a horse!"

This sally was too witty and too stinging to conciliate the minister. Ultimately Madame de Pompadour, who appreciated witty people, introduced Bougainville to the king and although he did not succeed in obtaining much for his general, he gained a colonelcy, and the order of St. Louis for himself, although he had only seen seven years' service. Returning to Canada he was anxious to justify Louis XIV.'s confidence, and distinguished himself in various matters. After the loss of the colony he served in Germany under M. de Choiseul-Stainville.

His military career was cut short by the peace of 1763. His active spirit and love of movement rebelled against a garrison life. He conceived the strange idea of colonizing the Falkland Islands in the extreme south of South America, and of conveying there free of expense the emigrants from Canada who had settled in France to escape the tyrannous yoke of England. Carried away by this idea, he addressed himself to certain privateers at St. Malo, who, from the commencement of the century, had been in the habit of visiting the group, and who had named them Malouine Islands.

Having gained their confidence, Bougainville brought the advantages (however problematical) of this colony to the minister's notice, maintaining that the fortunate situation of the island, would secure a good resting-place for ships going to the Southern Seas. Having high interest, he obtained the authority he desired, and received his nomination as ship-captain.

It was the year 1763. There is little reason to suppose, that marine officers, who had passed all the grades of the service, looked with gratification upon an appointment which no past event justified. But that mattered little to the Minister of Marine, M. de Choiseul-Stainville. Bougainville had served under him, and was far too grand a personage to trouble himself about the grumbling of the ship's officers.

Bougainville having brought his uncle and cousin, MM. de Nerville and d'Arboulin, to look favourably upon his venture, caused the *Eagle* of twenty guns, and the *Sphinx* of twelve, to be built at St. Malo, under the auspices of M. Guzot Duclos. Upon these he embarked several Canadian families.

Leaving St. Malo on the 15th of September, 1763, he rested at St. Catherine's Island, on the coast of Brazil, and at Montevideo, where he took horses and cattle, and landed at the Malouines in a large bay, which appeared to him wholly suited to his purpose, but he was not long in discovering that what had been taken by preceding navigators for woods of moderate height, were only reeds. Not a tree, not a shrub grew in the islands. Fortunately an excellent turf did for fuel in their stead, whilst fish and game offered good resources.

The colony consisted at first of only twenty-nine persons, for whom huts were built and also a provision warehouse. At the same time a fort, capable of holding fourteen guns, was planned and commenced. M. de Nerville agreed to remain at the head of the establishment, whilst Bougainville returned to France on the 5th of April. There he recruited some more colonists, and took a considerable cargo of provisions of every kind, which he disembarked on the 5th of January, 1765. He then went to the Strait of Magellan in search of a cargo of wood, and having, as we have already narrated, met Commodore Byron's squadron, followed it to Port Famine.

There he took in more than ten thousand saplings of different growths, which he intended to transport to the Malouines. When he left the group on the 27th of April following, the colony already numbered eighty persons, comprising a staff paid by the king. Towards the end of 1765, the same two vessels were sent back with provisions and new colonists.

The colony was beginning to make a show, when the English settled themselves in Port Egmont, reconnoitred by Byron. At the same time Captain Macbride attempted to obtain possession of the colony, on the ground that the land belonged to the English king, although Byron had not recognized the Malouines in 1765, and the French had then been settled there two years.

In the meantime Spain laid claim to it in her turn, as a dependency of Southern America. England and France were equally adverse to a breach of the peace, for the sake of this archipelago, which was of so little commercial value, and Bougainville was forced to relinquish his undertaking on condition that the Spanish Government indemnified him for his expenses. In addition, he was ordered by the French Government to facilitate the restoration of the Malouines to the Spanish Commissioners.

This foolish attempt at colonization was the origin and ground-work of Bougainville's good fortune, for in order to make use of the last equipment, the minister ordered Bougainville to return by the South Sea, and to make discoveries.

In the early days of November, 1766, Bougainville repaired to Nantes, where his second in command, M. Duclos-Guiyot, captain of the fire-ship, and an able and veteran sailor, who grew grey in the inferior rank because he was not noble, superintended the equipment of the frigate *La Boudeuse*, of twenty-six guns.

Bougainville left the roadstead of Minden at the mouth of the Loire, on the 15th of November, for the La Plata river, where he hoped to find two Spanish vessels, the *Esmeralda* and the *Liebre*. But scarcely had the *Boudeuse* gained the open sea when a furious tempest arose. The frigate, the rigging of which was new, sustained such serious damages that it was necessary to put for repairs into Brest, which she entered on the 21st November. This experience sufficed to convince the captain that the *Boudeuse* was, but little fitted for the voyage he had before him. He there-fore had the masts shortened, and changed his artillery for less heavy pieces, but in spite of these modifications, the *Boudeuse* was not fit for the heavy seas and storms of Cape Horn. However, the rendezvous with the Spaniards was arranged, and Bougainville was obliged to put to sea. The staff of the frigate consisted of eleven officers and three volunteers, among whom was the Prince of Nassau-Sieghen. The crew comprised 203 sailors, boys, and servants.

As far as La Plata the sea was calm enough to allow of Bougainville's making many observations on the currents, a frequent source of the errors made by navigators in their reckonings.

On the 31st of January, *La Boudeuse* anchored in Montevideo Bay, where the two Spanish frigates had been awaiting her for a month, under the command of Don Philippe Pelicis Puente.

The long stay Bougainville made in this part, and also at Buenos Ayres, enabled him to collect facts about the city, and the manners of the inhabitants, which are too curious to be passed over in silence. Buenos Ayres appeared to them too large for its population, which amounted only to 20,000, the reason being that the houses are of only one storey, and have large courts or gardens. Not only has this town no fort, but it has not even a jetty. Thus ships are forced to discharge their cargoes on to lighters, which convey them to the little river, where carts come to take the bales and convey them to the town.

The number of religious communities, both male and female, in Buenos Ayres, adds to the originality of its character.

Bougainville says, "The year is full of Saint days, which are celebrated by processions and fireworks. Religious ceremonies supply the place of theatres. The Jesuits incite the women to greater austerity in their piety than any other order. Attached to their convent they have an institution intitled, *Casa de los egericios de las mugeres*, that is, 'house for the devotion of women'. Women and girls, without the permission of husbands or fathers, enter the retreat for twelve days, to increase their sanctity."

They were lodged and boarded at the expense of the company. No man ever set foot in this sanctuary unless in the cowl of St. Ignatius. Servants even of the female sex were not allowed to accompany their mistresses. The devotional services consisted of meditation, prayer, catechizings, confession, and flagellation. "We were shown the stains on the walls of the chapel, made by the blood which flowed under the hands of these Magdalens as they did penance."

The environs of the town were well cultivated and brightened by a large number of country houses named "quentas", but scarcely two or at most three leagues from Buenos Ayres were immense plains, with scarcely a single undulation, given up to bulls and horses, which are almost the only inhabitatants. Bougainville says, –

"These animals were so abundant, that travellers, when they needed food, would kill a bull, consume what they could eat, and leave the rest to be devoured by wild dogs and tigers."

The Spaniards had not yet succeeded in subduing the Indian tribes on the two shores of the La Plata River. They were called "Indios bravos".

"They are of medium height, very ugly, and almost all infected with the itch. Their complexions are very dark, and the grease with which they perpetually rub themselves, makes them even blacker. Their sole garment is the skin of the roe-buck, which reaches to the heels, and in which they wrap themselves.

"These Indians pass their lives on horseback, at least near the Spanish settlement They occasionally come there with their wives to buy eau de cologne, and they never cease drinking until drunkenness literally deprives them of the power to move. Sometimes they assemble in droves of two or three hundred to carry off the cattle from the Spanish lands, or to attack the caravans of travellers.

"They pillaged, massacred, and carried off slaves. It was an evil without remedy. How was it possible to subdue a wandering nation in a vast and uncultivated country where it was difficult even to meet with them?

"Commerce was far from flourishing, as no European merchandise was allowed to pass by land to Peru or Chili."

Nevertheless Bougainville saw a vessel leaving Buenos Ayres carrying a million piastres, "And if," adds he, "all the inhabitants of this country had the traffic of their hides in Europe, that of itself would be enough to enrich them."

The anchorage of Montevideo was safe, although several times they were visited by "pamperos", a scourge of the South-West, accompanied by violent tempests. The town offered nothing of interest. The environs are so uncultivated that it is necessary to import flour, biscuits, and everything necessary for the boats. But fruits, such as figs, peaches, apples, lemons, &c., are plentiful, as well as the same quantity of butcher's meat as in the rest of the country.

These documents, which are a hundred years old, are curious when compared with those furnished by contemporary navigators, especially by M. Emile Daireaux, in his work on La Plata. In many respects this picture is still correct, but there are other details (such for instance as regards instruction, of which Bougainville could not speak, as it did not exist) in which it has made immense progress. When the victuals, the provision of water, and the cattle were embarked, the three vessels set sail on the 28th of February, 1767, for the Malouines. The voyage was not fortunate. Variable winds, heavy weather, and a running sea, caused much damage to the *Boudeuse*. On the 23rd of March she cast anchor in French Bay, where she was joined on the morrow by the two Spanish vessels, which had been much tried by the tempest.

Upon the 1st of April the restitution of the colony to the Spaniards was solemnized. Very few French profited by their king's permission to remain in the Malouines; almost all preferred to embark upon the Spanish frigates upon their leaving Montevideo. As for Bougainville, he was forced to await the provisions, which the fly-boat *Etoile* was to bring him, and which was to accompany him upon his voyage round the world.

However, the months of March, April, and May passed, and no *Etoile* appeared. It was impossible to cross the Pacific with only six months' provisions, which was all the *Boudeuse* carried.

Bougainville decided at last, on the 2nd of June, to reach Rio Janeiro, which he had mentioned to M. de la Gerandais, the commander of the *Etoile* as a rendezvous, should unforeseen circumstances prevent his reaching the Malouines.

The crossing was made with such favourable weather, that only eighteen days were needed to reach the Portuguese Colony. The *Etoile*, which had been awaiting her for four days, had left France later than was expected. She had been forced to seek shelter from the tempest at Montevideo, from whence, following her instructions she gained Rio.

Well received by the Count of Acunha, Viceroy of Brazil, the French had opportunities of seeing the comedies of Metastasio given at the opera by a Mulatto troupe, and of hearing the works of the great Italian masters executed by a bad orchestra, conducted by a deformed abbé in ecclesiastical dress.

But the cordial relations with the viceroy were not lasting. Bougainville, who with the viceroy's permission had made some purchase, found the delivery of it refused for no reason. He was forbidden to take wood he needed from the royal timber-yard although he had concluded a contract for it, and lastly, he was prevented from lodging with his staff, during the repairs of the *Boudeuse*, in a house near the town, placed at his disposal by a friend. To avoid altercation, Bougainville hurried the preparations for departure.

Before leaving the capital of Brazil, the French commander entered into various details of the beauty of the port, and the picturesque nature of its surroundings, and finished by a very curious digression upon the prodigious riches of the country of which the port was the emporium.

"The mines called 'general'," he says, "are the nearest to the town, although they are seventy-five leagues away from it. They yield the king a yearly revenue by his right to a fifth share of at least a hundred and twelve arobas of gold. In 1762, they brought him in a hundred and nineteen. Under the captaincy of the 'general' mines, those of the 'Rio des Morts', Sabara, and Sero Frio were included – the last named, in addition to all the gold it produces, yields all the diamonds which come from the Brazils. No precious stones, except diamonds, are contraband. They belonged to the speculators, who were obliged to keep an exact account of the diamonds they find and to restore them to the possession of an intendant named by the king for this purpose. He immediately places them in a casket bound with iron, and fastened with three locks. He retains one key, the king has another, and the 'Provedor de hacienda reale' the third. This casket is enclosed in a second, stamped with the seals of the three persons named, and containing the three keys of the smaller one."

But in spite of all these precautions, and the severe punishment visited upon diamond robberies, an enormous contraband trade was carried on. It was, however, not the only source of revenue; and Bougainville calculated, that deducting the maintenance of troops, the pay of the civil officers, and all the expenses of the administration, the King of Portugal drew no less than ten million francs from the Brazils.

From Rio to Montevideo no incident occurred, but upon the Plata, during a storm, the *Etoile* was run down by a Spanish vessel, which broke her bowsprit, her beak head, and much of her rigging. The damages and the shock increased the leak of the ship, and forced her to return to Encenada de Baragan, where repairs were more easily managed than at Montevideo. It was impossible therefore to leave the river until the 14th of November.

Thirteen days later, both ships came in sight of Virgin Cape at the entrance to the Strait of Magellan, which they hastened to enter.

Possession Bay, the first they met with, is a large space, open to all winds and offering very bad anchorage. From Virgin Cape to Orange Cape is about fifteen leagues, and the strait is throughout seven or eight leagues wide. The first narrow entrance was easily passed, and anchor cast in Boucault Bay, where half a score of officers and men landed.

They soon made acquaintance with the Patagonians, and exchanged a few trifles, precious to the natives, for swansdown and guanaco skins.

The inhabitants were tall, but none of them reached six feet.

"What struck me as gigantic in their proportions," says Bougainville, "was their enormous breadth of shoulder, the size of their heads, and the thickness of their limbs. They are robust and well-nourished, their muscles are sinewy, their flesh firm, and in fact they are men who, having lived in the open air and drawn their

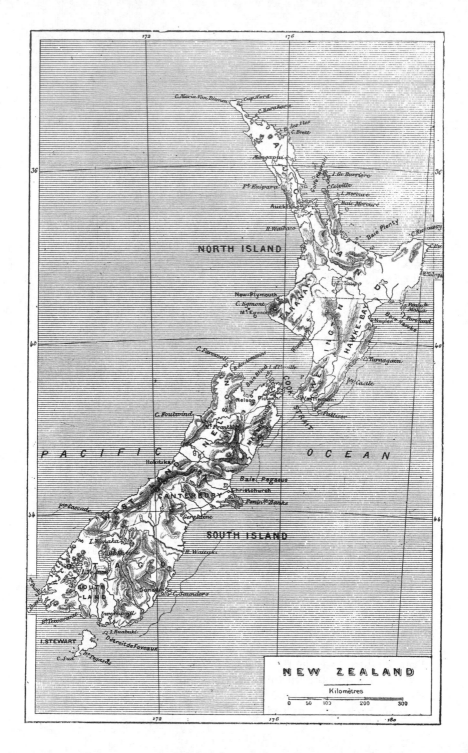

Gravé par E. Morieu.

nourishment from juicy aliments, have reached their highest point of development."

The distance from the first to the second opening may have been six or seven leagues, and was passed without accident. This opening is only one and a half leagues in width, and four in length. In this part of the strait the ships easily reconnoitred St. Bartholomew and St. Elizabeth Islands.

At the latter the French landed. They found neither wood nor water. It was an absolutely desert land.

Leaving this place, the American side of the strait is amply furnished with wood. But although the first advances had been fortunate, Bougainville was to find plenty to try his patience.

The distinctive character of the climate lies in the rapid atmospheric changes, which succeeded each other so quickly that it is quite impossible to forecast their sudden and dangerous variations. Hence the damages which it is impossible to foresee, which retard the passage of the ships, even if they do not force them to seek shelter for repairs.

Guyot-Duclos Bay provides an excellent anchorage, with six or eight fathoms of water and sound bottom. Bougainville remained there long enough to fill several casks, and endeavoured to procure fresh meat, but he only met with a few wild animals. St Anne's point was reached. At that place Sarmiento had founded the colony of Philippeville in 1581.

In a preceding volume we have narrated the fearful catastrophe which procured the name of Port Famine for this spot.

The French reconnoitred several bays, capes, and harbours at which they touched. They were Bougainville Bay, where the *Etoile* was repainted, Port Beau Bassin, Cormadière Bay, off the coast of Tierra del Fuego, and Cape Forward, which forms the most southerly point of the strait and of Patagonia, Cascade Bay in Tierra del Fuego, the safety, easy anchorage, and facilities for procuring water and wood of which, render it a most desirable haven for navigators.

The various ports which Bougainville discovered are particularly valuable, as they offer favourable points for doubling Cape Forward, one of the most difficult routes for sailors on account of the violent and contrary winds which prevail there.

The year 1768 opened for the adventurers in Fortescue Bay, below which is Port Galant, the plan of which had been taken with great exactitude by M. de Gennes. Detestable weather, of which the worst winter in Paris can give no idea, detained the French expedition for three weeks. It was visited by a band of Pecheians, the inhabitants of Tierra del Fuego, who boarded the ship.

"We made them sing," says the narrative, "dance, listen to instruments, and above all eat. Everything was pleasant to them, bread, salt meat, tallow, they devoured everything that was given them. They showed no surprise either at the sight of the vessels or that of the various objects which were shown to them, no doubt because to feel surprise at works of art, one must have elementary ideas. These men, akin to brutes, treated *chef-d'œuvres* of human industry as they treated the laws and phenomena of nature.

"These savages are small, ugly, thin, and smell abominably. They are all but naked, having only clothing of seal-skin too small to cover them.

"These women are hideous, and the men appear to care little for them. They live all together, men and women and children, in one hut, in the centre of which a fire is lighted.

"Their food is chiefly shell-fish. Still they have dogs and snares set with whalebone. On the whole they appear to be a good sort of people, but so weak that one overlooks their faults.

"Of all the savages I have met with, the Pecherais are the most destitute."

A painful event occurred whilst the crew were in this port. A child of about twelve years of age came on board, and glass beads and bits of glass were given to it, with no suspicion of the use to which they would be put. It would appear that these savages are in the habit of stuffing pieces of talc down their throats as talismans. This boy no doubt meant to do the same with the glass, for when they landed they found him vomiting violently and spitting blood. His throat and gums were lacerated and bleeding. In spite of the enchantments and violent rubbings of a juggler, or perhaps on account of this not too effective treatment, the poor child suffered dreadfully, and died shortly afterwards. This was the signal for a precipitate flight of the Pecherais. They no doubt entertained a fear that the French had cast a spell upon them, and that they would all die in a similar manner.

On the 16th of January, in endeavouring to reach Rupert Isle, the *Boudeuse* was driven by the currents half a cable's length from the shore. The anchor which was then heaved, gave way, and without the least land-breeze the vessel stranded.

It was necessary to regain Galant Harbour. It was just time, for next day a fearful storm was raging.

"After experiencing constantly adverse and variable winds for twenty-six days in Port Galant, thirty-six hours favourable breeze,

"We made them sing."

for which we had not dared to hope, sufficed to take us into the Pacific Ocean. This I believe to be a solitary instance of a voyage without anchorage from Port Galant to the narrow channel. I estimate the entire length of this strait, from Virgin Cape to Cape Peliers, at about 114 leagues.

"We took fifty-two days to accomplish it. In spite of the difficulties we met with in the passage of the Straits of Magellan" (and in this Bougainville entirely agrees with Byron), "I should advise this route, in preference to that by Cape Horn from September to the end of March. During the remaining months of the year I should prefer the open sea.

"Contrary winds and heavy seas are not dangerous, whilst it is not wise to grope one's way between two coasts. One is sure to be detained for some time in the strait, but this delay is not time wholly lost. One meets with water in abundance, wood and shell-fish, and occasionally very good fish. And I am decidedly of opinion that a crew reaching the Pacific by doubling Cape Horn suffers more from the ravages of scurvy than that which proceeds by the Straits of Magellan."

Bougainville's opinion has met with many opposers up to the present time, and the route which he lauds so highly has been almost abandoned by navigators. One strong reason for which is that steam has completely transformed maritime experience, and entirely changed nautical science.

Scarcely had he entered the Southern Sea, when Bougainville, to his intense surprise, found the winds southerly. He was therefore obliged to relinquish his intention of reaching Juan Fernandez.

Bougainville had agreed with M. de la Giraudais, captain of the *Etoile*, that if a larger stretch of sea was discovered, the two vessels should separate, but not lose sight of each other, and that every evening the bugle should recall them within half a league of each other, so that, in the event of the *Boudeuse* encountering danger, the *Etoile* might avoid it.

Bougainville for some time sought Easter Island in vain. At last he fell in during the month of March with the lands and islands erroneously marked upon M. Bellin's chart as Quiros Islands. On the 22nd of the same month he met with four islets, to which he gave the name of Quatre Facardins, which belonged to the Dangerous group, a set of madreporic islets, low and damp, which all navigators who have visited the Pacific Ocean by way of the Straits of Magellan appear to have noticed.

A little further discovery was made, of a fertile island inhabited

Lancers' Island.

by entirely naked savages, who were armed with long spears, which they brandished with menacing gestures, and thus it obtained the name of Lancers' Island.

We need not refer to what we have already repeatedly said of the nature of these islands, the difficulty of access to them, their wild and inhospitable inhabitants. Cook calls this very Lancers Island, Thrum Cape, and the island of La Harpe, which Bougainville found on the 24th, is identical with Cook's Bow Island.

The captain, knowing that Roggewein had nearly perished in these latitudes, and thinking the interest of their exploration not worth the risk to be run, proceeded southward and soon lost sight of this immense archipelago, which extends in length 500 leagues, aud contains at least sixty islands or groups.

Upon the 2nd of April Bougainville perceived a high and steep mountain, to which he gave the name of *La Boudeuse*. It was Maïtea Island, already called La Dezana by Quiros. On the 4th at sunrise the vessel reached Tahiti, a long island consisting of two peninsulas, united by a tongue of land no more than a mile in width.

More than 100 pirogues hastened to surround the two vessels. They were laden with cocoa-nuts and many delicious fruits which were readily exchanged for all sorts of trifles.

When night fell, the shore was illuminated by a thousand fires, to which the crew responded by throwing rockets.

"The appearance of this shore," says Bougainville, "raised like an amphitheatre, offered a most attractive picture. Although the mountains are high, the land nowhere shows its nakedness, being covered with wood. We could scarcely credit our sight, when we perceived a peak, covered with trees, which rose above the level of the mountains in the southern portion of the island. It appeared only thirty fathoms in diameter, and decreased in size at its summit. At a distance it might have been taken for an immense pyramid, adorned with foliage by a clever decorator, The least elevated portions of the country are intersected by fields and groves. And the entire length of the coast, upon the shore below the higher level, is a stretch of low land, unbroken and covered by plantations. There, amid the bananas, cocoa-nut and other fruit-trees we saw the huts of the natives."

The whole of the morrow was spent in barter. The natives, in addition to fruits, offered fowls, pigeons, fishing instruments, working implements, stuffs, and shells, for which they asked nails and earrings.

Upon the morning of the 6th, after three days devoted to tacking about and reconnoitring the coast in search of a roadstead, Bougainville decided to cast anchor in the bay he had seen the first day of his arrival.

"The number of pirogues round our vessels," he says, "was so great, that we had immense trouble in making way through the crowd and noise. All approached crying, 'Tayo', *friend*, and offering a thousand marks of friendship. The pirogues were full of women, who might vie with most Europeans in pleasant features and who certainly excelled them in beauty of form."

Bougainville's cook managed to escape, in spite of all prohibitions, and gained the shore. But he had no sooner landed, than he was surrounded by a vast crowd, who entirely undressed him to investigate his body. Not knowing what they were going to do with him, he thought himself lost, when the natives restored his clothes, and conducted him to the vessel more dead than alive. Bougainville wished to reprimand him, but the poor fellow assured him, that however he might threaten him, he could never equal the terrors of his visit on shore.

As soon as the ship could heave to, Bougainville landed with some of his officers to reconnoitre the watering-place. An enormous crowd immediately surrounded him, and examined him with great curiosity, all the time crying "Tayo! Tayo!". One of the natives received them in his house, and served them with fruits, grilled fish, and water. As they regained the shore, a native of fine appearance, lying under a tree, offered them a share of the shade.

"We accepted it," says Bougainville, "and the man at once bent towards us, and in a gentle way, sung, to the sound of a flute which another Indian blew with his nose, a song which was no doubt anacreontic. It was a charming scene, worthy of the pencil of Boucher. Four natives came with great confidence to sup and sleep on board. We had the flute, bassoon, and violin played for them, and treated them to fireworks composed of rockets and serpents. This display excited both surprise and fear."

Before giving further extracts from Bougainville's narrative, it appears *apropos* to warn the reader not to accept these descriptions *au pied de la lettre*. The fertile imagination of the narrator embellished everything. Not content with the ravishing scenes under his eyes, the picturesque reality is not enough for him, and he adds new delights to the picture, which only overload it. He does this almost unconsciously. None the less, his descriptions should be received with great caution. We find a strange example of this tendency of the age, in the narrative of Cook's second voyage. Mr. Hodges, the painter who was attached to the expedition, wishing to reproduce the disembarkation of the English on the island of Middleburgh, paints personages who have not the smallest resemblance to the dwellers in the ocean regions, and whose togas give them the appearance of being contemporaries of Caesar or of Augustus. Yet he had the originals before his eyes, and nothing could have been easier to him than to depict the scene as it really was.

We know better how to respect truth in these days. No additions, no embellishments are found in the narratives of our navigators. And if sometimes they prove but dry accounts, which give little pleasure to the general public, they are sure to contain the elements of earnest study for the scientific man, and the basis of works for the advancement of science.

With this preamble, let us follow the narrator.

Bougainville established his sick and his water-casks upon the shore of a small river which ran at the bottom of the bay, under a guard for their security. These precautions were not taken without arousing the susceptibility and distrust of the natives. They had no objection to seeing the strangers walk about their island all day but they expected them to return on board at night. Bougainville persisted, and at last he was obliged to fix the length of his stay.

At this juncture, harmony was restored. A large shed was prepared for the sufferers from scurvy, in number thirty-four, and for their guard, which consisted of thirty men. The shed was closed on all sides and only one opening left, to which the natives crowded with the wares they wished to exchange. The only trouble they had was in keeping an eye upon everything that was brought on shore, for "there are no more adroit sharpers in Europe than these folks". Following a laudable custom, now becoming general, Bougainville presented the chief of this settlement with a pair of turkeys, and ducks and drakes, and then cleared a piece of land, where he sowed corn, wheat, rice, maize, onions, &c.

On the 10th, a native was killed by a gunshot. All Bougainville's inquiries failed to find out the perpetrator of this abominable assassination. Apparently the natives thought the victim in the wrong, for they continued to frequent the market with their former confidence.

The captain, however, knew that the harbour was not well-sheltered, and the bottom was entirely coral.

On the 12th, during a storm of wind, the *Boudeuse*, whose anchor cable had been cut by the coral, caused great injuries to the *Etoile*, upon which she was driven. Whilst all on board were busily occupied in repairing these injuries, and a boat had been despatched in search of a second passage, by means of which the ships might have left with any wind, Bougainville learned that three natives had been killed or wounded in their cabins by bayonets, and that owing to the general alarm all the inhabitants had hurried to the interior.

In spite of the risk run by his ships, the captain at once landed, and put the supposed perpetrators of this outrage (which might have brought the entire population upon the French) into irons. Thanks to these rigorous measures the natives calmed down, and the night passed without incident.

Still, Bouganville's worst apprehensions were not upon this score. He returned on board as soon as possible. But for a breeze which opportunely sprang up, both vessels would have been driven on shore by a strong squall, accompanied by a swell and thunder. The anchor cables broke, and the vessels had a narrow escape of striking on the breakers, where they must speedily have been demolished. Fortunately the *Etoile* was able to gain the open, and was soon followed by the *Boudeuse*, leaving in this foreign roadstead six anchors, which might have been of great use during the rest of the voyage.

So soon as they perceived the approaching departure of the French, the natives came in crowds with provisions of every variety. One of them, named Aotourou, asked, and finally obtained, permission to accompany Bougainville on his voyage. After his arrival in Europe, Aotourou lived eleven months in Paris, where he was received with cordiality and welcome in the highest society. In 1770, when he returned to his native land, the government took an opportunity of conveying him to the Isle of France. He was to return to Tahiti as soon as the weather permitted, but he died in the island without having been able to convey to his land the useful implements, grains, and cattle, which had been given to him by the French Government.

Tahiti, which was named Nouvelle Cythère by Bougainville, on account of the beauty of the women, is the largest of the Society's group. Although it was visited, as we have already narrated, by Wallis, we will give a little information which we owe to Bougainville.

The principal productions were cocoas, bananas, bread fruits, yams, sugar cane, &c. M. de Commerson, naturalist, who was on board the *Etoile*, recognized the Indian flora. The only quadrupeds were pigs, dogs, and rats, who multiplied rapidly.

Bougainville says, "The climate is so healthy that in spite of our fatigues, although our people were perpetually in the water, and under a burning sun, sleeping on the naked soil under the stars, no one was ill. The sufferers from scurvy whom we disembarked, and who had not enjoyed a single night's sleep, regained their strength, and were so soon restored, that some of them were completely cured on board."

In addition to this, the health and strength of the natives, who live in cabins open to every wind, and who scarcely cover the ground, which serves them as a bed, with a few leaves, the happy old age to which they easily attain, the sharpness of all their senses, and the singular beauty of their teeth, which they preserve to the greatest age, all testify to the salubrity of the climate, and the efficiency of the rules followed by the inhabitants.

In character the people seem gentle and good. It would not appear that they have civil wars among themselves, although the country is divided into little portions under independent chiefs. They are constantly at war with the inhabitants of the neighbouring islands. Not satisfied with massacring the men and male children taken in arms, they skin their chins with the beard, and keep this hideous trophy. Bougainville, could only obtain very vague information of their ceremonies and religion. But he could at least assert the reverence they pay their dead. They preserve the corpses for a long time in the open air, on a sort of scaffold sheltered by a shed. In spite of the odour of decomposition, the women go every day to weep near the monuments, and bedew the sad relics of their beloved ones with their tears and with cocoa-nut oil.

The soil is so productive, and requires so little cultivation, that men and women live in a state of almost entire idleness. Therefore it is not astonishing that the sole care of the latter is to be pleasing. Dancing, singing, long conversations, teeming with gaiety, have developed a mobility of expression among the Tahitans, surprising even to the French, a people who themselves have not the reputation of being serious, possibly because they are more lively than those who reproach them with levity.

It is impossible to fix a native's attention. A trifle strikes them, but nothing occupies them. In spite of their want of reflection, they were clever and industrious. Their pirogues were constructed after a fashion equally ingenious and solid. Their fish-hooks and all their

Pirogue of the Marquesas Islands.

fishing implements were of delicate workmanship. Their nets were like those of Europeans. Their stuffs manufactured of the bark of a tree, were generally woven and dyed of various colours.

In fact Bougainville's impression of the Tahitan people was that they were "lazzaroni".

At eight o'clock on the 16th of April, Bougainville was about ten leagues north of Tahiti, when he perceived land to windward. Although it had the appearance of three islands, it was in reality but one. It was named Oumaita after Aotourou. The captain, not thinking it wise to stop there, steered so as to avoid the Pernicious Islands, of which Roggewein's disaster had made him afraid. During the remainder of the month of April the weather was fine, with little wind.

On the 3rd of May, Bougainville bore down towards a new land, which he had just discovered, and was not long in finding others on the same day. The coasts of the largest one wore steep; in point of fact, it was simply a mountain covered with trees to its summit, with neither valley nor sea coast. Some fires were seen there, cabins built under the shade of the coconut-trees, and some thirty men running on the shore. In the evening, several pirogues approached the vessels, and after a little natural hesitation, exchanges commenced. The natives demanded pieces of red cloth in exchange for cocoa-nuts, yams, and far less beautiful stuffs than those of the Tahitans; they disdainfully refused iron, nails, and earrings, which had been so appreciated elsewhere in the Bourbon Archipelago, as Bougainville had named the Tahitan group. The natives had their breasts and thighs painted dark blue; they wore no beards; their hair was drawn into tufts on the top of their heads.

Next day, fresh islands belonging to the archipelago were seen. The natives, who appeared very savage, would not approach the vessels.

"The longitude of these islands," says the narrative, "is pretty nearly similar to that which Abel Tasman reckoned it when he discovered Amsterdam and Rotterdam Islands, the Pilstaars, Prince William Island, and the low lands of Fleemskerk. It is also approximate to that assigned for the Solomon Islands. Besides the pirogues which we have seen rowing in the open sea, and to the south, indicate other islands in this locality. Thus it appears likely that these lands form an extended chain in the same parallel. The islands comprising the Navigator Archipelago, lie below the fourteenth southern parallel, between 17° and 172° west longitude from Paris."

As fresh victuals diminished, scurvy again began to appear. It was necessary to think of putting into a port again. On the 22nd and the following days of the same month, Pentecost Island, Aurora and Leper Islands, which belong to the archipelago of New Hebrides, were reconnoitred. They had been discovered by Quiros in 1606. The landing appearing easy, the captain determined to send an expedition on shore, which would bring back cocoa-nuts and other antiscorbutic fruits. Bougainville joined them during the day. The sailors cut wood, and the natives aided in shipping it. But in spite of this apparent good feeling, the natives were still distrustful, and carried their weapons in their hands. Those who possessed none, held large stones, all ready to throw.

As soon as the boats were laden with fruit and wood, Bougainville re-embarked his men. The natives then approached in great numbers, and discharged a shower of arrows, lances, and javelins, some even entered the water the better to aim at the French. Several gunshots, fired into the air, having no effect, a well-directed general volley soon put the natives to flight.

A few days later, a boat seeking anchorage upon the coast of the Leper Islands, was in danger of attack. Two arrows aimed at them served as a pretext for the first discharge, which was speedily followed by a fire so well directed, that Bougainville believed his crew in danger. The number of victims was very large, the natives uttered piercing cries as they fled to the woods. It was a regular massacre. The captain, uneasy at the prolonged firing, sent another boat to the help of the first, when he saw it doubling a point. He therefore signalled for their return. "I took measures," he said, "that we should never again be dishonoured by such an abuse of our superior forces."

The easy abuse of their powers by captains is truly sad! The mania for destroying life needlessly, even without any object, raises one's indignation! To whatever nation explorers belong we find them guilty of the same acts. The reproach, therefore, belongs not to a particular nation, but to humanity at large.

Having obtained the commodities he needed, Bougainville regained the sea.

It would appear that the navigator aimed at making many discoveries, for he only reconnoitred the lands he found very superficially and hastily, and of all the charts which accompany the narrative, and there are many of them, not one gives an entire archipelago, or settles the various questions to which a new discovery gives rise. Captain Cook did not proceed in this way. His explorations, always conducted with care, and with rare perseverance, are for that very reason far superior in value to those of the French explorer.

The lands which the French now encountered, were no other than St. Esprit, Mallicolo, and St. Bartholomew, and the islets belonging to the latter. Although he was perfectly aware that these islands were identical with the *Tierra del Espiritu Santo* of Quiros, Bougainville could not refrain from bestowing a new name upon them, and called them the Archipelago des "Grandes Cyclades", to which however, the name of New Hebrides has been given in preference. "I readily believed," he says, "that it was its extreme southern point which Roggewein saw under the eleventh parallel, and which he named *Tienhoven* and *Groningue*. But when we arrived there everything led us to believe that we were in the southern land of Espiritu Santo. Every appearance seemed to coincide with Quiros's narrative, and the discoveries we made every day encouraged us in our search. It is singular that precisely in the same latitude and longitude as that which Quiros gives to his St. Philip and St. James' Bays, upon a shore which at first sight appeared like a continent, we found a passage equal in size to that which he gives to the opening of his bays. Did the Spanish navigator see badly, or did he wish to hide his discoveries?

"Had geographers merely guessed in making the Tierra del Espiritu Santo identical with New Guinea? To ascertain the truth, we must follow the same parallel for over 350 leagues. I resolved upon doing so, although the state and quantity of our provisions warned us to seek a European settlement as soon as possible. It will be seen that we narrowly escaped being the victims of our own persistance."

Whilst Bougainville was in these latitudes certain business matters required his presence on board the *Etoile*, and he there found out a singular fact, which had already been largely discussed by his crew. M. de Commerson had a servant named Barré. Indefatigable, intelligent, and already an experienced botanist, Barré had been seen taking an active part in the herborising excursions, carrying boxes, provisions, the weapons, and books of plants, with endurance which obtained from the botanist, the nickname of his beast of burden. For some time past Barré had been supposed to be a woman. His smooth face, the tone of his voice, his reserve, and certain other signs, appeared to justify the supposition, when on arriving at Tahiti suspicions were changed into certainty. M. de Commerson landed to botanize, and according to custom Barré followed him with the boxes, when he was surrounded by natives, who, exclaiming that it was a woman, were disposed to verify their

Mdlle. Barré's adventure.

opinion. A midshipman, M. Bommand, had the greatest trouble in rescuing her from the natives, and escorting her back to the ship. When Bougainville visited the *Etoile*, he received Barré's confession. In tears, the assistant botanist confessed her sex, and excused herself for having deceived her master, by presenting herself in man's clothes, at the very moment of embarkation. Having no family, and having been ruined by a law-suit, this girl had donned man's clothes to insure respect. She was aware, before she embarked, that she was going on a voyage round the world, and the prospect, far from frightening her, only confirmed her in her resolution.

"She will be the first woman who has been round the world," says Bougainville, "and I must do her the justice to admit that she has conducted herself with the most scrupulous discretion. She is neither ugly nor pretty, and at most is only twenty-six or twenty-seven years old. It must be admitted that had the two vessels suffered shipwreck upon a desert island, it would have been a singular experience for Barré."

The expedition lost sight of land on the 29th of May. The route was directed westward. On the 4th of June, a very dangerous rock, so slightly above water that at two leagues' distant it was not visible from the look-out, was discovered in latitude 15° 50', and 148° 10' longitude. The constant recurrence of breakers, trunks of trees in large quantities, fruits and sea wrack, and the smoothness of the sea, all indicated the neighbourhood of extensive land to the southeast. It was New Holland. Bougainville determined to leave these dangerous latitudes, where he was likely to meet with nothing but barren lands, and a sea strewn with rocks and full of shallows. There were other urgent reasons for changing the route, provisions were getting low, the salt meat was so tainted, that the rats caught on-board were eaten in preference. Bread enough for two months, and vegetables for forty days alone remained. All clamoured for a return to the north.

Unfortunately the south winds had ceased, and when they recommenced, they brought the expedition within an inch of destruction.

On the 10th of June land was seen to the north. It was the bottom of the Gulf of the Louisiade, which had received the name of Cul-de-sac de l'Orangerie. The country was magnificent. On the sea shore, a low land covered with trees and shrubs, the balmy odours of which reached the ships, rose like an amphitheatre towards the mountains, whose summits were lost in the skies. However, it was impossible to visit this rich and fertile country, but, on the other hand, desirable to find to the east a passage to the south of New Guinea, which, by way of the Gulf of Carpentaria, would have led direct to the Moluccas. Did such a passage exist? Nothing was more problematic, for the notion was that land had been seen extending far to the westward. It was needful to hurry as fast as possible from the gulf where the ships had so incautiously involved themselves.

But there is a wide diference between a wish and its fulfilment! The two vessels strove in vain up to the 21st of June to transport themselves to the west, from this coast, which was so full of rocks and breakers, and upon which the wind and currents bade fair to swallow them up. The fog and rain continued so closely with them, that the frigate could only proceed in company with the *Etoile* by a constant firing of guns. When the wind changed, they profited by it, and immediately proceeded to the open sea – but it soon veered again, and continued east-south-east and thus they speedily lost the ground they had gained.

During this terrible cruise, the rations of bread and vegetables were obliged to be reduced, consumption of old leather was threatened with severe punishment, and the last goat on board was sacrificed.

It is difficult for the reader, tranquilly sitting in his chimney-corner, to imagine the anxiety of a voyage in these unknown seas, threatened with the unexpected appearance of rocks and breakers, with contrary winds, unknown currents, and a fog which concealed all dangers. Cape Deliverance was only rounded on the 26th. It was now possible to start for the north-north-east.

Two days later, when they had made about sixty leagues northward, some islands were perceived ahead. Bougainville imagined they were a part of the Louisiade group, but they are more generally accepted as belonging to the Solomon Archipelago, which Carteret, who saw them the preceding year, as little imagined that he had reached, as the French navigator.

Several pirogues speedily surrounded the two ships. They were manned by natives, blacker than Africans, with long curling red hair. Armed with javelins, they uttered shrill cries, and showed dispositions far from peaceful. It was useless to attempt to reach them. The surge broke violently, and the coast was so narrow that it scarcely seemed as if there were one at all.

Surrounded on all sides by islands, and in a thick fog, Bougainville steered by instinct in a passage only four or five leagues in width, and with a sea so rough that the *Etoile* was forced to close her hatchways.

Upon the eastern coast a pretty bay was perceived, which promised good anchorage. Boats were told off to sound it. Whilst they were thus engaged, ten or more pirogues, upon which some hundred and fifty men armed with bucklers, lances, and bows, were embarked, advanced against them. The pirogues divided into two parties to surround the French boats. As soon as they were within sufficient reach, the natives showered a storm of arrows and javelins upon the boats. The first discharge failed to stop them. A second was necessary to disperse them. Two pirogues, the crews of which had jumped into the sea, were captured. Of great length and well made, these boats were decorated in front with a man's head carved, the eyes of which were formed of mother of pearl, the ears of tortoise-shell, and the lips painted red.

The water in which this combat took place, was called the Warrior River, and the island received the name of Choiseul, in honour of the French Minister of Marine.

On leaving this strait a new land was discovered – Bougainville Island, the southern extremity of which, called Laverdy Cape, appears to join Bouka Island. The latter, which Carteret had seen the preceding year, and which he named Winchelsea, appeared densely populated – if the cabins which abounded were any criterion.

The inhabitants, whom Bougainville classifies as Negroes, probably to distinguish them from the Polynesians and Malays, are Papuans, of the same race as the inhabitants of New Guinea. Their short curly hair was painted red, and the betel-nut, which they perpetually chewed, had communicated the same colour to their teeth. The coast with its cocoanut and other trees, promised plentiful refreshments, but contrary winds and currents quickly drew the ships away.

On the 6th of July Bougainville cast anchor on the southern coast of New Ireland, which had been discovered by Schouten, in Port Praslin, at the very point where Carteret had stopped.

"We sent our casks on shore," says the narrative, "and began to collect water and wood, and commence washing, all of which was most necessary. The disembarkation was splendid – upon fine sand, with neither rock nor wave.

"Four streams flowed into the harbour in a space measuring four hundred paces. We selected three, according to custom; one to supply water for *La Boudeuse*, one for the *Etoile*, and one for washing purposes. Wood was plentiful on the shore, and there were various kinds of it, all good for burning, and several first-rate for carpentery, joinery, and even toy-making.

"The two vessels were in hearing of each other and close to the shore. Again this part and its neighbourhood to a great distance were uninhabited – a fact which secured us precious peace and liberty. We could not have hoped for a surer anchorage, or a more convenient spot for water, wood, or the various repairs needed by the vessels. We were able to send the sufferers from scurvy to range the woods. But with all these advantages, the port had a few inconveniences. In spite of active search, neither cocoanut-trees nor bananas were to be found, nor any of the resources which either by consent or by force, could have been gained in an inhabited country. Fish was not abundant, and we could expect only safety and strictly necessary things. There was every fear that the sick would not re-establish their health. We had indeed no serious cases, but several were infected, and no improvement took place, and their malady could not have increased more rapidly."

They had been only a few days in port, when a sailor found a leaden plate upon which was an inscription in English. It was easy to guess that they had found the very spot where Carteret had made a stay the preceding year.

The resources offered by this country to sportsmen were mediocre in the extreme. They did indeed catch sight of a few boars or wild pigs, but it was impossible to hit them. To make up for this they shot most beautiful pigeons, the bodies and necks of grey-white, and of golden green plumage, turtle-doves, parroquets, crested birds, and a species of crow, whose cry was so like the baying of a dog, as to be mistaken for it. The trees were large and magnificent, amongst them the betel, the areca, and the pepper-tree. Malignant reptiles swarm in these marshy lands, and in the ancient forests, serpents, scorpions, and other venomous reptiles abounded. Unfortunately, they were not only to be found on land. A sailor in search of *marteaux*, a very rare kind of bivalve mussel, was stung by a serpent. The fearful suffering and violent convulsions which followed only subsided at the expiration of five or six hours, and at last, the theriac which was administered to him after the bite, effected a cure. This accident was a sad damper to conchological enthusiasm. Upon the 22nd, after a severe storm, the ships were sensible of several slight earthquakes, the sea rose and fell several times in succession, which greatly alarmed the sailors who were occupied in fishing.

In spite of the rain and ceaseless storms which continued daily, a detachment started to search the interior for Bourbon palms, palm-trees, and turtle-doves. They expected to find wonders, but returned oftenest empty-handed and with the one result of being wet to the skin. A natural curiosity at some distance from the anchorage, a thousand times more beautiful than the wonders invented for the ornament of kingly palaces, attracted numberless visitors, who could never tire of admiring it. It was a waterfall, too beautiful for description! To form any idea of its beauty, it would be necessary to reproduce by the brush the sparkling gleam of the spray lit up by the rays of the sun, the vaporous shade of the trop-ical trees which dipped their branches into the water, and the fantastic display of light over a magnificent country, not yet spoiled by the hand of man!

As soon as the weather changed, the ships left Port Praslin, to follow the coast of New Guinea, until the 3rd of August. The *Etoile* was attacked by hundreds of pirogues, and forced to return the stones and arrows that assailed her by a few gunshots, which put the assailants to flight. On the 4th the islands named Matthias and Stormy by Dampier were sighted. Three days later Anchorite Island was recognized, so called because a number of pirogues occupied in fishing, took, no notice of the *Etoile* and *Boudeuse*, disdaining to enter into relations with the strangers. After passing a series of islets half under water, upon which the vessels nearly struck, and which were named the Echiquiers by Bougainville, the coast of New Guinea appeared. Steep and mountainous, it ran west-north-west. On the 12th a large bay was discovered, but the currents, which so far had been unfavourable, were equally so in carrying the boats far from it. It was visible at a distance of twenty leagues from two gigantic mountains, Cyclops and Bougainville.

The Arimoa Islands, the largest of which is only four miles in length, were next seen, but the bad weather and the currents forced the two vessels to remain in the open sea and relinquish all explor-ation. It was necessary, however, to maintain a close watch in order to avoid misssing the outlet into the Indian Ocean. Mispulu and Waigiou, the last at the extreme north of New Guinea, were passed in succession.

The "Canal des Français", the outlet for ships from this mass of little islands and rocks, was passed without mishap. From thence Bougainville penetrated to the Molucca Archipelago, where he reckoned upon finding the fresh provisions requisite for the forty-five sufferers from scurvy on board.

In absolute ignorance of the events which had occurred in Europe since he left it, Bougainville would not run the risk of visiting a colony in which he was not the strongest power. The small Dutch establishment, Boeton or Bouron Island, suited him perfectly, all the more that provisions were easily obtained there. The crew received orders to enter the Gulf of Cajeti with the greatest delight. No one on board had escaped scurvy, and half the crew, Bougainville says, were quite unfit for duty.

"The victuals remaining to us were so tainted and ill-smelling, that the worst moments of our sad days were those when we were obliged to partake of such disgusting and unwholesome viands.

"The charms of Boeton Island were enhanced by our wretched situation.

"About midnight a delicious odour, emanating from the aromatic plants with which the Molucca Islands are covered, had been wafted several leagues out to sea, and was hailed by us as a fore-runner of the end of our woes.

"The appearance of the moderately sized town, situated below the gulf, with vessels at anchor, and cattle grazing in the pastures that surrounded it, caused pleasure in which I participated, but which I cannot describe."

Scarcely had the *Boudeuse* and the *Etoile* cast anchor, than the resident governor sent two soldiers to inquire of the French captain what reason he could assign for stopping at this place, when he must be aware that entrance was permitted to the ships of the India Company only. Bougainville immediately sent an officer to explain that hunger and sickness forced him to enter the first port which presented itself in his route. Also, that he would leave Boeton as soon as he had received the aid of which he had urgent need. The resident at once sent him the order of the Governor of Amboyna, which expressly forbade his receiving any strange ship in his harbour, and begged Bougainville to make a written declaration of the reason for his putting into port, in order that he might prove to his superior that he had not infringed his orders except under paramount necessity.

As soon as Bougainville had signed a certificate to this effect, cordiality was established with the Dutch. The resident entertained the officers at his own table, and a contract was concluded for provisions and fresh meat. Bread gave place to rice, the usual food of the Dutch, and fresh vegetables which are not usually cultivated in the island, were provided for the crews by the resident, who obtained them from the Company's gardens. It would have been desirable for the re-establishment of the health of the crew, that the stay at this port could have been prolonged, but the end of the monsoon warned Bougainville to set out for Batavia.

The captain left Boeton on the 7th of September, convinced that navigation in the Molucca Archipelago was not so difficult as it suited the Dutch to affirm. As for trusting to French charts, they were of no use, being more qualified to mislead vessels than to guide them.

Bougainville therefore directed his course through the Straits of Button and Saleyer; a route which, though commonly used by the Dutch, is but little known to other nations. The narrative therefore carefully describes, with mention of every cape, the course he took. We will not dwell upon this part of the voyage, although it is very instructive, and on that account interesting to seafaring men.

On the 28th of September, ten months and a half after leaving Montevideo, the *Etoile* and the *Boudeuse* arrived at Batavia, one of the finest colonies in the world. After touching at the Isle of France, the Cape of Good Hope, and Ascension Island, near which he met Carteret, Bougainville entered St. Malo on the 16th of February, 1769, having lost only seven men, in the two years and four months which had elapsed since he left Nantes.

The remaining particulars of the career of this fortunate navigator do not concern our purpose, and may be dismissed briefly.

He took part in the American war, and in 1781 participated in an honourable combat before Port Royal of Martinique. Made Chief of the fleet in 1780, he, ten years later, received a commission to re-establish order in the mutinous fleet of M. d'Albert de Rions. Created vice-admiral in 1792, he did not think it right to accept a high rank, which was, to use his own words, "a title without duties".

Nominated first to the Bureau of Longitudes, and then to the Institute, raised to the rank of senator, created a count by Napoleon I., Bougainville died full of years and honours, on the 31st of August, 1811.

Bougainville acquired popularity as the first who accomplished a voyage round the world. Though the merit of discovering and reconnoitring, if not of exploring, many groups of islands little known and quite neglected before his time, has been ascribed to him, he owes his reputation rather to the charm and easy animation of his narrative, than to his labours. If he is better known than many other French naval officers, his competitors, it is not so much because he accomplished more than they, as because his style of narrating his adventures charmed his contemporaries.

As for Guyot Duclos, his secondary share in the enterprise, and his plebeian rank, excluded him from reward. He was afterwards given the cross of St. Louis, but he earned the title by his rescue of the *Belle Poule*. Although he was born in 1722, and had been in the navy since the year 1734, he was still only lieutenant in 1791. A succession of ministers of new views was needed to obtain the rank of ship-captain for him: a tardy recompense of long and signal services. Guyot Duclos died at St. Servan on the 10th March, 1794.

# CHAPTER III.

## CAPTAIN COOK'S FIRST VOYAGE.

### I.

The beginning of his maritime career – The command of the *Adventure* entrusted to him – Tierra del Fuego – Discovery of some islands in the Pomotou Archipelago – Arrival at Tahiti – Manners and customs of the inhabitants – Discovery of other islands in the Society group – Arrival at New Zealand – Interview with the natives – Discovery of Cook's Strait – Circumnavigation of two large islands – Manners and productions of the country.

In narrating the career of a distinguished man, it is well to neglect none of those details which may appear of but slight importance. They acquire significance as indications of a vocation unknown even to its subject, and throw a light upon the character under consideration. For these reasons we shall dwell a little upon the humble beginning of the career of one of the most illustrious navigators whom England boasts.

James Cook was born at Marton, in Yorkshire, on the 27th of October, 1728. He was the ninth child of a farm servant, and a peasant woman named Grace. When scarcely eight years of age little James assisted his father in the rough toil of the farm of Airy Holme, near Ayton. His amiability, and love of work, attracted the interest of the farmer, who had him taught to read.

When he was thirteen years of age, he was apprenticed to William Sanderson, a linendraper at Snaith, a fishing-hamlet of some importance. But young Cook found little pleasure in an employment which kept him behind a counter, and he spent every leisure moment in chatting with the sailors who visited the port. Gaining his father's consent, James soon left the linendraper's, to engage himself as ship-boy, to Messrs. Walker, whose boats carried coal from England to Ireland.

Successively ship-lad, sailor, and master, Cook rapidly learned all the details of his profession.

In the spring of 1755, as the first hostilities between England and France broke out, the boat upon which Cook served was anchored in the Thames. The navy was recruited in those days by means of pressgangs. At first Cook hid himself, but afterwards, urged no doubt by a presentiment, he engaged himself on board the *Eagle*, a vessel of sixty guns, to the command of which Sir Hugh Palliser was soon appointed.

Intelligent, active, thoroughly at home in all the details of the service, Cook was noticed by the officers, and attracted the attention of his captain, who in a short time received a letter of warm recommendation from the member for Scarborough, sent in accordance with the pressing solicitations of all the inhabitants of Ayton, for young Cook, who shortly afterwards received a warrant as boatswain. He embarked upon the *Mercury*, bound for Canada, upon the 15th of May, 1759, and joined the fleet of Sir Charles Saunders, who, in conjunction with General Wolfe, conducted the siege of Quebec.

In that campaign Cook found the first opportunity of distinguishing himself. Ordered off to sound the St. Lawrence between Orleans Island and the northern shore of the river, he executed his task with much skill, and drew up a chart of the channel in spite of the difficulties and dangers of the enterprise. His hydrographical sketch was acknowledged to be so exact and complete that he received orders to examine the channels of the river below Quebec. This duty he performed so well that his chart of the St. Lawrence was published by the English Admiralty. After the capture of Quebec, Cook passed on to the *Northumberland*, under command of Lord Colville, and profited by his stay on the shores of Newfoundland to devote himself to astronomy. Important operations were now entrusted to him. He drew up the plan of Placentia, and took the bearings of St. Peter and Miquelon.

In 1764 he was made naval engineer for Newfoundland and Labrador, and was employed for three consecutive years in hydrographical tasks, which obtained for him the notice of the ministry, and helped to correct innumerable errors in the maps of America.

At the same time he addressed a treatise to the Royal Society of London, upon an eclipse of the sun, which he had observed in Newfoundland in 1766.

This document appeared in the "Philosophical Transactions". Cook was not long in receiving a due reward for so much, and such

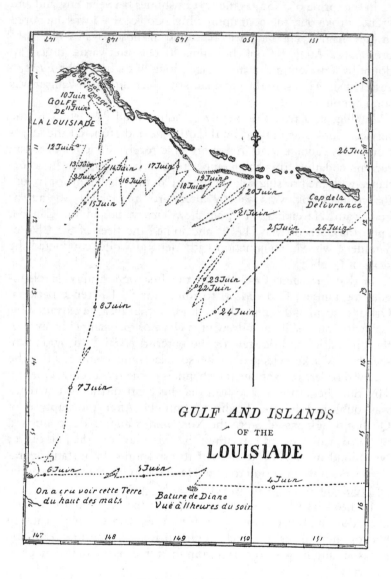

Louisiade Archipelago.
(Facsimile of early engraving.)

successful labour, and for his patient studies, the more meritorious, as he had had few opportunities, and was self-taught.

A scientific question of the highest importance, viz., the transit of Venus across the sun's disc, which had been announced for 1769, was eagerly discussed by all the scientists of the day. The English Government, confident that this observation could only be effectually made in the Pacific Sea, resolved to send a scientific expedition thither.

The command was offered to the famous hydrographer A. Dalrymple, equally celebrated for his astronomical investigations, and his geographical discoveries in the southern seas. But he was so exacting in his demands, and so persevering in his request for a commission as ship's captain, which Sir Edward Hawker as obstinately refused, that the Secretary of the Admiralty proposed another commander for the projected enterprise.

His choice fell upon James Cook, who was cordially recommended by Sir Hugh Palliser, and to him therefore the command of the *Endeavour* was given, whilst he was at the same time raised to the rank of ship's lieutenant.

Cook was now forty years of age. This was his first appointment in the Royal Navy. The mission entrusted to him called for varied qualifications, rarely to be met with in a sailor. For, although the observation of the transit of Venus was the principal object of the voyage, it was by no means the only one. Cook was also to make a voyage of discovery in the Pacific Ocean. But the humbly born Yorkshire lad was destined to prove himself equal to his task.

Whilst the *Endeavour* was being equipped, her crew of eighty-four men chosen, her store of eighteen months' provision embarked, her ten guns and twelve swivel guns, with the needful ammunition, shipped, Captain Wallis arrived in England. He had accomplished his voyage round the world. He was consulted as to the best spot for the observation of the transit of Venus, and he selected an island which he had discovered, and which was named by him after George III. It was later known by its native name of Tahiti. From this spot therefore Cook was to take observations.

Charles Green, assistant to Dr. Bradley, of Greenwich Observatory, embarked with him. To Green was entrusted the astronomical department, Doctor Solander, a Swedish doctor of medicine, a disciple of Linnæus, and professor at the British Museum, undertook the botanical part. Finally, Sir Joseph Banks joined the expedition, out of simple interest, anxious to employ his energy and fortune. After leaving Oxford, Sir Joseph Banks had visited the Newfoundland coast and Labrador, and had there acquired a taste for botany. Two painters accompanied the expedition, one a landscape and portrait painter, the other a scientific draughtsman. In addition to these persons, the company comprised a secretary and four servants, two of whom were negroes.

The *Endeavour* left Plymouth upon the 26th of August, 1768, and put into port at Funchal, in the island of Madeira, on the 8th of September, to obtain fresh fruit and make discoveries. The expedition met with a cordial reception.

During their visit to a convent, the staff of the *Endeavour* were entreated by the poor immured recluses to let them know when it would thunder, and to find a spring of fresh water for them, which they sorely needed, in the interior of the convent. With all their learning, Banks, Solander, and Cook found it impossible to satisfy these demands.

From Madeira to Rio de Janeiro, where the expedition arrived on the 13th of November, no incident interrupted the voyage, but Cook's reception by the Portuguese was hardly what he expected. The whole time of his stay in port was spent in disputes with the viceroy, a man of little knowledge, and quite incapable of understanding the scientific aspect of the expedition. However, he could not well refuse to supply the English with fresh provisions, of which they had absolutely none left. As, however, Cook was passing Fort Santa Cruz on leaving the bay, two shots were fired after him, whereupon he immediately cast anchor, and demanded the meaning of the insult. The viceroy replied that the Commandant of the Fort had orders to allow no vessel to leave the bay without his having received notice, and although Captain Cook had notified his intention to the viceroy, it had, by pure neglect, not been communicated to the Commandant of the Fort. Was this an intentional act of discourtesy on the part of the viceroy? or was it simple heedlessness?

If the viceroy was equally negligent in all the details of his administration, the Portuguese colony must have been well regulated!

Cook entered the Straits of Lemaire on the 14th of January, 1769. Kippis, in his Life of Captain Cook, gives the following account: –

"The sea ran so high, that the water was above Cape San Diego, and the vessel was so driven by the wind that her bowsprit was constantly under water. Next day anchor was cast in a small harbour, which was recognized as Port Maurice, and soon afterwards they anchored in the Bay of Good Success. Whilst the *Endeavour* remained off this spot a strange and untoward adventure befell Banks, Solander, Dr. Green, and Monkhouse, the surgeon of the vessel, and their attendants. They were proceeding towards a mountain in search of plants, and as they climbed it they were surprised by cold, so penetrating and sudden, that they were all in danger of perishing. Dr. Solander was seized with vertigo, two negro servants died on the spot, finally the gentlemen were only able to regain the vessel after a lapse of two days. They rejoiced in their deliverance, with a joy which can only be estimated by those who have escaped similar dangers, whilst Cook showed a lively pleasure in the cessation of the anxiety their absence had caused him. This event gave them a proof of the severity of the climate."

It was the middle of summer in this part of the world, and the day, when the cold surprised them, had begun as warmly as an ordinary May morning in England.

James Cook was enabled to make some curious observations upon the savage inhabitants of those desolate regions. Destitute of the necessaries of life, without clothes, without efficient shelter from the almost perpetual severity of this glacial latitude, unarmed, and unlearned in any industrial art which would enable them to construct the more necessary utensils, they passed a miserable life, and could only exist with difficulty. In spite of these facts, of all the articles offered in exchange they invariably chose the least useful. They joyfully accepted bracelets and necklaces, and rejected hatchets, knives, and fish-hooks. Careless of what we consider valuables, our superfluities were their neccessaries.

Cook had reason to congratulate himself upon the selection of this route. He took thirty days to double Tierra del Fuego, from the date of his entrance into the Straits of Lemaire to his arrival three degrees north of Magellan. No doubt a much longer time would have been needed, if he had followed the winding course of the Strait of Magellan. His very exact astronomical observations, in which Green joined him, and the directions he gave for this dangerous navigation, smoothed the difficulties of his successors, and rectified the charts of L'Hermite, Lemaire, and Schouten.

Cook noticed no current of any importance from the 21st January, the day upon which he doubled Cape Horn, to the 1st of March, in a distance of one hundred and sixty leagues of sea. He discovered a good many islands in the Dangerous Archipelago, which he respectively named, Lagoon, Arch, Groups, Birds, and Chain Islands. The greater number were inhabited and were covered with vegetation, which to sailors who for three months had seen only sea and sky, and the frozen rocks of Tierra del Fuego, appeared luxuriant. Soon they found Martea Island, which Wallis had named Osnaburgh, and on the next day, 11th of June, the island of Tahiti was reached.

Two days later, the *Endeavour* cast anchor in Port Matavai, called Port Royal by Wallis, and where that captain had had a struggle with the natives, over whom, however, he had triumphed without much difficulty. Cook, aware of the incidents of his predecessor's stay in this port, wished above all to avoid similar scenes. Moreover, it was essential to the success of his observations that no interruption or distraction should occur. His first care was to read out standing orders to his crew, which they were forbidden under heavy penalties to infringe. He first declared that he intended in every possible way to cultivate friendly relations with the natives, then he selected those who were to buy the needed provisions, and forbade all others to attempt any sort of traffic without special permission. Finally the men who landed were on no pretext to leave their posts, and if any soldier or workman parted with his arms or implements, not only would the price be deducted from his wages, but he would be punished in proportion to the exigency of the case.

In addition to this, to guard the observers from attack, Cook decided on constructing a sort of fort, in which they might be sheltered within gun range of the *Endeavour*. He then landed with Messrs. Banks, Solander, and Green, soon found a favourable spot, and in presence of the natives immediately traced out the extent of land he intended to occupy. One of them, named Owhaw, who had had friendly intercourse with Wallis, was particularly profuse in his protestations of friendship.

As soon as the plan of the fort was fixed, Cook left thirteen men and an officer in charge of the tents, and accompanied his associates into the interior of the island. But he was speedily recalled by the sound of firing.

A very painful incident, the consequences of which might have been serious, had occasioned this.

One of the natives had surprised a sentinel near the tents, and had possessed himself of his gun. A general discharge was immediately directed upon the inoffensive crowd, but fortunately no one was injured. The robber meantime was pursued and killed.

A great commotion ensued, and Cook was profuse in his protestations, to pacify the natives. He promised payment for all that he required for the construction of his fort, and would not allow a tree to be felled without their sanction. Finally, he had the butcher of the *Endeavour* mast-headed and flogged, for threatening the wife of one of the chiefs with death.

This proceeding effaced the recollection of the painful antecedents, and with the exception of some thieving by the natives, the friendly relations remained undisturbed.

And now the moment for the execution of the primary object of the voyage approached. Cook accordingly took steps for putting the instructions he had received into effect. With this view, he despatched observers with Sir Joseph Banks to Eimeo, one of the neighbouring isles.

Four others proceeded to a favourable distance from the fort, where Cook himself proposed to await the transit of the planet. Hence the point of observation was called Point Venus.

The night preceding the observation passed with many fears of unfavourable weather, but on the 3rd of June, the sun rose in all its glory, and not a cloud troubled the observers throughout the day.

The observations, according to W. de Tonnelle's article in "Nature", for the 28th of March, 1874, were most fatiguing for the astronomers, for they began at twenty-one minutes after nine in the morning, and only terminated at ten minutes after three in the afternoon, at which moment the heat was stifling. The thermometer registered 120 degrees Fahrenheit. Cook assures us, and we can readily believe it, that he himself was not certain of the end of his observation. In such thermetrical conditions, the human organism, admirable instrument as it is, loses its powers.

On passing the sun, the rim of Venus was elongated as though attracted. A black point or dark ligament, a little less dark than the body of the star, was formed; the same phenomenon occurred upon the second interior contact.

"The observation," says Cook, "was made with equal success at the fort, and by those I had sent to the east of the island. From the rising to the setting of the sun, not a single cloud obscured the sky, and Mr. Green, Dr. Solander, and myself, observed the entire transit of Venus with the greatest ease. Mr. Green's telescope and mine were of equal power, and that of Dr. Solander still stronger. We noted a luminous atmosphere or fog, surrounding the planet, which rendered the actual moment of contact and especially of interior contacts somewhat indistinct. To this fact it is owing that our observations varied somewhat one from the other."

Whilst the officers and *savants* were engaged in this important observation, some of the crew, forcing an entrance into the store-room, stole a hundredweight of nails. This was a grave offence, and one which might have had disastrous results for the expedition. The market was at once glutted with that one article of traffic, and as the natives testified an immoderate desire to possess it, there was every reason to anticipate an increase in their demands. One of the thieves was detected, but only seventy nails were found in his possession, and the application of eighty lashes failed to make him betray his accomplices.

Other incidents of this kind constantly occurred, but friendly relations were not seriously disturbed. The officers were free to make incursions into the interior of the island to prosecute scientific investigations, and to inquire into the manners of the inhabitants.

In one of these excursions, Sir Joseph Banks met a band of itinerant musicians and *improvisatori*. They were somewhat surprised to find that the arrival of the English, and the various incidents of their stay formed the subjects of native songs. Banks followed the river which flows into the sea at Matavai, some distance into the interior, and found traces of a long extinct volcano. He planted, and also distributed among the population a large number of kitchen-garden seeds, such as water-melons, oranges, lemons, &c., and planned a garden near the fort, where he sowed many of the seeds he had selected at Rio Janeiro.

Cook, and his principal assistants, wished to accomplish the circumnavigation of the island, which they estimated at thirty nautical leagues. During this voyage they entered into amicable relations with the chiefs of different districts and collected a mass of information as to the manners and customs of the natives.

A curious custom was that of allowing the dead to decompose in the open air, and of burying the bones only. The corpse was placed in a hut about fifteen feet in length, and eleven in height and of proportionate width. One end was closed up, and the three other sides shut in by trellis-work of twigs. The board upon which the corpse rested was five feet above the earth. There the dead

Captain James Cook.
(Facsimile of early engraving.)

body was laid, covered in stuffs, with its club and stone hatchet. Cocoa-nuts, wreathed together, were hung at the open end of the tent; half a cocoa-nut, filled with soft water, was placed outside, and a bag containing some bits of toasted bread, was attached to a post. This species of monument is called Toupapow. Whence could that singular method of raising the dead above the ground until the flesh was decayed by putrefaction have been derived! It is quite impossible to find out. Cook could only ascertain that the cemeteries called Morai, are places where the natives observe certain religious customs, and that they always betrayed some uneasiness when the English approached.

One of their most delicate dishes was dog. Those intended for the table never ate meat, but were fed upon bread-fruits, cocoa-nuts, yams, and other vegetables. The flesh placed in a hole upon hot stones covered with green leaves, was stewed down in four hours. Cook, who partook of it, says it has a delicious flavour.

On the 7th of July, preparations for departure began. In a short time the doors and palings were removed, and the walls demolished. At this moment, one of the natives, who had received the English with cordiality, came on board with a young lad of about thirteen years of age, who acted as his servant. He was named Tupia. Formerly first minister to Queen Oberea, he was afterwards one of the principal priests of Tahiti. He asked to be allowed to go to England. Many reasons combined to decide Cook upon permitting this. Thoroughly acquainted (as a necessary consequence of his high functions) with all the particulars concerning Tahiti, this native would be able to give the most circumstantial details of his compatriots, and at the same time to initiate them into the civilized customs of the Europeans. Finally, he had visited the neighbouring islands and perfectly understood the navigation of those latitudes.

On the 13th of July there was a crowd on board the *Endeavour*. The natives came to bid farewell to their English friends, and to their countryman Tupia. Some overcome with silent sorrow shed tears, others, on the contrary, uttered piercing cries, with less of true grief than of affectation in their demonstrations.

In the immediate neighbourhood of Tahiti were to be found, according to Tupia, four islands, Huaheine, Ulieta, Otalia, and Bolabola. He asserted that wild pigs, fowls, and other needful provisions could easily be obtained there. These commodities had become scarce in the latter part of the stay at Matavai. Cook, however, preferred visiting a small island called Tethuroa, about eight miles north of Tahiti, but the natives had no regular settlement, and he therefore considered it useless to wait there.

When they came in sight of Huabeine, several pirogues approached the *Endeavour*, and it was only after they had recognized Tupia that the natives consented to come on board. King Oreá, who was among the passengers, was greatly surprised at all the vessel contained. Soon reassured by the welcome of the English, he became so familiar as to wish to exchange names with Cook. During the entire stay in port, he always called himself "Cookee", and gave his own name to the captain. Anchor was cast in convenient harbour, and the officers of this vessel on landing found the manners, the language, and the productions of this island identical with those of Tahiti.

Seven or eight leagues south-west lay Ulietea. Cook landed there also, and solemnly took possession of this and the three neighbouring isles. He also profited by his stay to make hydrographical surveys of the shores, whilst a leak which had been found in the gun-room of the *Endeavour*, was attended to. After reconnoitring various other small islands, Cook gave the entire group the name of Society Isles.

Cook sailed on the 7th of August; six days later be reconnoitred the island of Oteroah. The hostile demonstrations of the natives prevented the *Endeavour* from remaining. She set sail for the south.

On the 25th of August, the anniversary of their departure from England was celebrated by the crew. On the 1st of September, in 40° 22' S. Lat., 174° 29' E. Long., the sea, agitated by a west wind, became very rough. The *Endeavour* was obliged to put her head to the north, and to run before the storm. Up to the 3rd the weather continued the same, then it abated and it was possible to resume the westward route.

In a few days, sundry indications of an island or a continent appeared, such as floating weeds, land-birds, &c.

On the 5th of October the colour of the sea changed, and on the morning of the 6th, a coast running west by north-west was perceived. Nearer approach showed it to be of great extent. Unanimous opinion decided that the famous continent, so long looked for, so necessary for the equipoise of the world, known to cosmographers, as the "Unknown land of the South", was at last discovered!

This land was the eastern shore of the most northerly of the two islands which have received the name of New Zealand.

Smoke was perceived at different points, and the details of the shore were soon mastered. The hills were covered with verdure, and large trees were distinguishable in the valleys. Then houses were perceived, then pirogues, then the natives assembled on the strand. And lastly, a pallisade, high and regularly built, surrounded the summit of the hill. Opinions varied as to the nature of this object; some declaring it to be a deer park, others a cattle enclosure, not to speak of many equally ingenious surmises, which were all proved false, when later it turned out to be a "pah".

Towards four o'clock on the afternoon of the 8th of October, anchor was cast in a bay at the mouth of a little river. On either side were white rocks; in the middle a brownish plain. rising by degrees, and joining by successive levels a chain of mountains, which appeared far in the interior. Such was the aspect of this portion of the shore.

Cook, Banks, and Solander entered two small boats, accompanied by a part of the crew. As they approached the spot where the natives were assembled, the latter fled; this, however, did not prevent the English from landing, leaving four lads to guard one of the boats, whilst the other remained at sea.

They had proceeded only a short distance from the boat, when four men, armed with long spears, emerged from the wood, and threw themselves upon it to take possession of it. They would have succeeded with ease, had not the crew of the boat out at sea perceived them, and cried out to the lads to let it drift with the current. They were pursued so closely by the enemy, that the master of the pinnace discharged his gun over the heads of the natives.

After a moment's hesitation, the natives continued their pursuit, when a second discharge stretched one of them dead on the spot. His companions made an effort to carry him away with them, but were obliged to abandon the attempt, as it retarded their flight. Hearing the firing, the officers who had landed went back to the vessel, whence they soon heard the natives returning to the shore, eagerly discussing the event.

Still Cook desired to have friendly intercourse with them. He ordered three boats to be manned, and landed with Banks, Solander, and Tupia. Fifty or more natives seated on the shore awaited them. They were armed with long lances, and an instrument made of green talc, and highly polished, a foot long, which perhaps weighed four or five pounds. This was the "patou-patou", or toki, a kind of battle-axe, in talc or bone, with a very

"They were pursued so closely."

sharp edge. All rose at once and signed to the English to keep their distance.

As soon as the marines landed, Cook and his companions advanced to the natives, whom Tupia told that the English had come with peaceful intentions, that they only wished for water and provisions, that they would pay for all that was brought them with iron, of which he explained the use. They saw, with pleasure, that the people, whose language was only a dialect of that spoken by the Tahitans, perfectly understood them. After some parleying, about thirty of the natives crossed the river. The strangers gave them iron and glass wares, on which they set no store; but one of them having succeeded in possessing himself secretly of Mr. Green's cutlass, the others recommenced their hostile demonstrations, and it was necessary to fire at the robber, who was hit, when they all threw themselves into the river to gain the opposite shore.

The various attempts at commercial intercourse with the people ended too unfortunately for Cook to persevere in them any longer. He therefore decided to find a watering-place elsewhere. Meanwhile, two pirogues, which were trying to regain the shore, were perceived. Cook took measures to intercept them; one escaped by rapid paddling, the other was caught, and although Tupia assured the natives that the English came as friends, they seized their weapons, and commenced attacking them. A discharge killed four, and three others, who threw themselves into the sea, were seized after a fierce resistance.

The reflections which this sad incident suggested to Captain Cook, are much to his honour. They are in strong contradistinction to the ordinary method of proceeding then in vogue, and deserve to be repeated verbatim.

"I cannot disguise from myself," he says, "that all humane and sensible people will blame me for having fired upon these unfortunate Indians, and I should be forced to blame myself for such an act of violence if I thought of it in cold blood. They certainly did not deserve death for refusing to trust to my proinises, and to come on board, even if they suspected no danger; but my commission by its nature obliged me to take observations of their country, and I could only do so by penetrating into the interior, either by open force or by gaining the confidence and good will of the natives. I had tried unsuccessfully by means of presents and my anxiety to avoid new hostilities led me to attempt having some of them on board, as the

Tahitian flute-player.
(Facsimile of early engraving.)

sole method of persuading them that far from wishing to hurt them, we were disposed to be of use to them. So far, my intentions were certainly not criminal. It is true that during the struggle, which was unexpected by me, our victory might have been equally complete without taking the lives of four of these Indians, but it must also be remembered that in such a situation, the command to fire having once been given, one is no longer in a position to proscribe it, or to lighten its effect."

The natives were welcomed on board, with every possible demonstration, if not to make them forget, at least to make them less sensible of the pain of remembering their capture, they were loaded with presents, adorned with bracelets and necklaces, but when they were told to land, they all declared, as the boats were directed to the mouth of the river, that it was an enemy's country, and that they would be killed and eaten. However, they were put on shore, and there is no reason to suppose that anything painful came of their adventure.

Next day, the 11th of October, Cook left this miserable settlement. He named it Poverty Bay, because of all that he needed he had been able to procure but one thing – wood. Poverty Bay, in 38° 42' S. Lat., and 181° 36' W. Long., is of horse-shoe shape, and affords good anchorage, although it is open to the winds between south and east.

Cook continued along the coast in a southerly direction, naming the most remarkable points, and bestowing the name of Portland upon an island which resembled that of the same name in the English Channel. His relations with the natives were everywhere inimical; if they did not break out into open outrage, it was owing to the English patience under every provocation.

One day several pirogues surrounded the ship, and nails and glassware were exchanged for fish; when the natives seized Tayeto, Tupia's servant, and quickly paddled off.

As it was necessary to fire at the robbers, the little Tahitan profited by the confusion, and jumping into the sea was soon picked up by the pinnace of the *Endeavour*.

On the 17th of October, Cook, not having been able to find a suitable harbour, and considering himself, as the sea became more and more rough, to be losing time which might be better employed in reconnoitring the northern coast, tacked round and returned the way he had come.

On the 23rd of October, the *Endeavour* reached a bay called

Tedago, where no swell was perceptible. The water was excellent, and it was easy to procure provisions, the more so as the natives appeared friendly.

After having arranged everything for the safety of the workers, Messrs. Banks and Solander landed and collected plants, and in their walk they found many things worthy of note. Below the valley, surrounded by steep mountains, arose a rock so perforated, that from one side the sea could be seen through it, and from the other the long range of hills.

Returning on board, the excursionists were stopped by an old man, who insisted upon their taking part in the military exercises of the country with the lance and the patou-patou.

In the course of another walk, Dr. Solander bought a top exactly resembling European tops, and the natives made signs to show him that he must whip it to make it go.

Upon an island to the left of the bay, the English saw the largest pirogue they had yet met with. It was no less than sixty-eight feet long, five wide, and three feet six inches high. It had in front a sculpture in relief, of grotesque taste, in which the lines were spiral and the figures strangely contorted.

On the 30th of October, as soon as he was supplied with wood and water. Cook set sail and continued along the coast towards the north.

Near an island, to which Cook had given the name of Mayor, the natives behaved most insolently, and were greater thieves than any previously encountered. It was, however, necessary to make a stay of five or six days in this district, to observe the transit of Mercury. With a view to impressing upon the natives that the English were not to be illused with impunity, a robber who had taken a piece of cloth was fired upon with grape shot, but although he received the discharge in the back, it had no more effect upon him than a violent blow with a rattan. But a bullet which struck the water and returning to the surface passed several times over the pirogues, struck such terror into the hearts of the natives, that they hastily paddled to the shore.

On the 9th of November, Cook and Green landed to observe the transit of Mercury. Green only observed the passing, while Cook took the altitude of the sun.

It is not our intention to follow the navigators in their thorough exploration of New Zealand.

The same incidents were endlessly repeated, and the recital of the similar struggles with the natives, with descriptions of natural beauty, however attractive in themselves, could not but pall upon the reader. It is better, therefore, to pass rapidly over the hydrographic portion of the voyage, in order to devote ourselves to our picture of the manners of the natives, now so widely modified.

Mercury Bay is situated at the foot of the long divided peninsula which, running from the east to the north-east, forms the northern extremity of New Zealand. On the 15th of November, as the *Endeavour* left the bay, several boats advanced towards her.

"Two of their number," says the narrative, "which carried about sixty armed men, approached within hearing, and the natives began their war-song, but seeing that this attracted little attention, they began throwing stones at the English, and paddled along the shore. Soon they returned to the charge, evidently determined to fight the navigators, and encouraging themselves with their war cry."

Without being incited to it, Tupia addressed them reproachfully, and told them that the English had arms, and were in a position to overpower them instantly. But they valiantly replied, –

"Come to land, and we will kill you all!"

"Directly," replied Tupia, "but why insult us as long as we are at sea? We have no wish to fight, and we will not accept your challenge, because there is no quarrel between us. The sea does not belong to you any more than to our ship."

Tupia had not been credited with so much simple and true eloquence, and it surprised Cook and the other English.

Whilst he was in the bay of the islands, the captain reconnoitred a considerable river, which he named after the Thames. It was shaded with trees, of the same species as those on Poverty Island. One, of them measured nineteen feet in circumference at the height of six feet above the ground, another was not less than ninety feet long from the root to the lowest branches.

Although quarrels with the natives were frequent, the latter were not invariably in the wrong.

Kippis relates as follows: –

"Some of the men on board, who, after the Indians had once been found in fault, did not fail to exhibit a severity worthy of Lycurgus, thought fit to enter a New Zealand plantation, and to carry off a quantity of potatoes. Captain Cook condemned them to a dozen stripes each. Two of them received them peaceably, but the third persisted that it was no crime for an Englishman to pillage

Indian plantations. Cook's method of dealing with this casuist was to send him to the bottom of the hold until he agreed to receive six additional stripes."

On the 30th of December the English doubled a cape which they took to be that of Maria Van Diemen, discovered by Tasman, but they were so assailed by threatening winds, that Cook only accomplished ten leagues in three weeks. Fortunately they kept at a uniform distance from shore all the time, otherwise we should probably have been spared the recital of their further adventures.

On the 16th of January, 1770, after naming various portions of the eastern shore, Cook arrived in sight of an imposing peak, which was covered with snow, and which he named Mount Egmont in honour of the earl of that name.

Scarcely had he doubled the peak, when he found that the coast described the arc of a circle. It was split up into numberless road-steads, which Cook determined to enter, in order to allow of his ship being repaired and keeled.

He landed at the bottom of a creek where he found a fine river and plenty of trees, for the forest only ceased at the sea for want of soil.

The amicable relations with the natives at this point enabled him to inquire if they had ever seen a vessel like the *Endeavour*. But he found that even the traditions of Tasman's visit were forgotten, although he was only fifteen miles south of Assassin Bay.

In one of the provision baskets of the Zealanders ten half gnawed bones were found. They did not look like a dog's bones, and on nearer inspection they turned out to be human remains. The natives in reply to the questions put to them, asserted that they were in the habit of eating their enemies. A few days later, they brought on board the *Endeavour* seven human heads, to which hair and flesh still adhered, but the brains as being delicate morsels, were already picked. The flesh was soft, and no doubt was preserved from decay by some ingredient, for it had no unpleasant odour. Banks bought one of these heads after some difficulty, but he could not induce the old man who brought it to part with a second, probably because the New Zealanders considered them as trophies, and testimonies to their bravery.

The succeeding days were devoted to a visit to the environs, and to some walks in the neighbourhood. During one of these excursions Cook, having climbed a high hill, distinctly perceived the whole of the strait to which he had given the name of Queen

Charlotte, and the opposite shore, which appeared to him about four leagues distant.

A fog made it impossible for him to see further to the south-east, but he had discerned enough to assure him that it was the final extent of the large island of which he had followed all the windings. He had now only to finish his discoveries in the south, which he proposed to do as soon as he had satisfied himself that Queen Charlotte's Sound was really a strait.

Cook visited a pah in the neighbourhood. Built upon a little island or inaccessible rock, the pah was merely a fortified village. The natives most frequently add to the natural defences by fortifications, which render the approach still more perilous. Many were defended by a double ditch, the inner one having a parapet and double palisade. The second ditch was at least eighty feet in depth. On the inside of the palisade, at the height of twenty feet, was a raised platform forty feet long by six wide. Supported on two large poles, it was intended to hold the defenders of the place, who from thence could easily overwhelm the attacking party with darts and stones, of which an enormous supply was always ready in case of need.

These strongholds cannot be forced, unless by means of a long blockade the inmates should be compelled to surrender.

"It is surprising," as Cook remarks, "that the industry and care employed by them in building places so well adapted for defence almost without the use of instruments, should not by the same means, have led them to invent a single weapon of any importance, with the sole exception of the spear they throw with the hand. They do not understand the use of a bow to throw a dart, or of a sling to fling a stone, which is the more astonishing, as the invention of slings, and bows and arrows is far more simple than the construction of these works by the people, and moreover these two weapons are met with in almost all parts of the world, in the most savage countries."

On the 6th of February, Cook left the bay, and set sail for the east, in the hope of discovering the entrance to the strait before the ebb of the tide. At seven in the evening, the vessel was driven by the violence of the current to the close neighbourhood of a small island, outside Cape Koamaroo. Sharply pointed rocks rose from the sea. The danger increased momentarily, one only hope of saving the ship remained.. It was attempted and sueceeded. A cable's length was the distance between the *Endeavour* and the rock when anchor was cast, in seventy-five fathoms of water. Fortunately the anchor found a hold, and the current changing its direction after touching the island, carried the vessel past the rock. But she was not yet in safety, for she was still in the midst of rocks, and the current made five miles an hour.

However, the current decreased, the vessel righted herself, and the wind becoming favourable, she was speedily carried to the narrowest part of the strait, which she crossed without difficulty.

The most northerly island of New Zealand, which is named Eaheinomauwe, was, however, as yet only partially known, there still remained some fifteen leagues unexplored.

A few officers affirmed from this that it was a continent, and not an island, which was contrary to Cook's view. But although his own mind was made up, the captain directed his navigation with a view to clear up any doubt which might remain in the minds of his officers. After two days' voyage, in which Cape Palliser was passed, he called them up on the quarter deck and asked if they were satisfied. As they replied in the affirmative, Cook gave up his idea of returning to the most southerly point he had reached on the eastern coast of Eaheinomauwe, and determined to prolong his cruise the entire length of the land which he had found, and which was named Tawai-Pounamow.

The coast was more sterile, and appeared uninhabited. It was necessary to keep four or five leagues from the shore.

On the night of the 9th of March the *Endeavour* passed over several rocks, and in the morning the crew discovered what dangers they had escaped. They named these reefs the Snares, as they appeared placed there to surprise unsuspecting navigators.

Next day Cook reconnoitred what appeared to him to be the extreme south of New Zealand, and called it South Cape. It was the point of Steward Island. Great waves from the south-west burst over the vessel as it doubled this cape, which convinced Captain Cook that there was no land in that quarter. He therefore returned to the northern route, to complete the circumnavigation of New Zealand by the eastern coast.

Almost at the southern extremity of this coast, a bay was discovered, which received the name of Dusky. This region was sterile, steep, covered with snow. Dusky Bay was three or four miles in width at its entrance, and appeared as deep as it was wide. Several islands were contained in it, behind which a vessel would have excellent shelter; but Cook thought it prudent not

A Fa-toka, New Zealand.

to remain there, as he knew that the wind, which would enable him to leave the bay, blew only once a month in these latitudes. He differed upon this point with several of his officers, who thinking only of the present advantage, did not reflect upon the inconveniences of a stay in port, the duration of which would be uncertain.

No incident occurred during the navigation of the eastern coast of Tawai-Pounamow.

From Dusky Bay, according to Cook, to 44° 20' latitude, there is a straight chain of hills which rise directly from the sea, and are covered with forests. Behind and close to these hills, are mountains which form another chain of prodigious height, composed of barren and jagged rocks, excepting in the parts where they are covered with snow, mostly in large masses. It is impossible to conceive a wilder prospect, or a more savage and frightful one than this country from the sea, because from every point of view nothing is visible but the summits of rocks; so close to each other that in lieu of valleys there are only fissures between them. From 44° 20' to 42° 81' the aspect varies, the mountains are in the interior, hills and fruitful valleys border the coast.

From 42° 8' S. to the 41° 30' the coast inclines vertically to the sea, and is covered with dark forests. The *Endeavour*, moreover, was too far from the shore, and the weather was too dark for it to be possible to distinguish minor details. After achieving the circumnavigation of the country, the vessel regained the entrance to Queen Charlotte Sound.

Cook took in water and wood; then he decided on returning to England, following the route which permitted him best to fulfil the object of his voyage. To his keen regret, for he had greatly wished to decide whether or no the southern continent existed, it was as impossible for him to return to Europe by Cape Horn as by the Cape of Good Hope.

In the middle of winter, in an extreme southerly latitude his vessel was in no condition to bring the enterprise to a successful issue. He had no choice, therefore, but to take the route for the East Indies, and to this end to steer westward to the eastern shores of New Holland.

But before proceeding to the narration of the incidents of the second part of the campaign, it will be better to glance backward and to summarize the information upon the situation, productions, and inhabitants of New Zealand which the navigators had accumulated.

We have already seen that this land had been discovered by Abel Tasman, and we have noted those incidents which were marked with traces of bloodshed when it was reconnoitred by the Dutch captain. With the exception of Tasman, in 1642, no European captain had ever visited its shores. It was so far unknown, that it was not oven decided whether it formed a part of the southern continent, as Tasman supposed, when he named it Staten Island. To Cook belongs the credit of determining its position and of tracing the coasts of these two large islands, situated between 34° and 48° S. Lat. 180° and 194° W. Long.

Tawai-Pounamow was mountainous, sterile, and apparently very sparsely populated. Eaheinomauwe presented an attractive appearance, in its hills, mountains, and valleys covered with wood, and watered by bright flowing streams. Cook formed an opinion of the climate upon the remarks made by Banks and Solander, that, –

"If the English settled in this country, it would cost them but little care and work to cultivate all that they needed in great abundance."

As for quadrupeds, New Zealand afforded an asylum for dogs and rats only, the former reserved for food. But if the fauna was poor, the flora was rich. Among the vegetable products which attracted the English most, was one of which the narrative says, –

"The natives used as hemp and flax, a plant which surpasses all those used for the same purposes in other countries. The ordinary dress of the New Zealanders is composed of leaves of this plant, with very little preparation. They fabricate their cords, lines, and ropes from it, and they are much stronger than those made with hemp, and to which they can be compared. From the same plant, prepared in another way, they draw long thin fibres, lustrous as silk and white as snow. Their best stuffs are manufactured from these fibres, and are of extraordinary strength. Their nets, of an enormous size, are composed of these leaves, the work simply consists in cutting them into suitable lengths and fastening them together." This wonderful plant, which was so enthusiastically described, in the lyrical account just quoted, and in the hardly less exuberant one which La Billadière afterwards gave of it, is known in our day as *phormium tenax*.

It was really necessary to subdue the expectations that these narratives excited! According to the eminent chemist Ducharte, the prolonged action of the damp heat, and above all bleaching,

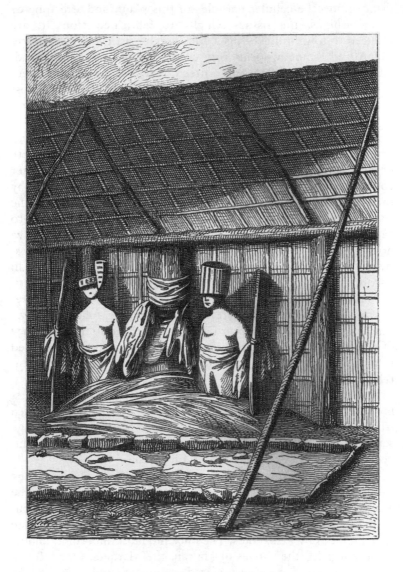

Interior of a morai in Hawaii.

disintegrates the cellular particles of this plant, and after one or two washings, the tissues which are fabricated from it, are reduced to tow. Still it forms a considerable article of commerce. Mr. Alfred Kennedy, in his very curious work on New Zealand, tells us that in 1685, only fifteen bales of *phormium* were exported, that four years later the export amounted to the almost incredible number of 12,162 bales, and in 1870 to 32,820 bales, valued at 132,578*l.*

The inhabitants were tall and well proportioned, alert, vigorous, and intelligent. The women had not the delicate organization, and grace of form, which distinguish them in other countries; dressed like the men. they were recognizable only by their sweetness of voice and liveliness of expression. Although the natives of the same tribe were affectionate in their relations to each other, they were implacable to their enemies, and they gave no quarter; the dead bodies of their enemies afforded horrible festivities, which the want of other animal food explains, but can hardly excuse.

"Perhaps," says Cook, "it appears strange that there were frequent wars in a country where so few advantages follow victory." But besides the need of procuring meat, which led to the frequency of these wars, another cause for them, unknown to Cook, existed in the fact that the population consisted of two distinct races naturally enemies of each other.

Ancient tradition has it that the Maories came in the first instance, some thirteen hundred years ago, from the Sandwich Islands. There is reason for believing this to be correct, when one reflects that the beautiful Polynesian race peopled all the archipelago sprinkled throughout the Pacific Ocean.

Leaving Haouaikai, which must be identical with Hawai, of the Sandwich Islands, or Sanaï of the Navigator Archipelago, the Maories had repelled or possibly driven back the aboriginal population. In truth, the earliest colonists noticed two distinctly separate types in the New Zealanders. The one, and most important, unmistakably recalled the natives of Hawaii, the Marquesas, and Tonga Islands, whilst the other offered many resemblances to the Melanesian races.

These particulars, collected by Freycinet, and recently confirmed by Hochsetten, are in perfect accord with the singular fact, recorded by Cook, that Tupia, a native of Tahiti, made himself readily understood by the New Zealanders.

The migrations of the Polynesian tribes are thoroughly understood in these days, thanks to the wider knowledge of languages and anthropology, but they were scarcely suspected in the time of Cook, who, indeed, was one of the first to collect legends on the subject.

"Every one of these tribes," he says, "traditionally believes that his forefathers came years ago from another country, and they all assert from the same tradition, that the country was called Heawise." The country at this time produced only one quadruped, the dog, and that was an alien. Thus the New Zealanders had no means of subsistence; but vegetables and a few fowls unknown to the English. Fortunately the inhabitants were saved from death by starvation by the abundance of fish. Accustomed to war, and looking upon all strangers as enemies, possibly seeing in them merely an edible commodity, the natives naturally attacked the English.

Once convinced, however, of the utter inadequacy of their weapons, and of the powers of their adversaries, once convinced that the new comers avoided using those instrument which produced such terrific effects, they treated the navigators as friends, and conducted themselves towards them with surprising loyalty.

If the natives usually met with by the navigators had little idea of decency or modesty, the same was not true of the New Zealanders, and Cook gives a curious example of this fact. Although not so clean as the natives of Tahiti, whose climate is much warmer, and although they bathed less often, they took a pride in their persons, and showed a certain coquetry. For instance, they greased their hair with an oil or fat obtained from fishes or birds, which becoming rank after awhile, made them as disagreeable to a refined sense of smell as the Hottentots.

They were in the habit of tatooing themselves, and some of their tatoo designs demonstrated wonderful skill, and taste certainly not to be expected among this primitive race.

The English were greatly surprised to find that the women devoted less attention to their attire than the men. Their hair was cut short and without ornament, and they wore clothes similar to those of their husbands. Their sole attempt at coquetry consisted in fastening the most extraordinary things to their ears, stuffs, feathers, fish-bones, bits of wood, not to mention green talc needles, the nails and teeth of their deceased parents, and generally everything they could lay hands on, which they suspended by means of thread.

Tatooed head of a New Zealander.
(Facsimile of early engraving.)

An I-pah.
(Facsimile of early engraving.)

A New Zealand family.

This recalls an adventure related by Cook, which happened to a Tahitan woman. This woman, envious of all she saw, wanted to have a padlock attached to her ear. She was allowed to take it, and then the key was thrown into the sea before her. After a certain time, either because the weight of this singular ornament worried her, or because she wished to replace it by another, she begged to have it removed. The request was refused, upon the ground that her demand was foolish, and that as she had wished for this singular ear-ring, it was fair that she should put up with its inconveniences.

The clothing of the New Zealanders consisted of one piece of stuff, something between reed or cloth, attached to the shoulders and falling to the knees, and of a second rolled round the waist, which reached to the ground. But the latter was not an invariable part of their dress. Thus, when they had on only the upper part of their costume, and they squatted, they presented the appearance of thatched roofs.

Their coverings were sometimes trimmed in a most elegant manner, by means of various coloured fringes, and more rarely with dogskin cut into strips. But the industry of these people was, especially shown in the construction of their pirogues.

Their war-vessels contained from forty to fifty armed men, and one of them, measured at Ulaga, was no less than sixty-eight feet long. It was beautifully ornamented with open work and decorated with fringes of black feathers. The smaller ones generally had poles. Occasionally two pirogues were joined together. The fishing-boats were ornamented at the prow and the poop by the face of a grinning man with hideous features, lolling tongue and eyes made of white shells. Two pirogues were often coupled, and the very smallest carried only the poles needed to preserve their equilibrium.

"The usual cause of illnesses," remarks Cook, "being intemperance and want of exercise, it is not surprising that these people rejoice in perfect health. Each time that we went to their settlements, men, women, and children surrounded us, excited by the same curiosity which caused us to look at them. We never saw one who appeared affected by illness, and amongst all that we saw naked we never remarked the smallest eruption on the skin, nor any trace of spots or sores."

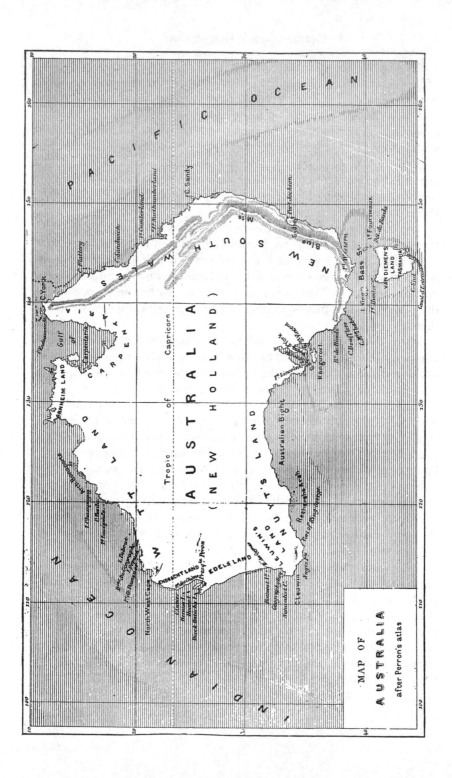

MAP OF
AUSTRALIA
after Perron's atlas

## II.

Reconnoitring the Eastern Coast of Australia – Remarks on the natives and productions of the country – The *Endeavour* stranded – Perpetual dangers of navigation – Crossing Torres Straits – The natives of New Guinea – Return to England.

On the 31st of March, Cook left Cape Farewell and New Zealand, steering westward. On the 19th of April, he perceived land which extended from north-east to west, in 37° 58' S. Lat. and 210° 39' W. Long.

In his opinion, judging by Tasman's chart, this was the country called Van Diemen's Land. In any case, he was unable to ascertain whether the portion of the coast before him belonged to Tasmania. He named all the points on his northern voyage, Hick's Point, Ram Read, Cape Howe, Dromedary Mount, Upright Point, Pigeon House, &c.

This part of Australia is mountainous, and covered with various kinds of trees.

Smoke announced it to be inhabited, but the sparse population ran away as soon as the English prepared to land.

The first natives seen were armed with long lances and a piece of wood shaped like a scimitar. This was the famous "boomerang", so effective a weapon in the hands of the natives, so useless in that of Europeans.

The faces of the natives were covered with white powder, their bodies were striped with lines of the same colour, which, passing obliquely across the chest, resembled the shoulder-belts of soldiers. On their thighs and legs they had circles of the same kind, which would have appeared like gaiters had not the natives been entirely naked.

A little further on the English once more attempted to land. But two natives whom they had previously endeavoured to propitiate by throwing them nails, glassware, and other trifles, made such menacing demonstrations, that they were obliged to fire over their heads. At first they seemed stunned by the detonation, but as they found that they were not wounded, they commenced hostilities by throwing stones and javelins. A volley of bullets struck the oldest in his legs. The unfortunate native rushed at once to one of the cabins, but returned with a shield to continue the fight, which was shortly ended, when he was convinced of his powerlessness.

The English seized the opportunity to land, and reach the houses, where they found several spears. In the same bay, they landed some casks for water, but communication with the natives was hopeless; they fled immediately on the advance of the English.

During an excursion on land, Cook, Banks, and Solander found traces of various animals. The birds were plentiful, and remarkably beautiful. The great number of plants discovered by the naturalists in this part, induced Cook to give it the name of Botany Bay. "This bay is," he says, "large, safe, and convenient; it is situated in 34° W. Lat., and 208° 37' W. Long." Wood and water were easily procurable there.

"The trees," according to Cook, "were at least as large as the oaks of England, and I saw one which somewhat resembled them. It is that one which distils a red gum like 'Dragon's blood.' "

No doubt this was a species of Eucalyptus. Among the various kinds of fishes which abound in these latitudes is the thorn-back skate, one of which, even after cleaning, weighed three hundred and thirty-six pounds.

On the 6th of May, Cook left Botany Bay, and continued to coast to the north at two or three miles distance from the shore. The navigation along this coast was sufficiently monotonous. The only incidents which imparted a slight animation, were the sudden and unexpected differences in the depth of the sea, caused by the line of breakers which it was necessary to avoid.

Landing a little further on, the navigators ascertained that the country was inferior to that surrounding Botany Bay.

The soil was dry and sandy, the sides of the hills were sparsely covered with isolated trees and free from brush-wood. The sailors killed a bustard, which was pronounced to be the best game eaten since leaving England. Hence, this point was named Bustard Bay. Numbers of bivales were found there, especially small pearl oysters.

On the 25th of May, the *Endeavour* being a mile from land, was opposite a point which exactly crossed the Tropic of Capricorn. The following day, it was ascertained that the sea rose and fell seven feet. The flow was westward, and the ebb eastward, just the reverse of the case in Botany Bay. In this spot islands were numerous, the channel narrow and very shallow.

On the 29th, Cook landed with Banks and Solander in a large bay, in search of a spot where he could have the keel and bottom of his vessel repaired, but they were scarcely on terra firma, when they found their progress impeded by a thick shrub, prickly and studded

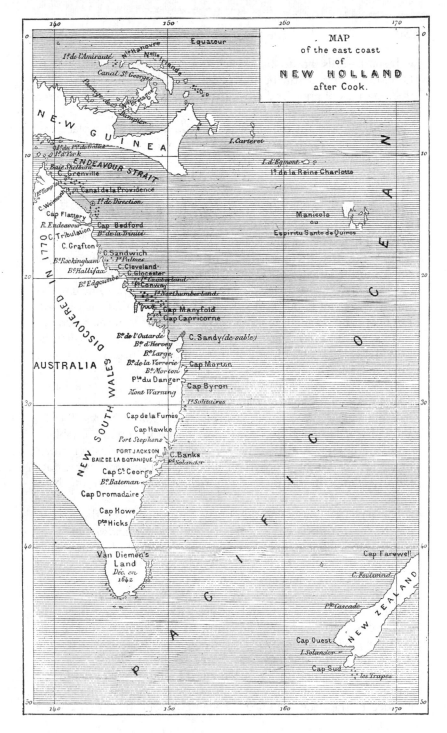

Gravé par E. Morieu.

with sharp seeds, no doubt a species of "spinifex", which clung to the clothes, pierced them, and penetrated the flesh. At the same time, myriads of gnats and mosquitoes attacked them, and covered them with painful bites.

A suitable spot for repairs was found, but a watering-place was sought in vain. Gum-trees growing here and there were covered with enormous ants' nests, and soon deprived of gum by those insects. Numerous brilliantly-coloured butterflies hovered over the explorers.

These were curious facts, interesting from more than one point of view, but they failed to satisfy the captain, who was eager to replenish his water supply.

From the first, the great defect of this country was apparent. It consists in the absence of streams, springs, and rivers!

A second excursion made during the evening of the same day was equally barren of good results. Cook ascertained that the bay was very deep, and decided on making the circuit of it in the morning.

He soon discovered that the width of the channel by which he entered increased rapidly, and that it ultimately formed a vast lake communicating with the sea to the north-west. Another arm stretched eastwards, and it was conceivable that the lake had a second outlet into the sea at the bottom of the bay.

Cook named this part of Australia New South Wales. Sterile, sandy, dry, it lacked all that was most necessary for the establishment of a colony. And the English could not ascertain from their cursory inspection or hydrographical examination that, mineralogically speaking, it was one of the richest countries of the New World.

The navigation was monotonously continued from the 31st of May to the 10th of June. On this latter date the *Endeavour*, after passing safely along an unknown coast, in the midst of shallows and breakers, for a space of 22° or 1,300 miles, was all at once exposed to a greater danger than any which had been apprehended.

They were in 16ºS. Lat. and 214° 39' W. Long. when Cook, seeing two islets lying low and covered with trees, gave orders to keep well out to sea during the night, so as to look for the islands discovered by Quiros in these latitudes, an archipelago which some geographers had maintained was united to the mainland.

Shortly after nine in the evening the soundings taken every quarter of an hour showed constantly decreasing depth. All crowded to the deck. The water became deeper. It was concluded that the vessel had passed over the extremity of the sandbanks seen at sunset, and all rejoiced at escape from danger. When the depth increased, Cook and all but the officers of the watch retired to their berths, but at eleven o'clock the sounding-line, after indicating twenty fathoms, suddenly recorded seventeen, and before it was possible to cast anchor, the *Endeavour* had touched, and beaten by the waves, struck upon a rock.

The situation was a serious one. The *Endeavour*, raised by a wave over the ridge of a reef, had fallen again into a hollow in the rock, and by the moonlight, portions of the false keel and the sheathing could be seen floating.

Unfortunately the accident happened at high water. It was useless therefore to count upon the assistance of the tide to release the ship. Without loss of time the guns, barrels, casks, ballast, and all that could lighten the vessel, were thrown overboard. The vessel still struck against the rock. The sloop was put to sea, the sails and topsails were lowered, the tow-lines were thrown to the starboard, and the captain was about to order the anchor to be cast on the same side, when it was discovered that the water was deeper at the stern. But although the capstan was vigorously worked, it was impossible to move the vessel.

Day-break disclosed the position in all its horrors. Land was eight leagues distant, not a single isle was visible between the ship and land where refuge might be found if, as was to be feared, the vessel broke up. Although she had been lightened of fifty tons weight, the sea only gained a foot and a half.

Fortunately the wind fell, otherwise the *Endeavour* must soon have been a wreck. However, the leak increased rapidly, although the pumps were worked incessantly. A third was put into action. The alternative was dreadful! If the vessel were freed, it must sink when no longer sustained by the rock, while if it remained fixed, it must be demolished by the waves which rent its planks asunder. The boats were too small to carry all the crew to land at one time.

Under such circumstances was there not danger that discipline would be thrown to the winds? Who could tell whether a fratricidal struggle might not ensue? And even should some of the sailors reach land, what fate could be in store for them upon an inhospitable shore, where nets and fire-arms would scarcely procure them nourishment?

What would become of those who were obliged to remain on board? Every one shared these fears, but so strong a sense of duty prevailed, so much was the captain beloved by his crew, that the terrors of the situation evoked no single cry, no disorder of any kind. The strength of the men not employed at the pumps was wisely harboured for the moment when their fate should be decided.

Measures were so skilfully taken, that when the sea rose to its height, all the officers and crew worked the capstan, and as the vessel was disengaged from the rock, it was ascertained that she drew no more water than when on the reef. But the sailors were exhausted after twenty-four hours of such terrible anxiety. It was necessary to change the hands at the pumps every five minutes.

A new disaster was now added. The man whose duty it was to measure the water in the hold, announced that it had increased to eighteen inches in a few moments. Fortunately the mistake of the measure taken was immediately ascertained, and the crew were so overjoyed that they fancied all danger over.

An officer named Monkhouse conceived an excellent idea. He applied a sort of cap to the stern, which he filled in with wool, rope-yarn, and the intestines of the animals slaughtered on board, and so effected a stoppage of the leak. From this time the men, who spoke of driving the vessel on a coast to reconstruct another from its ruins, which might take them to the East Indies, thought only of finding a suitable harbour for the purpose.

The desirable harbour was reached on the 17th of June, at the mouth of a current which Cook called *Endeavour* River.

The necessary labours for the careening of the vessel were at once begun and carried on with the utmost rapidity.

The sick were landed, and the staff visited the land several times, in the hope of killing some game, and procuring fresh meat for the sufferers from scurvy. Tupia saw an animal which Banks, from his description, imagined to have been a wolf. But a few days later several others were seen, who jumped upon their fore feet, and took enormous leaps. They were kangaroos, marsupial animals, only met with in Australia, and which had never before seen a European. The natives in this spot appeared far less savage than on other parts of the coast. They not only allowed the English to approach, but treated them cordially, and remained several days with them.

The narrative says, –

"They were usually of medium height, but their limbs were remarkably small. Their skin was the colour of soot, or rather, it might be described as of deep chocolate colour. Their hair was black and not woolly, and was cut short; some wore it plaited, some

They were kangaroos.

Tahitian fleet off Oparee.
(Facsimile of early engraving.)

curled. Various portions of their bodies were painted red, and one of them had white stripes on his lips and breast which he called 'carbanda'. Their features were far from disagreeable; they had very bright eyes, white and even teeth, and their voices, were sweet and musical. Some among them wore a nose-ornament which Cook had not met with in New Zealand. It was a bone, as large as a finger, passed through the cartilage.

"A little later a quarrel arose. The crew had taken possession of some tortoises which the natives claimed, without having in the least assisted in capturing them. When they found that their demand was not acceded to, they retired in fury, and set fire to the shrubs in the midst of which the English encampment was situated. The latter lost all their combustible commodities in the conflagration, and the fire, leaping from hill to hill, afforded a magnificent spectacle during the night."

Meantime Messrs. Banks, Solander, and others, enjoyed many successful hunts. They killed kangaroos, opossums, a species of pole-cat, wolves, and various kinds of serpents, some of which were venomous. They also saw numbers of birds, kites, hawks, cockatoos, orioles, paroquets, pigeons, and other unknown birds.

After leaving *Endeavour* River, Cook had good opportunities of testing the difficulties of navigation in these latitudes. Rocks and shallows abounded. It was necessary to cast anchor in the evening, for it was impossible to proceed at night through this labyrinth of rocks without striking. The sea, as far as the eye could reach, appeared to dash upon one line of rocks more violently than upon the others; this appeared to be the last.

Upon arriving there, after five days' struggle with a contrary wind, Cook discovered three islands stretching four or five leagues to the north. But his difficulties were not over. The vessel was once more surrounded by reefs and chains of low islets, amongst which it was impossible to venture.

Cook was inclined to think it would be more prudent to return and seek another passage. But such a detour would have consumed too much time, and have retarded his arrival in the East Indies. Moreover there was an insurmountable obstacle to this course. Three months' provisions were all that remained.

The situation appeared desperate, and Cook decided to steer as far as possible from the coast, and to try and pass the exterior line of rocks. He soon found a channel, which shortly brought them to the open sea.

"So happy a change in the situation," says Kippis, "was received with delight. The English were full of it, and openly expressed their joy. For nearly three months they had been in perpetual danger. When at night they rested at anchor, the sound of an angry sea forced them to remember that they were surrounded by rocks, and that, should the cable break, shipwreck was inevitable. They had travelled over 360 miles, and were forced to keep a man incessantly throwing the line and sounding the rocks through which they navigated. Possibly no other vessel could furnish an example of such continued effort."

Had they not just escaped so terrible a danger, the English would have had cause for uneasiness in reflecting upon the length of way that remained to them across a sea but little known, upon a vessel which let in nine inches of water in an hour. With pumps out of repair and provisions almost consumed, the navigators only escaped these terrible dangers to be exposed on the 16th of April to a peril of equal magnitude.

Carried by the waves to a line of rocks above which the sea spray washed to a prodigious height, making it impossible to cast anchor; without a breath of wind, they had but one resource, to lower boats to tow the vessel off. In spite of the sailors' efforts the *Endeavour* was still only 100 paces from the reef, when a light breeze, so slight that under better circumstances no one would have noticed it, arose and disengaged the vessel. But ten minutes later it fell, the currents strongly returned, and the *Endeavour* was once more carried within 200 feet of the breakers.

After many unsuccessful attempts, a narrow opening was perceived.

"The danger it offered was less imminent than that of remaining in so terrible a situation," says the narrative. "A light breeze which fortunately sprang up, the efforts of the boats, and the tide, conveyed the ship to the opening, across which she passed with frightful rapidity. The strength of the current prevented the *Endeavour* from touching either shore of the channel, which, however, was but a mile in width, and extremely unequal in depth, giving now thirty fathoms, now only seven of foul bottom."

If we have lingered somewhat over the incidents of this voyage, it is because it was accomplished in unknown seas, in the midst of breakers and currents, which, sufficiently dangerous for a sailor when they are marked on a map, become much more so when, as was the case with Cook, since leaving the coast of New Holland, the voyage is made in the face of unknown obstacles, which all the instinct and keen vision of the sailor cannot always successfully surmount.

One last question remained to be solved, –

Were New Holland and New Guinea portions of one country? Were they divided by an arm of the sea, or by a strait?

In spite of the dangers of such a course, Cook approached the shore, and followed the coast of Australia towards the north.

On the 21st he doubled the most northerly cape of New Holland, to which he gave the name of Cape York, and entered a channel sprinkled with islands near the mainland, which inspired him with the hope of finding a passage to the Indian Ocean.

Once more he landed, and planting the English flag, solemnly took possession in the name of King George, of the entire Eastern Coast from the eighteenth degree of latitude to this spot, situated in 107° south. He gave the name of New South Wales to this territory, and to fitly conclude the ceremony, he caused three salutes to be fired.

Cook next penetrated Torres Strait, which he called Endeavour Strait, discovered and named the Wallis Islands, situated in the middle of the south-west entrance to Booby Island, and Prince of Wales Island, and steered for the southern coast of New Guinea, which he followed until the 3rd of September without being able to land.

Upon that day Cook landed with about eleven well-armed men, amongst them Solander, Banks, and his servants. They were scarcely a quarter of a mile from their ship, when three Indians emerged from the wood, uttering piercing cries, and rushed at the English.

"The one who came nearest," says the narrative, "threw something which he carried at his side, with his hand, and it burned like gunpowder, but we heard no report."

Cook and his companions were obliged to fire upon the natives in order to regain their ship, from whence they could examine them at their leisure. They resembled the Australians entirely, and like them, wore their hair short, and were perfectly naked – only their skin was less dark; no doubt because they were less dirty.

"Meantime the natives struck their fire at intervals, four or five at a time. We could not imagine what this fire could be, nor their object in throwing it.

"They held in the hand a short stick, perhaps a hollow cane, which they flourished from side to side, and at the same instant we saw the fire and smoke exactly as it flashes from a gun, and it lasted no longer. We observed this astonishing phenomenon from the

Three Indians emerged from the wood.

vessel, and the illusion was so great that those on board believed the Indians had fire-arms, and we ourselves should have imagined they fired guns, but that our ship was so close that in such a case we must have heard the explosion."

This fact remains unexplained, in spite of the many commentaries it has occasioned, and which bear out the testimony of the great navigator.

Many of the English officers demanded immediate permission to land in search of cocoa-nuts and other fruits, but the captain was unwilling to risk his sailors' lives in so futile an attempt; he was, besides, anxious to reach Batavia, to obtain repairs for his vessel. He thought it useless, moreover, to remain a longer time in these latitudes. They had, been so often visited by the Spanish and Dutch, that there were no further discoveries to make.

In passing Arrow and Wesel Islands he rectified their positions, and reaching Timor, put into port in Savu Island, where the Dutch had been settled for some time. There Cook revictualled, and by accurate observations settled its position at 10° 35' southern latitude, and 237° 30' west longitude.

After a short interval the *Endeavour* arrived at Batavia, where she was repaired.

But the stay in that unhealthy country was fatal after such severe fatigue. Endemic fevers raged there; and Banks, Solander, and Cook, as well as the greater part of the crew, fell ill. Many died, amongst them Monkhouse, the surgeon, Tupia, and little Tayeto. Ten men only escaped the fever.

The *Endeavour* set sail on the 27th of December, and on the 15th of January, 1771, put into Prince of Wales Island for victuals.

From that moment, sickness increased among the crew. Twenty-three men died, amongst them Green, the astronomer, who was much regretted.

After a stay at the Cape of Good Hope, where he met with the welcome he so sorely needed, Cook re-embarked, touched at St. Helena, and anchored in the Downs on the 11th of June, 1772, after an absence of nearly four years.

"Thus," says Kippis, "ended Cook's first voyage, a voyage in, which he had experienced such dangers, discovered so many countries, and so often evinced his superiority of character. He was well worthy of the dangerous enterprise and of the courageous efforts to which he had been called."

# CHAPTER IV.

## CAPTAIN COOK'S SECOND VOYAGE.

### I.

Search for the Southern Continent – Second stay at New Zealand – Pomontou Archipelago – Second stay at Tahiti – Reconnoitring Tonga Isles – Third stay at New Zealand – Second crossing of The Southern Ocean – Easter Island reconnoitred – Visit to the Marquesas Islands.

Had the government not been desirous of rewarding James Cook for the way in which he had fulfilled the mission entrusted to him, the unanimous voice of the public would have constrained them. On the 29th of August he received the rank of commander in the Royal Navy. But the great navigator, proud of the services he had rendered to England and to science, thought the reward less than his achievements merited. He would have delighted in an appointment as ship's captain, but Lord Sandwich, who was then at the head of the Admiralty, pointed out to him, that it was not possible to gratify him without upsetting all established customs, and injuring the discipline of the Royal Navy.

However, Cook busied himself in putting together the necessary materials for the narration of his experiences; but, being soon occupied with still more important matters, he placed them in the hands of Dr. Hawkesworth, who was to superintend their publication.

At the same time, the observations he had taken on the transit of Mercury in concert with Mr. Green, his calculations and astronomical solutions, were submitted to the consideration of the Royal Society, and that learned body at once recognized his merit.

In one respect, however, the important results obtained by Cook were incomplete. He had not perfectly proved the impossibility of an antarctic continent. This chimera was still dear to the hearts of scientific men. Although obliged to admit that neither New Zealand nor Australia made part of such a continent, and that the *Endeavour* had navigated in latitudes in which it might have been found, they still affirmed that it would be found still more south, and reiterated all those advantages which its discovery would entail.

The government determined to settle a question which had been discussed for so many years, and to despatch an expedition for the purpose. Its commander was easily selected. The nature of the voyage demanded vessels of peculiar construction. As the *Endeavour* had been sent to the Falkland Islands, the Admiralty gave orders for the purchase of the two suitable vessels for the purpose.

Cook was consulted, and insisted that the ships should be solidly built, draw little water, and possess capacity for carrying provisions and ammunition in proportion to the number of the crew and the length of the voyage.

The Admiralty accordingly bought two vessels, constructed at Whitby, by the same ship-builder as the *Endeavour*. The larger was of 462 tons burden, and was named the *Resolution*, the second was only of 336 tons, and was called the *Adventure*.

Cook received command of the *Resolution*, and Captain Tobias Furneaux, second lieutenant of the Wallis, was raised to the command of the *Adventure*. The second and third officers, and several of the crew had already served in the *Endeavour*.

It may readily be imagined that every possible care was taken in the equipment of these ships. Lord Sandwich and Captain Palliser themselves superintended every detail.

Each of the ships was stocked with provisions of every kind for two years and a half.

Very extraordinary articles were provided at the instance of Captain Cook, who claimed them as anti-scorbutics, for instance, malt, sauerkraut, salted cabbages, soup-slabs, mustard and saloop, as well as carrot marmalade, and thickened and unfermented beer, which was tried at the suggestion of Baron Storch of Berlin, and Mr. Pelham, secretary to the Commissariat department.

Equal care was taken to ship two small boats, each of twenty tons, intended to carry the crew in case of shipwreck.

William Hodges, a landscape painter, two naturalists, John Reinhold Forster and his son George; two astronomers, W. Wales and W. Bayley, accompanied the expedition, provided with the best instruments for observation.

Nothing that could conduce to the success of the adventure was neglected. It was to return with an immense amount of collected information, which was to contribute to the progress of the natural and physical sciences, and to the ethnology of navigation and geography.

Cook says, "I received my instructions at Plymouth dated 25th June. They enjoined my immediate departure for the island of Madeira. To ship wine there, and thence to proceed to the Cape of Good Hope, where I was to let the crew have a spree on shore, and obtain the provisions and other stores I needed. To advance southwards and endeavour to find Circumcision Cape, which, was said to have been discovered by M. Bouvet, in the 54° southern parallel, and about 11° 20' east longitude, reckoning from Greenwich. If I found this cape, to ascertain whether it was part of the continent or an island. Should it prove the former, to neglect no opportunity of investigating its possible extent. To collect facts of every kind which might be useful to navigation and commerce, or would tend to the progress of the natural sciences. I was desired to observe the spirit, temperament, character, and means of the inhabitants, should there be any, and to use every fair means of forming friendly alliances with them.

"My instructions proceeded to enjoin me to seek discoveries in the east or west, according to the position in which I might find myself, and advised my nearing the south pole as much as possible, and as long as the condition of the ships, the health of the crew, and the provisions allowed of my doing so. To be careful in any case to reserve sufficient provisions to reach some known port, where I might refit for my return to England.

"In addition, I was ordered, if I found Circumcision Cape to be an island, or if I did not succeed in finding it, in the first case to take the necessary bearings, and in both to sail southward as long as I still hoped to find the continent. Then to proceed eastward, to look for this continent, and to discover the islands which might be situated in this part of the southern hemisphere. To remain in high latitudes and to prosecute my discoveries, as had been already said, as near the pole as possible, until I had completed the navigation of the world, and finally to repair to the Cape of Good Hope, and from thence to Spithead."

Cook left Plymouth harbour on the 13th of July, and on the 29th of the same month he arrived at Funchal, in Madeira. Here he took in provisions, and continued his route southwards. But being shortly convinced that his supply of water would not hold out until he reached the Cape of Good Hope, he determined to break the voyage by putting in at Cape Verd Islands, and on the 10th of August he anchored in Praya Port, which he left four days later.

Cook availed himself of his stay in this port, as he usually did, to collect every fact which might be useful to navigators. His description is the more valuable now, as these parts have completely changed in character, and the conditions of a stay in port have been greatly modified by the improvements accomplished there.

On the 23rd of the same month, after violent squalls which had driven every one on deck, Cook, aware of the pernicious effect of the damp of warm climates, and always on the alert to keep his crew in good health, gave orders to aerate (renew the air) in the between decks. He even had a fire lighted in order to smoke it, and dry it quickly, and not only took the precautions, advocated by Lord Sandwich, and Sir Hugh Palliser, but also those which the experience of his last voyage suggested to him.

Thanks to all these efforts at prevention there was not a single sick case on board the *Resolution* when she arrived at the Cape of Good Hope on the 30th of October. Cook, in company with Captain Furneaux, and Messrs. Forster, went to pay a visit to the Dutch governor, Baron de Plettemberg, who placed all the resources of the colony at his disposal. There he found that two French ships, which had left the island of Mauritius in March, had touched at the Cape before proceeding to the southern seas where they were to prosecute discoveries, under command of Captain Marion.

During this stay in port, which was longer than they expected, Forster met the Swedish botanist Sparman, a pupil of Linnæus, and engaged him to accompany him, by promising him large pay. It is difficult to praise Forster's disinterestedness under these circumstances too highly. He had no hesitation in admitting a rival, and even paid his expenses, in order to add completeness to the studies in natural history which he wished to make in the countries he was about to visit.

Anchor was weighed on the 22nd of December, and the two ships resumed their course southwards, in search of Cape Circumcision, discovered by Captain Bouvet, on the 1st of January, 1739. As the temperature would rapidly become colder, Cook distributed the warm clothes, furnished by the Admiralty, to his sailors. From the 29th of November till the 6th of December a frightful tempest prevailed. The ships, driven out of their course, were carried to the east, to such a degree that they were forced to resume the search for Circumcision Cape. Another consequence of the bad weather, and of the sudden change from heat to extreme cold was the death of all the animals embarked at the Cape.

And lastly, the sailors suffered so much from the damp, that it was necessary to increase the rations of brandy to stimulate them to work.

On the 10th of December, in 50° 40' southern latitude the first ice was met with. Rain and snow succeeded each other uninterruptedly. The fog soon became so dense, that the crews did not perceive a floating iceberg, until they were a mile past it. "One of these," says the narrative, "was not less, than 200 feet high, 400 wide, and 2,000 long.

"Taking it as probable, that this piece was of absolutely equal size, its depth beneath the water, would have been 1,800 feet, and its height about 2,000 feet, and from the dimensions just given its entire bulk must have contained 1,600 million cubic feet of ice."

As they proceeded further south the icebergs increased. The sea was so rough, that the waves climbed these glacial blocks, and fell on the other side in fine impalpable dust. The scene filled the observers with admiration. But this was soon succeeded by terror, upon the reflection that if the vessel struck one of these enormous masses, she must be dashed to pieces. The presence of danger soon, however, produced indifference, and more thought was bestowed upon the sublime beauty, than upon the strife with this terrible element.

Upon the 14th of December, an enormous iceberg, which closed in the horizon, prevented the two vessels from proceeding southwards, and it became absolutely necessary to skirt it.

It did not present an unbroken surface, for hillocks were visible on it, similar to those met on the previous days. Some thought they distinguished land under the ice, even Cook for the moment was deceived, but as the fog lifted the mistake was easily rectified.

Next day the vessels were driven before a strong current. The elder Forster and Wales, the astronomer, embarked in a small boat to ascertain its swiftness. Whilst thus engaged, the fog became so dense, that they completely lost sight of the ship. In this miserable boat, without instruments or provisions, in the midst of the wide ocean, far from any coast, surrounded by ice, their situation was dreadful. They left off rowing, lest they should get farther from the ship. They were losing all hope when the sound of a distant bell fell upon their ears. They rowed swiftly in the direction of the sound. The *Adventure* replied to their shouts and picked them up after several hours of terrible suspense.

The generally received opinion was that that the ice floats col-

Among the icebergs.

lected in the bays or mouths of rivers. The explorers, therefore, imagined themselves near land, which would prove to be situated in the south behind the vast iceberg.

They were thirty leagues to the west of it, before they found an opening in the ice which might lead to the south. The captain then determined to steer an equal distance to the east. Should he not find land, he at least hoped to double the iceberg, and penetrate in advance of it to the pole, and thereby settle the doubts of all the physicists.

But although it was the middle of summer in this part of the world, the cold became daily more intense. The sailors complained of it, and symptoms of scurvy appeared on board.

Warmer clothes were distributed, and recourse was had to the remedies usual in such cases, malt and lemon-juice, which soon overcame the malady, and enabled the crews to bear the severity of the temperature.

On the 29th of December, Cook ascertained positively that the iceberg was joined to no land. He therefore decided to proceed eastward as far as the parallel of Cape Circumcision, that is, if no obstacle prevented him.

He had scarcely put this resolve into execution when the wind became so violent, and the sea so rough, that navigation, in the midst of floating ice, which crashed with a fearful noise, became most perilous.

The danger increased, when a field of ice extending beyond the range of vision was seen to the north. There seemed every prospect of the ships being imprisoned for many weeks, "hemmed in", to use the expression of whalers, if indeed they did not run the risk of being crushed at once.

Cook neither tried to run to the west or east, he steered straight for the south. He was now in the latitude attributed to Cape Circumcision, and seventy leagues south of the position assigned to it. Hence he concluded that if land existed as stated by Bouvet (which is now known to be a fact) it could only be an inconsiderable island, and not a large continent.

The captain had no further reason for remaining in these latitudes. In 67° 15' southern latitude a new ice barrier, running from east to west closed the passage for him, and he could find no opening in it. Prudence enjoined his remaining no longer in this region, for two-thirds of the summer were already passed. He therefore determined to seek, with no further delay, the land recently discovered by the French.

New Zealand war canoe.
(Facsimile of early engraving.)

On the 1st of February, 1773, the vessels were in 48° 30' south latitude, and 38° 7' west longitude, very nearly the parallel attributed to St. Maurice Island.

After a fruitless cruise, productive of no results, they were forced to conclude, that if there really were land in these latitudes it could only be a small island, otherwise it could not have escaped their search.

On the 8th of February, the captain found to his dismay that the *Adventure* was no longer sailing with him. He waited in vain for two days, firing at close intervals and keeping great fixes upon the deck all night. The *Resolution* had to continue her voyage alone.

On the morning of the 17th of February, between twelve and three o'clock, the crew witnessed a magnificent spectacle, then first seen by European eyes. It was an aurora borealis. "The officer of the watch," says the narrative, "noticed that from time to time rays left it in spiral and circular forms, and that then its brilliancy increased, which gave it an extremely beautiful appearance. It appeared to have no particular bearing, but remained motionless in the heavens, which it filled entirely from time to time, by throwing its light to all parts."

After another attempt to pass the arctic circle, an attempt, which the fogs, the rain, the snow, and the ice-blocks forced him to relinquish, Cook resumed his course to the north, convinced that he left no large land behind him, and regained New Zealand, which he had agreed upon with the *Adventure* as a rendezvous in the event of separation.

On the 25th of March he cast anchor in Dusky Bay, after one hundred and seventy consecutive days of sea, in which he had not made less than three thousand six hundred and sixty leagues, without one sight of land.

As soon as he could find suitable anchorage, the captain hastened to avail himself of the resources for feeding his crew, which the country furnished in fowls, fish, and vegetables, whilst he himself, generally with the plumb-line in his hand, traversed the environs of the bay. He met only a few natives, with whom he had little intercourse. But one family becoming somewhat familiarized, established itself a hundred yards from the landing place. Cook gave a concert for them, in which the fife and cornet were lavished on them in vain, the New Zealanders awarded the palm to the drum!

On the 18th of April, a chief came on board with his daughter.

But before entering the ship he rapped her sides with a green wand he held in his hand, and addressed an harangue or invocation in modulated accents, to the strangers, a very general custom with the islanders of the southern sea. Scarcely was his foot on deck, when he offered the captain a bit of cloth, and a green talc hatchet, an unprecedented act of generosity for a New Zealander.

The chief visited every part of the ship. In order to testify his gratitude to the captain he plunged his fingers into a bag at his waist, and ofered to anoint his hair with the tainted oil it contained. Cook had much difficulty in escaping from this proof of affection, which had not been very pleasing to Byron in the Strait of Magellan, but the painter Hodges was forced to submit to the operation, to the amusement of the entire crew. The chief then departed, to return no more, taking with him nine hatchets, and thirty pairs of carpenter's scissors, which the officers had given him. Richer than all the New Zealanders put together, he no doubt hastened to stow away his treasures, in the fear that some one would deprive him of them.

Before leaving Cook landed five geese, the last of those he had brought from the Cape, thinking that they would multiply in this little inhabited spot, and he had a plot of land cleared in which he planted kitchen garden seeds. Thus he worked at the same time for the natives and for the future navigators who should find precious resources here.

When Cook had completed the hydrographical survey of Dusky Bay, he started for Queen Charlotte's Sound, the rendezvous assigned to Captain Furneaux.

On the 17th of May the crew witnessed a magnificent spectacle. Six water-spouts, one of them sixty feet wide at its base, were visible a hundred feet from the ship in succession, drawing the clouds and sea into communication by their powerful suction. This phenomenon lasted three quarters of an hour, and the first feeling of fear which it awakened in the breasts of the crew was soon merged in one of admiration, the greater as at this time such marvels were little known.

Next day, just as the *Resolution* entered Queen Charlotte's Sound, the *Adventure* was seen, and proved to have been waiting for six weeks. Furneaux, after reaching Van Diemen's Land on the 1st of March, had coasted it for seventeen days, but he was forced to desist before ascertaining whether it was, as he supposed, a part of New Holland. The refutation of this error was reserved for the surgeon, Bass. On the 9th of April after reaching Queen Charlotte's Sound, the captain of the *Adventure* had profited by his leisure to lay out a garden and to open relations with the natives, who had furnished him with irresistible proofs of their cannibalism.

Before he continued his voyage of discovery, Cook followed the same line of conduct as at Dusky Bay. He landed a ram and a sheep, a goat and a she-goat, a pig and a sow. He also planted potatoes, which only existed upon the more southerly of the two islands which form New Zealand.

The natives resembled those of Dusky Bay, but they appeared more thoughtless, ran from room to room during supper, and devoured everything that was offered to them. It was impossible to induce them to taste wine or brandy, but they were very partial to sugar and water. Cook says, –

"They laid hands on all they saw, but they gave up anything so soon as we made them understand by signs that we could not, or would not give it to them. They particularly admired glass bottles, which they called Tawhaw, but when the durability and use of iron was explained to them they preferred it to glass-ware, ribbons, or white paper. Amongst them were several women, whose lips were covered with little holes, painted a blueish black, whilst vivid red formed of chalk and oil, covered their cheeks. Like the natives of Dusky Bay, they had small legs and bodies, but thick knees, which proves that they take little exercise and sit cross-legged. The almost perpetual squatting in their pirogues no doubt also adds to these peculiarities.

"The colour of their skin is clear brown, their hair is very black, their faces are round, their nose and lips are somewhat thick but not flat, their eyes are black and bright enough, and tolerably expressive.

"Placed in a row, the natives took off their outer garments, and one of them sang a rough sort of song, the others accompanying him with gestures. They stretched out their hands, and alternately struck their feet against the ground with frantic contortions. The last words they repeated in chorus, and we easily distinguished a sort of metre, but I am not sure that there was any rhyme; the music was wild and monotonous."

Some of the New Zealanders begged for news of Tupia, and when they heard of his death, they expressed their grief by a kind of lamentation plainly artificial.

Cook did not recognize a single native whom he had met on his first voyage. He naturally concluded that the natives who in 1770 inhabited the Sound had been chased out, or had gone elsewhere of their free will. The number of inhabitants, too, was reduced by a third, the "pah" was deserted, as well as a number of cabins along the coast.

The two ships being ready to return to sea, Cook gave instructions to Captain Furneaux. He wished to advance southward between 41° to 46° S. lat. up to 140° west longitude, and if he found no land, to steer towards Tahiti, which was appointed as the place of rendezvous. He then proposed to return to New Zealand and survey all the unknown parts of the sea between that island and Cape Horn.

Towards the end of July, after a few days' hot weather, scurvy again broke out on board the *Adventure*. The *Resolution* escaped the scourge, owing to the precautions from which Cook never departed for a single day, and the example which he himself set of constantly eating celery and scurvy grass.

On the 1st of July, the two vessels were in S. lat. 25° 1', and 134° 6' W. long., the situation which Carteret attributed to Pitcairn Island. Cook endeavoured to find it, but, to his great regret, the illness on board the *Adventure* shortened his cruise.

He was anxious to verify or rectify the longitude of this island, and by so doing, that of all the surrounding lands discovered by Carteret, which had not been confirmed by astronomical observations. But having no longer any hope of finding an Antarctic continent, he set sail for the north-west, and soon reconnoitred several of the islands seen by Bougainville.

"The outlying islands with which the Pacific Ocean abounds between the tropics," he says, "are on a level with the waves in the low parts, and raised only a rood or two above them in the others. Their shape is often circular. In the centre they contain a basin of sea water, and the depth of water all round is not to be sounded. They produce little; cocoa-nuts appear to be the best of their productions; yet in spite of this sterility, and of their small extent, most of them are inhabited. It is not easy to conceive how these little settlements were peopled, and it is not less difficult to determine from whence the highest islands of the Southern Sea drew their inhabitants."

On the 15th of April, Cook reconnoitred Osnaburgh or Mairea Islands, discovered by Wallis, and set off for Otaiti-Piha, where he intended to embark as many provisions as possible before reaching Matavai.

"At daybreak," says Forster, "we rejoiced in one of those beautiful mornings which poets of every country have tried to paint. A light breeze brought a delicious perfume from the land, and ruffled the surface of the water. The forest-capped mountains elevated their majestic heads, over which the rising sun shed his beams. Close to us we saw a ridge of hills, of gentler ascent, but wooded like the first, and pleasantly intermixed with green and brown tints; below, a plain adorned with breadfruit-trees, and a quantity of palms in the background, overshadowing the delightful groves. All seemed still asleep. Dawn was but just breaking, and the country was wrapped in peaceful darkness. Yet we could perceive the houses amid the trees, and the pirogues on the shore. Half a mile from the beach, the waves broke over a reach of rocks level with the sea, and nothing could equal the tranquillity of the interior flow of the harbour. The day-star shed its lustre on the plain; the natives rose, and by degrees added life to this charming scene. At the sight of our vessels, several launched their pirogues in haste, and paddled towards us, as we were happily watching them. We little thought that we were going to run into great danger, and that destruction would soon threaten the vessels and their crews on this fortunate coast."

Skilful the writer, happy the painter, who knew how to find such fresh and varied colours! This enchanting picture is conveyed in a few words. One regrets not having accompanied this bold sailor, this scientist who so well understood Dame Nature! Unfortunately we could not visit these innocent and peaceable inhabitants in that age of gold to which our own century offers a painful comparison.

The vessels were half a league from a reef, when the wind fell. In spite of every effort, the ships were driven upon the rocks, in the very sight of the much-coveted land, when a clever manoeuvre of the captain's, ably seconded by the tide and the land breeze, came to their rescue. They had, however, received some injuries, and the *Adventure* lost three anchors.

The ships were surrounded by a crowd of pirogues, and every variety of fruit was exchanged for glass beads. Still the natives offered neither fowls nor pigs. Those that were seen near the cabins belonged to the king, and they had no right to sell them. Several of the Tahitans begged for news of Banks and the companions of Cook's earlier voyage. Some also inquired for news of Tupia, but they spoke no more of him when they had learned the circumstances of his death.

Next day, the two vessels anchored in the roadstead of Otaiti-

Piha, two cable-lengths from the shore, and were besieged by visitors and traffickers.

Some profited by the crush to throw the merchandize they had already sold into their canoes, that they might sell it over again. To put a stop to this trick, Cook drove the perpetrators away, after having flogged them, a punishment which they accepted without complaining.

In the afternoon the two captains landed, to examine the watering place, which they found very convenient. During their absence a crowd of natives came on board, and amply confirmed the unenviable reputation they had acquired in the earlier records of Bougainville and Cook.

"One of the officers, standing on the quarter-deck," says the narrative, "desiring to give a child six years old, in one of the pirogues, some glass beads, let them fall into the sea. The child at once jumped into the water and dived until he recovered them. To reward his skill, he threw other trifles to him, a generosity which tempted a crowd of men and women, who amused us by their surprising agility in the waves. Their easy attitudes in the water, and the suppleness of their limbs, made them like amphibious animals."

But the Tahitans who came on board were detected in several acts of theft. One of them, who remained for the greater part of the day in Cook's bedroom, hastened to jump into the sea, and the captain, enraged by his conduct, had shots fired over his head. A boat, sent to take the pirogues of the robbers, was assailed with stones until it reached the shore, and it was only after a discharge of shot that the assailants determined to retreat. These hostilities led to no result, the natives came on board as if nothing had occurred.

Cook learned from them that the greater part of his old friends from the neighbourhood of Matavai had fallen in a battle between the inhabitants of the two peninsulas.

The officers made many excursions on land. Forster, animated by an ardour for botanical research, missed none of them. In one of these he witnessed the method employed by the Tahitans in preparing their stuffs.

"We had gone but a few paces," he says, "when a noise from the forest struck upon our ears. Following the sounds, we reached a little tent, where five or six women sitting upon either side of a large square piece of wood, were thrashing the fibrous bark of mulberry-trees to fabricate their stuffs. For this purpose they used a bit of square wood, with long parallel grooves more or less hollowed, according to the different sides. They paused a moment to enable us to examine the bark, the hammer, and the beam which served them for a table.

"They also showed us a kind of gum-water in a large cocoa-nut which they used from time to time to join the various bits of bark together.

"This glue, which appears to us to be obtained from the 'Hibiscus Esculentus', is absolutely needful in the fabrication of the stuff, which being occasionally two or three yards wide and fifty long, are composed of small pieces of the bark. The women employed at this work wore very old and ragged clothes and their hands were hard and knotted."

The same day, Forster saw a man with very long nails, of which he was immensely proud, as proving that he was not obliged to work for his bread. In Annam, in China and other countries, this singular and ridiculous fashion is common. A single finger is kept with a shorter nail, being the one used to scratch with, a very frequent occupation in the extreme East.

In another of his walks Forster saw a native, who passed his days in being fed by his wives, quietly lying upon a carpet of thick shrubs. This melancholy person, who fattened without rendering any service to society, recalled Sir John Mandeville's anger at seeing "such a glutton who passed his days without distinguishing himself by any feats of arms, and who lived in pleasure, as a pig which one fattens in a sty".

On the 22nd of August, Cook having learned that King Waheatua was in the neighbourhood, and being desirous of seeing him, landed with Captain Furneaux, the Forsters, and several natives. He met him advancing towards him with a numerous suite, and recognized him at once as he had seen him several times in 1769.

This king was then a child, and was called Te Arée, but he had changed his name at the death of his father Waheatua. He made the captain sit down on his stool, and inquired solicitously for the various Englishmen he had known on the former voyage. Cook, after the usual compliments, presented him with a shirt, a hatchet, some nails, and other trifles. But of all his presents, that which appeared most precious to him, and which excited most cries of admiration from his followers, was a tuft of real feathers mounted upon iron wire.

Waheatua, king of Little Tahiti, was about seventeen or eighteen years of age. Tall and well made, his appearance would have been majestic, but for a look of fear and distrust.

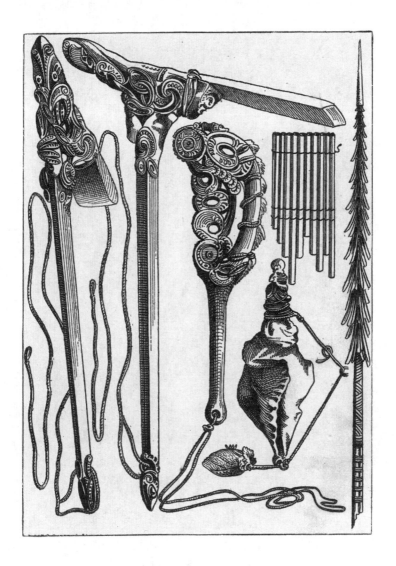

New Zealand utensils and weapons.

Who passed his days in being fed by his wives.

He was surrounded by several chiefs und noble personages, remarkable for their height, and one of whom, tattooed in a peculiar manner, was enormously stout. The king, who showed him great deference, consulted him every moment. Cook then learned that a Spanish vessel had put into Tahiti a few months previously, and he afterwards ascertained that it was that of Domingo Buenechea, which came from Callao.

Whilst Eteé, the king's confidant, conversed with some officers upon religious subjects, and asked the English if they had a god. Waheatua amused himself with the captain's watch. Astonished at the noise it made, and venting his surprise in the words, "It speaks!" he inquired of what use it was.

It was explained to him that it told the time, and in that respect resembled the sun. Waheatua gave it the name of the "little sun", to show that he understood the explanation.

The vessels sailed on the morning of the 24th, and were followed for a long time by numbers of pirogues bearing cocoa-nuts and fruit. Rather than lose this opportunity of obtaining European commodities, the natives parted with their wares very cheaply; a dozen cocoa-nuts could be obtained for one glass bead.

The abundant fresh provisions soon restored the health of all on board the vessels, and most of the sailors, who on reaching Osnaburgh could scarcely walk, could get about well when they left.

The *Resolution* and *Adventure* reached Matavai Bay on the 26th. A crowd of Tahitians soon invaded the deck. Most of them were known to the captain, and Lieutenant Pickersgill, who had accompanied Wallis in 1767, and Cook two years later, received a warm welcome from them.

Cook had tents erected for the sick, the sail-menders, and the coopers, and then left with Captain Furneaux and the two Forsters for Oparreé. The boat which took them soon passed a "morai" of stones, and a cemetery known as the "morai of Tootahah". When Cook called it by this name, one of the natives who accompanied him interrupted him by saying that since Tootahah's death it was called O-Too.

"A fine lesson for princes, who thus in their lives are reminded that they are mortal, and that after their death the earth which contains their corpse will not be their own. "The chief and his wife removed the upper garments from their shoulders as they passed, a mark of respect which natives of all ranks exhibit before a 'morai', as they appear to attach a particular idea of sanctity to these places."

Cook soon gained admittance to the presence of King O-Too. After many compliments he offered him all that he thought he had which would please him, because he appreciated the advantage this man's friendship would be to him, for his every word showed timidity of disposition.

Tall and well made, the king was about thirty years old. He inquired after Tupia and Cook's companions, although he had seen none of them. Many presents were distributed to those of his cortége who appeared the most influential.

"The women sent their servants to find large pieces of their finest stuffs, tinted scarlet, rose, and straw colour, and perfumed with the most odoriferous oil. They placed them over our outer clothing, and so loaded us that we could scarcely move."

O-Too paid the captain a visit on the morrow. He only came on board after Cook had been enveloped in a considerable quantity of the most costly native stuff, and he dared not go below until his brother had first done so. The king and his suite were seated for breakfast, at which the natives went into ecstasies over the usefulness of chairs. O-Too would not taste anything, but his companions were far from following his example. He greatly admired a beautiful spaniel belonging to Forster and expressed a wish to possess it. It was at once given to him, and he had it carried behind him by one of his lords-in-waiting. After breakfast the captain himself conducted O-Too to his sloop, and Captain Furneaux gave him a pair of goats. Upon an excursion to the interior, Mr. Pickersgill met the aged Oberea, who appeared to have lost all her honours, and she was so poor that it was impossible for her to give a present to her friends.

When Cook left on the 1st of September, a young Tahitian, named Poreo, begged to accompany him. The captain consented, hoping that he might prove useful. The moment he lost sight of land poor Poreo could not restrain his tears. The officers comforted him by promising to be like fathers to him.

Cook directed his course to Huaheine Island, which was only twenty-five leagues distant, and anchored there at three in the morning. The natives brought quantities of large fowls, which were the more acceptable as it had been impossible to obtain any at Tahiti. Pigs, dogs, and fruit were in the market, and were exchanged for hatchets, nails, and glass-ware.

O-Too, King of Otaheite.
(Facsimile of early engraving.)

This island, like Tahiti, showed traces of earlier volcanic eruptions, and the summit of one of its hills resembled a crater.

The appearance of the country is similar to that of Tahiti, but is on a smaller scale, for Huaheine is only seven or eight leagues in circumference.

Cook went to see his old friend Orea. The king, dispensing with all ceremony, threw himself on the captain's neck, and shed tears of joy; then he presented him to his friends, to whom the captain gave presents.

The king offered Cook all his most precious possessions, for he looked upon this man as a father. Orea promised to supply the English with all they needed and most loyally kept his word. However, on the morning of the 6th the sailors who presided over the traffic were insulted by a native covered with red, in war dress, and holding a club, who threatened every one. Cook, landing at this moment, threw himself on the native, struggled with him and finally possessed himself of his weapon, which he broke.

The same day another incident occurred. Sparrman had imprudently penetrated to the interior of the island to make botanical researches. Some natives, taking advantage of the moment when he was examining a plant, snatched a dagger, which was the only weapon he carried, from his belt, gave him a blow on the head, and rushing upon him, tore some of his clothes. Sparrman; however, managed to rise and run towards the shore, but, hampered by the bushes and briars, he was captured by the natives, who cut his hands to possess themselves of his shirt, the sleeves of which were buttoned, until he tore the wristbands with his teeth. Others of the natives, seeing him naked and half dead, gave him their clothes, and conducted him to the market-place, where there was a crowd assembled. When Sparrman appeared in this plight, they all took flight, without waiting to be told. Cook at first thought they intended to commit a theft. Undeceived by the appearance of the naturalist, he recalled the other natives, assured them that he would not revenge it upon the innocent, and carried his complaint straight to Orea. The latter, miserable and furious at what had occurred, loaded his people with vehement reproaches, and promised to do all in his power to find out the robbers and the stolen things.

In spite of the prayers of the natives, the king embarked in the captain's vessel, and entered upon a search for the culprits with him. The latter had removed their clothes, and for a while it was impossible to recognize them. Orea therefore accompanied Cook on board, dined with him, and on his return to land was received by his people, who had not expected his return, with lively expressions of joy.

"One of the most agreeable reflections suggested by this voyage," says Forster, "is that instead of finding the inhabitants of this island plunged in voluptuousness, as had been falsely affirmed by earlier navigators, we remarked the most humane and delicate sentiments among them. There are vicious characters in every society, but we could count fifty more sinners in England or any other civilized country than in these islands."

As the vessels were putting off, Orea came to announce that the robbers were taken, and to invite Cook to land and assist in their punishment. It was impossible. The king accompanied Cook half a league on his way, and left him with friendly farewells.

This stay in port had been very productive. The two vessels brought away more than three hundred pigs, and quantities of fowls and fruits. Probably they would not have procured much more, even had their stay been prolonged.

Captain Furneaux had agreed to take a young man named Omai on board. His conduct and intelligence gave a favourable idea of the inhabitants of the Society Islands. Upon his arrival in England this Tahitian was presented to the king by Earl Sandwich, first lord of the Admiralty. At the same time he found protectors and friends in Banks and Solander. They arranged a friendly reception for him among the first families of Great Britain. He lived two years in this country, and upon Cook's third voyage he accompanied him, and returned to his native land.

The captain afterwards visited Ulietea, where the natives gave him the most appreciative welcome. They inquired with interest about Tupia and the English they had seen in the *Endeavour*. King Oreo hastened to renew his acquaintance with the captain, and gave him all the provisions his island produced. During their stay, Poreo, who had embarked in the *Resolution*, landed with a young Tahitan girl, who had enchanted him, and would not return on board. He was replaced by a young man of seventeen or eighteen years of age, a native of Bolabola, named Œdidi, who announced his wish to go to England. The grief evinced by this native on leaving his native land spoke well for his good heart.

The vessels, laden with more than four hundred pigs, and also with fowls, and fruit, left the Society Islands on the 17th of September, and steered for the west. Six days later, one of the

Harvey Islands was sighted, and on the 1st of October anchor was cast off Eoa, called Middelbourg Island by Tasman and Cook.

The welcome by the natives was cordial. A chief named Tai-One came on board, touched the captain's nose with a pinch of pepper, and sat down without speaking. The alliance was concluded and ratified by the gift of a few trifles.

Tai-One guided the English into the interior. The newcomers were surrounded by a dense crowd of natives, offering stuffs and mats in exchange for nails as long as the walk lasted. The natives often even carried their liberality so far as to decline any return for these presents. Tai-One conducted his new friends to his dwelling, agreeably situated in a beautiful valley, in the shade of some "*sad-hecks*". He served them with a liquor extracted from the juice of the "*eava*", the use of which is common to the Polynesian islanders. It was prepared in the following manner: – Pieces of a root, a species of pepper, were first chewed, and then placed in a large wooden vase, over which water was poured. As soon as this liquor was drinkable, the natives poured it out into cups made of green leaves, shaped into form, and holding about half a pint. Cook was the only one who tasted it. The method of preparing the liquor had quenched the thirst of his companions, but the natives were not fastidious, and the vase was soon emptied.

The English afterwards visited several plantations or gardens, separated by intertwined hedges, which were connected by doors formed of planks and hung upon hinges. The perfection of culture, and the fully developed instinct of property, showed a degree of civilization superior to that of Tahiti.

In spite of the reception he met with, Cook, who could procure neither pigs nor fowls, left this island to reach that of Amsterdam, called Tonga Tabou by the natives. Here he hoped to find the provisions he needed. The vessels soon anchored in the roadstead of Van Dieman, in eighteen fathoms of water, a cable's length from the breakers which border the shore. The natives were friendly, and brought stuffs, mats, implements, arms, ornaments, and soon afterwards pigs and fowls. Œdidi bought some red feathers off them with much delight, declaring they would have a high value at Tahiti. Cook landed with a native named Attago, who had attached himself to him at once. During his excursion, he remarked a temple similar to a "morai", and which was called by the generic name of Faitoka. Raised upon an artificial butt, sixteen or eighteen feet from the ground, the temple was in an oblong form, and was reached by two stone staircases. Built like the homes of the natives, with posts and joists, it was covered with palm leaves. Two wooden images coarsely carved, two feet in length, occupied the corners.

"As I did not wish to offend either them or their gods," says the captain, "I dared not touch them, but I inquired of Attago if these, were 'Eatuas', or gods. I do not know if he understood me, but he instantly handled them, and turned them over as roughly as if he had merely touched a bit of wood, which convinced me that they did not represent a divine being."

A few thefts were perpetrated, but they did not interrupt cordiality, and a quantity of provisions were procured. Before leaving, the captain had an interview with a person who was treated with extraordinary respect, to whom all the natives accorded the rank of king. Cook says, –

"I found him seated, with a gravity of deportment so stupid and so dull, that in spite of all they had told me, I took him for an idiot, whom the people adored from superstitious motives. I saluted him, and talked to him, but he made no reply, and paid no attention to me. I was about to leave him, when a native made me understand that it was without doubt the king. I offered him a shirt, a hatchet, a piece of red stuff, a looking-glass, some nails, medals, and glassware. He received them, or rather allowed them to be placed upon his person or beside him, losing nothing of his gravity, and speaking no word, not even moving his head to the right or left."

However, next day, this chief sent baskets of bananas and a roast pig, saying that it was a present from the "ariki" of the island to the "ariki" of the ship.

Cook called this archipelago the Friendly Islands. They had formerly received various names from Schouten and Tasman, as, Cocoa-nut Islands, Traitor Islands, Hope Islands, and Horn Islands.

Cook not having been able to obtain fresh water, was obliged to leave Tonga sooner than he wished. He found time, however, to make a few observations as to the productions of the country, and the manners of the natives. We will mention the most striking.

Nature had showered its treasures with a liberal hand upon Tonga and Eoa Islands. Cocoa-nuts, palm-trees, breadfruit-trees, yams, and sugar-canes are most plentiful there. As for edible animals, pigs and fowls alone were met with, but dogs if not existing there, are known by name. The most delicate fish abounds on the coast. Of much the same form as Europeans, and equally white, the inhabitants of these islands are well-proportioned and of pleasant features. Their hair is originally black, but they are in the habit of tinting it with powder, so that white, red, and blue hair abounds, which produces a singular effect. Tattooing is a universal practice. Their clothes are very simple, consisting of one piece of stuff, rolled round the waist, and falling to the knees. The women, who at Tonga, as everywhere else, are more coquettish than men, make aprons of cocoa-nut fibres, which they ornament with shells, and bits of coloured stuffs and feathers.

The natives have some singular customs, which the English had not noticed before. Thus they put everything that is given them on their heads, and conclude a bargain with this practice. When a friend or relation dies, they slash their limbs, and even some of their fingers. Their dwellings are not collected in villages, but are separate and dispersed among the plantations. Built in the same style as those of the Society Isles, they differ from them only in being raised higher above the ground.

The *Adventure* and *Resolution* sailed on the 7th of October, and the following day reconnoitred Pylstart Island, discovered by Tasman. On the 21st, anchor was cast in Hawke's Bay, New Zealand. Cook landed a certain number of animals, which he wished to acclimatize, and set sail again to enter Queen Charlotte's Sound, but being caught in a great gale, he was separated from the *Adventure*, and did not meet her again until he reached England.

On the 5th of November the captain repaired the damages of his vessel, and before undertaking a new voyage in the southern seas, he wished to ascertain the extent and quality of his provisions. He reckoned that four thousand five hundred pounds of biscuits had been entirely spoiled, and that more than three thousand pounds were in scarcely better condition. During his stay here he obtained a new and still more convincing proof of the cannibalism of the natives of New Zealand. An officer had bought the head of a young man, who had been killed and eaten, and some natives seeing it, wished very much for a piece, Cook gave it up to them, and the avidity with which they threw themselves upon this revolting food, proved the pleasure that these cannibals took in eating food which they have difficulty in procuring.

The *Resolution* left New Zealand on the 26th of November, and entered the glacial regions which she had already traversed; but the circumstances attending her second voyage were distressing. The crew, though in good health, were overcome by fatigue, and less capable of resisting illness, the more so that they had no fresh food on board.

The *Resolution* had lost her consort, and the world was convinced that no Antartic continent existed. It was, so to say, a "platonic" voyage. It was necessary to prove beyond the possibility of doubt that no new land of any importance was to be discovered in these latitudes.

The first ice was encountered on the 12th of December, and farther to the south than in the preceding year. From this date, the usual incidents of navigation in these latitudes were repeated day by day. Œdidi was quite astonished by the "white rain", as he called the snow which fell on his hand, but the sight of the first ice was a still greater marvel to him; he called it "white earth".

"His mind had been struck by a phenomenon in the torrid zone," says the narrative. "As long as the ships remained in these latitudes, we had had scarcely any night, and he had seen that we could write at midnight by the light of the sun. Œdidi could scarcely believe his eyes, and he assured us that his fellow countrymen would put him down as a liar, if he talked to them of petrified rain, and of perpetual day."

The young Tahitan had time to become accustomed to this phenomenon, for the ship advanced as far as 76° south, amidst floating ice. Then, convinced that if a continent existed the ice made access to it impossible, Cook determined to proceed to the North.

General dissatisfaction prevailed; no one on board was free from severe colds, or from an attack of scurvy. The captain himself was seriously affected by bilious sickness, which kept him in bed. For eight days his life was in danger, and his recovery was likely to be equally painful and slow. The same route was followed until the 11th of March, when with the rising of the sun the joyful cry of "Land! land!" arose.

It was the Easter Island, of Roggewein's Davis' Land. Upon nearing it, the navigators were struck with astonishment, as the Dutch had been, by the enormous statues erected on the shore. Cook says that the latitude of Easter Island answers very closely to that marked in Roggewein's MS. journal, and its longtitude is only one degree wrong.

The shore, composed of black broken rock of ferruginous appearance, shows traces of violent subterranean eruption. A few scattered plantations were perceived in the centre of the island.

Singular coincidence! The first word spoken by the natives as the strangers approached the shore, was to ask in the Tahitan tongue for a rope. This again suggested that the origin of both races was the same. Like the Tahitans they were tattooed, and clothed in stuffs similar to those of the Society Islands.

"The action of the sun on their heads," says the narrative, "has forced them to find different means for protecting themselves. The greater number of the men wear a circular head-covering about two inches thick, twisted with grass from one side to the other, and covered with a great quantity of those long, black feathers which adorn the frigate bird. Others have enormous hats of brown gulls' feathers, almost as large as the wigs of European lawyers, and many have a simple wooden hoop, surrounded with white gulls' feathers, which wave in the air. The women wear large and wide hats of neat plaits, which come to a point in front, with a ridge along the top, and two great lobes on either side.

"The country was a picture of desolation. It was surveyed by two detachments, and was found to be covered with black and porous stones. The entire vegetation which could thrive on this mass of lava consisted of two or three kinds of rugose grass, which grew on the rocks, scanty bushes, especially the paper-mulberry, the 'hibiscus', and the mimosa, and some plantains. Close to the landing-place is a perpendicular wall, constructed of square stones, compactly and durably joined in accordance with art rules, and fitting in a style of durability. Further on, in the centre of a well-paved area, a monolith is erected, representing a half-naked human figure, some twenty[1] feet high, and more than five wide, very roughly hewn. The head is badly designed, the eyes, nose, and mouth scarcely indicated, but the ears are very long, as is the fashion in this country, and are better finished than the rest."

These monuments, which are numerous, do not appear to have been erected or hewn by the race the English found, or this race had degenerated; for these natives paid no respect to the statues, although they treated them with a certain veneration, and objected to any one's walking on the pavement near them.

It was not only on the sea-shore that these enormous sentinels were seen. Between the mountains, in the fissures of rocks, others existed, some erect or fallen to earth through some convulsion, others still imperfectly separated from the block from which they were being cut. What sudden catastrophe stopped the works? What do these monoliths represent? To what distant period do these testimonies of the industry of a race long disappeared, or the

---

[1] In the earlier editions of the French translation of Cook's Voyages (Paris, 1878, seven 4to vols.), the height of this statue is given as two feet, evidently by a typographical error. We now correct this mistake, which has been repeated in all subsequent editions.

Monuments in Easter Island.
(Facsimile of early engraving.)

recollection of whom has perished, seem to point? This problem must remain for ever insoluble.

Traffic proceeded easily. It was only necessary to repress the marvellous dexterity of the natives in emptying pockets. The few possessions which had been obtained had been very useful, though the want of drinkable water prevented Cook remaining long in Easter Island. He directed his course to the archipelago of the Marquesas of Mendana, which had not been visited since 1595. But his vessel had no sooner been put to sea than he was again attacked by the bilious fever, from which he had suffered so severely. The sufferers from scurvy relapsed, and all who had undertaken long walks across Easter Island had their faces burnt by the sun.

On the 7th of April, 1774, Cook sighted the Marquesas group, after seeking them in vain for five consecutive days in the different positions assigned to them by geographers. Anchor was cast at Tao Wati, the Santa Cristina of Mendana.

The *Resolution* was soon surrounded by pirogues, the foremost of which was full of stones, every man on board having a sling round his hand. However, friendly relations were formed, followed by barter.

"These natives," says Forster, "are well made, with handsome faces, yellowish or tanned complexions, and marks all over their bodies, which gives them an almost black appearance. The valleys of our harbour were filled with trees, and tallied in every particular with the description given by the Spaniards. We saw fire across the forests several times, very far from the shore, and concluded that the country was well populated."

The difficulty of procuring food decided Cook upon a hasty departure. But he had time to collect some interesting facts about the people, whom he considered the handsomest in Oceania. These natives appear to surpass all others in the regularity of their features. The resemblance in their speech, however, to that of the Tahitans, appears to point to a common origin.

The Marquesas are five in number, Magdalena, San Pedro, Dominica, Santa Cristina, and Hood Island, the latter so called after the volunteer who first discovered it. Santa Cristina is divided by a chain of mountains of considerable elevation, to which the hills that rise from the sea lead. Deep, narrow, and fertile valleys, filled with fruit-trees, and watered by streams of excellent water, intersect this mountain isle. Port Madre de Dios, called by Cook Resolution Harbour, is about the centre of the eastern coast of Santa Cristina. It contains two sandy creeks, into which two streams flow.

## II.

A fresh visit to Tahiti and the Friendly Islands – Exploration of New Hebrides – Discovery of New Caledonia and Pine Island – Stay in Queen Charlotte's Sound – South Georgia – Accident to the *Adventure*.

After leaving these islands, on the 12th of April, and sailing for Tahiti, Cook fell in, five days later, with the Pomotou archipelago. He landed on the Tioukea Island of Byron. The inhabitants, who had cause to complain of earlier navigators, received the advances of the English coldly. The latter could only obtain about two dozen cocoa-nuts and five pigs, which appeared plentiful in this island. In another settlement a more friendly reception was met with. The natives embraced the new-comers, and rubbed their noses in the same fashion as the New Zealanders. Œdidi bought several dogs, the long and white hair of whose skins serves as an ornament for cuirasses in his native land.

Forster relates: –

"The natives told us that they broke up scurvy grass, mixed it with shell-fish, and threw it into the sea on the approach of a shoal of fish. This bait intoxicated the fish for a time, and when they came to the surface it was easy to take them. The captain afterwards saw several other islands of this immense archipelago, which were similar to those he had left, especially the Pernicious Islands, where Roggewein had lost his sloop, the *African*, and to which Cook gave the name of Palliser Islands."

He then steered for Tahiti, which the sailors, certain of the good-will of the natives, regarded as a home. The *Resolution* cast anchor in Matavai Bay on the 22nd of April, and their reception was as friendly as had been anticipated. A few days later, King O-Too and several other chiefs visited the English, and brought them a present of ten or a dozen large pigs and some fruit.

Cook's first idea was to remain in this spot only just long enough for Mr. Wales, the astronomer, to take observations, but the abundance of provisions induced him to prolong his stay.

On the morning of the 26th, the captain, who had been to Oparrée with some of his officers, to make a formal visit to the king, observed a fleet of more than 300 pirogues, drawn up in order on the shore. They were all completely equipped. At the same time a number of warriors assembled on the beach.

Natives of Easter Island.
(Facsimile of early engraving.)

The officers' suspicions were excited by this formidable armament, collected in one night, but they were reassured by the
welcome they received.

This fleet consisted of no less than sixty large double pirogues,
decorated with flags and streamers, and 170 smaller ones, intended
for the transport of provisions, and the flotilla was manned with no
fewer than 7,760 men, warriors or paddlers.

"The sight of this fleet," says Forster, "increased our ideas of the
power and wealth of this island. The entire crew was astonished.
When we reflect upon the implements possessed by this people, we
can but admire the patience and toil necessary to cut down these
enormous trees, separate and polish the branches, and then to carry
the heavy constructions to such perfection. These works are produced by them by means of a stone hatchet and saw, a piece of
coral, and the hide of whales. The chiefs, and all who occupied a
prominent fighting rank, were dressed in military style – that is to
say, in a quantity of stuffs, turbans, helmets, and breastplates. The
height of some of the helmets was most embarrassing to the
wearers. The entire equipment appeared more appropriate for
scenic effect than suitable for a battlefield. But, in any case, it added
to the grandeur of the display, and the warriors did not fail to show
themselves with a view to the most striking effect.

"Upon reaching Matavai, Cook learned that this formidable
armament was destined for an attack upon Eimio, whose chief had
revolted against the Tahitan yoke, and become independent.

"During the following days the captain was visited by some of his
old friends. All showed a desire to possess red feathers, which were
of considerable value. One only attached more importance to a
glass bead or a nail. The Tahitans were so impressed that they
offered in exchange the strange mourning garments, which they
had refused to sell during Cook's first voyage.

"These garments are made of the rarest productions of the
islands and the surrounding sea, and are worked with care and great
skill, and no doubt are of great value to themselves. We bought no
less than ten, which we brought to England."

Œdidi, who had taken good care to procure some feathers for
himself, could indulge in any caprice he liked. The natives looked
upon him as a prodigy, and listened eagerly to his tales. The principal personages of the island, and even the king sought his society.
He married a daughter of the chief of Matavai, and brought his wife
on board. Every one was delighted to make him a present. Finally

he decided to remain at Tahiti, where he had found his sister married to a powerful chief.

In spite of the thefts, which more than once caused unpleasantness, the English procured more provisions on their stay in this port than ever before. The aged Oberea, who was like a queen in the island during the stay made by the *Dauphin* in 1767, herself brought pigs and fruits, in the secret hope of obtaining red feathers, which had so great a success. Presents were liberally given, and the Indians were amused with fireworks and military manœuvres.

Just before he left, the captain witnessed a curious naval review. O-Too ordered a sham fight, but it lasted so short a time that it was impossible to observe the movements. The fleet was to commence hostilities five days after Cook's departure, and he would much have liked to have waited for it; but, fearing the natives might suspect him of an attempt to overcome both conquered and victors, he determined to leave.

The *Resolution* had scarcely left the bay, when one of the gunners, seduced by the delights of Tahiti, and possibly by the promises of King O-Too, who, no doubt, thought a European might be of use to him, threw himself into the sea, but he was soon retaken by a boat launched by Cook in his pursuit.

Cook very much regretted the fact that discipline obliged him to act in this way. The man had no relations or friends in England, and, had he requested permission to remain in Tahiti, it would not have been refused.

On the 15th, the *Resolution* anchored in Wharre harbour, in Huaheine Island. The old chief Orea was one of the first to congratulate the English upon their return, and to bring them presents. The captain presented him with red feathers, but the old chief appeared to prefer iron, hatchets, and nails. He seemed more indolent than upon the previous visit. His head was weaker, no doubt owing to his immoderate love for an intoxicating drink extracted from pepper by the natives. His authority was evidently despised, and Cook sent in pursuit of a band of robbers, who had not refrained from pillaging the old king himself, and who had taken refuge in the centre of the island.

Orea showed himself grateful for the consideration the English had always shown him. He was the last to leave the vessel before she sailed, on the 24th of April, and when Cook said that they should never meet again, he shed tears and replied, –

"Send your children here, we will treat them well."

Natives of the Marquesas.

On another occasion, Orea asked the captain where he should be buried. "At Stepney," said Cook. Orea begged him to repeat the word until he could pronounce it. Then a hundred voices cried at once, "Stepney morai no Toote", "Stepney the grave of Cook". In giving this reply the great navigator had no prevision of his fate, or of the difficulty his fellow countrymen would have in finding his remains.

Œdidi, who at the last moment had accompanied the English to Huaheine, had not met with so cordial a welcome as at Tahiti. His riches had strangely diminished and his credit suffered in consequence. The narrative says, –

"He soon proved the truth of the proverb, that a man is never a prophet in his own country. He left us with regrets, which proved his esteem for us, and when the moment of separation arrived, he ran from cabin to cabin embracing every one. It is impossible to describe the mental anguish of the young man when he left. He gazed at the vessel, burst into tears, and crouched in despair in the bottom of his pirogue. We saw him again, stretching out his arms to us, as we left the reefs."

Cook reconnoitred Hove Island (so called by Wallis) on the 6th of June. It is named Mohipa by the natives. A few days later he found several uninhabited islets, surrounded by a chain of breakers, to which he gave the name of Palmerston, in honour of one of the Lords of the Admiralty.

Upon the 20th a steep and rocky island was discovered crowned with large woods, and bushes; the beach was narrow and sandy, and several natives of very dark complexion were seen upon it.

They made menacing demonstrations, and were armed with lances and clubs. As soon as the English landed they retired. Champions, however, advanced, and endeavoured to provoke the strangers, assailing them with a storm of arrows and stones. Sparrman was wounded in the arm, and Cook just escaped being struck by a javelin. A general volley soon dispersed these inhospitable islanders, and the uncivil reception which was thus accorded well deserved the name bestowed upon their land of Savage Island.

Four days later Cook reached the Tonga archipelago once more. He stopped this time at Nomouka, called Rotterdam by Tasman.

He had scarcely cast anchor before the ship was surrounded by a crowd of pirogues, filled with bananas and every kind of fruit, which were exchanged for nails and old pieces of stuff. This friendly reception encouraged the naturalists to land and penetrate to the interior, in search of new plants and unknown productions. Upon their return they enlarged upon the beauty of this picturesque and romantic country, and upon the affability and cordiality of the natives.

In spite of it, however, various thefts continued to take place, until a more important larceny than usual obliged the captain to resort to severity.

A native, who opposed the seizure of two pirogues by the English, as hostages until the stolen arms were restored, was wounded severely by a gunshot. During this second visit Cook bestowed the name of Friendly Islands upon this group, no doubt with a sarcastic meaning. Now-a-days they are better known by the native name of Tonga.

The indefatigable navigator continued his route in a westward direction, passed in succession Lepreux, Aurora, Whitsunday and Mallicolo Islands, to which archipelago Bougainville had given the name of the Grandes Cyclades.

Cook gave his usual order, to enter into friendly and commercial relations with the inhabitants.

The first day passed quietly, and the natives celebrated the visit of the English by games and dancing, but on the morrow an incident occurred which led to a general collision.

A native, who was refused access to the ship, prepared to launch an arrow at one of the sailors. His fellow-countrymen at first prevented him. At the same moment Cook appeared on deck, his gun in his hand. His first step was to shout to the native, who again aimed at the sailor. Without replying, the native was about to let his arrow fly at him, when a shot anticipated and wounded him. This was the signal for a general discharge of arrows, which struck on the vessel and did but little damage. Cook then ordered a gun to be fired over the natives' heads with a view to dispersing them. A few hours later the natives again surrounded the ship, and returned to their barter as if nothing had happened.

Cook took advantage of these friendly indications to land an armed detachment for wood and water. Four or five natives were collected on the beach. A chief, leaving the group, advanced to the captain, holding in his hand, as Cook also did, a green bough. The two branches were exchanged, and peace thus concluded, a few slight presents helped to cement it. Cook then obtained permission to take wood, but not to go far from the shore, and the naturalists, who were anxious to prosecute their investigations in the interior,

Typical natives of the Sandwich Islands.
(Facsimile of early engraving.)

were brought back to the beach, in spite of their protestations.

Iron implements had no value for these people. This made it extremely difficult to obtain provisions. Only a few agreed to exchange arms for stuffs, and exhibited an honesty in their transactions to which the English were unaccustomed.

The exchanges continued after the *Resolution* had set sail, and the natives hurried in their pirogues to deliver the articles for which they had received the price. One of them, after vigorous efforts, succeeded in gaining the vessels, carrying his weapons to a sailor who had paid for them and forgotten it, it was so long ago. The native refused the recompense the sailor would have given, making him understand that he had been paid already. Cook gave the name of Port Sandwich to this harbour of refuge, which he left on the morning of the 23rd of July.

He was most favourably impressed by the moral qualities of the natives of Mallicolo, but by no means so in regard to their physical powers.

Small and badly proportioned, bronze in colour, with flat faces, they were hideous. Had Darwinian theories been in vogue in those days, no doubt Cook would have recognized in them that missing link between man and monkey, which is the despair of Darwin's followers.

Their coarse, crinkly black hair was short, and their bushy beards did not add to their beauty. But the one thing which made them most grotesque was their habit of tying a cord tightly across the stomach, which made them appear like great emmets. Tortoise-shell ear-rings, bracelets made of hogs' teeth, large tortoise-shell rings, and a white flat stone which they passed through the cartilage of the nose, constituted their ornaments. Their weapons were bows and arrows, spears and clubs. The points of their arrows, which were occasionally two or three in number, were coated with a substance which the English thought was poisonous, from observing the care with which the natives drew them out of a kind of quiver.

The *Resolution* had only just left Port Sandwich when all the crew were seized with colic, vomiting, and violent pains in the head and back. Two large fish had been caught and eaten by them, possibly whilst they were under the influence of the narcotic mentioned above. In every case, ten days elapsed before entire recovery. A parrot and dog which had also eaten of the fish died next day. Quiros' companions had suffered in the same way, and since Cook's voyage similar symptoms of poisoning have been noticed in these latitudes.

After leaving Mallicolo, Cook steered for Ambrym Island, which appeared to contain a volcano, and shortly afterwards discovered a group of small islands, which he named Shepherd Islands, in honour of the Cambridge Professor of Astronomy.

He then visited the Islands of Two Hills, Montagu and Hinchinbrook Islands, and the largest of all, Sandwich Island, which must not be mistaken for the group of the same name. All the islands, lying among and protected by breakers, were covered with rich vegetation and were largely populated.

Two slight accidents interrupted the calm on board. A fire broke out, which was soon extinguished, and one of the sailors falling overboard, was at once rescued.

Koro Mango was discovered on the 3rd of August. Next day Cook reached its shore, hoping to find a watering-place, and facility for landing. The greater part of the sufferers from the poisonous fish had not yet recovered their health, and they looked forward to its speedy re-establishment on shore. But the reception accorded to them by the natives, who were armed with clubs, lances, and arrows, seemed wanting in sincerity.

Cook was on his guard. Finding that they could not lure the English into landing, the natives endeavoured to force them. A chief and several men tried to snatch the oars from the sailors. Cook wished to fire his musket, but the priming would not go off. The English were immediately overwhelmed with stones and arrows. The captain at once ordered a general volley; fortunately half of the shots missed, or the slaughter would have been terrific.

Forster says, "These natives appear to be of different race to those living in Mallicolo. They speak a different language. They are of medium height, but well-shaped, and their features are not disagreeable. They were bronze in complexion, and they paint their faces black or red; their hair is somewhat woolly and curly. The few women I saw appeared very ugly. I have seen no pirogues on any part of the coast. They live in houses covered with palm-leaves, and their plantations are in straight lines and are surrounded by a hedge of reeds."

It was useless to make a second attempt to land. Cook having bestowed the name of Cape Traitor upon the scene of the collision, reached an island, which he had seen the previous evening, and which the natives called Tanna.

"The highest hill of the same range is of conical shape," says Forster, "with a crater in the centre. It is reddish brown, and composed of a mass of burnt stones, perfectly sterile. From time to time it emitted a thick column of smoke like a great tree, increasing in width as it ascended."

The *Resolution* was at once surrounded by a score of pirogues, the largest of which contained twenty-five men. The latter sought to appropriate everything within their reach, buoys, flags, the hinges of the rudder, which they tried to knock off. They only returned to the shore after a four-pounder had been fired over their heads.

The vessel made for the shore, but all the trifles that were distributed could not induce the natives to relinquish their attitude of defiance and bravado. It was clear that the smallest misunderstanding would lead to bloodshed.

Cook imagined these people to be cannibals, although pigs, fowls, roots, and fruits abounded.

During the stay prudence prevented any one leaving the shore. Forster, however, ventured a little way and discovered a spring of water, so hot that he could not hold his finger in it longer than a second. In spite of all their wishes, the English found it impossible to reach the central volcano, which emitted torrents of fire and smoke as high as the clouds, and projected enormously large stones into the air. The number of extinct volcanoes in every direction was considerable, and the soil was decidedly subject to volcanic eruptions. By degrees, though without losing their reserve, the Tannians became more at home with the strangers, and intercourse was less difficult.

"These people," says Cook, "showed themselves hospitable, civil, and good-hearted, when we did not excite their jealousy. We cannot blame their conduct greatly, for after all, from what point of view can they have judged us? They could not possibly know our real intentions. We entered their country, as they dared not oppose us; we endeavoured to disembark as friends, but we landed and maintained our superiority by force of arms. Under such circumstances what opinion could the natives form of us? It doubtless appeared far more plausible that we came to invade their country, than that we visited them as friends. Time only, and intimate relations, could teach them our good intentions."

However that might be, the English were at a loss to guess why the natives prevented their penetrating to the interior of the country. Was it owing to a naturally shy nature? or possibly because they were threatened with constant inroads from their neighbours.

Their address in the use of arms and their bearing supported this idea, but it was impossible to know with any certainty.

As the natives did not value anything the English offered, they did not bring any great quantity of the fruits and roots the latter longed for. They would not consent to part with their pigs even for hatchets, the utility of which they had proved.

The productions of the island included bread-fruits, cocoa-nuts, a fruit like a peach, called "parre", yams, potatoes, wild pigs, nutmegs, and many others of which Forster did not know the names.

On the 21st Cook left Tanna, discovered successively, Erromam and Annatom islands, and coasted Sandwich Island. He passed Mallicolo and Quiros' Land of the Holy Spirit, where he easily recognized St. James and St. Philip Bays, and left this archipelago after having named it New Hebrides, by which appellation it is now known.

A new discovery was made on the 5th of September. No European foot had ever trodden the soil he now sighted. It was the northern extremity of New Caledonia. The first point recognized was called Cape Colnett, after one of the volunteers who saw it first. The coast was bordered by a chain of breakers, behind which two or three pirogues appeared to be paddling, so as to reconnoitre the new-comers. But at sunrise they brailed their sails and were seen no more.

Having cruised for two hours along the outer reefs, Cook perceived an opening which would he thought would enable him to draw near. He steered for it and landed at Balade.

The country appeared sterile, and uniformly covered with a whitish grass. Some trees with white trunks, like the willow in shape, were seen here and there. They were "niaoulis". At the same time several houses like bee-hives were perceived.

No sooner was anchor cast than fifteen or more pirogues surrounded the vessel. The natives had sufficient confidence to approach and begin traffic. Some of them even entered the ship, and inspected all the various parts of it with extreme curiosity. They refused to touch the dishes offered them, stewed peas, beef, and salt pork, but they voluntarily tasted the yams. They were most surprised at the goats, pigs, dogs, and cats, which were so strange to them that they had no words to designate them. Nails, all iron implements, and red stuffs, appeared precious to them. Tall, strong, and well-proportioned, with curly hair and beard, and of dark chocolate colour, they spoke a language which bore no resemblance to any which the English had hitherto heard.

The natives had sufficient confidence.

When the captain landed he was received with joyful demonstrations, and with the surprise natural to people who are brought face to face with objects of which they have had no previous idea. Some of the chiefs, enjoining silence, made short harangues, and Cook began the usual distribution of ironmongery and hardware. His officers mixed with the crowd to make observations.

Many of the natives appeared afflicted with a kind of leprosy, and their arms, and legs were greatly swollen. They were all but naked, wearing merely a cord tightened to the figure, from which hung scraps of stuff made from the fig-tree. A few wore enormous cylindrical hats, open on two sides, like the hats of the Hungarian hussars. They hung tortoiseshell earrings or rolls of the leaves of the sugar-cane in their ears, which were pulled out and split.

The English soon perceived a little village above the mangroves which bordered the shore. It was surrounded by sugar-cane plantations, yams, and banana-trees, and watered by little canals, cleverly diverted from the large river.

Cook soon discovered that he need expect nothing of this race but permission to survey the country.

"These natives," he says, "taught us a few words of their language, which bore no resemblance to that of any other tribe. They were mild and peaceable in character, but extremely lazy. If we addressed them they replied, but if we continued our way seldom joined us in our excursions. If we passed their cabins without remark they took no notice of us. The women were slightly more curious, and hid themselves in the bushes to look after us, but they would only approach in the company of the men. They appeared neither vexed nor alarmed when we shot birds. Indeed, if we were near their huts, the young people would point them out to us, for the pleasure of seeing us fire. They appeared to have very little to do at this time of year. Having tilled the ground, and sown roots and bananas, they awaited their crops next summer.

"Perhaps in this fact lay the explanation of their having no provisions to offer in traffic, for in other respects we found them fully alive to the hospitable instinct which more particularly commends the islanders of the southern seas to navigators."

Cook's assertion of the indolence of the New Caledonians is perfectly true. But his stay amongst them was too short to enable him to appreciate their character thoroughly; and he certainly never suspected that they indulged in the horrible practice of cannibalism. He noticed no birds living in a wild state there excepting quails, turtle-doves, pigeons, turkeys, ducks, teal, and a few smaller ones. He could not ascertain the presence of any quadrupeds, and he entirely failed in his endeavours to procure provisions.

At Balade the captain made several excursions into the interior, and climbed the mountains to gain a general view over the country. From the summit of a rock he clearly saw the two coasts and ascertained that New Caledonia in this part was only ten leagues in width.

In its general features the country resembled various portions of New Holland, which is in the same latitude. The productions of both appear to be the same, and there is an absence of brushwood in the forests of both.

Cook also observed the presence of minerals on the hills, and his discovery has been verified in late years by the proved existence of gold, iron, copper, coal, and nickel.

A few of the crew met with a similar adventure here to that which had been almost fatal to some of them in the neighbourhood of Mallicolo.

Cook relates it thus: –

"My secretary bought a fish which had been harpooned by a native, and sent it to me on board. This fish was of an entirely new species, and resembled that known as sun-fish, it was of the order called 'tetrodon' by Linnæus. Its head was hideous, wide and long. Never suspecting that it might be poisonous, I ordered it to be served at table the same evening. Fortunately so much time was consumed in drawing and describing it that no time was left for the cooking, and only the liver was served.

"The two Forsters and myself partook of it, and towards three in the morning we experienced a sensation of weakness and want of power in our limbs. I all but lost the sense of touch, and could no longer distinguish light from heavy objects when I desired to move them. A pot full of water and a feather appeared to me equally heavy. We first resorted to emetics, and afterwards we succeeded in inducing perspiration, which relieved us greatly. In the morning, a pig which had eaten the entrails of the fish was found dead. When the natives came on board, and saw the fish hanging up, they made us understand that it was unwholesome. They showed their disgust of it, but neither in selling it, or even after having been paid for it, had they given the slightest hint of such aversion."

Cook next proceeded to the survey of the greater part of the eastern coast. During this excursion he met with a native as white as a European. His complexion was attributed to illness. This man was an Albino, like those already met with in Tahiti and the Society Islands.

The captain was anxious to acclimatize pigs in New Caledonia, but he had the greatest difficulty in inducing the natives to accept a hog and a sow. He was forced to insist upon their usefulness, the facility of breeding them, and to exaggerate their value before the natives would consent to their being landed.

Cook describes the New Caledonians as tall, robust, active, polite, and peaceable. He gives them the rare character of honesty. But his successors in this country, more especially Entrecasteaux, discovered to their detriment that they did not preserve this quality. Some of them had the thick lips, flat nose, and general appearance of the negro. Their naturally curly hair added to the resemblance.

"If I were to guess," says Cook, "at the origin of this people, I should take them to be an intermediate race between the people of Tanna and the Friendly Islands, or between those of Tanna and New Zealand, or possibly between all three, for their language is in some respects a sort of mixture of that of these different countries."

The frequency of war amongst them is indicated by the number of their offensive weapons, clubs, spears, lances, slings, javelins, &c. The stones used for their slings are smooth and oval. Their houses are built on a circular plan, most of them being like beehives, with the roof of considerable height, and terminating in a point. They always have one or two fires alight, but as there is only one outlet for the smoke, through the doorway, no European could live in them.

They subsisted entirely upon fish and roots, such as yams, and the bark of a tree, which was but little succulent. Bananas, sugar-canes, and bread-fruit were rare, and cocoa-nuts did not flourish so well as in the island previously visited by the English. The number of inhabitants appeared considerable. But Cook justly remarked that his arrival had brought about a general reunion of all the tribes, and Lieutenant Pickersgill decided during his hydrographical excursions that the country was sparsely populated.

The New Caledonians buried their dead. Many of the crew visited their cemeteries, and especially the tomb of a chief, which was a kind of mound, decorated with spears, javelins, arrows, and darts, which were stuck around it.

Cook left the harbour of Balade, and continued to coast New Caledonia, without finding fresh provisions. The aspect of the

With the roof of considerable height.

country was universally sterile. But quite to the south of this large
land a smaller one was discovered, to which the name of Pine Island
was given, on account of the number of pine trees upon it.

They were a species of Prussian pine, very appropriate for the
spars needed for the *Resolution*. Cook accordingly sent a sloop and
some men to choose and cut the trees he needed. Some of them
were twenty inches in diameter, and seventy feet high, so that a
mast could have been formed of one had it been needed. The discovery of this island had a certain value, as, with the exception of
New Zealand, it was the only one in the entire Pacific Ocean which
produced wood fit for masts and poles.

In steering southwards towards New Zealand, Cook sighted a
small uninhabited island on the 10th of October, upon which the
botanists reaped a plentiful harvest of unknown vegetables. It was
Norfolk Island, so named in honour of the Howard family. It was
afterwards colonized by a part of the mutineers of the *Bounty*.

The *Resolution* anchored again in Queen Charlotte's Sound. The
gardens so anxiously planted by the English had been entirely
neglected by the New Zealanders, but in spite of this several plants
had grown marvellously.

The natives were very shy of appearing at first, and seemed to
care little for any intercourse with the strangers; but when they recognized their old friends, they testified their delight most
extravagantly. When asked why they had been so reserved at first,
they evaded a reply, and there was no doubt that they were thinking
of murder and combats.

This aroused Cook's apprehensions for the fate of the *Adventure*,
of which he had heard nothing since his last stay in this port, but he
could obtain no reply to the questions he put. He was only to learn
what had occurred in his absence, when he reached the Cape of
Good Hope, and found letters from Captain Furneaux.

After once more landing some pigs, with which he wished to
endow New Zealand, the captain set sail for Cape Horn on the
10th of November. After a vain cruise, he at last sighted the eastern
shore of Tierra del Fuego, near the entrance to the Straits of
Magellan.

"The portion of America which now met our view," says Cook,
"was dreary enough. It seemed to be cut up into small islands,
which though by no means high, were very black, and almost
entirely barren. In the background, we saw high ground covered
with snow, almost to the water's edge. It is the wildest shore I have

ever seen, and appears entirely composed of mountains and rocks, without a vestige of vegetation. The mountains overhang horrible precipices, the sharp peaks of which arise to great height. Probably there is nothing in nature which presents so wild an appearance. The interior mountains are covered with snow, but those bordering the sea are not. We imagined the former to belong to Tierra del Fuego, and the latter to be ranged over the small islands in such a way as to present the appearance of an uninterrupted coast."

The captain still thought it better to remain some time in this desolate region, to procure fresh victuals for his crew. He found safe anchorage in Christmas Sound, where as usual, he made a careful hydrographical survey.

Several birds were shot, and Mr. Pickersgill brought three hundred seagull's eggs and fourteen geese on board.

"I was thus enabled," says Cook, "to distribute them to the entire crew, a fact which gave the greater satisfaction as it was near Christmas. Without this timely supply, they must have contented themselves with beef and salt pork."

Some of the natives, belonging to the nation called "Pecherais" by Bougainville, came on board without any pressing. Cook's description of these savages recalls that of the French explorer. They preferred the oily portions of the flesh of the seals upon which they lived – a taste which Cook attributed to the fact that the oil warmed their blood, and enabled them to resist the intense cold.

"If," he adds, "the superiority of a civilized to a savage life could ever be called in question, a single glance at one of these Indians would be sufficient to settle the question. Until it is proved that a man perpetually tortured by the rigour of a climate is happy, I shall never give in to the eloquent declamations of those philosophers who have never had the opportunity of observing human nature in all its phases, or who have not felt what they have seen."

The *Resolution* at once set sail and doubled Cape Horn. The Strait of Lemaire was then crossed, and Staten Island reconnoitred. Here a good anchorage was found. Quantities of whales abound in these latitudes. It was now their pairing season, and seals and sea-lions, penguins and gannets appeared in shoals.

"Dr. Sparman and myself," says Forster, "narrowly escaped being attacked by one of these sea-monsters, upon a rock where several of them were assembled, appearing to wait the upshot of the struggle. The doctor had fired at a bird, and stooped to pick it up, when the sea-lion growled, and showing his tusks, seemed disposed to attack

View of Christmas Sound.

my companion. From where I was posted I shot the animal stark dead, and at the report of my gun the herd, seeing their companion fall, fled along the coast. Several of them threw themselves into the sea with such haste, that they jumped ten or fifteen roods, straight upon the pointed rocks. But I do not think they hurt themselves much, for their skin is very hard and their fat is so elastic that it is easily compressed."

After leaving Staten Island, Cook set sail on the 3rd of January, for the south-east, to explore the only part of the ocean which had hitherto escaped him. He soon reached Southern Georgia, seen in 1675 by Laroche, and again by M. Guyot Duclos in 1756, when in command of the Spanish vessel the *Leön*. This discovery was made on the 14th of January, 1775. The captain landed in three places and took possession in the name of King George III. of England, bestowing his name upon the newly-found country. Possession Bay is bordered by pointed rocks of ice exactly similar to those which had been met with in the high southern latitudes.

"The interior of the country," says the narrative, "is no less savage and frightful. The summits of the rocks are lost in the clouds and the valleys are covered with perpetual snow. Not a tree or even the smallest shrub is to be seen."

After leaving Georgia, Cook penetrated further to the southeast, amidst floating ice. The continual dangers of the voyage overcame the crew. Southern Thule, Saunder's Island, and Chandeleur Islands, and finally Sandwich Land were discovered. These sterile and deserted archipelagoes have no value for the merchant or geographer. Once certain of their existence, it was unnecessary to remain, for to do so was to risk in exploring them the valuable records the *Resolution* was taking to England.

Cook was convinced by the discovery of these isolated islands "that near the pole there is a stretch of land, where the greater part of the floating ice spread over this vast southern ocean is formed". This ingenious theory has been confirmed in every particular by the explorers of the 19th century.

After another fruitless search for Cape Circumcision, mentioned by Bouvet, Cook decided to regain the Cape of Good Hope, and he arrived there on the 22nd of March, 1775.

The *Adventure* had put into this port, where Captain Furneaux had left a letter relating all that had happened in New Zealand. Captain Furneaux arrived in Queen Charlotte's Sound on the 13th of November, 1773, and took in wood and water. He then sent one of his boats under Lieutenant Rowe to gather edible plants. As the lieutenant did not return on board either in the evening or the next morning, Captain Furneaux, feeling sure that an accident had happened, sent in search of him. The following is a short account of what he learned.

After various useless searchings, the officer in command of the sloop came upon some traces, as he landed upon the shore, near Grass Creek. Portions of a boat and some shoes, one of which had belonged to an officer of the watch, were found. A sailor, at the same time, noticed a piece of fresh meat, which was taken to be the flesh of a dog, for it was not known then that the people of the place were cannibals. "We opened," says Furneaux, "about eight baskets which we found on the beach, tightly corded. Some were full of roast flesh, and others of roots used by the natives for bread. Continuing our search, we found more shoes, and a hand, which we recognized as that of Thomas Hill, because T.H. was tatooed upon it in the Tahitan fashion.

"At a short distance an officer perceived four pirogues and a number of natives, assembled round a large fire. The English landed and fired a volley, which put the Zealanders to flight, with the exception of two, who left with the greatest *sang-froid*. One of them was severely wounded, and the sailors advanced up the beach.

"A frightful scene was soon presented before our eyes. We saw the heads, hearts and lungs of many of the crew upon the sands, and at a little distance dogs were devouring the entrails."

The officer had not a sufficient force with him, being backed by only ten men, to meet this fearful massacre with fitting vengeance. The weather, too, became bad, and the savages collected in large numbers. It was necessary to regain the *Adventure*.

"I do not believe," says Captain Furneaux, "that this butchery was premeditated on the part of the natives, for in the morning Mr. Rowe said that he observed two vessels pass us, and remain all the forenoon in sight of the ship. The bloodshed was most likely the result of a quarrel which was instantly fought out, or possibly as our men took no measures for their own safety, their want of caution tempted the Indians."

The natives having heard one discharge, were encouraged by observing that a gun was not an infallible instrument, that it sometimes missed fire, and that once fired it was necessary to reload before firing again.

In this fearful ambuscade the *Adventure* lost ten of her best sailors.

Furneaux left New Zealand on the 23rd, of December, 1773, doubled Cape Horn, put into the Cape of Good Hope, and reached England on the 14th of July, 1774.

After Cook had taken in provisions and repaired his vessel, he left False Bay on the 27th of May, put into St. Helena, Ascension Island, and Fernando de Noronha, at Fayal, one of the Azores, and finally at Plymouth, on the 29th of July, 1775. During his voyage of three years and eighteen days, he had only lost four men, that is to say, without reckoning the ten sailors who were massacred at New Zealand.

No former expedition had reaped such a harvest of discoveries and hydrographical, physical, and ethnological observations. The learned and ingenious investigations pursued by Cook elucidated many of the difficulties of earlier navigators. He made various important discoveries, amongst others, that of New Caledonia and Easter Island. The non-existence of an antarctic continent was definitely ascertained. The great navigator received the fitting reward of his labours almost immediately. He was nominated ship's captain nine days after his landing, and was elected a member of the Royal Society of London on the 29th of February, 1776.

# CHAPTER V.

## CAPTAIN COOK'S THIRD VOYAGE.

### I.

Search for the lands discovered by the French – Kerguelen Islands – Stay at Van Diemen's Land – Queen Charlotte's Strait – Palmerston Island – Grand rejoicings in the Tonga Islands.

At this date the idea which had sent so many explorers to Greenland was in full force. The question of the existence of a northern passage between the Atlantic and the Pacific, by way of the Asiatic or American coasts, was eagerly discussed: and should such a passage exist, was it practicable for ships? The attempt had quite lately been made, to discover this outlet in Hudson or Baffin Bays, and it was now determined to seek it in the Pacific.

The task was an arduous one. The Lords of the Admiralty felt that it was essential to send out a navigator who had experience of the dangers of the Polar Seas, and one who had shown presence of mind in the face of danger; one moreover, whose talents, experience, and scientific knowledge might be of use in the powerful equipment then in course of preparation.

In Captain Cook alone were all the requisite qualities to be found. The command was offered to him, and although he might have passed the remainder of his days in peace at his post in the Greenwich Observatory, in the full enjoyment of the honour and glory he had gained by his two voyages round the world, he did not hesitate for a moment.

Two ships, the *Resolution* and the *Discovery*, were placed under his command The latter was under the orders of Captain Clerke; and the equipment of both was similar to that of the last expedition.

The instructions given to the commander of the expedition, enjoined his reaching the Cape of Good Hope, and steering south in search of the islands recently discovered by the French, in 48 degrees of latitude, towards the meridian of the island of Mauritius. He was then to touch at New Zealand, if he thought well, to take in refreshments at the Society Islands, and to land the Tahitan Mai there; then to proceed to New Albion, to avoid landing in any of the Spanish possessions in America, and from thence to make his way by the Arctic Ocean to Hudson and Baffin Bays. In other words he was to look in an easterly direction for the north-west passage. This once effected, after a stay at Kamschatka, he was to make another attempt to reach England by the route he might judge most productive of good results for geography and navigation.

The two vessels did not start together. The *Resolution* set sail from Plymouth on the 12th of July, 1776, and was rejoined at the Cape by the *Discovery* on the 10th of the following November, she having left England only on the 1st of August.

The two ships were detained at the Cape until the 30th of November, by the repairs needed by the *Discovery*. Much damaged by tempest, she required calking. The captain profited by this long delay, to buy live stock, which he intended to land at Tahiti and New Zealand, and also to stock his vessels with the necessary stores for a two-years' voyage.

After steering southwards for twelve days, two islands were discovered in 46° 53' south latitude, and 37° 46' east longitude. The strait which separates them was crossed, and it was found that their steep sterile coasts were uninhabited. They had been discovered with four others, from nine to twelve degrees further east, by the French Captains Marion-Dufresne and Crozet, in 1772.

On the 24th of December, Cook found the islands which M. de Kerguelen had surveyed in his two voyages of 1772, 1773.

We will not here relate the observations made by Cook upon this group. As they agree in every particular with those of M. de Kerguelen, we can reserve them until we relate the adventures of that navigator, and content ourselves with remarking that Cook surveyed the coasts carefully, and left them on the 1st of December. The vessels were enveloped in a thick fog, which accompanied them for more than 300 leagues.

Anchor was cast in Adventure Bay, in Van Diemen's Land, on the 26th of January. It was the same spot at which Captain Furneaux had touched four years earlier. The English were visited by a few natives, who received the presents offered to them, without showing any satisfaction.

The narrative says, –

"They were of ordinary height, but rather slightly built. Their skin was black and their hair of the same colour, and as woolly as that of the negroes of New Guinea, but they had not the thick lips or flat noses of African negroes. There was nothing disagreeable in their features, and their eyes struck us as beautiful, so did their teeth, but they were very dirty. Most of them anointed their hair and beards with a yellow ointment, and some even rubbed their faces with the same stuff."

Concise as this account is, it is not the less valuable. The race of Tasmanians is extinct, the last of them died a few years ago.

Cook weighed anchor on the 30th of January, and took up his station at his usual point in Queen Charlotte's Strait. The vessels were soon surrounded by pirogues, but not a single native ventured to go on board, they were so fully persuaded that the English had come to avenge their murdered comrades. Once convinced that the English had no such intention, they banished their mistrust and reserve. The captain soon found out by Mai's interpretation (he understanding the Zealand tongue) the right cause of this terrible catastrophe.

It appeared that the English had been seated on the grass, taking their evening meal when the natives committed several thefts. One of them was caught and struck by a sailor. At his cry, his companions rushed upon the sailors of the *Adventure*, who killed two of them, but unfortunately succumbed to numbers. Several of the Zealanders pointed out to Cook the chief who had directed the carnage, and urged Cook to kill him. But to the great surprise of the natives and the stupefaction of Mai, the captain refused.

Mai remarked, "In England they kill a man who assassinates another; this fellow killed ten, and you take no revenge!"

Before he left, Cook landed pigs and goats, hoping that these animals might at length become acclimatized to New Zealand

Mai had a wish to take a New Zealander to Tahiti. Two offered to go, and Cook agreed to receive them, warning them at the same time that they would never see their native land again. But no sooner had the vessels lost sight of the shores of New Zealand than they began to weep. Sea-sickness added to their distress. But as they recovered from it their sadness disappeared, and they soon attached themselves to their new friends.

An island named Mangea was discovered on the 29th of March. At Mai's representations the inhabitants decided to come on board. Small, but vigorous and well-proportioned, they wore their hair knotted upon the top of the head. They wore long beards, and were

Kerguelen Islands.

tatooed in all parts of their bodies. Cook could not carry out his earnest wish to land, as the people were too hostile.

A new island, similar to the last, was discovered four leagues further on. The natives appeared more friendly than those of Mangea, and Cook profited by this fact, and landed a detachment under Lieutenant Gore, with Mai as interpreter. Anderson, the naturalist, an officer named Barnes, and Mai landed alone and unarmed, running the risk of being maltreated.

They were received with solemnity, and conducted through a crowd of men, with clubs on their shoulders, to the presence of three chiefs, whose ears were adorned with red feathers. They soon perceived a score of women, who danced in a grave and serious fashion, paying no attention to their arrival.

The officers were separated from each other, and observing that the natives hastened to empty their pockets, they began to entertain fears for their safety, when Mai reappeared. They were detained all day, and forced several times to take their clothes off, and allow the natives to examine the colour of their skin; but night arrived at last, without the occurrence of any disagreeable incident. The visitors regained their sloop, and cocoa-nuts, bananas, and other provisions were brought to them.

The English may have owed their safety to the description Mai had given of the power of their weapons, and the experiment he made before them of setting fire to a cartridge.

Mai had recognized three of his fellow countrymen in the crowd on the beach.

These Tahitans had started in a pirogue to reach Ulitea Island, and had been driven out of their course by contrary winds. As they expected a short voyage, they had not provided themselves with food. Famine and fatigue had reduced their number to four men, all of them half dead, when the pirogue capsized. The unfortunate wretches managed to seize the side of their boat and support themselves in the water until they were picked up by the inhabitants of this island, Wateroo. It was now twelve years since fate threw them upon this shore, more than two hundred leagues from their native island They had contracted family ties and friendly alliances with these people, whose manners and language were not unlike their own. They refused to return to Tahiti.

Cook says, "We may find in this incident a better explanation of the way in which detached portions of the globe, and particularly the islands of the Pacific, have been peopled, than in any theories;

especially in regard to those which are far from any other continent, and at a great distance from each other."

Wateroo Island is situated in 20° 1' south latitude, and 201° 45' east longitude.

The two vessels afterwards reached a neighbouring island called Wenooa, upon which M. Gore landed to get fodder. Although the ruins of houses and tents were seen, it was uninhabited.

On the 5th of April, Cook arrived in sight of Harvey Island, which he had discovered during his second voyage in 1773. At that time it appeared to him deserted. He was, therefore, astonished to see several pirogues leave the shore and approach the ships. But the natives could not find courage to go on board.

Their fierce appearance and noisy offers did not promise well for their friendly intentions.

Their language was still more like that of Tahiti, than that of the last islands they had visited.

Lieutenant King was sent in search of good anchorage, but could not succeed in finding a suitable harbour. The natives, armed with spears and clubs, appeared disposed to resent any attempt at landing.

Cook, in his great need of wood and water, determined to reach the Friendly Islands. He was sure of finding refreshments for his men and forage for his beasts there. The season was too far advanced, and the distance between these latitudes and the pole too great to allow of anything being attempted in the southern hemisphere.

The wind obliged him to relinquish his idea of reaching Middlebourgh or Eoa, as he had at first intended. He therefore, directed his course towards Palmerston Island, where he arrived on the 14th of April, and where he found birds in abundance, scurvy grass, and cocoa-nuts. This island was merely a collection of nine or ten islets, very slightly raised, appearing almost like the points of reefs, belonging to one coral bank.

The English reached Komango Island on the 28th of April, and the natives brought them quantities of cocoa-nuts, bananas, and other stores.

They then proceeded to Annamooka, which is also part of the Tonga, or Friendly archipelago.

On the 6th of May, a chief of Tonga Tabou, named Finaou, visited Cook. He called himself king of all the Friendly Islands.

"I received," says Cook, "a present from this great personage of two fish, which were brought to me by one of his servants. I paid him a visit after dinner. He came to meet me as soon as he saw me land. He appeared some thirty years of age, tall and of slender form, and I have met no countenance in these islands so European in 'type'."

When all the provisions of this island were exhausted, Cook visited a group of islets called Hapaee, where his reception was friendly, owing to the orders given by Finaou, and where he procured pigs, water, fruits, and roots. Some of the native warriors exhibited their skill in various singular combats, with clubs and boxing.

"What most surprised us," says the narrative, "was to see two great women enter the lists, and attack each other with their fists, without the least ceremony, and with as much skill as the men. Their fight lasted about half a minute, when one of them declared herself beaten. The victorious heroine received as much applause from the assembled multitude as is usually accorded to a man who has overcome his rival by his skill and address."

There was no cessation of the fêtes and games. A dance was executed to the sound of two drums, or rather of two hollow trunks, by a hundred and five performers, supported by a vocal choir. Cook reciprocated these demonstrations by putting his soldiers through their artillery exercises, and letting off fireworks, which produced indescribable astonishment in the minds of the natives.

Not wishing to be out-done in the attempt at display, the natives gave a concert, and then a dance, executed by twenty women crowned with China roses. This magnificent ballet was followed by another performance by fifteen men. But we shall never end, if we attempt to give an account of the wonders of this enthusiastic reception. It justly gained for the Tonga archipelago the name of Friendly Islands.

On the 23rd, Finaou, who had represented himself as king of the entire archipelago, came to inform Cook of his departure for the neighbouring island of Vavaoo. He had excellent reasons for this, as he had just heard of the arrival of the real sovereign, named Futtafaih or Poulaho.

Cook at first refused to recognize the new-comer in this character, but he soon had irrefutable proof that the title of king belonged to him.

Poulaho was extremely stout, which with his short height made him look like a barrel. If rank is proportioned to size in these islands, he was without exception the *greatest* chief the English had met with. Intelligent, grave, and dignified, he examined the vessel and everything that was new to him in detail, put judicious questions, and inquired into the motives of the arrival of these vessels. His followers objected to his descending below decks, saying it was "*tabu*," and that it was not allowed for any one to walk over his head. Cook, however, promised through the interpreter Mai that no one should be allowed to walk over his cabin, and so Poulaho dined with the captain. He ate little and drank still less, and invited Cook to land with him. The marks of respect lavished upon Poulaho by all the natives, convinced Cook that he had been entertaining the real sovereign of the archipelago.

On the 29th of May, Cook set sail on his return to Annamooka, thence to Tonga Tabou, where a feast or "*keiva*", more magnificent than any he had seen, was given in his honour.

"In the evening," he said, "we had the spectacle of a '*bomai*', that is to say, the dances of the night were performed in front of Finaou's house. We saw twelve dances during the time. They were executed by women, and in the midst of them we noticed the arrival of a number of men, who formed a ring within that of the dancing women. Twenty-four men, who executed a third, made a movement with the hands, which was greatly applauded, and which we had not previously seen. The orchestra was renewed once. Finaou appeared upon the scene at the head of fifty dancers, most magnificently apparelled. His garment consisted of cloth and a large piece of gauze, and round his neck small figures were suspended."

Cook, after a stay of three months, thought it well to leave these enchanting islands, he distributed a share of the cattle he had bought at the Cape, and explained, through Mai, the way to feed them, and their utility. Before leaving he visited a cemetery or "Fiatooka", belonging to the king, composed of three good-sized houses, placed on the edge of a sort of hill. The planks of these buildings, and the artificial hills which supported them, were covered with pretty movable pebbles, and flat stones, placed erect, surrounded the whole.

"One thing which we had not previously seen, was that the buildings were open on one side, and within there were two wooden busts, roughly carved, one at the entrance, and the other a little within. The natives followed us to the door, but dared not pass the threshold. We asked them the meaning of the busts: they assured us that they did not represent any divinity, but were intended to recall two chiefs who were buried in the 'Fiatooka'."

Leaving Tonga Tabou on the 10th of July, Cook repaired to the small island of Eoa, where his old friend Tai-One received him cordially. The captain learned from him that the property of the various islands in the archipelago belonged to the chiefs of Tonga Tabou, which was known as the land of the chiefs. Thus Poulaho had a hundred and fifty islands under his rule. The most important are Vavao and Hamao. As for the Viti Islands, which are comprised in this number, they were inhabited by a warlike race, very superior in intelligence to those of the Friendly Islands.

We can only refer to some of the many and interesting particulars collected by the captain and the naturalist Anderson, which relate to the gentleness and docility of the natives.

Cook could do nothing but praise the welcome accorded to him, each time he stayed in the archipelago. But then he did not guess the project entertained by Finaou, and the other chiefs, of assassinating him during the nocturnal feast of Hapaee, and of seizing his vessels.

The navigators who succeeded him were not lavish in their praises, and if we did not know his sincerity, we should be tempted to think that the illustrious mariner gave the name of Friendly Islands to this group satirically.

The inhabitants of Tonga Island always mourned the death of a relation, by hitting themselves on their cheeks, and by tearing them with whale's teeth, a custom which explains the many tumours and cicatrices they have on the face. If their friends are dangerously ill, they sacrifice one or two joints of their little finger, to propitiate the divinity, and Cook did not meet with one native in ten who was not mutilated.

"The expression 'tabu,' he says, "which plays so great a part in the language of this people, has a very wide significance. When they are not allowed to touch anything they say it is tabu. They also told us that if the king enters a house belonging to one of his subjects, the house becomes 'tabu', and the owner of it may not live in it any longer."

Cook fancied he had made out their religion. Their principal god was Kallafoutonga, and in his anger, he destroys plantations and scatters illness and death. The religious ideas of all the islands are not alike, but the immortality of the soul is unanimously admitted. Although they do not offer fruit or other productions of the earth to their divinity, they sacrifice human victims.

Cook lost sight of the Tonga Islands on the 17th of July, and the

Fête in Cook's honour at Tonga.

expedition arrived in sight of an island called Tabouai by the inhabitants, upon the 8th of April, after a series of tempestuous winds which caused serious damage to the *Discovery*. All the eloquence of the English failed to bring the natives on board. Nothing would induce them to leave their boats, and they contented themselves with inviting the strangers to visit them. But as time pressed, and Cook had no need of provisions, he passed the island without stopping, although it appeared to him fertile and the natives assured him that it abounded in pigs and fowls. Strong, tall, and active, the natives had a hardy and savage appearance. They spoke the Tahitan language, which made intercourse with them easy.

Some days later, the verdant summits of Tahiti appeared on the horizon, and the two vessels were not slow in stopping opposite the peninsula of Tairabon, where the welcome Mai received from his compatriots was as indifferent as possible. His brother-in-law, chief Outi, would scarcely consent to recognize him, but when Mai showed him the treasures he brought back, amongst them all the famous red feathers, which had been so successful in Cook's last voyage, Outi changed his demeanour, treated Mai affably, and proposed to change names with him.

Mai was overcome by these demonstrations of tenderness, and, but for Cook's interference, would have been robbed of all his treasures.

The ships were well supplied with red feathers. Therefore fruits, pigs, and fowls appeared in great abundance during the stay in port. Cook, however, soon proceeded to Matavai Bay, where King Otoo left, his residence at Pané, to pay his old friend a visit. Mai was disdainfully received by his friends there also, and although he threw himself at the king's feet, when he presented him with a tuft of red feathers, and three pieces of gold cloth, he was scarcely noticed. But as at Taqabou, the treatment changed suddenly upon the discovery of Mai's fortune, but he being only happy in the company of vagabonds, who laughed at him good-naturedly, even while they robbed him, was unable to acquire the influence over Otoo, and the principle chiefs, which was necessary to the development of civilization.

Cook had long heard that human sacrifices were common in Tahiti, but he had always refused to believe it. A solemn ceremonial which he saw at Atahour, no longer allowed him to doubt the existence of the practice. In order to gain the favourable assistance of the Atoua or Godon in an expedition against the island of Eimèo, a man of the lowest social rank was killed by blows with clubs in the

Human sacrifice at Tahiti.
(Facsimile of early engraving.)

king's presence. As an offering the hair and one eye of the victim was placed before the king; last signs of the cannibalism which formerly existed in this archipelago. At the end of this barbarous ceremony, which was a blot in the memoirs of so peaceable a people, a kingfisher alighted in the foliage. "It is Atoua!" cried Otoo, delighted at the happy augury.

Next day the ceremony was to be continued by a holocaust of pigs. The priests, like the Roman augurs, sought to read the history of the expedition in the dying struggles of the victims.

Cook, who had silently assisted at the ceremony, could not conceal the horror with which it inspired him. Mai interpreted for him, eloquently and forcibly. Towha could scarcely contain his anger.

"If the king had killed a man in England," said Mai, "as he has done the unhappy and innocent victim he has offered to his gods, it would have been impossible to save him from hanging, a punishment reserved for murderers and assassins." Mai's severe reflection was a little out of place, Cook should have remembered that manners vary with countries. It is absurd to attempt to apply to Tahiti, as punishment for that which is their custom, a punishment reserved in London for what is considered a crime. "Every man's house is his cattle", says a popular proverb, which European nations have too often forgotten. Under the pretext of civilization, they have often shed more blood than would have flowed if they had not interfered.

Before he left Tahiti, Cook bestowed all the animals he had had so much difficulty in bringing from Europe upon Otoo. They were geese, ducks, turkeys, goats, sheep, horses, and cattle. Otoo was at a loss to express his gratitude to the "Areeke no Pretonne", (King of Britain) especially when he found that the English could not take a large pirogue on board which he had constructed as an offering for his friend the King of England, it being too large.

The *Resolution* and the *Discovery* left Tahiti on the 30th of September, and anchored at Eimeo.

In this place their stay was marked by a painful incident. Frequent thefts had occurred for several days, when a goat was stolen. To make an example, Cook burnt five or six cabins, and set fire to a large number of pirogues, threatening the king with his anger if the animal were not immediately produced. As soon as he had obtained satisfaction the captain started for Huaheine with Mai who was to settle on that island

A sufficiently large space of land was ceded by the chiefs of the

Ouare settlement in return for such presents. Upon this Cook had a house built, and planted a garden, where he planted European cabbages. Mai was left with two houses, two goats, and fowls. At the same time he was presented with a present of a coat of mail, of a complete set of armour, powder, balls, and guns. A portable organ, an electrical machine, fireworks, and domestic and agricultural implements completed the collection of useful and ornamental presents intended to give the Tahitans an idea of European civilization. Mai had a sister married at Huaheine, but her husband occupied too humble a position for him to attempt to despoil him. Cook then solemnly declared that the native was his friend, and that in a short time he should return to ascertain how he had been treated, and that he should severely punish those who had acted badly to him.

His threats were likely to be effective, as a few days earlier, some robbers, caught in the act by the English, had had their heads shaved and their ears cut. A little later at Raiatea, in order to force the natives to send back some deserters, Cook had carried off the entire family of the chief Oreo on one rope.

The moderation exhibited by the captain in his first voyage, constantly diminished; every day he became more severe and exacting. This change in his conduct was fatal to him.

The two Zealanders who had asked to accompany Mai were landed with him. The elder readily consented to live at Huaheine, but the younger conceived such an affection for the English, that it was necessary to use force, as it were, to land him, amid the most touching demonstrations of affection. At the last moment as anchor was weighed Cook bid farewell to Mai, whose expression and tears testified to his comprehension of all he was to lose.

Although Cook left satisfied with having loaded the young Tahitan who had trusted himself to him with benefits, he was also full of anxious fears as to his future. He knew his light and inconstant character, and he left him weapons with some regret, fearing that he might make a bad use of them. The King of Huaheine gave Mai his daughter in marriage and changed his name to Paori, by which he was afterwards known. Mai profited by his high station to show his cruelty and inhumanity. Always armed, he began to try his skill with pistol and gun upon his fellow-countrymen. His memory therefore is hated in Huaheine, and the memory of his crimes was for a long time associated with that of the English.

Cook visited Raiatea before leaving the island. He found his

Tree, from beneath which Cook observed the transit of Venus.
(Facsimile of early engraving.)

friend Oreé deprived of supreme authority. Then he went to Bolabole on the 8th of December, and bought of the King Pouni an anchor, which Bougainville had lost in the roadstead.

During his long sojourns in the different islands of the Society archepelago, Cook completed his geographical, hydrographical, and ethnological investigations, as well as his studies of natural history.

In this difficult task he was seconded by Anderson, and by his entire staff, who invariably showed the greatest zeal in their efforts for the advancement of science.

On the 24th of December Cook discovered another low island. It was uninhabited and the crew obtained abundance of turtle there. It was named Christmas Island, in honour of the solemn anniversary of the morrow.

Although seventeen months had passed since he left England Cook considered his voyage as only begun. Indeed he had not as yet been able to put the part of his instructions relating to the exploration of the Southern Atlantic and the search for a north passage, into execution.

## II.

Discovery of the Sandwich Islands – Exploration of the Eastern shore of America – From thence to Behring Straits – Return to the Hawaiian Group – History of Rono – Death of Cook – Return of the Expedition to England.

On the 18th of January, 1778, in longitude 160° and latitude 20° north, the two vessels perceived the first islands of the Sandwich or Hawain archipelago.

It did not take long to convince the navigators that they were inhabited. A large number of pirogues left Atooi or Tavaï Island and surrounded the ships.

The English were not a little surprised at hearing these natives speak in the Tahitan language. On this account the intercourse between them was soon friendly, and next day numbers of the islanders agreed to go on board. They showed their astonishment and admiration, at the sight of so many unknown objects, by their looks, gestures, and continual exclamations. Iron they were acquainted with, and called "hamaite".

But their covetousness was soon excited by so many curiosities and precious things, and they tried to appropriate them both by honest and by illicit means.

Their cleverness and their taste for thieving was as keen as is usual with the natives of the southern seas. It was necessary to take a thousand precautions, and they were often taken in vain, to guard against their larceny. The English, when they approached the shore, under charge of Lieutenant Williamson, to sound and search for anchorage, were forced to repulse the attempts of the natives by force. The death of one of them repressed their turbulence in a measure, and gave them an exalted opinion of the strength of the new arrivals.

As soon, however, as the *Resolution* and *Discovery* had cast anchor in Ouai Mea Bay, Cook had himself taken on shore. He had scarcely touched land, when the natives assembled in a crowd upon the strand, prostrated themselves at his feet, and welcomed, him with signs of the most profound respect.

This extraordinary reception gave promise of a pleasant stay, for provisions appeared to be abundant; fruits, pigs, fowls, began to arrive from all parts. At the same time a party of natives assisted the English sailors in filling the casks with water, and in carrying them on board.

Anderson and the draughtsman Weller were encouraged by this friendly conduct to advance into the interior. They were not long in coming upon a *moraï*, similar in every respect to the Tahitian *moraïs*. This discovery confirmed the English in the ideas induced by the similarity of the language with that of Tahiti. An engraving in Cook's narrative represents the interior of this *moraï*. In it two figures may be seen, standing, the top of the heads disappearing in high cylindrical hats, similar to those on the statues in Easter Island In any case, the singular resemblance gives rise to reflection.

Cook remained two days more in this anchorage and could only extol the traffic with the natives. He then explored the neighbouring Island of Oneeheow. In spite of his great wish to explore this interesting archipelago, he set sail, and from a distance perceived Ouahou Island, and the reef of Tahoora which he designated by the general appellation of Sandwich Archipelago. This name has been superseded by the native appellation of Hawai. Strong and vigorous, although of medium height, the Hawaians are represented by Anderson as being of frank and loyal character. Not so serious as the natives of the Friendly Isles, they are less frivolous than the Tahitans.

Cook's reception by the natives.

Clever, industrious, and intelligent, their plantations showed a knowledge of rural economy, and an extensive taste for agriculture. They not only abstained from showing the childish and common curiosity which the English had so often noticed, but they inquired into their customs and evinced a certain regret for their own inferiority.

The population appeared considerable, and was estimated at 30,000 in Tavai Island alone. In their style of dress, their choice of food, their manner of preparing it, and their general habits, they conform to the customs of Tahiti. This identity of two populations separated by a large stretch of sea gave the English much food for reflection.

During his first stay Cook did not become acquainted with any chief, but Captain Clerke, of the *Discovery*, at last received a visit from one. He was a young and well-made man, wrapped up from head to foot. The natives testified their respect by kneeling before him Clerke made him several presents, and in return received a vase decorated with two small figures, fairly well sculptured, which served for the "kava", a favourite drink of the Hawaians, as well as the natives of Tonga. Their weapons comprise bows, clubs, and lances, the latter made of a strong and durable wood, and a sort of poignard called "paphoa", terminating in a point at both ends. The custom of "tabu" was just as universally practised as in the Friendly Islands, and the natives were always careful to ask if things were "tabu" before they touched them.

On the 27th of February, Cook continued his course to the north, and soon fell in with the sea wrack of the rocks mentioned by the narrator of Lord Anson's voyage. On the 1st of March he steered for the east, in order to approach the American coast, and five days later he recognized New Albion, so named by Francis Drake.

The expedition, coasting at a distance, surveyed Cape Blanc, already seen by Martin d'Aguilar on the 19th of January, 1603, and near which the geographers placed a large opening, to the strait, the discovery of which they attributed to him. Shortly afterwards the latitude of Juan de Fuca was reached, but nothing resembling it was discovered, although this strait really exists, and divides the continent from Vancouver's Island.

Cook soon reconnoitred a bay in latitude 49° 15, to which he gave the name of Hope Bay. He anchored there to obtain water, and give a little rest to his worn-out crews. This coast was inhabited, and three boats approached the vessels.

"One of the savages," he says, "rose up, and with many gesticulations made a long speech, which we understood as an invitation to land. In addition, he threw feathers towards us, and many of his companions threw us handfuls of dust or red powder. The native who usurped the post of orator was clothed in a skin, and in each hand he held something which he shook, and which emitted a sound like that of a child's rattle.

"When he was tired of haranguing and exhorting, of which we did not understand a word, he rested, but two other men took up the speech in succession. Their speeches were not so long, and they did not acclaim so vehemently.

"Many of the natives had their faces painted in an extraordinary way, and feathers fixed in their heads. Although they appeared friendly, it was impossible to persuade any of them to come onboard. However, as the vessels had cast anchor, the captain had the sails furled, took in the topmasts, and unrigged the mizzen mast of the *Resolution*, in order to allow of repairs. Barter with the Indians soon commenced, and the most rigorous honesty prevailed. The objects offered were bear and wolf skins, and those of foxes, deers, and polecats, weasels, and especially otters, which are found in the islands east of Kamschatka. Also clothes made of a kind of hemp, bows, lances, fish-hooks, monstrous figures, and a kind of stuff of hair or wool, bags filled with red ochre, bits of sculptured wood, trinkets of copper and iron shaped like horse-shoes, which they wore hung from the nose.

"Human ears and hands, not yet free from flesh, struck us most among the things they offered us. They made us clearly understand that they had eaten the portions that were missing, and we indeed perceived that these hands and ears had been on the fire."

The English were not long in ascertaining that these natives were as habitual robbers as any they had hitherto met with. They were even more dangerous, as possessing iron implements, they could easily cut the cords. They combined their thefts with intelligence, and one of them amused the sentinel at one end of the boat, whilst another snatched the iron from the other end. They sold a quantity of very good oil, and a great deal of fish, especially sardines.

When the numerous repairs needed by the ships were made, and the grass required for the few goats and sheep remaining on board had been shipped, Cook set sail on the 26th of April, 1778.

He gave the name of King George's Sound to the spot where he had stayed, although it was called Nootka, by the natives.

The vessels had scarcely gained the open sea when a violent tempest overtook them, during which the *Resolution* sprung a leak on the starboard side below the water line.

Carried away by the storm, Cook passed the spot selected by geographers as the situation of the Strait of Admiral de Fonte, though he greatly wished to dispel all doubt on the subject.

The captain therefore continued along the American coast, surveying and naming the principal points. During this cruise he had constant intercourse with the Indians, and was not slow in noticing that their canoes had been replaced by boats, of which only the framework was wood, and over which were spread seal-skins.

After a stay at Prince William's Sound, where the leak of the *Resolution* was repaired, Cook resumed his voyage, reconnoitred and named Elizabeth and Saint Hermogene Capes, Bank's Point, Capes Douglas and Bede, Saint Augustine's Mount, the River Cook, Kodiak Island, Trinity Island, and the islands called Schumagin by Behring. Afterwards he passed Bristol Bay, Round Island, Calm Point, Newenham Cape, where Lieutenant Williamson landed, and Anderson Island, so called in honour of the naturalist who died there of disease of the chest; later, King island, and Prince of Wales's Cape, the most western extremity of America. Cook then passed the Asiatic coast and entered into communication with the Tchouktchis, entered Behring Strait on the 11th of April, and next week came in contact with ice.

He tried in vain to survey in various directions. The iceberg presented an insuperable barrier. On the 17th of April, 1778, the expedition was in latitude 70° 41'. During an entire month he coasted the iceberg, in the hope of finding an opening which might enable him to proceed to the north, but in vain. It was remarked that "the ice was clear and transparent except in the upper part, which was slightly porous".

"I supposed," says Cook, "that it was frozen snow, and it appeared to me that it must have been formed in the open sea, both because it is improbable, or rather impossible, that such enormous masses could float down rivers which contain too little water for a boat, and also because we perceived no produce of the earth, which we must have done if it was so formed."

Up to this date the passage through Behring's Strait had been the least used to reach the northern latitudes. Cook's observation is valuable, as it proves that beyond this aperture a vast extent of sea without land must exist. It may possibly be (this was the view held

Prince William's Sound.

Captain Cook's chart of Otahiti.

by the lamented Gustave Lambert) that this sea is open. No greater distance north has ever been attained since Cook's time, except on the Siberian coast – where Plover and Long Islands were discovered, and where at this moment, as we write, Professor Nordenskjold is exploring.[1]

After most careful exploration and repeated efforts to reach higher latitudes, Cook, seeing that the season was advanced, and encountering more icebergs daily, had no choice but to seek winter quarters in a more clement country, before continuing his expedition the following summer. He therefore retraced his route as far as Ounalaska Island, and on the 26th of October steered towards the Sandwich Islands, hoping to complete his survey of them during his wintering there.

An island was discovered on the 26th of November. The natives sold a quantity of fruits, roots, bread-fruits, potatoes, "taro" and "eddy" roots, which they exchanged for nails and iron implements. It was Mowee Island, which forms part of the Sandwich Archipelago. Shortly afterwards Owhyhee or Hawai was sighted, the summits of which were covered with snow.

The captain says: –

"We never met savages so liberal as these in their views. They usually sent the different articles they wished to sell to the ships. They then came on board themselves, and finished their 'trade' on the quarter-deck. The Tahitans, in spite of our constant stays there, have not the same confidence in us. I conclude from this that the inhabitants of Owhyhee are more accurate and true in their reciprocal trade than those of Tahiti, for the latter have no honour among themselves, and are thus not inclined to believe in the honour of others."

On the 17th of January Cook and Clerke cast anchor in a bay, called by the natives Karakakooa. The sails were unbent from the yard, the yards and the top-mast struck. The vessels were crowded with visitors and surrounded by pirogues, and the shore was covered by a curious multitude. Cook had never previously seen so much excitement. Among the chiefs who came on board the *Resolution*, a young man named Pareea was soon remarked. He said

[1] [On the 5th September, 1879, a telegram from Stockholm announced that the Swedish Arctic Expedition under Professor Nordenskjold had made the North-East Passage from Europe to Japan, and that the Swedish exploring vessel, the *Vega*, had arrived at Yokohama by way of Behring's Straits] *Translator.*

he was "Iakanee", but it was not known that was his title of office, or if it suggested a degree of relationship or alliance with the king. However, he evidently had great authority over the common people. Some presents, opportunely given, attached him to the English, and he rendered them more than one service.

If Cook on his first visit to Hawai pronounced that the natives were little disposed to robbery, he was not of the same opinion this time. Their large numbers gave them many facilities for thieving trifles, and encouraged them to think that their larceny would not be punished. It became evident at last that they were encouraged by their chiefs, for several stolen objects were found in the possession of the latter.

Pareea and another chief named Kaneena brought an old man on board, whose name was Koah. He was very thin and his body was covered with white scurf from immoderate use of "ava". He was a priest. When he was presented to Cook, he put a sort of red mantle which he had brought upon his shoulders, and gravely delivered a long discourse as he gave him a little pig. It was soon proved that it was intended as a form of adoration, for all the idols were clothed in similar stuff. The English were immensely astonished at the whimsical ceremonies of homage presented to Cook. They only understood them later, through the researches of the learned missionary, Ellis. We shall give a brief account of his interesting discovery. It will make the recital of the events that followed plainer.

According to tradition, a certain Rono, who lived under one of the ancient kings of Hawai, had killed his wife, whom he tenderly loved, in a transport of jealousy. The grief and sorrow which followed upon his act, drove him mad; he ran about the island, quarrelling with, and striking everybody. At last, tired out, but not satiated, with murder, he embarked, promising to return one day, upon a floating island, bringing cocoa-nuts, pigs, and dogs.

This legend had been embodied in a national song, and became an article of faith with the priests, who added Rono to their list of deities. Confident in the fulfilment of the prediction, they awaited his coming every year, with a patience which nothing could exhaust.

Is not there a strange resemblance between this legend and that relating to the Mexican god Quetzalcoatl, who, forced to fly from the wrath of a more powerful god, embarked upon a skiff of serpent skin, promising those who accompanied him to return at some later time, and visit the country with his descendants?

They gave him a little pig.

As soon as the English ships appeared, the high priest Koah and his son One-La declared that it was Rono himself, fulfilling his prediction. From that moment Cook was a divinity for the entire population. As he went about, the natives prostrated themselves. The priests made him speeches or addressed prayers to him. They would have sprinkled him with incense had that been fashionable at Hawaï. The captain felt that there was something extraordinary in these demonstrations, but, unable to understand it, he resigned himself for the sake of his crew and for the advancement of science to the mysterious circumstances he was unable to unravel.

He was obliged to give himself up to all kinds of ceremonies, which appeared, to him at least, ridiculous. Thus he was taken to a moraï, a solid construction of stone forty roods long and fourteen high. The summit was well built and was surrounded by a wooden balustrade, upon which were hung the ears of the captives sacrificed to the gods. At the opening of the platform were two large wooden figures with grinning faces, and bodies draped in red stuff, the heads surmounted by a large piece of sculptured wood, the shape of a reversed cone. There Koah mounted with Cook upon a sort of table, under which lay a rotten pig and a quantity of fruit. Some men brought a living pig in a procession, and some scarlet cloth in which it was wrapped. The priests then sang some religious hymns, while the assistants were devoutly prostrated at the entrance of the moraï. After various ceremonies, which it would take too long to describe, a pig, cooked in the oven, was presented to the captain, with fruits and the roots which were used in the preparation of "ava".

"The ava," says Cook, "was then handed round, and when we had tasted it, Koah and Pareea divided the flesh of the pig into several pieces, which they placed in our mouths."

"I felt no repugnance when Pareea, who is very clean, gave me something to eat," says Lieutenant King, "but Cook, to whom Koah offered the same attention, could not swallow a morsel, as he thought of the putrid pig. The old man, wishing to redouble his politeness, tried to give him pieces already chewed, and one can easily imagine that the disgust of our captain increased."

After this ceremony Cook was conducted to his boat, by four men carrying sticks, who repeated the same words and phrases as at the landing, in the midst of a kneeling host of the natives. The same ceremonies were observed every time the captain landed. One of the priests always walked before him, announcing that Rono had landed, and ordering the people to prostrate themselves.

If the English had reason to feel satisfied with the priests, who loaded them with attentions and presents, it was otherwise with the "carees", or warriors. The latter encouraged the robberies which were perpetrated daily, and in other ways exhibited disloyalty. Still, up to the 24th of January, 1779, no important event occurred. Upon that day the English were surprised to see that none of the pirogues left the river to trade with the ships. The arrival of "Terreoboo" had made the bay "tabu", and prevented any communication with the strangers. Upon the same day, the chief, or rather king, went without ceremony to the ships. He had but one pirogue, in which were his wife and children. On the 26th, Terreoboo paid a second visit, which was official.

"Cook," says the narrative, "noticing that the prince landed, followed him and arrived about the same time. He conducted them to the tent; they were scarcely seated when the prince rose, and in a graceful manner threw his mantle over the captain's shoulders. He further placed a hat of feathers upon his head, and a curious fan in Cook's hands, at whose feet he also spread five or six very pretty mantles of great value."

Terreoboo and the principal chiefs of his suite asked many questions of the English as to the time of their leaving. The captain wished to ascertain the opinion the Hawaians had formed of the English; but he could only learn that they supposed them to be the natives of a country where provisions were scarce, and that they had simply come there "to fill their stomachs". This conviction arose from the emaciated appearance of some of the sailors, and from the desire to ship fresh victuals.

There was no fear, however, of exhausting their provisions, in spite of the immense quantity which had been consumed since the English arrived. It is very likely that the king wished for time to prepare the present he intended to offer the strangers upon their leaving; and, accordingly, the day before the one fixed upon, the king begged Captains Cook and Clerke to accompany him to his residence. Enormous heaps of every kind of vegetable, parcels of stuffs, yellow and red feathers, and a herd of pigs were collected together.

All this was a gratuitous gift to the king from his subjects. Terreoboo chose about a third of these articles, and gave the rest to the two captains – a more valuable present than they had ever received either at Tonga or Tahiti.

On the 4th of February the vessels left the bay, but the damage received by the *Resolution* forced her to put in again in a few days.

The vessels had scarcely cast anchor before the English noticed a change in the conduct of the natives. Still all went on peaceably until the afternoon of the 13th. Upon that day several chiefs wished to prevent the natives from assisting the English in filling their casks. A tumult ensued. The natives armed themselves with stones, and became threatening.

The officer in command of the detachment was ordered by Cook to draw upon the natives, if they persisted in throwing stones, or became insolent. Under these circumstances, a pirogue was fired into, and it was soon apparent that a robbery had been committed by its crew.

At the same time a still more serious dispute arose. A sloop belonging to Pareea was seized by an officer, who took it to the *Discovery*. The chief hastened to claim his belongings, and to protest his innocence. The discussion grew animated, and Pareea was overthrown by a blow from an oar.

The natives who had hitherto been peaceable observers, armed themselves with stones, forced the sailors to retire precipitately, and took possession of the pinnace which had brought them. Pareea, forgetful of his resentment at this moment, interposed, and restored the pinnace to the English, together with several things which had been stolen.

"I am afraid the Indians will force me to violent measures," said Cook, upon learning what had passed. "We must not allow them to believe that they have gained an advantage over us."

The boat of the *Discovery* was stolen upon the 13th or 14th of February. The captain determined to possess himself of the person of Terreoboo, or some others of the leading persons, and to keep them as hostages until the stolen objects were restored to him.

He therefore landed with a detachment of marines, and pursued his way to the king's residence. He was received with the usual marks of respect on the road, and perceiving Terreoboo and his two sons, to whom he said a few words on the theft of the sloop, he decided to pass the day on board the *Resolution*.

The matter took a happy turn, and the two young princes embarked upon the pinnace, when one of Terreoboo's wives begged him with tears not to go on board. Two other chiefs joined her, and the natives, frightened by the hostile preparations they saw, began to crowd round the king and captain. The latter hurried to embark, and the prince appeared willing to follow him, but the chiefs interposed, and used force to prevent his doing so.

Cook, seeing that his project had failed, and that he could only put it into execution by bloodshed, gave it up, and walked quietly along the shore to regain his boat, when a rumour spread that one of the principal chiefs had been killed. The women and children were therefore sent away and all directed their attention to the English.

A native armed with a "pahooa" defied the captain, and as he would not cease his threats, Cook discharged his pistol. The native, protected by a thick mat, did not feel himself wounded, and so became more audacious. Several others advanced, and the captain discharged his gun at the nearest and killed him. This was the signal for a general attack.

The last that was seen of Cook was his signing to the boats to cease firing, and to approach, that his small troop might embark. In vain! The captain was struck and fell to the earth.

"The natives," says the narrative, "uttered cries of joy when they saw him fall. They at once dragged his body along the shore, and taking the poniard one after the other, they all attacked him with ferocious blows until he ceased to breathe."

Thus perished this great navigator, assuredly the most illustrious produced by England. The boldness of his undertakings, his perseverance in carrying them out, and the extent of his knowledge, all made him a type of the true sailor of discovery.

What immense service he has rendered to geography! In his first voyage he reconnoitred the Society islands, proved that New Zealand is formed of two islands, explored the strait that separates them, and surveyed its coast, and lastly he visited the entire eastern coast of New Holland.

In his second voyage he proved the chimerical character of the long-talked-of Antarctic continent, the dream of stay-at-home geographers. He discovered New Caledonia, Southern Georgia, the Sandwich Islands, and penetrated farther into the southern hemisphere than any one had done before him.

In his third expedition he discovered the Hawaian archipelago, and surveyed the eastern coast of America, to the forty-third degree, that is to say, an extent of 3,500 miles. He passed through Behring Straits, and ventured into the Arctic Sea, which was the horror of navigators, until the icebergs opposed an impenetrable barrier to his progress.

It is needless to praise his qualities as a seaman; his hydrographical works remain, but above all his careful treatment of his crews

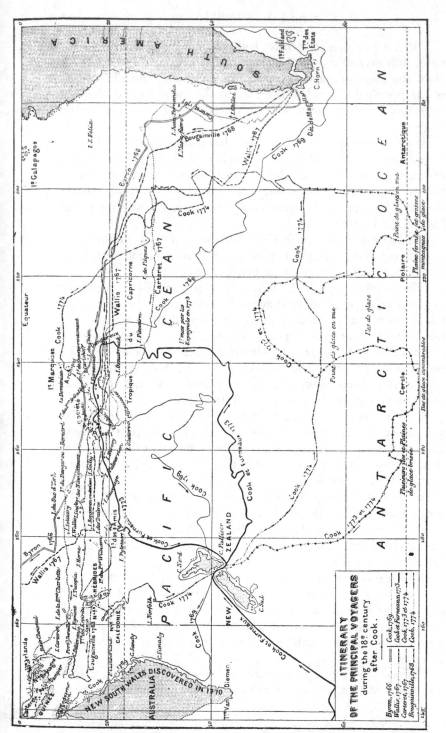

(Facsimile of early engraving.)

deserves to be remembered. To it was due their ability to bear the long and trying voyages, which he made with so little loss of life.

After this fatal day the English folded their tents and returned on board. Their offers for the recovery of the body of their unfortunate captain were in vain. In their anger they were about to have recourse to arms, when two priests, friends of Lieutenant King, brought a piece of human flesh at the instance of the other chiefs, which weighed from nine to ten pounds. It was all, they said, that remained of Rono's body, which had been burnt according to custom. This sight of course made the English still more anxious for reprisals, and the natives on their side had to avenge the death of five chiefs and a score of men. Every time the English landed at their watering place they found a furious crowd armed with stones and sticks. In order to make an example, Captain Clerke, who had taken the command of the expedition, set fire to the abodes of the priests, and massacred those who opposed them.

On the 19th of February, however, an interview was arranged, and the remains of Cook, his hands, recognizable by a large scar, his head, stripped of flesh, and various other debris, were made over to the English, who three days later paid them the last honours.

After that, barter was resumed as if nothing had happened, and no other incident occurred during the remainder of the stay in the Sandwich Islands.

Captain Clerke had relinquished the command of the *Discovery* to Lieutenant Gore, and hoisted his flag upon the *Resolution* After completing the survey of the Hawaian Islands, he set sail for the north, touched at Kamschatka, where the Russians made him heartily welcome, passed through Behring Strait, and advanced as far as latitude 69° 50' north, where his further progress was barred by icebergs.

On the 22nd of April, 1779, Captain Clerke died of pulmonary phthisis, aged thirty-eight.

Captain Gore then assumed the command in chief, put in again at Kamschatka, again at Canton, and at the Cape of Good Hope, and anchored in the Thames on the 1st of October, 1780, after more than four years' absence.

The death of Captain Cook caused a general mourning throughout England. The Royal Society of London, of which he was a member, struck a medal in his honour, the cost of which was covered by public subscription, to which persons of the highest rank subscribed.

The Admiralty petitioned the king to provide for the family of the deceased captain. The king granted a pension of 200*l*. to his widow, and 25*l*. to each of his three sons. The charts and drawings, relating to his last voyage were engraved at the expense of the government, and the proceeds of their sale divided among Cook's family, and the heirs of Captain Clerke and Captain King.

Although the family of the great navigator is extinct, a proof of the esteem in which his memory is held was given in the solemn meeting of the French Geographical Society on the 4th of February, 1879.

A large number assembled to celebrate the centenary of Cook's death. Amongst them were many representatives of the Australian colonies, which are now so flourishing, and of the Hawaian Archipelago, where he met his death. A quantity of relics belonging to the great navigator, his charts, Webber's magnificent watercolours, and the instruments and weapons of the Oceanic islanders decorated the walls.

This touching homage, after the lapse of a hundred years, was accorded by a people whose king had bidden them not to thwart Cook's scientific and civilizing mission, and was well calculated to awake an echo in England, and to draw yet closer the bonds of that good fellowship which exists between England and France.

END OF THE FIRST PART.

# PART II.

Death of Captain Cook.

# CHAPTER I.

## FRENCH NAVIGATORS.

### I.

Discoveries made by Bouvet de Lozier in the Southern Seas – Surville – The land of the Arsacides – Incident during the stay at Port Praslin – Arrival upon the coast of New Zealand – Death of Surville – Marion's discoveries in the Antarctic Ocean – He is murdered at New Zealand – Kerguelen in Iceland and the Arctic regions – The contest between the watches – Fleurien and Verdun de la Crenne.

In the earlier half of the eighteenth century, a discovery had been made which was designed to exercise a favourable influence upon the progress of geographical science. Jean Baptiste Charles Bouvet de Lozier, a captain of one of the East India Company's ships, was so struck by the immensity of the space surrounding the Southern Pole, known to geographers as the *Terra australis incognita*, that he begged for the privilege of prosecuting discoveries in these unkown regions. His importunities were long disregarded, but at length, in 1738, the Company consented, in the hope of opening new facilities for trade.

Two small frigates, the *Aigle* and the *Marie*, fully equipped, left Brest upon the 19th of July, 1738, under command of Bouvet de Lozier. After a stay of a month at St. Catherine's Island, upon the coast of Brazil, they put to sea again upon the 13th of November, and steered for the south-east.

On the 26th, heavy fog set in, so that the vessels could only keep in company by constant firing, and were obliged to tack about continually, at the risk of running foul of each other. Upon the 5th of December, although it would have appeared impossible, the fog increased in density to such an extent that those on board the *Aigle* could hear the movement of the *Marie* though they could not see her. The sea was covered with kelp, and seagulls, never found at a distance from land, were shortly afterwards seen.

"Upon the 15th of December," says M. Favre, in his Memoir the Bouvets, in 48° 50' S. lat. (Paris is in N. lat. 48° 50') and in 7° E. long. (the meridian of Teneriffe), an enormous iceberg was perceived towards five or six in the morning; shortly afterwards many others were seen, surrounded by ice-floes of various sizes.

The *Marie*, signalling danger, tacked about, but Bouvet, annoyed by this action, which was likely to affect the confidence of the crews, crowded sail on the *Aigle*, and, by passing the *Marie*, showed his determination to maintain his southern course. To reassure his men, he asserted that it was considered a lucky omen to meet with ice, as it was a certain indication of land at hand.

The course was continued to the south, and Bouvet's perseverance was soon rewarded by the appearance of land, to which he gave the name of Cape Circumcision. It was steep, covered with snow, and so shut in by large icebergs, that it was impossible to approach to within seven or eight leagues. It appeared to measure from four to five leagues from north to south.

"This land was supposed," says M. Favre, judging from Pietergos' charts, which were used by Bouvet, "to be situated in 54° S. lat. and 26° and 27° east of the meridian of Teneriffe, or between 5° 30' and 6° 3' east of that of Paris."

Bouvet would much have liked to make closer acquaintance with this region, but the fogs and contrary winds prevented his reaching it, and he was obliged to satisfy himself with observing it from a distance.

"Upon the 3rd of January, 1739," says Bouvet, in his report to the Company, "we made up for what we had lost during the preceding days, and about four in the afternoon, the fog clearing somewhat, we distinctly saw land. The coast, broken throughout its entire length, formed several bays. The summits of the mountains were covered with snow; the sides appeared wooded."

After several fruitless attempts to near the coast, Bouvet was forced to relinquish the idea. His sailors were worn out with fatigue, discouraged, and enfeebled by scurvy. The *Marie* was sent to the Isle of France, and the *Aigle* directed her course to the Cape of Good Hope, which she reached upon the 28th of February.

"We had penetrated," says Bouvet, in the report already cited, "twelve or fifteen hundred leagues into an unknown sea. For seventy days we had encountered almost continuous fog. We had been for forty days in the midst of ice, and we had had snow and hail almost every day. Several times our decks and rigging were covered with them. Our shrouds and sails were frozen. On the 10th January, it was impossible to work our fore-topsail. The cold was severe, for men accustomed to a warm climate, and who were lightly clad. Many had chilblains on the hands and feet. Still they were forced constantly to tack about, bring to, get under weigh, and take soundings at least once a day. One of the sailors belonging to the *Aigle*, having been sent to loosen the fore-topsail, became frozen in the fore-top. He had to be lowered by a whip, and circulation was with difficulty restored. I have seen others with tears gushing from their eyes as they handled the sounding-line. And all this was in the fine season, and I ameliorated their condition by every means in my power."

We can readily understand that such small results did not tempt the East India Company to continue their efforts in these latitudes. If they were productive of no good, they cost heavily in the loss of men and ships they entailed. Still Bouvet's discovery was a first blow to the existing belief in an Antarctic continent. He gave the start, and various navigators, amongst them two Frenchmen, followed it up.

In our short record of this expedition, which is scarcely known, we have testified to an appreciation of our countryman, who was the pioneer of Antarctic navigation, and who deserves the credit of furnishing an example to the great English explorer, James Cook.

Another of the East India Company's captains, who had distinguished himself in various battles against the English, Jean François Marie de Surville, was destined to make important discoveries in Oceania some thirty years later, and to re-discover, almost simultaneously with Cook, the lands first seen by Tasman, and which he called Staten Island. The following is an account of the circumstances.

Messrs. Law and Chevalier, governors in French India, determined to send a vessel at their own risk to trade in the southern seas. They admitted Surville to their schemes, and sent him to France to obtain the needful authority from the Company, and to superintend the equipment of the vessel.

The *Saint-Jean Baptiste* was made ready for sea at Nantes, and provisioned for three years, with every requisite for a distant expedition. Surville then reached India, where Law provided him with twenty-four native soldiers.

Leaving Angley Bay on the 3rd of March, 1769, the *Saint-Jean Baptiste* put in successively at Masulipatam, Yanaon, and Pondicherry, where her equipment was completed.

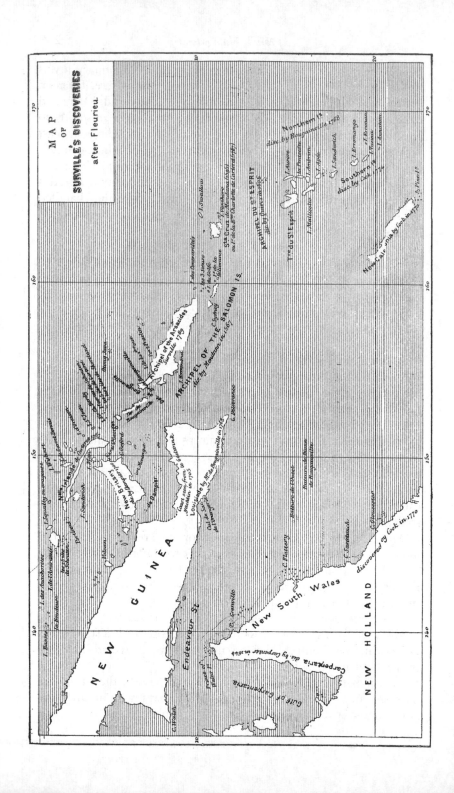

MAP
OF
SURVILLE'S DISCOVERIES
after Fleurieu.

NEW GUINEA

NEW SOUTH WALES

NEW HOLLAND

Carpentaria dis: by Carpenter in 1644

Gulf of Carpentaria

Endeavour St.

ARCHIPEL OF THE SALOMON IS.
disc: by Mendana in 1567

Archipel of the Arsacides
Surville 1769

ARCHIPEL DU St ESPRIT
dis: by Quiros in 1606

Northern Is.
disc: by Bougainville 1768

Southern Is.
disc: by Cook 1774

New ZEALAND dis: by Capt. Tasman

discovered by Cook in 1770

Surville left the last-named port on the 2nd of June, and steered his course for the Philippines. On the 20th of August, he cast anchor off the Bashees, or Baschy Islands. Dampier had so named them after an intoxicating drink, which the natives compounded from the juice of the sugar-cane, into which they infused a certain black seed.

Several of Dampier's crew had formerly deserted in these islands; they had received from the natives a field, agricultural instruments, and wives. The recollection of this fact incited three of the sailors belonging to the *Saint-Jean Baptiste* to follow their example. But Surville was not the man to allow his crew to melt away in such a manner. He seized twenty-six Indians, and signified his intention of keeping them as hostages until his men were brought back to him.

"Among the Indians thus seized," says Crozet, in his narrative of Surville's voyage, "there were several courageous enough to throw themselves into the sea, and, much to the surprise of the crew, they had sufficient courage and skill to swim to one of their pirogues, which was far enough from the vessel to be secure from danger."

Pains were taken to make the savages understand that they had been treated in this way in order to make their comrades bring back the three deserters. They made signs that they understood, and were then released, with the exception of six, who had been taken on shore. The haste with which they left the ship, and flung themselves into their pirogues, augured badly for their return. Much surprise was therefore felt when in a short time they were seen returning with joyful acclamations. Doubt was no longer possible, they could only be bringing the deserters back to the commander. They came on board, and proceeded to deposit on deck – what? – three magnificent pigs, tied and bound. Surville did not appreciate, and he objurgated the natives so fiercely, that they jumped into their pirogues, and disappeared. Twenty-four hours later the *Saint-Jean Baptiste* left the Bashees, taking three captive Indians to replace the deserters.

Upon the 7th of October, after a lengthened route to the south-east, land, to which the name of "Prémiere Vue" was given, was sighted in 6° 56' S. lat., and 157° 30' long. east of Paris.

The explorers coasted along it until the 13th October, upon which day an excellent port was discovered, sheltered from every wind, and formed by a number of small islands. M. de Surville cast anchor and named it Port Praslin. It is situated in 70° 25' S. lat. and 151° 55' E. long. reckoning from the Paris meridian.

Upon entering this port, the French saw several Indians, armed with spears, and carrying a sort of shield. The *Saint-Jean Baptiste* was very soon surrounded by pirogues, manned by a crowd of Indians, who were profuse in menacing gestures. However, they were pacified at last. About thirty of the boldest clambered on to the deck, and examined everything they saw with close attention. It soon became needful to check their advances, as there were many sick among the crew, and it was unwise to allow too many natives on board.

In spite of the welcome they received, the natives were still doubtful, and their looks expressed distrust. The slightest movement on board the vessel was sufficient to make them jump into their pirogues, or the sea. One only showed a little more confidence, and Surville gave him several presents. The Indian acknowledged the attention, by saying he could point out a spot where good water was to be had.

The captain gave orders to arm the boats, and entrusted the command to his lieutenant Labbé.

"The savages appeared impatient for the departure of the boats from the ship," says Fleurien, in his "Découvertes des Français", "and they were no sooner lowered than they were followed by all the pirogues. One of these appeared to lead the others; in it was the Indian who had offered his services to Surville. At the back of the pirogue, a man stood erect, holding in his hands a bunch of herbs, raising them above his head, with a rhythmical movement. In the centre of the same pirogue stood a young man, resting upon a spear, who gravely watched all that went on. Red flowers were in his ears, and passed through the cartilage of his nose, and his hair was powdered with white lime."

Certain trifling symptoms aroused the suspicions of the French, who soon found themselves in a cul-de-sac, where the natives persisted in declaring that fresh water was to be found. Labbé, in spite of all the persuasions of the natives, did not wish to imperil his boats in two or three feet of water, with a muddy bottom, and therefore allowed only a corporal and four soldiers to disembark. They soon returned, asserting that they had seen on all sides nothing but marsh, in which the men would sink to the waist.

It was evident that the natives had meditated treason. Labbé took good care not to let them suspect that he had detected their design, and asked them to point out a spring.

Pirogues of the Admiralty Islands.
(Facsimile of early engraving.)

The natives then led the boats some three leagues away, to a spot from whence it was impossible to see the ship. The corporal was again sent forward with some men, but he found only a very poor spring, barely affording sufficient water to slake the thirst of his party. During his absence, the natives did all in their power to induce Labbé to land, pointing out to him the abundant cocoa-nut and other fruit trees, and even attempting to possess themselves of the boat-hook.

"More than two hundred and fifty of these natives," says the narrative, "armed with spears, from seven to eight feet long, with swords, or wooden clubs, arrows and stones, and some carrying shields, were assembled on the shore, observing the movements of the boats. When the detachment, consisting of five men, proceeded to re-embark, the natives fell upon them, wounding one soldier with a blow from a club, the corporal with a spear, and many others in different ways. M. Labbé himself was hit by two arrows in the thigh, and on the leg by a stone. The traitors were fired upon. The first volley so astonished them that they remained motionless. It was the more fatal, as, being fired only three or five fathoms from the boats, every shot took effect. The amazement of the natives gave the opportunity for a second discharge, which completely routed them, the death of their chief greatly hastening their flight. M. Labbé, who had recognized him, apart from the others, with his hands raised to heaven, striking his breast, and encouraging the assailants by his voice, aimed at him and shot him dead. The natives carried off their wounded, leaving thirty or forty dead upon the field of battle. It was then possible to land, and, picking up such of the enemy's weapons as were scattered about, the victors contented themselves with towing away one of their pirogues and destroying the others."

Surville was extremely anxious to capture an Indian, who might serve him as a guide, and who, convinced of the superiority of European weapons, might warn his countrymen against opposing the French. With this view, he hit upon a singular expedient. He ordered two negro sailors to be placed on board the pirogue he had seized, had their heads powdered, and disguised them so cleverly that the natives were likely to be deceived.

In fact, a pirogue soon after approaching the *Saint-Jean Baptiste*, the men who were in seeing what they took to be two of their own people trafficking with the strangers, drew nearer. So soon as the French imagined they were at a fair distance, they launched two

Picking up the enemies' weapons.

boats in pursuit. The natives gained ground; it was then decided to fire, in order to stop them. One of the natives was killed at once, and his boat capsizing, he fell into the sea, and the other, who was only fourteen or fifteen years of age, endeavoured to reach the shore by swimming.

"He defended himself most courageously," says the narrative, "sometimes making believe to bite himself, but really biting those who held him. His hands and feet were tied, and he was taken on board. He counterfeited death for an hour, but when he was made to sit up, and he fell back on deck, he took good care to fall on his shoulders instead of his head. When he was tired of playing this game he opened his eyes, and, seeing that the crew were eating, he asked for a biscuit, ate it with a good appetite, and made many expressive signs. He was bound securely, so that he might not throw himself overboard."

During the night, it was necessary to resort to firing, to disperse the pirogues, which approached with a view to surprising the ship. Next day, the native was taken in a boat to a small islet, since called Aiguade Island. Scarcely had he landed when it was perceived that he had almost cut through the ropes with a sharp shell.

The young savage was taken by a different route to the shore; when he perceived that he was to re-embark, he rolled upon the ground, shrieking, and biting the sand in his fury.

The sailors succeeded at last in finding an abundant spring, and plenty of wood. One of the trees they cut appeared to have dyeing properties, for it tinged the sea with red. Some of the bark was boiled, and pieces of cotton steeped in the decoction turned deep red.

Welcome refreshment was afforded to the crew by the palm cabbages, good oysters, and various shell-fish which abounded. There were indeed many sufferers from scurvy on board the *Saint-Jean Baptiste*. Surville had looked forward to this stay to cure them, but the rain, which fell ceaselessly for six days, aggravated their complaint to such a degree that three of them died before they left the anchorage.

This port was named Praslin, and the large island or archipelago, which it belonged, Arsacides, in reference to the deceitful nature of its inhabitants.

"Port Praslin," says Fleurien, "would be one of the finest ports in the world, if the bottom were better. It is of circular shape, reckoning all the islands discovered from the spot where the *Saint-Jean*

*Baptiste* cast anchor. The ferocity of the people inhabiting the islands of Port Praslin was such that it was impossible to penetrate into the interior, and it was only possible to examine the sea-coast. We perceived no cultivated ground, either in the trip we made to the further end of the port, nor upon Aiguade Island which was explored throughout."

Such are the superficial particulars which Surville and his crew were able to collect. Fortunately, they were supplemented by those furnished by the captive native, whose name was Lova-Salega, and who possessed a great faculty for learning languages.

According to his account, the island produced palms, cocoa-nut trees, various almond trees, wild coffee, the ebony tree, the tacamahac, as well as numerous resinous or gum trees, the banana, sugar-cane, yams, aniseed, and lastly a plant called "Binao", which is used by the natives as bread. Cockatoos, wood pigeons, Lories, and black-birds, somewhat larger than those of Europe, abounded in the woods. In the marshes the curlew, sea lark, a species of snipe, and ducks were to be found. The only quadrupeds the country produced were goats and half-wild pigs.

"The natives of Port Praslin," says Fleurien, quoting from the manuscripts in his possession, "are of ordinary height, but strong and muscular. They do not appear to be all of one origin (a valuable remark), for some are perfectly black, whilst others are copper-coloured. The former have woolly hair, which is very soft to the touch, their foreheads are small, their eyes slightly sunken, whilst the lower part of their face is pointed, and adorned with a small beard; their expression is fierce. Some of the copper-coloured natives have smooth hair. They usually cut it round the head as high as the ear. A few only retain a little, shaped like a cap, on the top of the head, shaving off the remainder with a sharp stone, and leaving only a circular fringe about an inch deep at the bottom. Their hair and eyebrows are powdered with lime, which gives them a yellowish hue.

"Both men and women are stark naked; but it must be allowed that their nudity is not so startling as would be that of an European without clothes, for the faces, arms, and generally every part of their bodies are tattooed. Sometimes the taste of these designs is really wonderful. They pierce their ears and the cartilage of their nose, and the nostrils often hang down, from the weight of the ornaments, to the upper lip."

The commonest ornament worn by the natives of Port Praslin is a necklace made of men's teeth. It was at once concluded that they were cannibals, although the same custom had been met with among people who were not. Lova's confused replies, and the half-broiled head of a man, found by Bougainville in a pirogue in Choiseul Island, placed the existence of this barbarous practice beyond the possibility of doubt.

On the 21st of October after nine days' rest, the *Saint-Jean Baptiste* left Port Praslin.

On the next and ensuing days, lofty and mountainous land was constantly in sight. Upon the 2nd of November Surville descried an island, which received the name of Contrariétés, from the contrary winds which for three days checked the progress of the ship.

This island presented a delightful appearance. It was well cultivated, and, judging from the number of pirogues, which constantly surrounded the *Saint-Jean Baptiste*, it must have been well populated.

The natives could scarcely be persuaded to go on board. At last a chief sprang on deck. His first act was to possess himself of a sailor's clothes. He next visited the poop and took the white flag, which he wished to appropriate. It was only after some difficulty that he was dissuaded from the attempt. Lastly, he climbed up the mizen mast, and from that elevated position observed all parts of the vessel. Then, coming down, he began to jump about, and, addressing himself to those he had left in the canoes, he invited them, by words and gestures, to join him on deck.

About a dozen ventured. They resembled the natives of Port Praslin, but they spoke a different language, and could not make themselves understood by Lova-Salega. Their stay on board did not last long, for one of them having possessed himself of a bottle and thrown it into the sea, the captain showed some annoyance, which induced them to return to their pirogues.

The land appeared so inviting, and the sufferers from scurvy were in such pressing need of green provisions, that Surville determined to send a boat to test the disposition of the natives.

It had no sooner left the vessel than it was surrounded by pirogues, manned by a number of warriors. Hostilities were imminent, but a few shots dispersed the assailants. During the night a flotilla advanced towards the *Saint-Jean Baptiste*, and Surville, from motives of humanity, did not wait until the natives were close, but at once fired several pieces charged with grape shot, which put them to flight.

It was useless to think of landing, and Surville regained the open sea. He discovered successively the Three Sisters Island, and Gulf and Deliverance Islands, the last of the group.

The archipelago, just explored by Surville, was no other than that of the Solomon Islands, which, as we have mentioned, was discovered in the first instance by Mendana. That skilful navigator had traced and surveyed a hundred and forty leagues, besides drawing a series of fourteen very curious views of this sea coast.

If Surville's crew, were not to be decimated by death, it was necessary at all risks to reach land, where he might disembark the sick, and procure fresh provisions for them.

He resolved to steer for New Zealand, which had not been visited since the time of Tasman.

On the 12th of December, 1769. Surville descried land in 35° 37' S. lat., and five days later he cast anchor in a bay which he called Lauriston. At the extremity was a creek which received the name of Chevalier. Cook had been in search of this land since the beginning of October, and was fated to pass by Lauriston Bay a few days later without observing the French vessel.

Whilst anchored in Chevalier Creek, Surville was overtaken by a frightful tempest, which brought him within an ace of destruction, but his sailors had such confidence in his nautical ability that they felt no anxiety, and obeyed his orders with a *sang froid* of which, unfortunately, the Maoris were the sole spectators.

The sloop which was conveying the sick to land had no time to reach the shore, before the storm broke in all its fury, and she was driven into Refuge Creek. The sailors and invalids were cordially welcomed by a chief called Naginoui, who received them into his cabin, and bestowed upon them all the green provisions which he could procure during their stay.

One of the boats which was towed behind the *Saint-Jean Baptiste* was carried away by the waves. Surville saw it stranded in Refuge Creek. He sent in search of it, but only the rudder was found. The natives had carried it off. The river was searched in vain; there was no trace of the boat. Surville would not allow this theft to go unpunished. He made signs to some Indians who were near their pirogues to approach him. One of them ran to him at once, and was immediately seized and carried on board. The others fled.

"He seized one pirogue," says Crozet, "and burnt the other; set fire to the huts and returned to the ship. The Indian who was taken was recognized by the surgeon as the chief who had so generously assisted them during the storm. It was the unfortunate Naginoui, who, after the services he had rendered the whites, could hardly have anticipated such treatment at their hands, when he obeyed Surville's signal."

He died on the 24th of March, 1770, near the island of Juan Fernandez.

We will pass over the observations made by the French navigator upon the natives, and the productions of New Zealand, as they are merely a repetition of those of Captain Cook.

Surville, convinced that he could not obtain the provisions he needed, put to sea a few days later, and steered between the parallels of 27° and 28° S. lat.; but the ravages of the scurvy, which increased daily, decided him on steering for the coast of Peru without delay.

He sighted it on the 5th of April, 1770, and three days later cast anchor off the Chilica Bar at the entrance of Callao.

In his haste to reach the land, and seek help for his sick, Surville was unwilling to allow any one else to visit the governor. Unfortunately his boat was capsized by the waves that break over the bar, and only one of the crew was saved. Surville and all the rest were drowned.

Thus miserably perished this great navigator, too early for the services he might have rendered to his country and to science. As for the *Saint-Jean Baptiste*, she was detained "for three years" before Lima by the interminable delays of the Spanish customs. Labbé assumed the command, and took her back to Lorient on the 23rd of August, 1773.

As we have already related, M. de Bougainville had taken a Tahitan named Aoutourou to Europe. When this native expressed a desire to return to his native land, the French administration had sent him to Mauritius, with orders to the governor of that colony to facilitate his return to Tahiti.

A naval officer, Marion Dufresne, availed himself of this opportunity, and offered Poivre, the Governor of Mauritrus and Bourbon, to send the young Aoutourou to Tahiti at his own expense and in a vessel belonging to him. He only required that a vessel belonging to the state might be assigned to him, and a small sum of money advanced to assist him in the preparations for the expedition.

Nicholas Thomas Marion Dufresne was born at St. Malo on the 22nd of December, 1729, and had entered the naval service very young. On the 16th of October, 1746, he was made lieutenant of a frigate, and at the time of his offer was still only captain of a fire ship. Still he had served everywhere with distinction, and nowhere more successfully than in the Indian Seas.

The mission for which he offered himself was merely a pretext for a voyage of discovery in the Southern Seas.

Poivre, an intelligent governor and a friend to progress, approved of Dufresne's projects, and gave him detailed instructions for the enterprise he was about to undertake in the Southern Hemisphere. At this time Cook had not yet proved the non-existence of an Antarctic Continent.

Poivre would clearly have liked to have discovered the northern portion of the lands he imagined to lie near the French colonies, and where he hoped to meet with a more temperate climate. He calculated upon finding timber for masts, and many other necessaries there, such as provisions, which he was now obliged to obtain at heavy cost from the metropolis. Moreover, there might be a safe port, where vessels could find shelter from the storms which almost periodically ravaged the islands of Mauritius and Bourbon.

The government had just sent a ship's lieutenant, M. Kerguelen, to make discoveries in these unknown seas. Marion's expedition, which was to try a different route, could not fail to aid in the solution of the problem.

On the 18th of October, 1771, the *Mascarin*, commanded by Marion, and the *Marquis de Castries*, under the Chevalier Du Clesmeur, midshipman, set sail. They put in first at Bourbon Island. There they took Aoutourou on board. He was unfortunately infected with small-pox, which he had caught in the Mauritius; and the illness soon declared itself, so that it was necessary to leave Bourbon lest he should communicate it to the inhabitants. The two vessels then made for Port Dauphin, on the coast of Madagascar, in order to allow the malady to run its course, before proceeding to the Cape, where they were to complete provisioning. Young Aoutourou soon died of the disease.

Under these circumstances, was it necessary to return to Mauritius, disarm the ships, and give up the expedition? Marion thought not. With greater freedom of action, he determined to make himself famous by a new voyage, and he inspired his companions with enthusiasm like his own.

He soon reached the Cape of Good Hope, where he completed in a few days the provisioning necessary for an eighteen months' voyage.

A southerly route was chosen towards the land, discovered in 1739 by Bouvet de Lozier, and which was to be looked for east of the meridian of Madagascar.

Nothing remarkable occurred from the 28th of December, 1771, the day upon which the vessels had left the Cape, until the 11th of January. It was then discovered by taking the latitude 20° 43' east of the Paris meridian, that they were in the parallel (40° to 41° south) of the islands named in Van Keulen's chart as Dina and Marvezen, and not marked at all upon French maps.

Although the presence of land-birds induced Marion to suppose that he was not far from the islands, he left these latitudes on the 9th of January, convinced that his search for the southern continent ought to occupy his entire attention. The 11th of January found him in 45° 43' S. lat., and, although it was summer in these regions, the cold was severe, and snow fell without ceasing. Two days later, in a dense fog, which was succeeded by rain, Marion discerned land which extended a distance of five leagues from the W.S.W. to the E.N.E. The sounding gave a depth of eighty fathoms with a bottom of coarse sand mixed with coral. This land stretched away till it could be seen behind the vessels, that is to say, over a distance of six to seven leagues. It appeared to be very lofty and mountainous. It received the name of Hope, marking Marion's great desire to reach the southern continent. Four years later Cook called it Prince Edward's Island.

To the north lay another territory.

Crozet, editor of Marion's voyage, says, –

"I noticed, in coasting along this island, that to the N.E. there existed a creek, opposite to what appeared to be a large cavern. All around this cavern he remarked a number of large white spots, which looked like a flock of sheep. Had time allowed, he might have found anchorage opposite the creek. I fancied I saw a cascade issuing from the mountains. In rounding the island we discovered three islets detached from it, two of them situated in the large bay formed by the coast, and the third on its northern extremity. The island itself was about seven or eight leagues in circumference, without verdure, and apparently barren. The coast was healthy and safe. M. Marion named it Cavern Island.

"These two southern territories are situated in 45° 45' S. lat. by 34° 31' east of the Paris meridian, half a degree east of the route pursued by Bouvet. Next day, about six leagues of the coast of the land of Hope was made out. It looked fertile. The mountains were lofty and covered with snow. The navigators were about to look for anchorage, when, during the sounding operations, the two ships ran foul of each other and were both damaged. Three days were occupied in repairs. The weather, which had hitherto been fine, broke up, and, the wind becoming violent, it was necessary to continue the course following the forty-sixth parallel. New lands were discovered on the 24th of January.

"At first," says Crozet, "they appeared formed of two islands; I took a sketch at a distance of eight leagues, and shortly afterwards we took them for two capes, imagining we could see in the far distance a stretch of land between them. They are situated in 40° 5' S. lat. and about 42° E. long. reckoning from the meridian of Paris. M. Marion named them Les Îles Froides, or the Cold Islands.

"Although little progress was made during the night, the islands were invisible next morning. Upon this day the *Castries* signalled land, which stretched some ten or twelve leagues E.S.E.; but a dense fog, lasting no less than twelve hours, continued rain, and cold, which was severe and trying to lightly-clad men, made any approach nearer than six or seven leagues impossible.

"This coast was seen again upon the 24th, as well as new land, which received the name of the Arid Island, and is now known as Crozet Island. Marion was at length able to lower a boat, and ordered Crozet to take possession of the larger of the two islands in the name of the king. It is situated in 46° 30' S. lat., and 43° E. long., reckoning from the Paris meridian. M. Marion called this island La Prise de Possession (it is now known as Marion Island). This was the sixth island discovered by us in these southern waters. From a height I discerned snow in many of the valleys. The land appeared barren, and covered with very small grass. I found neither tree nor bush in the island. Exposed to the continual ravages of the stormy west winds which prevailed the entire year in these latitudes, it appeared unhabitable. I found nothing there but seals, penguins, sea-gulls, Mother Carey's chickens and every variety of aquatic birds, usually met with by navigators in the open sea, when passing the Cape of Good Hope. These creatures, never having seen a man, were not wild, and allowed us to take them in the hand. The female birds sat tranquilly upon their eggs, others fed their young, whilst the seals continued their gambols in our presence, without appearing in the least alarmed."

Marion continued to steer between 46° to 47° lat. in the midst of a fog so dense that it was impossible to see from one end of the deck to the other, and without constant firing the ships must have parted company. Upon the 2nd of February the two ships were in 47° 22' E. long., that is to say within 1° 10' of the lands discovered upon the 13th of the same month by the king's vessels *La Fortune* and *Le Gros Ventre*, commanded by MM. de Kerguelen and Saint Allouarn. Doubtless, but for the accident to the *Castries*, Marion would have fallen in with them.

Having reached 90° east of the Paris meridian, Marion changed his route, and directed his course to Van Diemen's Land. No incident occurred during the cruise, and the two vessels cast anchor in Frederick Henry Bay.

Boats were at once lowered, and a strong detachment made its way to the shore, where some thirty natives were found; and the country, judging from the fires and smoke, must have been well populated.

"The natives of the country," says Crozet, "came forward willingly. They picked up wood and formed a sort of pile. They then presented the new comers with pieces of dried wood which they had lighted; and appeared to invite them to set fire to the pile. No one knew what the ceremony might mean, and it was accordingly tried. The natives did not appear surprised. They remained about us, without making any demonstration either of hostility or friendship, and their wives and children were with them. Both men and women were of ordinary height, black in colour, with woolly hair, and all were naked. Some of the women carried their children tied on to their backs with rushes. All the men were armed with pointed sticks and stones, which appeared to us to be sharp, like hatchets.

"We attempted to win them over by small presents. They disdainfully rejected all that we offered, even iron, looking-glasses, handkerchiefs, and pieces of cloth. Fowls and ducks which had been brought from the ship were shown to them as evidence that we wished to trade. They took them, looked at them as if they had never seen such things before, and threw them aside with an angry air."

An hour had been spent in the attempt to gain the good-will of the savages, when Marion and Du Glesmeur landed. A lighted brand was also presented to them, and fully persuaded that it was a peaceful ceremony, they did not hesitate to light the pile which was prepared. They were mistaken, for the natives immediately retired and flung a volley of stones, which wounded the two captains. They retaliated by a few shots, and the whole party re-embarked.

A lighted brand was also presented to them.

After another attempt at landing, which the natives opposed with great bravery, it was necessary to repulse them by a volley which wounded several and killed one. The crew then landed and pursued the natives, who made no attempt to resist them.

Two detachments were sent in search of a watering place, and of trees suitable for repairing the masts of the *Castries*. Six days passed in fruitless search; fortunately not wholly wasted, as many curious observations were made on behalf of science.

"From the considerable number of shells which we found at short distances," says Crozet, "we concluded that the ordinary food of these savages was mussels, cockles, and various shell-fish."

Is it not strange to find, among the New Zealanders, the remains of food similar to that with which we are familiar on the Scandinavian coasts? Is not man everywhere the same, and incited by the same needs to the same actions?

Finding it waste of time to seek for water and wood with which to remast the *Castries* and repair the *Mascarin*, which leaked a good deal, Marion started on the 10th of March for New Zealand, and reached that island fourteen days later.

New Zealand, discovered by Tasman in 1642, and visited by Cook and Saville in 1772, was now becoming known.

The two vessels made for land at Mount Egmont, but the shore was so steep at this point, that Marion put back to sea and returned to reconnoitre the land upon the 31st of March in 36° 30' latitude.

He coasted along the shore, and, in spite of contrary winds, returned northward as far as the Three Kings Islands. He found it impossible to land there. It was therefore necessary to reach the mainland, and anchor was cast opposite Cape Maria-Van-Diemen, the most northerly extremity of New Zealand. The anchorage was soon perceived to be bad, and after many attempts Marion stopped at Cook's Island Bay on the 11 of May.

Tents were erected on one of the islands, where wood and water were found, and the sick were installed there under a strong guard. The natives came on board, some of them even slept there, and trade, facilitated by the use of a Tahitan vocabulary, was carried on in grand style.

"I remarked with surprise," says Crozet, "that among the savages who came on board were three distinct species of men. One of these appeared to be the original native, and was of a yellowish white colour, taller than the others, the usual height being from five foot nine to five foot ten inches; he had smooth black hair. The more swarthy and somewhat smaller men had slightly curling hair. And lastly the genuine negro, with woolly hair and of smaller stature than the others, but usually broader chested. The first have very little beard, whilst the negroes have a great deal."

This curious observation was afterwards verified. It is unnecessary to linger over the customs of the New Zealanders, or over Marion's minute description of their fortified villages, their arms, clothing and food; these details are already known to our readers.

The French pitched three camps on land. The first for the sick, upon Matuaro Island, the second upon the mainland, which served as a depôt, and a means of communication with the third, which was the workshop of the carpenters, and was some two leagues away in the midst of a wood. The crew, persuaded by the friendliness of the natives, made long excursions into the interior, and received a hearty welcome everywhere. Confidence was at length so fully established that, in spite of Crozet's representations, Marion ordered the sloops' boats to be disarmed. This was unpardonable imprudence in a country where Tasman had given the name of Assassin Bay to the first point on which he landed, where Cook had met with cannibals, and had been nearly massacred.

On the 8th of June, Marion landed, and was received with even greater demonstrations of friendship than usual. He was proclaimed head chief of the country, and the natives placed four white feathers in his hair, as insignia of royalty.

Four days later he again landed with two young officers. MM. de Vaudricourt and Le Houx, a volunteer and captain of arms, and a few sailors, seventeen persons in all. Evening approached, but no one came back to the ship. At first no anxiety was felt, for the hospitable customs of the natives were well-known. It was supposed that Marion had slept on shore, to be ready to visit the workshops in the morning.

On the 13th of June the *Castries* sent her boat for the daily supply of wood and water. At nine o'clock a man was seen swimming towards the ships. A boat was lowered to help him on board. It was one of the rowers, the only one who had escaped from the massacre of his comrades. He had received two lance thrusts in the side, and been much ill-treated.

From his account, it appeared that the natives had at first shown their usual friendliness. They had even carried the sailors, who feared getting wet, ashore upon their shoulders. But, when the crew dispersed to pick up their cargo of wood, the natives reappeared, armed with spears, tomahawks, and clubs, and threw themselves in parties

The only one who had escaped.

of six and seven upon each of the sailors. The survivor had been attacked by two men only, who had wounded him with two lance thrusts, and as, fortunately, he was not far from the sea, he had succeeded in reaching the shore, where he hid himself in some brushwood. From thence he had witnessed the massacre of all his companions. The savages had the bodies stripped, and commenced cutting them up, when he stole noiselessly from his concealment, and threw himself into the sea, hoping to reach the ship by swimming. Had all the sixteen men who accompanied Marion, and of whom no news was received, met a like fate? It seemed probable. In any case, it was needful to take immediate precautions for the safety of the three camps. Chevalier Du Clesmeur at once took the command, and, thanks to his energy, the disaster did not assume worse proportions.

The sloop of the *Mascarin* was armed and sent in search of Marion's boat and sloop, with orders to warn all the camps, and carry help to the most distant, where masts and spars were being made. On the road, upon the shore, the two boats were discovered near the village of Tacoury. They were surrounded by natives, who had pillaged them after massacring the sailors.

Without waiting to regain possession of the boats, the officer put on all speed in the hope of reaching the workshop in time. Fortunately, it had not yet been attacked by the natives. All work was immediately stopped, the utensils and weapons were collected, the guns were loaded, and such objects as could not be removed were buried beneath the ruins of the shed, which was set on fire.

The retreat was accomplished amongst crowds of natives, crying in sinister tones, "Tacouri maté Marion", "Tacouri has killed Marion". Two leagues were traversed in this manner, during which no aggression was attempted against the sixty men who composed the detachment. Upon their arrival at the sloop, the natives approached them; Grozet first sent all the sailors who carried loads on board, then, tracing a line on the ground, he made it understood that the first native who passed it would immediately be fired upon. An order was then given to the natives to seat themselves; and it must have been an imposing spectacle to see thousands obeying unresistingly, in spite of their desire to seize the prey which was escaping before their eyes.

Crozet embarked last, and no sooner had he set foot in the sloop than the war-cry was uttered; whilst javelins and stones were thrown from every direcection. Hostilities had succeeded threats, and the savages rushed into the water the better to aim at their foes. Grozet found himself obliged to prove to these wretches the superiority of his weapons, and gave orders to fire. The New Zealanders, seeing their comrades fall wounded or dead, without their appearing to have been touched, were quite amazed. They would all have been killed had not Crozet stopped the firing. The sick were taken on board without accident, and the encampment, reinforced and put on guard, was not molested.

Next day, the natives, who had an important village upon Matuaro Island, endeavoured to prevent the sailors from fetching the water and wood they needed. The latter then marched against them, bayonet in hand, and followed them up to their village, where they shut themselves in. The voice of the chief inciting them to battle was heard. Firing was commenced as soon as the village was within range, and this was so well directed that the chiefs were the first victims. As soon as they fell, the natives fled. Some fifty were killed, the rest were driven into the sea, and the village was burned.

It was useless to dream of bringing to the shore the five masts, made with great difficulty from the cedars which had been cut down, and the carpenters were obliged to repair the mast with pieces of wood collected on the ships. The provisioning of the ships with the seven hundred barrels of water, and seventy loads of wood, necessary for the voyage, would infallibly occupy at least a month, for there remained only one sloop.

The fate of Marion, and the men who had accompanied him, was still unknown. A well-armed detachment therefore started for the village of Tacouri.

It was abandoned! Only men too old to follow the flight of their companions remained, and were seated in the doors of their huts. An effort was made to take them. One of them, without any apparent effort, at once struck a soldier with a javelin he held in his hand. He was killed, but no injury was inflicted upon the others who were left in the village. All the houses were thoroughly searched. In Tacouri's kitchen a man's skull was found which had been cooked some days before. Some fleshy parts still remained which bore the impress of the cannibal's teeth. On a wooden spit, a piece of a human thigh, three parts eaten, was found. In another house, a shirt was recognized as having belonged to the unfortunate Marion. The collar was soaked in blood, and two or three holes were found in the side, also blood-stained. In various other houses, portions of the clothes, and the pistols belonging to young Vaudricourt, who had accompanied the Captain, were brought to light. The boat's arms, and quantities of scraps of the unfortunate sailors' clothing, were also discovered.

A man's skull was found.

Doubt was unfortunately no longer possible. An account of the death of the victims was drawn up, and Chevalier Du Clesmeur searched Marion's papers to discover his projects, and the plans for the prosecution of the voyage. He found only the instructions given by the Governor of Mauritius.

A council was held with the ship's officers, and, bearing in mind the lamentable condition of the vessels, it was decided to abandon the search for new lands, and to make for Amsterdam or Rotterdam island, then for the Mariana and Philippines, where there was a chance of disposing of the cargo, before returning to Mauritius. On the 14th of July, Du Clesmeur left Treason Port, as he named the bay of these islands, and the vessels steered towards Amsterdam and Rotterdam Islands, to the north of which they passed on the 6th of August. Navigation was aided by splendid weather, a fortunate circumstance, as scurvy had made such ravages among the sailors, that very few of them were in a condition to work. At length, on the 20th of September, Guaham Island, the largest of the Mariana group, was discovered. It was impossible to cast anchor until seven days later.

The account published by Crozet contains very precise and circumstantial details regarding this island, with its productions and inhabitants. We will only transcribe from it one phrase, as explicit as it is short.

"Guaham Island," he says, "appeared to us a terrestrial paradise. The air was excellent, the water good, the vegetables and fruits were perfect, the herds of cattle, goats, and pigs, innumerable; every species of fowl abounded." Amongst the vegetable productions, Crozet mentions "Rima", the fruit of which is good to eat, when it has attained its full growth and is still green.

"In this condition," he says, "the natives gather it for food. They remove the rough skin, and cut it in slices like bread. When they wish to preserve it, they cut it in round pieces, and dry it in the sun or in an oven, in the form of very small cakes. This natural biscuit preserves its bread-like qualities for several years, and far longer than our best ship's biscuits."

From Port Agana, Crozet reached the Philippine Islands, and anchored off Cavite, in Manilla Bay. This was the spot where the *Castries* and *Mascarin* parted, to go back to Mauritius separately.

Some years previously a gallant officer of the royal navy, Chevalier Jacques Raymond de Geron de Grenier, who was one of that group of distinguished men – the Chazelles, the Bordas, the

Fleuriens, the Du Martz de Gormpy, the Chaberts, the Verduns de la Crenne, who contributed so zealously to the progress of navigation and geography – had employed his leisure, during a stay in the Isle of France, in exploring the adjacent seas.

He had made a very profitable cruise in the corvette, the *Heure du Berger*, during which he rectified the position of Saint Brandon's rock, and of the Saya-de-Malha sandbank, examined separately Saint Michael, Rocque-pire, and Agalega in the Seychelles archipelago, and corrected the charts of Adu and Diego Garcia Islands. Convinced of the connexion of the currents with the monsoon, which he had thoroughly studied, he proposed a shortened route, always open, from the Isle of France to the Indies. It would be a saving of eight hundred leagues, and was well worth serious consideration.

The minister of Marine, who had seen Grenier's proposition well received by the Naval Academy, decided to entrust its examination to a ship's officer, who was accustomed to work of the kind.

He selected Yves-Joseph de Kerguelen. During two expeditions, undertaken in 1767 and 1768, for the encouragement and protection of the cod-fisheries on the coast of Iceland, this navigator had surveyed a great number of ports and roadsteads, collected astronomical observations, rectified the map of Iceland, and accumulated a mass of particulars concerning this little-known country. It was he, indeed, who gave the earliest authentic account of "geysers", those springs of warm water which occasionally reach to such great heights, and he also supplied curious details of the existence of fossil wood, which prove that at an early geological period, Iceland, now entirely devoid of trees, possessed enormous forests.

Kerguelen had at the same time published novel details of the manners and customs of the inhabitants.

"The women," he said, "have dresses, jackets, and aprons made of a cloth called 'wadmal' which is made in Iceland. They wear an ample robe above their jackets, rather like that of the Jesuits, but not so long as the petticoats, which they allow to be seen. These robes are of different colours, but generally black; they are called 'hempe.' They are trimmed with velvet or some other ornament. The head-dresses look like pyramids or sugar-loaves, two or three feet high. The women ornament the head with a large handkerchief of very coarse cloth, which stands upright, and they cover it with another finer one, which forms the shape of which I spoke." Lastly, Kerguelen had collected very interesting documents, relating to

Denmark, the Laplanders, the Samoyedes, the Farœ Islands, the Orkney and Shetland Islands, which he had thoroughly explored.

Kerguelen, entrusted with the examination of the route proposed by Grenier, asked permission of the minister to employ his ship to explore all the southern lands discovered in 1739 by Bouvet de Lozier. The Abbé Terray, who had just succeeded the Duke of Praslin, gave him command of the ship *Le Berryer*, which brought 300 able-bodied seamen and provisions for fourteen months from Lorient, together with some ammunition for Mauritius. The Abbé Rochon was associated with Kerguelen, for making astronomical observations. Upon reaching Mauritius, on the 20th of August, 1771, Kerguelen exchanged the *Berryer* for the *La Fortune*, to which a small vessel, the *Gros-ventre*, with sixteen guns and a crew of a hundred men, was attached under command of M. de Saint Allouarn.

As soon as the two vessels were equipped, Kerguelen set sail and steered northward in search of the Mahé Islands. During a great storm, the sounding lines of the *Fortune* gave an ever-decreasing depth, first thirty, then twenty, and at last only fourteen fathoms. Anchor was then cast, and it held fast throughout the tempest.

"Daybreak at last relieved our anxieties," says Kerguelen; "we perceived neither land nor rock. The *Gros-ventre* was three leagues distant; her captain could not believe that I was at anchor, for the noise of the thunder, and the dazzling lightning, prevented his hearing or seeing my signals. This is the sole instance of a vessel anchoring in the night in the open sea upon an unknown coast. I set sail, and allowed the vessels to drift, taking constant soundings. I at first found fourteen, then twenty, then twenty-five, at last twenty-eight fathoms. Then I suddenly lost the bottom altogether, proving that we had passed above a submarine mountain. This new bank, I called Fortune Bank, stretched, N.W. and S.E. It is situated 7° 16' S. lat. and 55° 50' E. long."

The *Fortune* and the *Gros-ventre* then made for 50° S. lat., which was the route recommended by the Chevalier de Grenier. The two captains were aware that the winds constantly blew from the east, at this season of the year, and therefore went to the Maldives, and coasted along Ceylon from Point de Galle, to Trincomalée. Upon their return the monsoon had changed. The prevailing winds were W. and S.W. as Grenier had predicted. The route suggested by him had undeniable advantages, and these have been so amply confirmed by experience that no other now followed.

Returning to Mauritius on the 8th of December, Kerguelen hurried his preparations for departure to such an extent that he was able to start upon the 12th of January, 1772. He steered southwards, for, supposing that he found land in that direction, the nearest would naturally be the most useful for the French colony.

From the 1st of February, numbers of birds seemed to indicate the proximity of land. Hail succeeded snow. The vessels experienced foul weather, boisterous winds, and a heavy sea. The first land was sighted upon the 12th. Next day a second was discovered, and shortly afterwards a very lofty and extensive cape. The following day at seven o'clock in the morning, the sun having dispelled the clouds, a line of coast extending some twenty-five leagues was clearly seen. The vessels were then in 49° 40' S. lat. and 61° 10' E. long.

Unfortunately storm succeeded storm, and the two vessels with great difficulty escaped being cast ashore. Kerguelen was driven northward by currents, shortly after he had sent a boat to attempt a landing.

"Finding myself so far from land," says Kerguelen, "I reflected upon the best course to be pursued. I remembered that the state of my mast was too bad to allow me to crowd sail, and leave the coast, and that, having no sloop to carry my anchors, I was exposed to extreme danger whilst near the shore, that in the dense fog it was all but impossible to find the *Gros-ventre*, from which I had been separated for several days. It was the more difficult on account of the tempest we had experienced, and the variable winds that prevailed. These reflections and my conviction that the *Gros-ventre* was an excellent sailer, and that she was provisioned for seven months, determined me to return to Mauritius, which I reached upon the 16th of March." Fortunately no accident had happened to the *Gros-ventre*. Her boat had returned in time; M. de Boisgue-Henneuc, who had landed, had taken possession of the land with all the usual formalities, and left some writing in a bottle, which was found by Captain Cook in 1776.

Kerguelen returned to France, but his successful enterprise had gained him many enemies. When upon the 1st of January, 1772, the the king nominated him captain, and Chevalier de Saint Louis, the attacks upon him increased. The most malignant slanders were circulated. They even went the length of accusing him of having scuttled the *Gros-ventre* in order to derive all the benefit accruing from the discovery which he had made in concert with M. de Saint Allouarn.

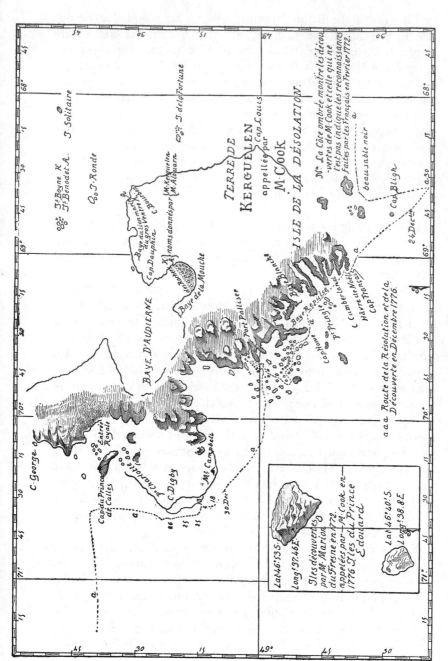

Islands discovered by M. Marion du Fresne in 1772, called Prince Edward's Island by Cook in 1776.

The minister, however, was not influenced by these slanders, and decided to entrust the command of a second expedition to Kerguelen. The *Roland*, and the frigate *Oiseau*, left Brest upon the 26th of March, 1772, the latter under command of M. de Saux de Rosnevet.

Upon reaching the Cape, Kerguelen was obliged to put in for forty days. The entire crew was suffering from putrid fever, probably owing to the dampness of the new vessel.

"This appeared the more probable," says the narrative, "because all the dried vegetables, such as peas, beans, lentils, &c., together with the rice, and a quantity of biscuits, were spoiled in the storeroom. The vegetables emitted a kind of steam which was infectious, and the store-rooms became infested with numbers of white worms. The *Roland* left the Cape upon the 11th of July, but she was almost immediately overtaken by a frightful tempest, which carried away two topsails, the jib, and the mizen mast. Finally Mauritius was reached by means of jury-masts."

MM de Roches and Poivre, who had contributed so essentially to the success of the first expedition, had been succeeded by M. de Ternay and the Intendant Maillard. They appeared determined to offer every possible obstacle to the execution of Kerguelen's orders. They gave him no fresh victuals, of which the crew had pressing need, and there were no means of replacing the masts destroyed by the tempest. In lieu of the thirty-four sailors who had to go to the hospital, he was provided only with disgraced or maimed soldiers, of whom he was glad to rid himself. An expedition to the southern seas, so equipped, could only come to a disastrous end; and that was precisely what happened.

On the 5th of January, Kerguelen sighted the lands he had discovered in his first voyage, and between that date and the 16th he recognized various points, Croy Island, Re-union island, *Roland* Island, which in his estimation made more than eighty leagues of coast. The weather continued extremely severe; thick fogs, snow, hail, and gales succeeded each other. On the 21st, the vessels could only keep in company by constant firing. Upon that day the cold was so severe that several of the sailors fainted on deck.

"The officers," says Kerguelen, "insisted that the ordinary ration of biscuit was not enough, and that without more the crew could not possibly resist the cold and fog. I increased each man's rations by four ounces of biscuit daily."

Upon the 8th of January, 1774, the *Roland* signalled the frigate at Re-union Island. Communication with her was opened, and M. Rosnevet declared that he had found an anchorage in a bay behind Cape Français, that he had sent a boat on the 6th to take soundings, and that, upon landing to take possession, the men had killed a sea-lion and some penguins.

Once again, the prostrate condition of the crew, the bad quality of the victuals, and the dilapidated state of the vessels, prevented Kerguelen from making a thorough investigation of this desolate archipelago. He was forced to return; but, instead of returning to Mauritius, he landed in Antongil Bay, Madagascar, where he was sure of obtaining lemons, limes, custard apples, and other anti-scorbutics, as well as fresh meat.

An adventurer named Beniowski, whose history is sufficiently curious, had just founded a French colony there. But he was in need of everything. Kerguelen gave him ammunition, bricks, iron implements, shirts, blankets, &c., and finally ordered his carpenters to build a store-shed for him.

Thirty-four of the crew of the *Roland* had died since leaving the southern regions, and if Kerguelen had remained another week in these latitudes, he would have lost a hundred men! On his return to France, Kerguelen met with nothing but ill-will and calumny, in return for so much fatigue, so bravely born. The feeling against him was so strong that one of his officers was not ashamed to publish a memoir, in which all the facts were dressed up in the most unfavourable shape, and the failure of the enterprise thrown upon Kerguelen. We do not assert that he was entirely free from blame, but we consider the verdict of the council of war which deprived him of his rank, and condemned him to detention in the Château of Saumur, most unjust. No doubt the judgment was found to be excessive, and the government discerned more malice than justice in it, for a few months later Kerguelen was restored to liberty. The gravest charge against him was that of having abandoned his sloop and a portion of his crew, in the southern seas, who, but for the opportune arrival of the *Fortune*, must have perished. Probably, however, even this was much exaggerated, for a letter exists from the abandoned officer, M. de Rosily (afterwards vice-admiral), in which he begs to serve again under Kerguelen. The account of these expeditions is an extract from the apology published by Kerguelen during his imprisonment, a work which was confiscated by government, and on that account is extremely rare.

We must now turn our attention to the account of expeditions which, although they did not result in discoveries, had an importance of their own. They contributed to the rectification of charts, to the progress of navigation and geography, but, above all, they solved a long-standing problem, the determination of longitude at sea.

To decide upon the position of a locality it is first necessary to obtain its latitude, that is to say, its distance N. or S. from the equator, and its longitude, or in other words its distance E. or W. from some known meridian.

At this period, no instrument for determining the position of a ship existed but the rope known as a log, which, thrown into the sea, measured the distance which the ship made every half minute; the proportionate speed of the vessel per hour was deduced from it. But the log is far from immoveable, and the speed of a vessel is not always the same, hence arose two important sources of error. The direction of the route was determined by the mariner's needle or compass. But every one knows that the compass is subject to variations, and that the vessel does not invariably follow the course it indicates, and it is no easy matter to determine the exact difference. These inconveniences once admitted, the question was to find a method exempt from them.

With Hadley's quadrant, latitude could be determined within a minute, that is to say, to the third of a league. But such an approximate exactitude was not possible in deciding longitudes. When once the different phenomena of the variations of the magnetic needle, either of declination or inclination, should be fully understood, it would be easy; but how to obtain this knowledge? It was well known that in the Indian Sea, between Bourbon, Madagascar, and Rodriguez, a variation of four degrees in the declination of the needle was equivalent to a variation of five degrees in the longitude, but it was equally admitted that the declination of the magnetic needle was subject to variations, in the same localities, for which no cause could be assigned.

Verdun de la Crenne, writing in 1778, says a declination of twelve degrees, from N. to W. twenty years ago, indicated a longitude of 61° W. of Paris, in any given latitude. It is very probable that within the last twenty years the declination has varied two degrees, which makes the longitude deduced from it wrong by two and a half degrees, or nearly fifty nautical miles.

If the right time is known on board, that is to say, the correct time by which the meridian could be computed at the moment of any given observation, and if at the same time, the exact time at the port from which the ship had started, or that if any known meridian could be ascertained, the difference of time would evidently give that of the meridians, at the rate of fifteen degrees per hour, or one degree per four minutes. The problem of the longitude could thus be reduced to a determination, at a given moment of the time at any given meridian.

To achieve this it was necessary to have a watch or clock which should preserve a perfect isochronism, in defiance of the state of the sea or differences of temperature.

Many attempts had been made. Besson in the sixteenth century, Huyghens in the seventeenth century, and again Sully, Harrison, Dutertre, Gallonde, Rivas, Le Roy, and Ferdinand Berthould had attempted to solve the problem.

The English and French Governments, moreover, convinced of the value of a perfect instrument, had offered a high reward for its invention. The Academy of Science had instituted a competition. In 1765 Le Roy sent in two watches for competition, whilst Berthould, who was in the king's service, was unable to do so. Le Roy's watches passed successfully through the various trials to which they were subjected on land. It remained to be proved whether they would be equally trustworthy at sea.

The Marquis de Constanvaux had the frigate *Aurora* built at his own cost for this experiment. Le Roy, however, decided that a cruise, with constant stoppages, at Calais, Dunkirk, Rotterdam, Amsterdam and Boulogne, lasting only from the 25th of May to the 29th of August, was far too short, and he demanded a second trial. This time his watches were sent on board the frigate, the *Enjouée*, which, leaving Havre, put in at St. Pierre near Teneriffe, at Salee in Africa, at Cadiz, and finally, after a voyage of four months and a half, at Brest. The trial had been a serious one, the latitudes and the state of the sea having both changed constantly. If the watch had neither lost or gained, it won the prize, which was in fact assigned to Le Roy.

The Academy, however, knew that many other scientific men had bestowed their attention upon the subject, and for various causes had been unable to exhibit. They therefore proposed the same subject for the competition of 1771, and in 1773 they doubled the prize.

F. Berthould imagined that he had reached perfection, but his watch had still to be tested by the trial of a long sea voyage.

The *Isis* a frigate of eighteen guns, was equipped at Rochefort at the latter end of 1768, and placed under command of Chevalier d'Eveux de Fleurien, known later as Caret-de Fleurien. Fleurien, then a midshipman, was already, though only thirty years of age, a well known *savant*. We have already mentioned his name, and shall find further occasion to do so. At this juncture, fascinated by mechanics, Fleurien had assisted Berthould in his undertaking, but that his disinterestedness might be above suspicion, he selected several officers to assist him in observing the motions of the watch which was entrusted to him.

Starting in November, 1768, the *Isis* put in successively at Cadiz, the Canary Islands, Goree, the Cape Verde Islands, Martinique, St. Domingo, Terra Nuova, the Canaries, Cadiz again, and reached Aix Island on the 31st of October, 1769.

The watches, carried through climates alternately cold, hot, and temperate, had experienced every vicissitude of climate, and at the same time had been exposed to all the variations of the sea, in the roughest season of the year.

After this trial, which had redounded so much to his honour, Berthould obtained the rank and pension of an inspector of nautical watches.

This expedition had other results which concern us more particularly. Fleurien took a number of astronomical observations, and hydrographical surveys, which resulted in a well-founded condemnation of the maps of his country.

"For a long time," he says, in his account of his voyage, "I did not attempt criticism of the maps belonging to the Society; I wished to limit myself to giving new details by which they might be rectified; but I found such numberless and dangerous mistakes, that I should have considered myself culpable towards mariners if I had neglected fully to point them out."

A little further on he justly criticizes the maps of a geographer who had at one time been famous.

"I will not undertake," he says, "to enumerate all the errors which I have found in M. Bellin's maps. Their number is infinite. I shall content myself simply with proving the necessity for the work I did, by indicating the more glaring faults, either by comparing the positions of various places upon his maps, with the positions they should have occupied if M. Bellin had been willing to use the astronomical observations which have been published at various times; or by comparing other positions with those which we have determined by our own observations."

Lastly, after giving a long list of errors in the situation of the most frequented places of Europe, of Africa and America, he winds up with these judicious words: –

"Upon glancing at a list of the various errors I have discovered in M. Bellin's maps, one is led to a reflection, sad but true and inevitable – if the maps of the best known part of the globe, and on which the greater number of observations have been taken, are so far from correct, what exactitude can we hope to find in maps representing less frequented shores and islands, drawn and arranged by guess-work?"

Up to this time the watches had been examined separately and by different judges. Now arose the question of submitting them simultaneously to the same test, and of seeing which would come out victorious.

For this purpose the frigate *La Flore* was equipped at Brest, and the command was given to a most distinguished officer, Verdun de la Crenne, who was to become vice-admiral in 1786. The various stages of the expedition were Cadiz, Madeira, the Salvage Islands, Teneriffe, Goree, Martinique, Terra Nuova, Iceland – which our explorers had some trouble to find – the Faroe Islands, Denmark and Dunkerque. The narrative published by Verdun de la Crenne, like that of Fleurien, abounds in rectifications of every kind. It is easy to see how carefully and exactly the soundings were taken, with what care the coasts were surveyed; but not little interesting also is that which is altogether wanting in Fleurien's publication, descriptions of the countries and critical reflections upon the manners and customs of the different peoples visited.

Amongst the most interesting particulars contained in two large 4to volumes, we must mention those relating to the Canary Islands and their ancient inhabitants the Serères and Yolof, on Iceland, and the accurate remarks made by Verdun upon the subject of the meridian of Faroe Islands.

"It was the most easterly meridian of these islands," he says, "that Ptolemy chose for the first meridian. It would doubtless have been easy for him to have selected Alexandria for the first meridian; but this great man was aware that such a choice would bring no real honour to his country, that Rome and other ambitious towns might covet this imaginary glory, that every geographer, every narrator of voyages, arbitrarily choosing his own meridian, would engender confusion or at least embarrassment in the mind of the reader."

Clearly Verdun regarded the question of the first meridian from a high standpoint, as all really disinterested minds still do. It gives him yet another claim to our sympathy.

Let us conclude with a quotation from this author: "The watches came out of the contest with honour. They had borne heat and cold, they had been becalmed, they had endured shocks as well as the vessel which carried them when it was wrecked at Antigua, and when it received charges of artillery. In a word, they fulfilled the hopes we had indulged, they deserve the confidence of navigators, and lastly they are of great service in the determination of longitude at sea."

The solution of the problem was found!

## II.

The Expedition of La Perouse – St. Catherine's Island – Conception Island – The Sandwich Islands – Survey of the American coast – French Port – Loss of two boats – Monterey and the Indians of California – Stay at Macao – Cavite and Manilla – *En route* for China and Japan – Formosa – Quelpaert Island – The coast of Tartary – Ternay Bay – The Tartars of Saghalien – The Orotchys – Straits of La Perouse – Ball at Kamschatka – Navigator Islands – Massacre of M. de Langle and several of his companions – Botany Bay – No news of the Expedition – D'Entrecasteaux sent in search of La Perouse – False News – D'Entrecasteaux Channel – The coast of New Caledonia – Land of the Arsacides – The natives of Bouka – Stay in Port Carteret – Admiralty Islands – Stay at Amboine – Lewin Land – Nuyts Archipelago – Stay in Tasmania – Fête in the Friendly Islands – Particulars of the stay of La Perouse at Tonga Tabou – Stay at Balado – Traces of La Perouse in New Caledonia – Vanikoro – Sad fate of the Expedition.

The result of Cook's voyage, except the fact of his death, was still unknown, when the French government resolved to make use of the leisure which the peace just concluded had secured to the navy. The French officers, desirous of emulating the success of their old rivals the English, were fired with a noble emulation to excel them in some new field. The question arose as to the fittest person for the conduct of an important expedition. There was no lack of deserving candidates. Indeed, in the number lay the difficulty.

The Minister's choice fell upon Jean François Galaup de la

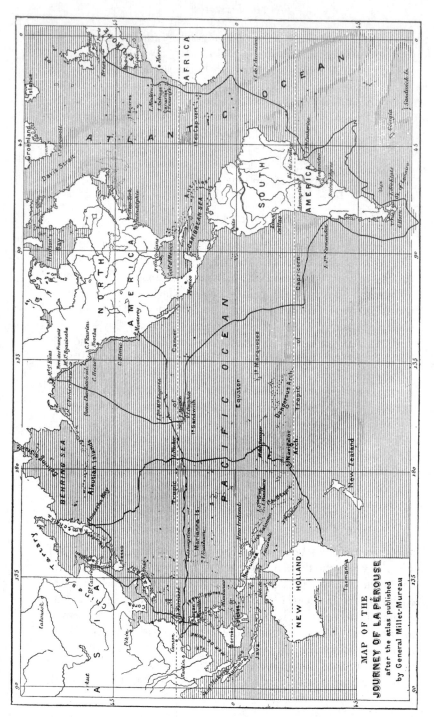

Journey of La Pérouse.

Perouse, whose important military services had rapidly advanced him to the rank of captain. During the last war he had been intrusted with the difficult mission of destroying the English posts in Hudson's Bay, and in this task he had proved himself not only an able soldier and sailor, but a man who could combine humanity with professional firmness. Second to him in the command was M. de Langle, who had ably assisted him in the expedition to Hudson's Bay.

A large staff embarked upon the two frigates *La Boussole* and *L'Astrolabe*. On board the *Boussole* were La Perouse; Clenard, who was made captain during the expedition: Monneron, an engineer; Bernizet, a geographer; Rollin, a surgeon; Lepante Dagelet, an astronomer of the Academy of Sciences; Lamanon, a physicist; Duché de Vancy and Prevost the younger, draughtsmen; Collignon, a botanist; and Guéry, a clock maker. The *Astrolabe*, in addition to her commander, Captain de Langle, carried Lieutenant de Monte, who was made captain during the voyage, and the celebrated Monge, who, fortunately for the interests of science, landed at Teneriffe upon the 30th of August, 1785.

The Academy of Sciences and the Society of Medicine had drawn up reports for the Minister of Marine, in which they called the attention of the navigators to certain points. Lastly, Fleurien, the superintendent of ports and naval arsenals, had himself drawn up the maps for the service of the expedition, and added to it an entire volume of learned notes, and discussions upon, the results of all known voyages since the time of Christopher Columbus.

The two ships carried an enormous amount of merchandise for trade, as well as a vast quantity of provisions and stores, a twenty-ton boat, two sloops, masts, and reserve sets of sails and rigging.

The two frigates sailed upon the 1st of August, 1785, and anchored off Madeira thirteen days later.

The French were at once charmed and surprised at the kind and cordial welcome accorded them by the English residents. Upon the 19th La Perouse put into Teneriffe.

"The various observations," he says, "made by MM. de Fleurien, Verdun, and Borda, upon Madeira, the Salvage Islands, and Teneriffe leave nothing to be wished for. Our attention was therefore confined to testing our instruments."

This remark proves that La Perouse was capable of doing justice to his predecessors. And we shall have other opportunities of observing that quality in him.

While the astronomers devoted themselves to estimating the regularity of the astronomical watches, the naturalists, with several officers, ascended the Peak, and collected some curious plants. Monneron succeeded in measuring this mountain with much greater accuracy than his predecessors, Herberdeen, Feuillée, Bouguer, Verdun, and Borda, who calculated its height respectively at 2,409, 2,213, 2,100, and 1,904 fathoms. Unfortunately his work, which would have settled the discussion, never reached France.

Upon the 16th of October, the isles, or rather rocks, of Marten Vas were seen. La Perouse ascertained their position, and afterwards made for the nearest, Trinity Island, which was only some nine leagues to the west. The commander of the expedition sent a sloop on shore in charge of an officer, in the hope of finding water, wood, and provisions. The officer had an interview with the Portuguese governor, whose garrison consisted of about two hundred men, fifteen of whom wore uniforms, and the rest merely shirts. The poverty of the land was obvious, and the French re-embarked without having obtained anything.

After a vain search for Ascension Island, the expedition reached Saint Catherine's Island, off the coast of Brazil.

"After ninety-six days' navigation," we read in the narrative of the voyage published by General Millet-Mureau, "we had not one case of illness on board. The health of the crew had remained unimpaired by change of climate, rain, and fog; but our provisions were of first-class quality; I neglected none of the precautions which experience and prudence suggested to me; and above all, we kept up our spirits by encouraging dancing every evening among the crew, whenever the weather permitted, from eight o'clock till ten."

Saint Catherine's Island, of which we have more than once had occasion to speak in the course of this narrative, extends from 27° 19' 10" S. lat. to 27° 49'. It is only two leagues wide, and is divided in its narrowest part from the mainland by a channel of two hundred fathoms. The town of Nostra Señora del Desterra, the capital of the colony, where the governor resides, is built at the point of this narrow entrance. The population amounts, at the utmost, to three thousand, and there are about four hundred houses. The appearance of the town is very pleasant. According to Frezier's account, this island was a refuge in 1712 for the vagabonds who fled there from different parts of Brazil. They were Portuguese subjects in name only, and recognized no other authority. The country is so fertile that the inhabitants can live quite independently of any neighbouring

Portrait of La Pérouse
(Facsimile of early engraving.)

colony. The ships in the harbour gave them shirts and coats, of which they had absolutely none, in exchange for provisions.

This island is extremely fertile, and the soil could easily be made to grow sugar-cane, but the inhabitants are so poor that they cannot buy the needful slaves for the labour.

The French vessels found all that they needed in this spot, and their officers were cordially received by the Portuguese authorities.

The following fact will give an idea of the hospitality of these people. "My boat," says La Perouse, "having been upset in a creek where I was having wood cut, the inhabitants, after assisting in saving it, insisted on our shipwrecked sailors using their beds, and themselves slept on mats upon the floor of the room where they received them so hospitably. A few days later they brought to my vessel the sails, mast, grapnel, and flag of the boat, which would have been of great use to them for their pirogues."

The *Boussole* and the *Astrolabe* weighed anchor upon the 19th of November, and directed their course to Cape Horn. After a violent storm, during which the frigates behaved very well, and after forty days' fruitless search for the large island discovered by a Frenchman, Antoine de la Roche, and called Georgia by Captain Cook, La Perouse crossed the Straits of Lemaire. Finding the winds favourable, he decided not to remain in Good Success Bay at this advanced season of the year, but immediately to double Cape Horn, in the hope of avoiding a possible delay that would have exposed his ships to injury and his crew to useless fatigue.

The friendly demonstrations of the Fuegians, the abundance of whales, which had never before been disturbed, the immense flocks of albatross and petrels, did not change his resolve. Cape Horn was rounded more easily than could have been expected. Upon the 9th of February the expedition was in the Straits of Magellan, and upon the 24th anchor was cast in Concepcion Harbour, which La Perouse preferred to that of Juan Fernandez, on account of the exhaustion of his provisions. The robust health of the crews astonished the Spanish governor. Possibly this was the first time a vessel had rounded Cape Horn and arrived in Chili without any sick on board.

The town, which was destroyed by an earthquake in 1757, had been rebuilt three leagues from the sea, upon the shore of the river Biobio. The houses are of one storey, and the town of La Concepcion contains ten thousand inhabitants. The bay is one of the most commodious in the world; the sea is smooth, and almost free from currents. This part of Chili is wonderfully fertile. One ear

Costumes of the inhabitants of Concepcion.

of corn reproduces sixty; vines are equally prolific; and the country teems with innumerable flocks, which multiply beyond all credence.

In spite of these prosperous conditions the country made no progress, on account of the prohibitive system which at this time prevailed. Chili, with its productions, which might easily have fed the half of Europe; its wool, which might have sufficed for the manufactures of France and England; its meats, which might have been preserved – had no commerce whatever. At the same time the duty upon imported goods was excessive, so that living was very dear. The middle class, as the "bourgeoisie" are now called, did not exist; the population consisted of two classes, the rich and the poor, as the following passage shows: –

"The dress of the women consists of a plaited skirt, of the ancient gold or silver tissues which were formerly manufactured at Lyons. These petticoats, which are kept for grand occasions, are often inherited like diamonds, and are handed down from generation to generation. They are only worn by a small number of the higher class; the others have scarcely the means of clothing themselves at all."

We will not follow La Perouse into his details of the enthusiastic reception given to him, and we will pass over in silence his description of balls and toilettes, which never for a moment induced him to lose sight of the object of his voyage. So far the expedition had only passed through regions often before visited by Europeans. It was now about to penetrate to less-known realms. Anchor was raised upon the 15th of March, and, after a voyage entirely free from incident, the two frigates anchored upon the 9th of April in Cook's Bay, Easter Island.

La Perouse affirms that Mr. Hodges, the painter, who accompanied the celebrated English navigator, has given a very unjust representation of the inhabitants. Generally their physiognomies are pleasing, but they cannot be said to have much character.

This is by no means the only point upon which the French navigator differs from Captain Cook. He believed the famous statues, of which one of the draughtsmen made an excellent sketch, to have been the work of the present generation, whose numbers he estimates at two thousand. It appeared to him also that the absolute lack of trees, and therefore of lakes and rivers, was due to the extravagant waste of wood by the earlier races. No disagreeable incident occurred during the stay. Robberies, it is true, were frequent; but as the French intended remaining only one day on the island, they thought it superfluous to give the population stricter ideas of honesty.

Inhabitants of Easter Island.

After leaving Easter Island, upon the 10th of April, La Perouse followed much the same route as Cook had done in 1777, when he sailed from Tahiti to the American coast; but he was a hundred leagues farther west. La Perouse indulged in the hope of making discoveries in this little-known region of the Pacific Ocean, and he promised to reward the sailor who should first sight land. Upon the 29th of May the Hawaian archipelago was reached.

The naval watches proved of great assistance upon this occasion, and justified the opinion entertained of them. Upon reaching the Sandwich Islands La Perouse found a difference of five degrees between the longitude given and that obtained by him. Without the watches he would have placed this group five degrees too far east. This explains why the islands discovered by the Spanish – Mendana, Queros, &c. – are much too near the American coast, and also the non-existence of the group called by the Spaniards La Mesa, Los Majos, and La Disgraceada, which there is every reason to suppose was none other than the Sandwich archipelago, as Mesa in Spanish means "table", and Captain King compares the mountain called Mauna Loa to a plateau or table-land. He did not, however, trust to conjecture; he crossed the reputed site of Los Majos, and found not the slightest trace of land.

"The aspect of Monee," says La Perouse, "is delightful. We saw water tumbling in cascades from the summit of the mountains, and reaching the sea after watering the Indian plantations, of which there are so many that each village extends over three or four leagues. All the huts are, however, on the sea-shore; and the mountains are so close that the habitable portion of the land appeared to me to be less than half a league in depth. One must be a sailor, and, like us, have been reduced to a bottle of water per day in a burning climate, to realize the sensations we experienced. The trees which crowned the mountains, the green fields, the banana-trees which surrounded the dwelling, all combined to charm our senses with an inexpressible delight; but the sea broke violently on the shore, and, like Tantalus, we were obliged to devour with our eyes what was completely beyond our reach."

The two frigates had no sooner anchored than they were surrounded by pirogues, full of natives, offering pigs, potatoes, bananas, "taro", &c. Clever traders, they attached most value to bits of old iron rings. Their acquaintance with iron and its use, for which they were not indebted to Cook, is a another proof that this people had known the Spaniards, to whom the discovery of the group is probably due.

The welcome accorded to La Perouse was most cordial, in spite of the military force by which he had thought proper to protect himself. Although the French were the first to land on Monee Island, La Perouse did not think it his duty to take possession.

"The usual European custom in such matters," he says, "is perfectly ridiculous. Philosophers may well sigh when they see men, simply because they have guns and bayonets, thinking nothing of sixty thousand of their fellow-men, and, without the least respect for the most sacred rights, looking upon a land whose inhabitants have cultivated it in the sweat of the brow, and whose ancestors he buried there, as an object fit for conquest."

La Perouse does not pause to give any details about the inhabitants of the Sandwich Islands. He only passed a few hours there, whilst the English remained for four months. He therefore rightly refers to Captain Cook's narrative.

During their short stay the French bought more than a hundred pigs, mats, fruits, a pirogue, ornaments made of feathers and shells, and handsome helmets decorated with feathers.

The instructions furnished La Perouse before his departure enjoined him to survey the American coast, of which a portion, extending to Mount Elias had, with the exception of Nootka port, been merely sighted by Captain Cook.

On the 23rd of June he reached 60° N. lat., and, in the midst of a long chain of snow-covered mountains, recognized the Mount Elias of Behring. After skirting along the coast for some time, La Perouse sent three boats, under command of one of his officers, M. de Monte, who discovered a large bay, to which he gave his name.

Following the coast at a short distance, surveys were taken, which were uninterrupted as far as an important river, which received the name of Behring. Apparently it was that to which Cook had given this name.

Upon the 2nd of July, in 58° 36' lat., and 140° 3' long., what appeared to be a fine bay was discovered. Boats, under command of MM. de Pierrevert, de Flassan, and Boutevilliers, were sent to examine it.

Their report being favourable, the two frigates arrived at the entrance of the bay, but the *Astrolabe* was driven back to the open sea by a strong current, and the *Boussole* was forced to join her. At six o'clock in the morning, after a night passed under sail, the vessels again approached the bay. "But," says the narrative, "at seven in the morning, when we were close to it, the wind veered so suddenly to

W.N.W. and N.N.W., that we were forced to give way, and even to bring our ships to the wind. Fortunately the tide carried our frigates into the bay, and we escaped the rocks on the east by half a pistol's range. I anchored in three and a half fathoms, with a rocky bottom, half a cable's length from shore. The *Astrolabe* had anchored in the same depth, and upon a similar bottom. In all the thirty years I have spent at sea, I have never seen two vessels in greater danger. Our situation would have been safe had we not anchored upon a rocky bottom, which extended several cables' length around us, and which was different from what MM. de Flasson and Boutevilliers had reported. We had no time to make reflections; it was above everything necessary to get out of our dangerous anchorage, to which the rapidity of the current was a great obstacle." However, by dint of much skilful tacking, La Perouse succeeded.

Ever since their entry into the bay the vessels had been surrounded by pirogues swarming with savages. The natives showed a decided preference for iron, in exchange for fish and the skins of otters and other animals. After a few days' stay their number increased rapidly, and they became, if not dangerous, at least a nuisance.

La Perouse established an observatory upon one of the islands in the bay, and set up tents for the sail makers and smiths. Although these posts were most carefully watched, the natives, gliding along the ground like snakes, scarcely stirring a leaf, managed in spite of our sentinels to commit various thefts; and one night they were clever enough to enter the tent where MM. de Launston and Darbaud (who were in charge of the observatory) slept. They carried off a silver-mounted gun, as well as the clothes belonging to the two officers, who had placed them for safety under their pillows. They escaped the notice of a guard of twelve men, and the two officers were not even awakened.

But now the stay of the expedition in this port drew to a close. The soundings, surveys, plans, and astronomical observations were completed; but, before finally leaving the island, La Perouse wished thoroughly to explore the depths of the bay. He imagined that some large river must empty itself into it, which would enable him to penetrate into the interior; but in all the openings he entered he found only vast glaciers, which extended to the very summit of Fair Weather Mount.

No accident or sickness marred the success which had so far attended the expedition.

Typical native of the Port des Français.

"We thought ourselves," says La Perouse, "the most fortunate of navigators, for having reached so great a distance from Europe without having had one invalid or a single sufferer from scurvy. But the greatest misfortune, and one it was impossible to foresee, now awaited us."

Upon the chart of the Port des Français, drawn up by MM. Monneron and Bernizet, the soundings alone remained to be indicated. The naval officers were bound to accomplish the task, and three boats, under the orders of MM. d'Escures, de Marchainville, and Boutin, were selected for the undertaking. La Perouse, acquainted with the somewhat rash zeal of M. d'Escures, advised him on the eve of departure to act with most careful prudence, and only to attempt the soundings in the channel if the sea were smooth.

The boats left at six o'clock in the morning. It was as much a party of pleasure as of duty, as the crews were to hunt, and breakfast under the trees.

"At ten in the morning," says La Perouse, "I saw our little boat return. Somewhat surprised, for I had not expected it so soon, I asked M. Boutin, before he came on deck, whether he had any news. At first I feared an attack from the natives, and M. Boutin's expression was not calculated to reassure me, for it was profoundly sad.

"He soon related to me the terrible disaster he had just witnessed, and from which he had escaped by the presence of mind which enabled him to see the best course to pursue in the dreadful peril. Carried, whilst following his commander, into the midst of breakers caused by the tide rushing with a speed of three or four leagues per hour out of the channel, he thought he could place his boat stern on the breakers; the boat yielding to their force, and being impelled by the tide, would not fill, but would be carried safely outside.

"Soon, however, he saw breakers ahead of his boat, and found himself in the open sea. More concerned for the safety of his companions than for his own, he again approached the breakers, and in the hope of saving some life he again braved them, but was repulsed by the tide; finally, he mounted on M. Mouton's shoulder, in the hope of finding a wider opening. All was in vain; everything had been swallowed up, and M. Boutin returned with the ebb of the tide.

"The sea becoming quieter, this officer had still some hope of finding the boat of the *Astrolabe*; he had only witnessed the loss of ours. M. de Marchainville was now a quarter of a mile from the danger, that is to say, in a sea as still as the quietest harbour; but, impelled by an imprudent generosity – for all help was quite impossible under the circumstances – this rash young officer, being too high-spirited and too courageous to pause in presence of his friends' danger, flew to their help, threw himself among the breakers, and, a victim to his imprudence and disregard of his chief's orders, perished with him.

"M. de Langle shortly after came on board my ship, as much overcome as myself, and informed me with tears that the misfortune was even greater than I had supposed. We had always made a point, ever since leaving France, of never allowing the two brothers, M. la Borde Marchainville and M. la Borde Boutevilliers, to go on the same service, but on this one occasion he had yielded, as they desired to hunt together; and it was almost wholly on this account that we had, both of us, directed our boats in the way we did, thinking there was as little danger as there is in Brest Harbour in fine weather.

"Several boats were at once despatched in search of the ship-wrecked crew. Rewards were offered to the natives if they saved any one; but the return of the sloops destroyed all hope. All had perished."

Eighteen days after this catastrophe, the two frigates left the Port des Français. La Perouse erected a monument to the memory of his unfortunate countrymen, in the middle of the bay, on an island which he called the Cenotaph. It bore the following inscription: –

"At the entrance of this port, twenty-one brave sailors perished.
Whoever you are, mingle your tears with ours."

A bottle, containing an account of this deplorable accident, was buried at the foot of the monument.

The Port des Français, which is situated in 58° 37 N. lat., and 139° 50' W. long., presents many advantages, but also many inconveniences – foremost amongst them the currents of the channel. The climate is much milder than in Hudson's Bay, which is in the same latitude. The vegetation is vigorous; pines six feet in girth, and a hundred and forty in height, are not rare. Celery, sorrel, lupine, wild pea, chicory, and mimulus are met with in every direction, as well as many pot-herbs, the use of which helped to keep the crews in health.

Shipwreck of French boats outside the Port des Français.
(Facsimile of early engraving.)

The sea supplied abundance of salmon, trout, cod, and plaice.

In the woods are found black and brown bears, the lynx, ermine, weasel, minever, squirrel, marmot, beaver, fox, elk, and the wild goat. The most precious skins are those of the otter, wolf, and sea-bear.

"But if the vegetable and animal productions of this country," says La Perouse, "are similar to those of many others, its aspect cannot be compared with them, and I doubt whether the deep valleys of the Alps and Pyrenees offer so terrible, and at the same time so picturesque, a prospect. Were it not at one of the extremities of the world, it should be visited by every one."

As to the inhabitants, La Perouse gives an account of them which is worth preserving.

"The Indians in their pirogues surrounded our frigates, hovering about for three or four hours before beginning to exchange a few fish, or two or three otter skins; they seized every opportunity of robbing us; they tore off all the iron which could be easily carried away, and they took every precaution to elude our vigilance at night. I invited some of the principal personages on board my frigate, and loaded them with presents; and the very men I distinguished in this manner did not scruple to steal a nail or an old pair of trousers. Whenever they assumed a particularly lively and pleasant air, I was convinced that they had committed a theft, and I often pretended not to see it."

The women make an opening in the thick part of the lower lip, the whole length of the jaw. They wear a sort of wooden bowl without a handle, which rests on the gums, "to which this split lip forms an outer cushion, in such a way that the lower part of the mouth protrudes some two or three inches".

The forced stay which La Perouse had just made in Port des Français prevented his stopping elsewhere and reconnoitring the indentations of the coast, for at all hazards he was to reach China during the month of February, in order to secure the following summer for the survey of the coast of Tartary.

He successively reconnoitred, upon this coast, Cross Sound, where the high snow-covered mountains cease, Cook's Island Bay, Engamio Cape, low land partly submerged and containing Mount Hyacinthine, Mount Edgecomb of Cook, Norfolk Sound, where the following year the English navigator Dixon was to anchor, ports Neeker and Guibert, Cape Tschiri-Kow, Croyère Islands, so called after the brother of the famous geographer Delisle, companion of Tschiri-Kow, the San Carlos Islands, La Touche Bay, and Cape Hector.

La Perouse imagined that these various coast lines were formed by a vast archipelago; and in this he was correct. They contained George III.'s Island, Prince of Wales and Queen Charlotte's Islands Cape rector forming the southern extremity of the latter.

The season was far advanced, and too short a time remained at La Perouse's disposal to allow of his making detailed observations of these countries; but his instinct had justly led him to imagine that the series of points he had discovered indicated a group of islands, and not a continent. Beyond Cape Fleurien, which formed the extremity of an elevated island, he passed several groups, which he named Sartines, and then returning, he reached Nootka Sound on the 25th of August. He afterwards visited various parts of the continent which Cook had been unable to approach, and which had left a blank on his chart. This navigation was attended with a certain amount of danger, on account of the currents, "which rendered it impossible to make more than three knots an hour at a distance of five leagues from land".

Upon the 5th of September new islets were discovered, about a league from Cape Blanco, to which the captain gave the name of Necker Islands. The fog was very thick, and more than once the fear of running upon some islet or rock, the existence of which could not be suspected, obliged the vessels to deviate from the land. Until they reached Monterey Bay the weather continued bad. At that port La Perouse found two Spanish vessels.

At this time Monterey Bay abounded in whales, and the sea was literally covered with pelicans, which were very common upon the Californian coast.

A garrison of two hundred and eighty men was sufficient to keep in order a population of fifty thousand Indians, wandering about this part of America. It must be admitted that these Indians were usually small and insignificant, and not endowed with that love of independence which characterizes the northern tribes; and, unlike them they have no appreciation of art, and no industry.

"These Indians," says the narrative, "are very expert in the use of the bow and arrow. They killed the smallest birds in our presence. It is true that they approach them with wonderful patience, hiding themselves, gliding, somehow, close to their prey, and aiming at them only when within fifteen paces.

"Their skill in the capture of larger animals is even more wonderful. We saw an Indian with a stag's head over his own, walking on all fours, appearing to graze, and carrying out the pantomime

"An Indian with a stag's head over his own."

with such truth to life that our hunters would have fired at him at thirty paces had they not been prevented. By this means the natives approach quite close to a herd of deer, and then kill them with arrows."

La Perouse gave many details of the presidency of Loretto and of the Californian missions, but these are rather of historical interest, and are out of place in a work of this kind. His remarks upon the fertility of the country are more within our programme. "The harvest of maize, barley, corn, and peas," he says, "is comparable only to that of Chili. Our European husbandmen could not conceive of such abundance. The most moderate yield of corn is at the rate of from seventy and eighty to one, and the largest from sixty to a hundred."

Upon the 22nd of September the two frigates returned to sea after a cordial welcome from the Spanish governor and the missionaries. They carried with them a quantity of provisions of all sorts, which would be of the greatest value to them during the long trip to be taken before reaching Macao.

The portion of the ocean now to be crossed by the French was almost unknown. The Spaniards had navigated it previously, but their political jealousy prevented their publishing the discoveries and observations they had made. La Perouse wished to steer S.W. as far as 28° lat., where some geographers had placed the island of Nuestra Señora-de-la-Gorta.

But he looked for it in vain during a long and difficult cruise, with contrary winds, which sorely tried the patience of the navigators.

"We were daily reminded," he says, "by the condition of our sails and rigging, that we had been sixteen months at sea. Our ropes gave way, and the sail makers could not repair the sails, which were fairly worn out."

Upon the 6th of November a small island, or rather rock, some five hundred fathoms long, upon which not a single tree-grew, and which was thickly covered with guano, was discovered. It was named Necker Island, and is in 166° 52' long. W. of Paris, and 23° 34' N. lat.

Never had the expedition, seen a more lovely sea, or a more exquisite night, when suddenly, at about half-past one in the morning, breakers were perceived two cable lengths ahead of the *Boussole*. The sea, only broken here and there by a slight ripple, was so calm that it scarcely made any sound. The ship's course was altered immediately; but the manœuvre took time, and when it was accomplished the vessel was but a cable's length off the rocks.

"We had just escaped one of the most imminent dangers to which navigators are subject," says La Perouse, "and I must do my crews the justice to say that less disorder and confusion in such a position would have been impossible. The slightest neglect in the execution of the manœuvres which were necessary to carry us from the breakers would have been fatal."

These rocks were unknown; it was therefore needful to determine their exact position, for the safety of succeeding navigators. La Perouse, after fulfilling this duty, named them the "Reef of the French Frigates".

Upon the 14th of December the *Astrolabe* and the *Boussole* sighted the Mariana Islands. A landing was effected upon the volcanic island of Assumption. Here the lava had formed ravines and precipices, bordered by a few stunted cocoa-nut trees, alternately with tropical creepers and a few shrubs. It was almost impossible to advance a couple of hundred yards in an hour. Landing and re-embarkation were difficult, and the few cocoa-nut shells and bananas, of a new variety, which the naturalists obtained, were not worth the risk.

It was impossible to remain longer in this archipelago if China were to be reached before the vessels returned to Europe. They were to take back an account of the results of the expedition upon the American coast, and of the crossing to Macao.

After taking the position of the Bashees, without stopping, La Perouse sighted the coast of China, and next day cast anchor in the roadstead of Macao.

Here La Perouse met with a small French cutter, commanded by M. de Richery, midshipman, whose business it was to cruise about the eastern coast, and protect French trade.

The town of Macao is so well known that it is needless for us to give La Perouse's description of it. The constant outrages and humiliations to which Europeans were daily subjected under the most despotic and cowardly government in the world, aroused the indignation of the French captain, and made him heartily wish that an international expedition might put a stop to so intolerable a state of things.

The furs which had been collected upon the American coasts were sold at Macao for ten thousand piastres. The sum produced should have been divided among the crews, and the head of the

Swedish company undertook to ship it at Mauritius; but the unfortunate sailors themselves were never to receive the money.

Leaving Macao on the 5th of February, the vessels directed their course to Manilla, and, after sighting the shoals of Pratas, Bulinao, Manseloq, and Marivelle, wrongly placed upon D'Apres' maps, they were forced to put into the port of Marivelle, to wait for better winds and more favourable currents. Although Marivelle is only one league to windward of Cavito, three days were consumed in reaching the latter port.

"We found," says the narrative, "different houses where we could repair our sails, salt our provisions, construct two boats, lodge the naturalists and geographical engineers, and the governor kindly lent us his own for the establishment of our observatory. We enjoyed as much liberty as if we had been in the country; and in the market and arsenal we found the same resources as in the best European ports."

Cavito, the second town of the Philippine islands, and the capital of the province of the same name, was then but a miserable village, where only Spanish military and government officers resided; but although the town was nothing but a mass of ruins, it was none the less a port, and afforded the French every possible resource. Upon the morrow of his arrival La Perouse, accompanied by De Langle and his principal officers, paid a visit to the governor, reaching Manila by boat.

"The environs of Manila are delightful," he says. "A most beautiful river flows through it, separating into different canals, one of which leads to the famous Bay Lake, which is distant seven leagues in the interior, surrounded by more than a hundred Indian settlements in the midst of a most fertile territory.

"Manila, built upon the shore of the bay of that name, which is more than twenty-five leagues in circumference, is at the mouth of a river navigable as far as the lake in which it rises. It is probably the most fortunately situated town in the whole world. Provisions are found there in the greatest profusion, and very cheap; but clothing, European cutlery, and furniture fetch an enormous price.

"Want of competition, the prohibitive tariffs, and commercial restrictions of every sort, tend to make the productions and manufactured goods of India and China at least as dear as in Europe; and although the various duties on imports bring to the treasury some eight hundred thousand piastres, the colony costs the Spanish government at least fifteen hundred thousand francs per annum, which are sent from Mexico. The immense possessions of the Spanish in America have prevented the government from bestowing much attention upon the Philippines. They are still like the possessions of great lords, which remain uncultivated, though they might provide fortunes for many families.

"I do not hesitate to state, that a great nation with no colony but the Philippine Islands, supposing that colony to be as well governed as possible, need not envy all the European colonies in Africa and America."

Upon the 9th of April – after having heard of the arrival at Macao of M. D'Entrecasteaux, who had come from Mauritius with the contrary monsoon, and received despatches from Europe by the frigate *La Subtile*, MM. Guyet, midshipman, and Le Gobien, naval officer, and a reinforcement of eight sailors – the two vessels set out for the coast of China.

Upon the 21st La Perouse sighted Formosa, and at once entered the channel which separates that island from China. He discovered a very dangerous bank unknown to navigators, and carefully examined the soundings and approaches. Shortly afterwards he passed in front of the bay of the ancient Dutch fort of Zealand, where the capital of the island, Tai-wan, is situated.

The monsoon was unfavourable for ascending the channel, and La Perouse therefore resolved to pass to the east of the island. He rectified the position of the Pescadores Islands, a mass of rocks which assume various shapes, reconnoitred the small island of Botol-Tabaco-Xima, where no navigator had landed, coasted Kinin Island, which forms part of the kingdom of Liken, whose inhabitants are neither Chinese nor Japanese, but appear to be of both races, and sighted Hoa-pinsu and Tiaoy-su Islands. The latter form part of the Liken Archipelago, known only through the letters of Father Goubil, a Jesuit.

The frigates then entered the Eastern Sea, and directed their course to the channel which divides China and Japan. La Perouse there encountered fogs as thick as those which prevail upon the coast of Labrador, with variable and violent currents. The first point of interest before entering the Sea of Japan was Quelpaert Island, first made known to Europeans by the shipwreck of the *Sparrow Hawk* upon its coast in 1635. La Perouse determined its southerly extremity, and surveyed it for a distance of twelve leagues.

"It is scarcely possible," he says, "to find an island of pleasanter aspect. A peak of about four thousand five hundred feet high, vis-

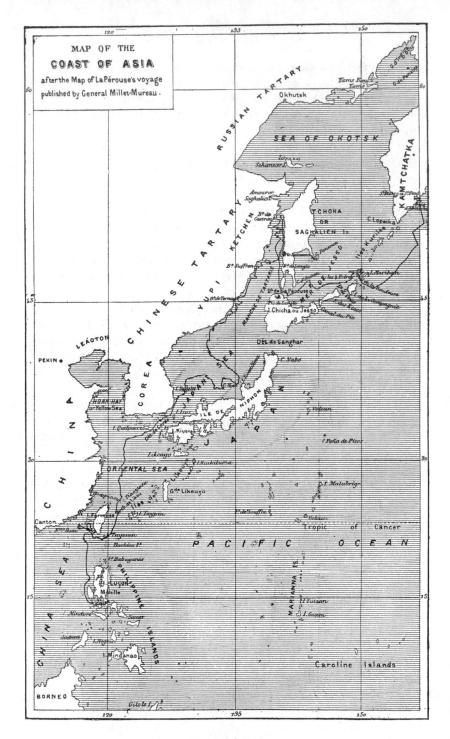

Coast of Asia.

ible at a distance of eighteen or twenty leagues, rises in the centre of the island; the land slopes gently from thence to the sea, so that the houses look like an amphitheatre. The soil seemed to be highly cultivated. By the aid of our glasses we clearly made out the divisions of the fields. They are in very small allotments, which augurs a large population. The different shades of the various cultivated patches give a very agreeable variety to the view."

The explorers had ample opportunity for taking the longitude and latitude, which was the more important, as no European vessel had navigated these seas, which were only indicated upon the maps in accordance with the Chinese and Japanese maps published by the Jesuits.

Upon the 25th of May the frigates entered the channel of Corea, which was minutely explored, and in which soundings were taken every half hour.

As it was possible to keep close in shore, it was easy to observe some fortifications in the European style, and to note all their details.

On the 27th an island was perceived which was not to be found upon any map, and which seemed to be about twenty leagues distant from the coast of Corea. It received the name of Dagelet Island.

The course was now directed towards Japan, but it was very slow, on account of the contrary winds that prevailed.

On the 6th of June Cape Noto and the island of Tsus Sima were discovered.

"Cape Noto, upon the Japanese coast," says La Perouse, "is a point on which geographers may rely. Reckoning from it, to Cape Kona on the eastern coast, the position of which was determined by Captain King, the width of the northern half of the empire may be ascertained. Our observations have the greater value for geographers as they determine the width of the Gulf of Tartary, to which I now directed my course."

Upon the 11th of June La Perouse sighted Tartary. He made land precisely at the boundary between the Corea and Manchuria. The mountains appeared to be six or seven thousand feet high. A small quantity of snow was visible on the summits. No trace of inhabitants or cultivation could be seen; nor was any river's mouth found, upon a length of coast extending for forty leagues. A halt would have been desirable, to enable the naturalists and lithologists to make observations.

"Up to the 14th of June the coast had run to the N.E. by N. We were now in 44° lat., and had reached the degree which geographers assign for the so-called Strait of Tessoy, but we were five degrees farther west than the longitude given for this spot. These five degrees should be taken from Tartary, and added to the channel which separates it from the islands north of Japan."

Whilst coasting along this shore no sign of habitation had been perceived – not a pirogue left the shore. The country, although covered with magnificent trees and luxuriant vegetation, appeared to be uninhabited.

On the 23rd of June the *Boussole* and the *Astrolabe* cast anchor in a bay situated in 45° 13' N. lat. and 135° 9' E. long. It was named Ternay Bay.

"We burned with impatience," says La Perouse, "to reconnoitre this land, which had occupied our imagination ever since we left France. It was the only portion of the globe which had escaped the indefatigable activity of Captain Cook; and perhaps we owe the small advantage of having first landed there to the sad event which ended his days.

"This roadstead was formed of five little creeks, separated one from the other by hillocks covered with trees of a more delicate and varied green than is to be seen in France in the brightest spring. Before our boats reached the shore, our glasses had been directed to the coast, but we perceived nothing but stags and bears, quietly grazing. Our impatience to disembark increased at the sight. The ground was carpeted with plants similar to those of our climate, but more vigorous and green; most of them were in flower. At every step we found roses, red and yellow lilies, lilies of the valley, and almost all our field flowers. The summits of the mountains were crowned with pines and oak-trees grew half way up, decreasing in size and vigour as they neared the sea. The rivers and streams were planted with willows, birches, and maples; and skirting the larger woods we saw apple-trees and azaroles in full bloom, as well as clumps of nut-trees, the fruit of which was beginning to form."

Upon returning from a fishing excursion the French met with a Tartar tomb. Curiosity induced them to open it, and they found in it two skeletons, lying side by side. The heads were covered with stuff caps, the bodies were wrapped in bearskins, and from the waists hung several little Chinese coins and copper ornaments. They also found half-a-score of silver bracelets, an iron hatchet, a knife, and other things, amongst which was a small bag of blue nankeen filled with rice.

Upon the morning of the 27th La Perouse left this solitary bay, after depositing there several medals, with an inscription giving the date of his arrival.

A little further on, more than eight hundred cod, which were at once salted, were caught, and an immense quantity of oysters with superb mother of pearl were also obtained.

After a stay in Saffren Bay, situated in 47° 51' N. lat. and 137° 2WE. long., La Perouse discovered, upon the 6th of July, an island, which was no other than Saghalien. The shore here was as wooded as that of Tartary. Lofty mountains arose in the interior, the highest of which was called Lamanon peak. As huts and smoke were seen, M. de Langle and several officers landed. The inhabitants had recently fled, for the ashes of their fires were scarcely cold.

Just as the French were re-embarking, after leaving some presents for the natives, a pirogue landed seven natives, who showed no signs of fear.

"Amongst them," says the narrative, "were two old men with long white beards, dressed in stuff made from the bark of trees, very like the cotton drawers worn in Madagascar. Two of the seven natives had coats of padded nankeen, differing little in shape from those of the Chinese. Others wore long gowns, which were fastened by means of a waist-belt and some little buttons, so that they had no need of drawers. Their heads were bare, but one or two of them wore bearskin bands. They had their forelocks and faces shaven, but the back hair kept about eight or ten inches long in a different fashion from the Chinese, however, who leave only a round tuft of hair, which they call 'pen-t-sec'. All had sealskin boots with the feet artistically worked *à la Chinoise*.

"Their weapons were bows, spears, and arrows, tipped with iron. The oldest of the natives, to whom the others showed the most respect, had his eyes in a dreadful state; he wore a shade round his head, to protect them from the sun. These natives were grave in manner, and friendly."

M. de Langle appointed a meeting for the morrow. La Perouse and most of his officers attended. The facts they learned about these Tartars were important, and decided La Perouse to pursue his discoveries further north.

"We succeeded in making them understand," he says, "that we wished them to draw their country, and that of Manchuria. One of the old men then arose, and with the point of his spear traced the coast of Tartary westward, running nearly N. and S. To the east, *vis-*

*à-vis* in the same direction, he represented his island, and, placing his hand upon his breast, made us understand that he had indicated his own country. He left an opening between his island and Tartary, and, pointing to our vessels, showed us by signs that they could pass through it. At the south island he delineated another, and left a second opening, indicating that this too was a route for our ships.

"His quickness in understanding us was great, but not equal to that of another islander, about thirty years of age, who, seeing that the figures traced on sand were rubbed out, took one of our pencils and some paper. He traced out his island, which he called Tchoka, and made a line for the little river upon the shore of which we were – placing it two-thirds of the length of the island from north to south. He then drew Manchuria, leaving, as the old man had done, a strait at the extreme end; and to our surprise he added the river Saghalien, the name of which the natives pronounce like ourselves. He placed the mouth of this river a little to the south of the northerly point of his island.

"We afterwards wished to ascertain whether this strait was very wide. We tried to make him understand our idea. He caught at it at once, and, placing his two hands upright at a distance of three inches one from the other, he made us understand that he meant to indicate the width of the little river which formed our watering place; and then, holding them wider apart, he indicated that the second width was to represent that of the river Saghalien; and, separating them still more, he gave the breadth of the strait which divides his country from Tartary.

"M. de Langle and I thought it of the greatest importance to ascertain whether the island we were coasting was that to which geographers had given the name of Saghalien, without guessing its extension southwards. I ordered all hands on board, and prepared to sail in the morning. The bay in which we had anchored received the name of Langle, from the captain who discovered it, and was the first to put foot on land.

"In another bay upon the same shore, called Estaing Bay, the boats landed close to ten or twelve huts. They were larger than those we before had seen, and were divided into two rooms. That at the back contained the stove, cooking utensils, and the bench running all round. That in front was absolutely bare, and probably destined for the reception of strangers. The women fled when they saw the French land. Two of them, however, were caught, and, whilst they were being re-assured, time was found to sketch them.

He traced the coast of Tartary.

Their faces were peculiar, but pleasant; they had small eyes and thick lips, the upper one being painted or tattooed."

M. de Langle found the natives gathered about four boats, that were loaded with smoked fish, which they were helping to put in water. They were Manchurians, from the shores of Saghalien River. In the corner of the island was a kind of circus, planted with fifteen or twenty stakes, each surmounted by the head of a bear. It was supposed, not without some show of reason, that these trophies were intended to pepetuate the memory of a victory over this wild beast.

Quantities of cod-fish were obtained upon this coast; and at the mouth of the river a prodigious quantity of salmon was caught. After reconnoitring the bay of La Jonquière, La Perouse cast anchor in Casters Bay. His water supply was nearly exhausted, and he had no more wood. The further he penetrated into the strait which separates Saghalien from the continent, the more the depth diminished. La Perouse, recognizing that he could not double the island of Saghalien by the north, and afraid of not being able to leave the defile in which he now found himself excepting by the strait of Sangaar, which was much further south, determined to remain only five days in Casters Bay, a period which he absolutely needed to take in provisions.

The observatory was set up in a small island, while the carpenters cut down wood, and the sailors filled the water-barrels.

"The huts of these islanders, who call themselves Orotchys," says the narrative, "are surrounded by a drying ground for salmon, which were exposed to the sun upon perches, after having been smoked for three or four days at the stove which is in the centre of the hut. The women who have charge of this operation take them, as soon as they are smoked through, into the open air, where they become as hard as wood.

"The natives joined us in our fishing with nets or hooks, and we saw them voraciously devouring the head, gills, and sometimes the skin, of raw salmon, tearing it up very cleverly. They sucked out the mucilage, much as we eat oysters. Their fish seldom reach the shore without having first paid toll, unless the catch is very large; and the women show the same eagerness to seize upon the whole fish, and in the same ravenous way devour the mucilaginous parts, which appear to be their tid-bits.

"These people are revoltingly dirty. It would be impossible to find a race farther removed from our ideas of beauty. In height they are less than four foot ten, their bodies are emaciated, their voices are weak and shrill like children's. They have projecting cheek-bones, bleared and sunken eyes, large mouths, flat noses, short and almost beardless chins, and olive skins, shining with oil and smoke. They allow their hair to grow long, and dress it somewhat in the European style. The women wear it loose over their shoulders, and the description we have given applies to them as well as to the men, from whom they are scarcely to be distinguished, except for a slight difference in their apparel. The women are not subject to any labour, which, as in the case of the American Indians, might have accounted for the inelegance of their appearance. All their time is occupied in cutting out and making their clothes, in drying fish and nursing their children, whom they suckle to the age of three or four years. It rather astonished me to see a child of this age, who had been shooting with bow and arrows, beating a dog, &c., throw himself upon his mother's bosom, and take the place of an infant of five or six months who was lying asleep upon her knees."

The Bitchys and the Orotchys confirmed much of the information which La Perouse had already obtained. From them he ascertained that the northern point of Saghalien was connected with the continent merely by a sand-bank, on which grew seaweed, and where there was but little water.

This concurrence of testimony left no room for doubt, especially as he never found more than six fathoms in the canal. There remained but one point of interest to determine, and that was the survey of the southern point of Saghalien, which he had only explored as far as Langle Bay in 47° 49'.

Upon the 2nd of August the *Astrolabe* and the *Boussole* left Casters Bay, and returned southwards, successively discovering and reconnoitring Monneron Island and Langle Peak, doubling the southern point of Saghalien called Cape Crillon, which led to a strait between Oku-Jesso and Jesso; this they named after La Perouse. Hitherto the geography of this part of the world had been most fanciful and imaginary. Sansen was of opinion that Corea was an island, and that Jesso, Oku-Jesso, and Kamschatka existed only in imagination; whilst Delisle insisted that Jesso and Oku-Jesso were merely an island, ending at Sangaar Strait; and lastly, Buache, in his "Considérations Géographiques", page 105, says, "Jesso, after being placed first in the east, then in the south, and finally in the west, was at last found to be in the north."

To this confusion the discoveries of the French expedition were destined to put an end.

Typical Orotchys.
(Facsimile of early engraving.)

La Perouse had some intercourse with the natives of Crillon Cape, and stated that they were handsome men, far more industrious than the Orotchys of Casters Bay, but less liberal in their dealings.

"They have," he says, one most important article of commerce – unknown in the channel of Tartary – from which they derive their riches, namely, whale oil. Of this they collect considerable quantities. They extract it in a way which is far from economical. They cut the flesh into pieces, and dry it upon a slope in the open air, by exposing it to the sun. The oil which flows from it is caught in vessels made of bark, or into bottles of dried scalskin."

After sighting the Cape Arniva of the Dutch, the vessels coasted along the barren, treeless, uninhabited country in possession of the Dutch Company, and shortly reached the Kurile Islands. They then passed between Marikon Island and the Island of the Four Brothers, calling the strait – the finest amongst the Kurile Islands, through which they penetrated – La Boudeuse.

On the 3rd of September the coast of Kamschatka was reached. This coast was uninviting enough. "There the eyes rest painfully, and often fearfully, upon enormous masses of rock, which are already covered with snow in the beginning of September, and which never appear to have had any vegetation."

Three days later Avatscha Bay, or the Bay of Saint Peter and Saint Paul, was reached. The astronomers at once proceeded to take observations; the naturalists made the perilous and arduous ascent of a volcano, some eight leagues inland; whilst those of the crew who were not engaged upon the vessels gave themselves up to hunting and fishing. Thanks to the welcome accorded by the governor, their pleasures were varied.

"We were invited," says La Perouse, "to a ball which the governor wished to give to all the women, whether from Kamschatka or Russia. If the ball was not large, it was at least mixed. Thirteen females, clothed in silk, ten of whom were natives of Kamschatka, with large faces, small eyes, and flat noses, were seated upon benches round the room. Both they and the Russians wore silk handkerchiefs wrapped round the head, in a way similar to those worn by mulattoes. The ball opened with Russian dances, the airs for which were very lively, and like those of the Cossack dances given a short time since in Paris. These were followed by Kamschatka dances, which were comparable only to the convulsionists of the famous tomb of Saint Médard. The dancers of this part of Asia scarcely require legs, they make such vigorous use of the shoulders and arms. The impression made upon the spectators by the convulsive and contorted movements of the Kamschatka dancers is painful, and is rendered more so by a pitiful cry which escapes them at intervals, and which is the sole music by which they measure their time. The exertions they made are so formidable that they are completely covered with sweat, and at the conclusion they lie upon the ground unable to move a limb. The exhalations from their bodies permeate the atmosphere with the smell of fish and oil, so strong as to be disagreeable to the unaccustomed nostrils of Europeans."

The arrival of a courier from Okotsk interrupted the ball. The news he brought was pleasant for every one, but particularly for La Perouse, who learned that he was promoted.

During their stay in this port, the navigators found the tomb of Louis Delisle de la Croyère, Member of the Academy of Sciences, who died in Kamschatka in 1741, upon his return from an expedition undertaken by command of the Czar for the survey of the American coast. His fellow-countrymen honoured his memory by placing an engraved copper slab over his grave. They paid the same homage to Captain Clerke, Captain Cook's second in command and successor.

"Avatscha Bay," says La Perouse, "is certainly the best, most commodious, and safest to be found in any part of the world. The entrance is narrow, and forts might easily be constructed to command vessels entering it. The anchorage is excellent, the bottom muddy; and two large harbours, one on the eastern shore and one on the west, would hold all the vessels of the French and English navy."

The *Boussole* and the *Astrolabe* set sail upon the 29th of September, 1787. M. de Lesseps, Vice-Consul for Russia, who had accompanied La Perouse thus far upon his expedition, was charged to return to France by land (at that time a most perilous journey), and to convey despatches, from the expedition to the government.

The question now arose of finding land discovered in 1620 by the Spaniards. The two frigates passed south of 37° 30' some three hundred leagues, without finding any trace of it. Crossing the line for the third time, they passed the site given by Byron as that of the Dangerous Islands, without finding them; and, upon the 6th of December, entered the Navigator Archipelago, the merit of discovering which belongs to Bougainville. The vessels were at once surrounded by pirogues. The natives who manned them did not give La Perouse a very favourable idea of the beauty of the inhabitants.

"I saw but two women," he says, "and they had no delicacy of feature; the younger, who may have been eighteen years of age, had a frightful ulcer upon her leg. Many of these islanders were covered with sores, which may have been the commencement of leprosy; for I noticed two men, whose ulcerated and swollen legs left no doubt as to their malady. They approached us fearlessly and unarmed, and appeared as peaceable as the natives of the Society or Friendly Islands."

Upon the 9th of December anchor was cast off Maouna Island. Next day the weather was so promising that La Perouse resolved to land to take in water, and then set sail at once, as the anchorage was too bad to admit of a second night's stay. Every precaution having been taken, La Perouse landed, and proceeded to the spot where his sailors were obtaining water. Captain Langle penetrated to a small creek about a league from the watering place, "and this excursion, from which he returned delighted with the beauty of the village he had seen, was, as will be seen, the cause of our misfortunes."

"Upon the shore, meantime, a brisk trade was going on. Men and women sold hens, parrots, fruits, and pigs. At the same time a native, getting into one of the sloops, possessed himself of a hammer, and commenced dealing vigorous blows upon a sailor's back. He was speedily seized, by four strong fellows, and thrown into the sea.

La Perouse penetrated into the interior, accompanied by women, old men, and children. He enjoyed a delightful excursion through a charming country, which rejoiced in the double advantage of a soil which required no culture, and a climate in which clothing was superfluous.

"Bread-fruits, cocoa-nuts, bananas, guavas, and oranges afforded a wholesome and sufficient nourishment to the inhabitants; while chickens, pigs, and dogs, which lived upon the surplus fruits, afforded the necessary change of diet.

"The first visit passed over without serious danger. There were a few quarrels, it is true; but, thanks to the prudence and reserve of the French, who kept on their guard, they did not amount to anything serious. La Perouse had given orders to re-embark, when M. de Langle insisted upon sending for a few more casks of water.

"He had adopted Captain Cook's views: he thought fresh water preferable to all other things which he had on board; and as some of his crew showed signs of scurvy, he was right in thinking that every help should be given them."

La Perouse from the first had a presentiment against consenting. But he yielded when M. de Langle persisted that a captain is responsible for the health of his crew, that the spot which he named was perfectly safe, that he himself would command the expedition, and that three hours would suffice for the work.

"M. de Langle," says the narrative, "was a man of so much judgment, that his representation influenced my decision more than anything else.

"Next day two boats, under command of M. Boutin and M. Mouton, conveying all the sufferers from scurvy, under charge of six armed soldiers and a captain, in all twenty-eight men, left the *Astrolabe*, to be under M. de Langle's orders. M. de Langle was accompanied in his boat by M. de Lauranon and M. Collinet, who were invalids, and M. de Varignas, who was convalescent. M. de Gobien commanded the sloop, M. de la Martinière, M. Lavant, and the elder Receveur, were amongst the thirty-three persons sent by the *Boussole*. The entire force amounted to sixty-one, and those the picked men of the expedition.

"M. de Langle ordered every one to be armed with guns, and six swivel-guns were placed in the sloop, M. de Langle and all his companions were greatly surprised when, instead of a large and commodious bay, they found a creek filled with coral, which it was only possible to reach through a tortuous channel, where the surf broke violently. M. de Langle had only seen this bay at high tide, and as soon as this new sight met his view his first idea was to regain the former watering-place.

"But the friendly appearance of the natives, the number of women and children he observed among them, the quantities of pigs and fruit they ofered for sale, put his prudent resolutions to flight.

"The water-casks of the four boats were landed quietly, the soldiers keeping order upon the shore, and forming a barrier which left a free space for the workers. But this peaceful condition of affairs did not last long. Many of the pirogues, having disposed of their wares to our vessels, returned to the shore, and, landing in the bay of our watering-place, it was soon entirely filled by them. In place of the two hundred natives, counting women and chil-

those who, less fortunate, had fallen overboard upon the side near the Indians, were killed instantaneously.

"The safety of forty-nine of the crew is due to the good order which M. de Varignas was wise enough to maintain, and to the punctuality with which M. Mouton, who commanded the boats of the *Boussole*, carried out his orders.

"The boat belonging to the *Astrolabe* was so overloaded that it grounded. The natives at once decided to harass the wounded in their retreat. They hastened in great numbers towards the reefs, within six feet of which the boats must necessarily pass. The little ammunition which remained was exhausted upon these savages, and the boats at last emerged from the creek."

La Perouse's first idea was naturally to avenge the death of his unfortunate companions; but M. de Boutin, who, although severely wounded, retained all his faculties, begged him to desist, representing to him that if by any mishap one of the boats ran aground, the creek was so situated, being bordered with trees which afforded secure shelter to the natives, that not a Frenchman would come back alive. La Perouse remained for two days upon the scene of this terrible disaster, without being able to gratify the vindictive desires of his crew.

"No doubt," says La Perouse, "it will appear incredible that during this time five or six pirogues left the shore, bringing pigs, pigeons, and cocoa-nuts, and offering them in exchange. I was forced to control myself, or I should have disposed of these natives summarily enough."

It may readily be supposed that an event which deprived La Perouse of a large number of officers, and of thirty-two of his best sailors, was calculated to upset the plans of the expedition. At the slightest approach of danger it would now be necessary to destroy one frigate, in order to arm the other. But one course remained for La Perouse – to set sail for Botany Bay, reconnoitring the various islands he passed, and taking their astronomical positions.

Upon the 14th of December, Oyolava, another island belonging to the same group, and which Bougainville had seen from a distance, was sighted. It was larger than Tahiti, and exceeded that island in beauty, fertility, and in the number of its inhabitants.

The natives resembled those of Maouna in every particular, and quickly surrounded the two frigates, offering the multifarious productions of their island. It appeared that the French must have been the first to trade with them, for they were quite unacquainted with

dren, whom De Langle had found an hour and a half previously, there were now, at the end of three hours, a thousand or twelve hundred.

"M. de Langle's situation became more perilous every moment. He succeeded, however, seconded by M. de Varignas, M. Boutin, M. Collier, and Gobien, in embarking the water-casks. But the bay was almost dry, and he could not hope to get his boats off before four o'clock in the afternoon. However, followed by his detachment, he attempted it, and, leading the way with his gun and the soldiers, he forbade firing until he should give the order.

"He felt that he would soon be forced to fire. Already stones were flying; and the Indians who were in shallow water surrounded the sloops for a distance of at least two hundred yards. The soldiers who were already in the boats tried in vain to drive them back.

"M. de Langle was anxious to avoid beginning hostilities, and fearful of being accused of barbarity; otherwise he would, no doubt, have ordered a general discharge, which would effectually have scattered the multitude. But he believed he could subdue the natives without bloodshed, and he was the victim of his humanity.

"Very soon a storm of stones, thrown at short distances with the force of a sling, struck almost all who were in the sloop. M. de Langle had only time to discharge his gun. He was thrown over and unfortunately fell outside the sloop. He was at once massacred by more than two hundred Indians, who assailed him with clubs and stones. As soon as he expired they fastened him by one arm to the sloop, no doubt with a view to despoiling the body.

"The sloop of *La Boussole*, under M. Boutin, was run aground within four yards of that of the *Astrolabe*, and parallel between them was a narrow channel not yet occupied by the Indians. By this outlet, all the wounded who were fortunate enough to avoid falling into the open sea, escaped by swimming. They reached our boats, which fortunately had remained afloat, and we succeeded in saving forty-nine out of the sixty-one men who had composed the expedition.

"M. Boutin had imitated M. de Langle. He would not fire, and only gave orders for a discharge after his commander's shot. Naturally, at the short distance of four or five paces, every shot killed an Indian; but there was no time to re-load. M. Boutin was knocked down by a stone, and fortunately fell between the two stranded boats. Those who had escaped by swimming towards the two boats had received many wounds, mostly on the head; whilst

the use or value of iron, and preferred a single coloured bead to a hatchet, or a nail six inches long.

Some of the women had pleasant features and elegant figures; their eyes were gentle, and their movements quiet, whilst the men were wild and fierce in appearance.

Pola Island, also belonging to the Navigator Archipelago, was passed upon the 17th of December. Probably the news of the massacre of the French had already reached this people, for no pirogue approached the vessels.

Cocoa-nut island and Schouten's Traitor island were recognized upon the 20th of December. The latter is divided by a strait, which the navigators would not have perceived, had they not coasted close in shore. About a score of natives appeared, bringing the finest cocoa-nuts La Perouse had ever seen, with a few bananas and one small pig.

These islands, which Wallis calls Boscawen and Keppel Islands, and which he places 1° 13' too far west, may also be considered part of the Navigator Archipelago. La Perouse considers the natives of this group as belonging to the finest Polynesian race. Tall, vigorous, and well-formed, they are of finer type than those of the Sandwich Islands, whose language is very similar to theirs. Under other circumstances, the captain would have proceeded to explore Oyolava and Pola Islands; but the memory of the disaster at Maouna was too recent, and he dreaded another encounter which might end in massacre.

"Painful associations," he says, "met us with every succeeding island. In the Recreation Islands, east of the Navigator Archipelago, Roggewein's crew had been attacked and stoned to death; at Traitor Island, which was now in sight, Schouten's crew were the victims; and in the south was Maouna Island, where we ourselves had met with so shocking a calamity.

"These recollections affected our way of dealing with the Indians. We now punished every little theft and injustice severely; we demonstrated by force of arms that flight would not save them from our vengeance; we refused to allow them to come on board, and threatened to punish all who did so without permission with death."

These remarks prove that La Perouse was right in preventing all intercourse between his crews and the natives. We cannot sufficiently praise the prudence and humanity of the commander who, in the excited condition of his men's minds, knew how to curb the desire for vengeance.

From the Navigator Islands the route was directed to the Friendly Archipelago, which Cook had been unable to explore entirely. Upon the 27th of December, Vavao Island was discovered, one of the largest of the group, which had not been visited by the English navigator. As large as Tonga Tabou, it is higher, and not wanting in fresh water. La Perouse reconnoitred many of these islands, and entered into relations with the natives, who, however, did not offer sufficient provisions to make it worth his while to trade. He therefore resolved upon the 1st of February, 1788, to go to Botany Bay, following a route not yet attempted by any navigator.

Pilstaart Island, discovered by Tasman – or rather, the rock of Pilstaart, for its entire length is but a quarter of a league – presents but a steep and broken appearance, and serves only as a resting-place for sea birds. On this account La Perouse, having no reason for remaining, wished to hasten on to New Holland; but there was another power to be consulted – the wind, and by it La Perouse was detained for three days before Pilstaart.

Norfolk Island and its two islets were sighted upon the 13th of January. La Perouse cast anchor within easy distance of shore, intending to allow the naturalists to land, and inspect the productions of the island; but the waves broke with such violence upon the beach that landing was impossible. Yet Cook had landed there with the greatest facility.

An entire day was passed in vain attempts, and was quite unproductive of scientific results.

Next day La Perouse started afresh, and upon entering the roadstead of Botany Bay encountered an English vessel, under command of Commodore Phillip, who was engaged in constructing Port Jackson, the embryo of that powerful colony which in our day, after only a quarter of a century's growth, has attained to such a height of civilization and prosperity.

Here the journal kept by La Perouse terminates. A letter, written by him from Botany Bay, upon the 5th of February, to the Naval Minister, informs us that he intended building two sloops, to replace those which had been destroyed at Maouna. All his wounded, amongst them M. Lavaux, the surgeon of the *Astrolabe*, who had been trepanned, were perfectly recovered. M. de Clenard had assumed command of the *Astrolabe*, and had been succeeded upon the *Boussole* by M. de Monti.

In a letter of two days' later date, giving particulars of his intended route, La Perouse says, –

"I shall regain the Friendly Islands, and carry out the instructions I have received with regard to the northern portion of New Caledonia, to Santa Cruz de Mendana, to the land south of the Arsacides of Survillle, and to the Louisiade of Bougainville, and also ascertain, if possible, whether the latter constitutes portion of New Guinea, or is a separate continent. At the end of July, 1788, I shall pass between New Guinea and New Holland by some other channel than the Endeavour; that is to say, if there be another. During September, and the early part of October, I propose to visit the Gulf of Carpentaria, and the eastern coast of New Holland, as far as Van Diemen's Land, so as to allow of my return to the north in time to arrive at Mauritius in the beginning of December, 1788."

Not only did La Perouse fail to keep the rendezvous he himself appointed, but two entire years passed away, and no news whatever of his expedition were received.

Although at that epoch France was passing through a terrible crisis, the interest of the public in the fate of La Perouse was so intense that it found vent in an appeal to the National Assembly from the members of the Society of Natural History in Paris. Upon the 9th of February, 1791, a decree was passed enjoining the fitting out of two or more armed vessels, to be sent in search of La Perouse. It was argued, that had shipwreck overtaken the expedition a number of the crews might still survive, and that it was only just to carry help to them as soon as possible. Men of science, naturalists, and draughtsmen, were to take part in the expedition, with the view to obtaining valuable information for navigation, geography, and commerce, as well as for the arts and sciences. Such were the terms of the decree to which we have alluded.

The command of the expedition was entrusted to Vice-admiral Bruny D'Entrecasteaux, who had attracted the attention of government by his conduct in India. Two vessels, the *Recherche*, and the *Espérance*, the latter under the orders of M. Huon de Kermadec, ship's captain, were placed at his command. The staff of these vessels comprised many officers who later attained to high military positions. Amongst them were, Rossel, Willaumez, Trobriand, La Grandière, Laignel, and Jurien. Amongst the men of science on board were, La Billardière, naturalist, Bertrand and Pierson, astronomers. Ventenat and Riche, naturalists, Beautemps-Beaupré, hydrographer, and Jouveney, engineer.

The vessels were stocked with provisions for eighteen months, and a quantity of merchandise, for trading purposes. Leaving Brest

Portrait of D'Entrecasteaux.
(Facsimile of early engraving.)

upon the 28th of September, they reached Teneriffe upon the 13th of October. An ascent of the famous Peak followed as a matter of course. La Billardière noticed a phenomenon which had already been observed by him in Asia Minor: his figure was reflected upon the clouds below him, opposite to the sun, in every colour of the rainbow.

Upon the 23rd of October, the necessary provisions having been shipped, anchor was weighed, and the start made for the Cape. During the cruise, La Billardière discovered that the phosphorescent appearance of the sea is caused by minute globular animalculi, floating in the waves. The voyage to the Cape, where the vessels arrived upon the 18th of January, 1792, was barren of incident, if we except the unusual quantity of bonitos, or tunny, and other fish that were met with, and a small leakage which occurred, but was quickly remedied.

At the Cape, D'Entrecasteaux found a letter from M. de Saint Felix, commanding the French forces in India, which seemed likely to upset all his plans, and exercise an unfavourable influence upon the expedition. From this communication it appeared that two French captains, from Batavia, had stated that Commodore Hunter, in command of the English frigate *Syrius*, had seen, "near the Admiralty Islands, in the Pacific Ocean, men dressed in the European style, and in what he took to be French uniforms". "It is clear," wrote M. de Saint Felix, "that the commodore was convinced they were the remnants of La Perouse's company."

When D'Entrecasteaux arrived at the Cape, Hunter was still in the roadstead; but within two hours of the arrival of the French vessels he weighed anchor. This conduct, appeared very strange. The commodore had had time to hear that the vessels just arrived were those sent in search of La Perouse, and yet he had made no communication to the commander upon the subject. But it was soon ascertained that Hunter had declared himself quite ignorant of the facts stated by M. de Saint Felix. Were they then to be regarded as unfounded? Incredible as M. de Saint Felix's communication appeared, D'Entrecasteaux could not suppose so.

The naturalists had availed themselves of their stay at the Cape to make many excursions in the neighbourhood: La Billardière had penetrated as far into the interior as the short stay of the frigates in the roadstead permitted.

Anchor was weighed upon the 16th of February, and D'Entrecasteaux decided upon reaching the southern seas by doubling Cape Horn, and steered for the passage between St. Paul and Amsterdam Islands. Captain Valming had discovered these islands in 1696, and they had been recognized by Cook in his last voyage. When the *Recherche* and the *Espérance* passed St. Paul island it was enveloped in a thick smoke, through which the summits of the mountains were visible. The forests were on fire.

Upon the 21st of April the two vessels entered a bay upon the coast of Van Diemen's Land, which was supposed to be Adventure Bay, but which in reality was Storm Bay. The extreme point of this bay was named after D'Entrecasteaux. Wood was easily obtained there, and fish was very abundant. Amongst the magnificent trees of the country, La Billlardière mentions various species of the eucalyptus, the many uses of which were then unknown. The hunting-parties caught black swans and kangaroos, creatures also but little known.

Upon the 16th of May the vessels left the port, and made for a strait, afterwards named after D'Entrecasteaux.

"M. Creton and M. Auribeau," says the narrative, "were encouraged to land by the sight of fires close to the shore. They had gone but a short distance when they came upon four natives, attending to three small fires, by which they were seated. They took to flight on seeing the strangers, in spite of every friendly demonstration, leaving the lobsters and shell-fish which they had been broiling. As many huts as there were fires were close by.

"One of the natives, in his hurry, left a small basket, full of pieces of silica, behind him. He was not afraid to return in search of it, but approached Creton with a bold air, possibly owing to his confidence in his own strength. Some of these savages were naked, and others wore only a kangaroo skin upon the shoulders. In colour they were nearly black; they had woolly hair, and allowed the beard to grow."

Upon leaving D'Entrecasteaux Strait, the vessels proceeded to survey the south-western coast of New Caledonia, which La Perouse should have visited. A portion of Pine Island, which stretches to the north of that country, was the first to be recognized.

The *Recherche* narrowly escaped destruction upon the coral reefs which surround the coast, leaving only a narrow passage between them and the main land. At the northern extremity several mountainous islands and detached rocks were perceived, which rendered the navigation extremely dangerous. The navigators, grateful for their escape, named them the Entrecasteaux Reefs and Huon Islands.

They came upon four natives.

The survey of this perilous coast lasted from the 16th of June to the 3rd of July. A true service was thus rendered to geographers and navigators, though it was, perhaps, the least profitable part of the voyage of discovery.

As the favourable season was now approaching, D'Entrecasteaux determined to avail himself of it to reach the land of the Arsacides, which had been seen by Surville, and visited some years later by Shortland, who, imagining he was making a new discovery, named it New Georgia.

"Upon the 9th of July," says La Billardière, "towards half-past four o'clock, we perceived, about ten miles to the N.W., a rock called Eddystone. "We took it at first, as Shortland had done, for a sailing vessel. The illusion was the greater, as in colour it much resembles the sails of a ship; a few shrubs crowned the summit. The land of the Arsacides, opposite this rock, is steep, and covered with large trees."

After rectifying the position of Eddystone rocks, and that of the Treasury islands – which are five in number, though so close together that Bougainville took them for one island – D'Entrecasteaux coasted Bougainville Island. It is separated from Bouka Island by a narrow strait, and is covered with plantations. It appeared to be well populated. Some trade was done with the natives, but nothing would induce them to venture on board the vessels.

"The colour of their skins," says La Billardière, "is nearly black. They are of medium height, and wear no clothes. They are muscular and strong. Although their features are not pleasant, they are very expressive. They have large heads, and broad fore-heads. Their faces, especially in the lower part, are flat; they have thick chins, rather prominent cheek bones, flat noses, large mouths, and thin lips.

"Their ugliness is increased by the colour with which the betel-nut stains their mouths. They appear very skilful in the use of bows and arrows. One of them brought a gannet which he had just killed, on board, and the hole made by the arrow could easily be seen.

"These natives have bestowed particular attention upon their weapons, which are very well finished. We could not but admire the skill with which they coated the strings of their bows with resin, in such a way that at first sight they looked like catgut. The centre was protected with a piece of bark, to lessen the wear in projecting the arrows."

The survey of the western coast of these two islands was completed upon the 15th of July. Bougainville had already surveyed the eastern shore.

Next day the French navigators sighted first the island to which Carteret had given the name of Sir Charles Hardy, and then the south eastern extremity of New Ireland.

The two vessels cast anchor in Carteret Bay, and the crews were established upon Cocoa Island. This island is covered with evergreen trees, which, in spite of the volcanic nature of the soil, grow vigorously.

The cocoa-nuts from which it received its name were procured with difficulty. On the other hand, it afforded the naturalists so many varieties of plants and insects as to charm Billardière.

Rain fell abundantly during the stay; it was like a ceaseless torrent of tepid water.

After obtaining the necessary wood and water, the *Recherche* and *Espérance* set sail from Port Carteret upon the 24th of July, 1792. In so doing the *Espérance* unfortunately lost an anchor, the cable having been cut by the coral reefs. The two vessels then entered St. George's Strait, which at the southern extremity is only about forty-two miles in width, about half the extent assigned to it by Carteret. The currents were so rapid that the ships were carried past Man and Sandwich Islands, without being able to stop.

After sighting Portland Islands, low lands, seven in number, which stretch from 2° 39' 44" S. lat. to 147° 15' E. long., D'Entrecasteaux continued his route towards the Admiralty Islands, which he intended to visit. It was upon the most easterly of these islands that, according to the report received by Commodore Hunter, the natives wearing French naval uniforms had been seen.

"The natives appeared in crowds," says the narrative. "Some ran along the shore, others, fixing their eyes upon our vessels, invited us by signs to land. The cries they uttered were intended to express their joy. At half-past one the vessels anchored, and a boat was despatched from each, containing articles for distribution among the natives of this small island. The frigates were so placed as to protect the boats as they neared the land, in the event of any attack by the savages, for our recollection of the treachery of the natives of the islands south of the Admiralty made us distrustful."

The coast abounded in reefs; the boats could only approach within a hundred yards of the shore. Numbers of the natives crowded to the beach, and invited the French by signs to land.

One of the savages, distinguished by a double row of small shells upon his forehead, appeared to exercise a good deal of authority. He ordered one of the natives to jump into the water, and bring us some cocoa-nuts. Fearing to approach strangers swimming and defenceless, he hesitated for a moment. The chief, evidently quite unaccustomed to resistance to his wishes, followed up his command by blows from his club, and compelled obedience.

"As soon as the islander returned to land, curiosity brought the natives around him in crowds. Each wished to participate in our presents. Pirogues were immediately launched, and many natives swam to the boats, which were shortly surrounded by quite a crowd. We were surprised that the violence of the surf upon the breakers did not intimidate them."

Perhaps the French may have attempted that which the Indians accomplished. It seems probable that they would never have observed these people if the vessels, or at least a small boat, had not been wrecked in the archipelago.

The only remark made by them is to the effect that the natives understood and appreciated the use of iron.

D'Entrecasteaux then proceeded to reconnoitre the northern portion of the archipelago, and to trade with the natives. He did not land anywhere, and does not appear to have executed this part of his task with the minute care and attention which might have been expected of him.

The *Recherche* and the *Espérance* afterwards visited the Hermit Islands, discovered in 1781 by a Spanish frigate, *La Princesa*. The natives, like all those they had encountered, showed a great desire to induce the strangers to land, but did not succeed in persuading them to do so.

The Exchequer Islands, discovered by Bougainville, several unknown low islands, covered with luxuriant vegetation, Schouten Island, and the coast of New Guinea, were successively sighted. In the interior of the last-named a large chain of mountains was distinguished, the loftiest of which appeared at least three thousand five hundred feet high.

After coasting this large island, the *Recherche* and the *Espèrance* entered Pitt Strait to reach the Moluccas.

Upon the 5th of September, 1792, the French joyfully anchored in the roadstead of Amboyna. There were many sufferers from scurvy on board and officers and crew alike needed a lengthened rest. The naturalists, astronomers, and other scientific men immediately landed, and took the necessary steps for the prosecution of their various observations. The naturalists were particularly successful in acquiring new facts. La Billardière congratulates himself upon the multiplicity of new plants and animals that he was able to obtain.

"Once when upon the shore," he says, "I heard what appeared to be wind instruments, the tones now harmonious, now discordant, yet never unpleasing. These harmonious and distinct sounds appeared to come from a distance, and I imagined the natives were making music some six or seven miles beyond the roadstead. But my ear deceived me, for I found that I was not a hundred yards from the instrument. A bamboo cane, at least sixty feet high, was fixed vertically upon the shore. At each notch a slit had been made, about two and a half inches long and one and a quarter broad. These slits made so many openings for the wind, which, passing through them, produced varied and pleasant sounds. As the notches in this cane were very numerous, the slits had been made all round, so that whichever way the wind blew it went through some of them. I can only compare the sound of this instrument to that of an harmonium."

During this long stay of a month in one place the vessels were well caulked, the sails and rigging attended to, and every precaution taken for a voyage in tropical and damp climates.

A few details on the roadstead of Amboyna, and the manners and customs of the native population, will not be out of place.

"Amboyna roadstead," says La Billardière, "forms a channel some thirteen or fourteen miles in length, and about two and a half miles in breadth. It affords good anchorage, although the bottom is partly of coral.

"The fort, called Victory Fort, is built of bricks; the governor and some of the members of government reside there. It was at this time falling into ruins, and every discharge of cannon did evident damage.

"The garrison consisted of about two hundred men, of which the natives of the island composed a considerable part; the remainder consisted of a few retired European soldiers and a small detachment of a Wurtemberg regiment.

The mortality amongst officers living in the Indies makes the lives of those who have been some time in the climate precious; the Dutch Company is therefore seldom true to its promise to allow them to return to Europe at the expiration of their time of service. I met with several of these unfortunate men who had been detained for more than twenty years, when, according to agreement, they ought to have been freed long before.

"The language of the natives of Amboyna is Malay. It is very soft and musical. The country produces spices, coffee, which is inferior to that of Reunion Island, and sago; the latter is largely cultivated in the marshy districts.

"The rice consumed at Amboyna is not indigenous to the soil, but still it might be successfully cultivated in the low lands. The Dutch Company, however, prohibit the growth of this article of commerce, because its sale enables them to keep back a part of the sum which they are obliged to pay for cloves furnished by the blacks. They thus prevent the increase of pay, and obtain the fruits of native labour at a moderate price.

"Thus the company, consulting their own interest only, discourage all industry in the population, by forcing them, as it were, to relinquish everything but the cultivation of spices.

"The Dutch are careful to limit the cultivation of spices within the compass of ordinary consumption. Their efforts, which are destructive of all enterprise, chime in with the *nonchalant* character of the natives."

On the 23rd of "Vendémiaire"[1] of the year 1, if we conform to the new style, as Bougainville does, the two vessels left Amboyna, amply provisioned with fowls, ducks, geese, pigs, goats, potatoes, yams, bananas, and pumpkins. Meat, however, they obtained in but small quantities, the flour was of a bad quality, and the sailors could never accustom themselves to the sago which was shipped in its stead; bamboos, cloves, and arrack may be added to the list of shipments.

"Young bamboo shoots, cut in slices, and preserved in vinegar," says La Billardière, "made an excellent store for a long voyage. These young shoots are generally very tender. They are gathered early, and sold in the market as vegetables, for which they are a good substitute. They are often a yard long, and half an inch thick.

"These young bamboo shoots are much appreciated by the Chinese, who think them similar to asparagus in flavour.

"We were also provided with cloves and nutmegs preserved in sugar. The shell of the nutmeg is the only edible portion; unfortunately, ignorant preservers had chosen full-grown nutmegs. Cloves, when once as large as ordinary olives, retain too much flavour to be a pleasant sweetmeat. One must be endowed with an Indian palate

[1] First month of the Republican calendar.

to enjoy them. I might say the same of our ginger preserves.

"The only spirituous liquor obtainable was arrack, several casks of which were bought. Many travellers have spoken in praise of this liquor, which is, in reality, not equal to the poorest brandy."

Upon leaving Amboyna, the expedition sailed for the south-west coast of Australia. Shortly afterwards, Kisser Island, the north shore of Timor, Baton Islahd, and the delightful Sauva Island, were successively passed; and finally, upon the 16th "Frimaire", the western extremity of the south-western coast of New Holland, which was discovered by Leuwin in 1622, was sighted.

The coast presented a succession of sandy dunes, in the midst of which arose pointed rocks, apparently utterly sterile. Navigation upon this unsheltered coast was extremely dangerous. The sea ran high, the wind was boisterous, and it was necessary to steer amongst the breakers. During a strong gale the *Espérance* was nearly driven upon the coast, when one of the officers fortunately distinguished from the main-mast an anchorage, where, he declared, the ships would be in safety.

"The safety of the two ships," says the narrative, "was due to this discovery, for the *Recherche*, after battling as long as she could against the storm, had been forced to tack about all night amidst these perilous breakers, hoping for a change of wind which would make it possible for her to reach the open sea, and must infallibly have perished. This bay, named Legrand, after the able seaman who first discovered it, will always recall his invaluable service to the expedition."

The islets surrounding this coast were reconnoitred by the navigators. A geographical engineer, named Riche, belonging to the *Recherche*, landing upon the mainland to make observations, lost his way, and only reached the vessels after two days' absence, nearly dead of fatigue and hunger.

This small archipelago concluded the discoveries of Nuyts.

"We were surprised," says La Billardière, "at the exactitude with which the latitude had been determined by this navigator, at a time when instruments were very imperfect. The same remark applies to nearly all Leuwin's discoveries in this region."

Upon the 15th Nivose[2] 31° 52' lat. and 129° 16' E. long., Captain Huon de Kermadec informed D'Entrecasteaux that his rudder was

[2] Fourth month of the Republican calendar, from 21st December to 21st January.

injured, that he was obliged to limit his crew to three quarters of a bottle of water per day, that he had been forced to discontinue the distribution of anti-scorbutic drinks, and that he had only thirty casks of water remaining. The *Recherche* was hardly in better case. D'Entrecasteaux accordingly made for Cape Diemen, after navigating for about six hundred and seventy miles along a barren coast, which offered no object of interest or value.

Upon the 3rd Pluviose,[3] the vessels anchored in the Bay of Rocks, in Tempest Bay, which they had visited the preceding year. This spot was very rich in points of interest. La Billardière was amazed at the varied products of this portion of Van Diemen's Land, and was never tired of admiring the vast forests of gigantic trees, and the many unknown shrubs and plants, through which he had to force his way. During one of his numerous excursions he picked up some fine pieces of beautiful bronze red hæmatite, and further on some earth containing ochre, of so bright a red as to denote the presence of iron. He soon encountered some natives, and his remarks upon this race, which is now quite extinct, are interesting enough for repetition; moreover, they complete the particulars already given by Captain Cook.

He says, "There were about forty-two natives; seven grown men, and eight women, the others appeared to be their children; many of them were girls already arrived at maturity, who were even more lightly clad than their mothers. They have woolly hair, and the men let their beards grow long. In the children the upper jaw projects, but in adults it is about even with the lower. No doubt these people consider it a beauty to be black; for, not being very dark to begin with, they powder the upper part of the body with coal dust.

"We noticed rows of spots on the skin, especially of the shoulders and breast, now in lines above three inches long, now in equidistant dots. These people do not appear to observe the custom which many travellers have thought to be universal amongst their tribes, of extracting the incisor teeth, for we saw no native with any missing from the upper jaw, and they all had very fine, strong teeth. These people swarm with vermin. We could not but admire the patience of a woman, whom we watched freeing her child of them; nor could we avoid feeling shocked when she crushed the disgusting insects with her teeth, and then swallowed them. Monkeys have the same habit!

[3] Fifth month of the Republican calendar, from 20th January to 20th February.

"The young children greatly admired everything shining, and they did not hesitate to take the metal buttons off our coats. I must not omit to mention a trick played upon a sailor by a young savage. The man had collected a number of shells, and left them in a bag at the foot of a rock. The native furtively removed them, and allowed the sailor to search for them vainly for some time; then quietly replacing them, he seemed much amused at the trick he had played."

Early in the morning of the 26th Pluviose the two vessels weighed anchor, entered D'Entrecasteaux Strait, and, on the 5th of Ventose,[4] anchored in Adventure Bay. After a stay of five days, spent in taking observations, D'Entrecasteaux set sail for New Zealand, and reached its southern extremity. After an interview with the natives, too short to admit of additions being made to the many and precise observations of Captain Cook, D'Entrecasteaux started for the Friendly Islands, which La Perouse had intended visiting. He anchored in Tonga Tabou Bay. The vessels were at once surrounded by a crowd of pirogues, and literally boarded by the natives, who came to sell pigs and every variety of fruit.

One of the sons of Poulao, the king Cook had known, received the navigators cordially, and scrupulously superintended the trade with the islanders. This was no easy task, for they developed surprising talents for stealing everything which came in their way.

La Billardière describes rather a good joke of which he was the victim. He was followed to the provision tent by two natives, whom he took to be chiefs.

"One of them," he says, "was very anxious to choose the best fruits for me. I had placed my hat on the ground, thinking it safe there; but these two rogues understood their business. The one behind me was clever enough to hide my hat under his clothes, and was off before I perceived the theft; the other speedily followed. I was the more surprised at this attempt, because I should have supposed they would not have had the courage to steal so large an object, running the risk of being caught, in the enclosure to which we had admitted them. Moreover, a hat could not be a very useful article to those people, who generally go bare-headed. Their dexterity in robbing me, convinced me that it was by no means their first attempt."

The French entered into relations with a chief named Finau, probably the same who is mentioned as Finauo in Captain Cook's

---

[4] Sixth month of French Republican calendar.

voyage, and who called him Touté. But he was only a secondary chief. The real king, supreme chief of Tonga Tabou, Vavao, and of Annamooka, was named Toubau. He visited the ships, and brought back a gun which had been stolen a day or two previously from a sentinel. He presented D'Entrecasteaux with two pieces of stuff made from the bark of the mulberry-tree, so large that if opened out either would have covered the vessel. In exchange for mats and pigs he received a fine hatchet and a general's red coat, which he immediately put on.

Two days later, an extraordinarily stout female, at least fifty years of age, and to whom the natives paid great respect, came on board. This was Queen Tina. She tasted everything that was offered to her, but preferred preserved bananas. The steward stood behind her chair, and waited to clear away, but she saved him the trouble by appropriating the plate and napkin.

King Toubau was anxious to give an entertainment to D'Entrecasteaux. The admiral was received upon landing by two chiefs, Finau and Omalai, and conducted by them to an extensive esplanade. Toubau arrived with his two daughters. They had sprinkled a quantity of cocoa-nut oil upon their heads, and each wore a necklace made of the pretty seeds of the *arbus peccatorius*.

"The natives," says the narrative, "arrived from all parts in great crowds; we estimated that the number amounted to at least four thousand.

"The seat of honour was evidently to the left of the king, for he invited D'Entrecasteaux to take his place there. The captain then offered the presents he had brought for the king which were gratefully accepted. A piece of crimson damask excited the most vivid admiration from all the assembled natives. "Eho! Eho!" they exclaimed repeatedly, in accents of the greatest surprise. They uttered the same admiring cry when we unfolded some pieces of coloured ribbon, in which red predominated. The captain then presented a couple of goats, and a pair of rabbits, of which the king promised to take every care. D'Entrecasteaux also bestowed various presents upon Toubau's son Omalai, and several other chiefs.

"To our right, on the north-east, under a shady bread-fruit tree laden with fruit, thirteen musicians were seated, who sang together in different parts. Four of the musicians played the accompaniment by striking bamboo canes, a yard and a yard and a half long, upon the ground, the holder of the longest bamboo occasionally acting as

Fête in honour of D'Entrecasteaux at the Friendly Islands.
(Facsimile of early engraving.)

conductor. These bamboo canes emitted a sound not unlike that of a tambourine, and they were arranged in the following order. The two medium-sized canes were in unison, the longest a tone and a half lower, and the shortest two tones and a half higher. The voice of the alto was heard far above all the others, although he was a little hoarse; he accompanied himself by striking with two little sticks upon a bamboo cane, some six yards long, and split throughout its entire length. Three musicians stationed in front of the others appeared to explain the song by gestures, which had apparently been well studied, as they all acted in unison. Occasionally gracefully moving their arms, they turned towards the king; whilst sometimes they suddenly sunk their heads upon their breasts, and as suddenly tossed them back.

"After these entertainments Toubau offered the captain several pieces of stuff made from the bark of the mulberry-tree. He had them unrolled with great ostentation, that we might fully appreciate the value of his gift. The minister seated upon his left ordered the preparation of 'kava', which was soon brought in an oval-shaped wooden vase, about three feet long.

"The musicians had reserved their best pieces for this moment, for at each succeeding effort we heard applauding cries of 'Mâli, Mâli'; and it was evident that the music had an agreeable and inspiriting effect upon the natives. The 'kava' was then offered to the various chiefs by those who had prepared it."

This concert, it will be seen, was by no means equal to the splendid entertainment, which had been given to Captain Cook.

Queen Tina followed it up by giving a grand ball, which was preceded by a concert, fully attended by the natives, amongst whom, we may incidentally mention, were numbers of thieves, who became so bold that they ended by forcibly taking possession of a cutlas. As the blacksmith of the *Recherche* pursued the thieves, they turned, and seeing him alone, struck him on the head with a club. Fortunately his danger was perceived by those on board the *Espérance*, and a well-directed shot dispersed his assailants. Several natives were killed upon this occasion by the officers and sailors, who, not seeing exactly what had happened, treated all the islanders they met as dangerous. Fortunately, concord was soon restored; and the relations were so friendly when the time came for the French to leave, that many of the natives begged to accompany them to France.

"The intelligent account which these islanders gave of the vessels which had anchored in this archipelago," says the narrative, "convinced us that La Perouse had not visited any of these islands. They remembered perfectly every occasion upon which they had seen Captain Cook, and they indicated the intervals between his visits by the crops of yams, reckoning two in each year."

It is true that their information, as far as it related to La Perouse, was in direct contradiction to the facts which Dumont-Durville collected thirty-six years later, when Tamaha was queen.

"I was anxious to know," he says, "if any Europeans had visited Tonga between Cook and D'Entrecasteaux. After a few moments' reflection, she explained to me very clearly that a few years before D'Entrecasteaux's visit, two large vessels, like his in every respect, carrying guns and many Europeans, had anchored off Annamooka, and remained there six days. They showed a white flag, quite unlike the English one. The strangers had been very friendly with the natives, and had had a house on the island and entered into trade. She related that a native who had agreed to exchange a wooden bolster for a knife, was shot by an officer because he wanted to take back his merchandise when he had been paid for it. However, the incident had not broken the peace, because in that instance the native was in the wrong."

Although it is impossible to suspect Dumont-Durville of any attempt at imposition, many portions of this circumstantial account bear the impress of truth, more especially that relating to the flag, as being different to that of the English. Must we then charge D'Entrecasteaux with want of thoroughness in his work? This would be a very serious charge. Yet two circumstances, which we shall presently relate, appear to point to that conclusion.

The natives witnessed the departure of the French with keen regret. The expedition left upon the 21st Germinal,[5] and six days later the *Espérance* signalled Erronan, the most easterly of the islands of Santo Espiritu, discovered by Quiros in 1660. Beyond this Annatom, Tanna, with its volcano in constant eruption, and the Beautemps-Beaupré Islands were passed. Carried onwards by the currents, the vessels were soon in sight of the mountains of New Caledonia, and anchored in Balade harbour, where Captain Cook had cast anchor in 1774.

[5] Seventh month of the Republican calendar, from 21st March to 19th April.

The natives were acquainted with the use of iron, but they did not appear to value it as highly as others had done, probably because the stones they used instead were very hard and answered admirably for their purposes. Their first demand upon going on board was for something to eat; and their need was unmistakable, for they pointed to their manifestly empty stomachs. Captain Cook had already remarked that they managed their pirogues, which were far less ingeniously constructed than those of the Friendly Islands, unskilfully. The greater number of these natives had woolly hair, and skins almost as black as those of the inhabitants of Van Diemen's Land. Their weapons were assegais and clubs; and in addition to these they carried at the waist a little bag, full of the oval stones which they throw from their slings.

After a short excursion inland, during which they visited the huts of the natives, which were shaped like beehives, the officers and naturalists prepared to re-embark.

"Upon returning to our boat," says the narrative, "we found more than seven hundred natives, who had assembled from all directions. They began by demanding stuffs and iron in exchange for their wares, and soon some of them proved themselves arrant thieves.

"I will mention one of their many manœuvres. A man offered to sell me the little bag of stones which he carried at his waist. He unfastened it, and pretended to offer it to me in one hand, whilst he held out the other for the price upon which we had agreed. But at the same moment another native, who had taken up his stand behind me, uttered a shrill scream, which made me turn my head in his direction, whereupon the rogue made off with his bag, and hid himself in the crowd. We were unwilling to punish him, although most of us carried our guns.

"Unfortunately our leniency might be regarded as a proof of our weakness, and so add to the native insolence; and an incident which shortly occurred indicates this was so.

"Some natives were bold enough to throw stones at an officer who was only about two hundred paces away from us. We were still unwilling to act harshly, as we had heard so much in their favour from Forster's narrative, and had such confidence in their good will that still more evidence was required to convince us of their real character.

"One of them, who was enjoying a broiled bone, and busily devouring the meat which still clung to it, offered a share of his meal to a sailor named Piron. He, thinking it to be the bone of some animal, accepted it, but before eating it showed it to me. I at once

Typical native of New Holland.
(Facsimile of early engraving.)

recognized that it had belonged to the body of a child, of probably fourteen or fifteen years of age. The natives crowding round us, showed us upon a living child the position of the bone, owning without hesitation that the man had been making his meal of it, and giving us to understand that it was a great delicacy.

"Those of our company who had remained on board, could hardly credit our account of this disgusting fact. They refused to believe that a people who had been so differently described by Captain Cook and Captain Forster could be capable of so degrading a practice, but the most incredulous were soon convinced. I had retained possession of the gnawed bone, and our surgeon at once recognized it as that of a child. To make still more sure of the cannibalism of the natives, I offered it to one of them. He seized it eagerly, and tore the remaining flesh from it with his teeth; after he had done with it, I passed it to another, who still found something upon it to relish."

The natives who visited the vessel, committed so many thefts, and became so impudent, that we were forced to drive them away. Upon landing next day, the French found the natives feasting.

They immediately offered a share of their meal to the strangers. It proved to be human flesh recently cooked.

Many of them even came close up to the French and felt the muscles of their arms and legs, uttering the word Karapek, with an expression of admiration and longing which was anything but reassuring.

Many of the officers were assaulted and robbed with the greatest effrontery. There remained no doubt of the intentions of the natives. They even attempted to possess themselves of the hatchets the sailors had brought on shore to cut wood, and were only made to desist by being fired upon.

These constantly recurring hostilities always ended in the repulse of the natives, many of whom were killed or wounded. But in spite of the repulses they met with, they let no favourable opportunity pass of recommencing their attacks.

La Billardière was witness to a fact which has since been frequently observed, but was long disbelieved. He saw the natives eating steatite. This mineral substance serves to deaden the sense of hunger, by filling the stomach and sustaining the viscera of the diaphragm, and although it contains no nourishment whatever, it is useful to them, because they have long periods when food is scarcely procurable, as they bestow very little cultivation upon their

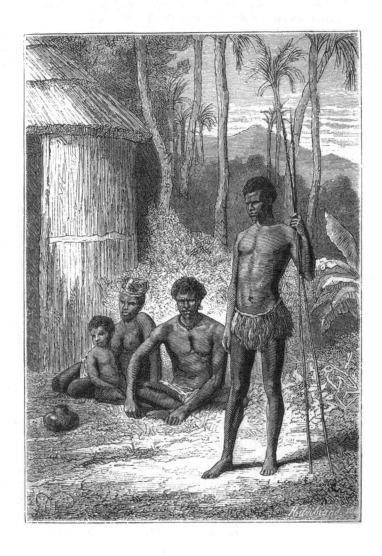

Natives of New Caledonia.

land, which is naturally very sterile. Yet, one would scarcely have expected hungry cannibals to resort to such an expedient.

No news of La Perouse had been obtained during the stay in New Caledonia. But M. Jules Garnier states that a tradition exists of the appearance of two large ships, which had sent boats on shore, near the northern extremity of Pine Island.

"After the first alarm," says M. Jules Garnier, in a communication which appeared in the Bulletin de la Société de Géographie" for November, 1869, "the natives approached the strangers and fraternized with them; they were quite astonished at their riches, and their cupidity induced them to oppose the departure of the French sailors by force; but their ardour was moderated by a volley which killed a few of them. Little pleased with their reception, the French vessels proceeded to the mainland, after letting off a cannon, which the natives took to be a clap of thunder."

It is strange that D'Entrecasteaux, who entered into communications with the natives of Pine Island, should have heard nothing of these events. The island is small, and its population has always been scanty. The natives must have kept secret the fact of their dealings with La Perouse.

Had D'Entrecasteaux, in his navigation among the coral reefs which protect the eastern coast of New Caledonia, succeeded in entering one of the many openings he met with, he might have found some trace of the course taken by La Perouse, who was a careful navigator, and anxious to emulate Cook, who had touched at several points of that coast. A whaler, whose account is quoted by Rienzi, declared that he had seen medals and a cross of St. Louis, relics of the French expedition, in possession of the natives of New Caledonia.

M. Jules Garnier, during a voyage from Noumea to Canala, in March, 1865, observed in the hand of one of their native escort, "an old rusty sword in the fashion of the last century", which bore the impression of the "fleur-de-lys". He could obtain no account of it from its possessor, except that he had had it a long time.

There is no evidence that any member of the expedition gave a sword, still less a cross of the order of St. Louis, to a savage. No doubt an officer had fallen in some encounter, and thus these articles had come into native hands.

This hypothesis accords with M. Garnier's explanation of the contradictory accounts given by Cook and D'Entrecasteaux of the people of Balade. According to the former, they are peaceable, honest, and friendly; according to the latter, they are robbers, traitors, and cannibals. Jules Garnier suggests that some extraordinary event must have changed the disposition of the natives between the two visits. Most likely an encounter had taken place. The Europeans may have been driven to the use of arms: they may possibly have destroyed plantations and burnt huts. In such a case their hostile reception of D'Entrecasteaux would be explicable.

La Billardière, in his account of an excursion to the mountains forming the water-shed of the northern extremity of New Caledonia, and from which the sea can be seen on either side, says, –

"We were followed by three natives, who had no doubt seen us a year previously, when we coasted the eastern shores of their island, for before they left us they spoke of two ships, which they had seen upon that coast."

La Billardière ought to have pressed the natives upon this subject. Were the vessels seen by them those of La Perouse or of D'Entrecasteaux: and was it really "a year previously"?

From these details we see how much it is to be regretted that D'Entrecasteaux did not pursue his investigations more zealously. No doubt, had he done so, he would have found traces of his fellow-countrymen. We shall shortly see, that with a little perseverance he would have found some at least, if not all of them alive.

During the stay in this port Captain Huon de Kermadec succumbed to a hectic fever from which he had long been suffering. He was succeeded in the command of the *Espérance* by M. D'Hesminy d'Auribeau.

Leaving New Caledonia upon the 21st Floréal,[6] D'Entrecasteaux sighted successively Moulin and Huon Islands, and Santa Cruz de Mendana, which is separated from New Jersey by a strait, in which the French vessels were attacked by the natives.

To the south-east D'Entrecasteaux observed an island, which he named after the *Recherche*, and which he might have called Discovery if he had approached it. It was Vanikoro, an islet surrounded by coral reefs, upon which La Perouse's vessels had been wrecked, and which at this time, in all probability, was inhabited by some of the unfortunate seamen. It was most unfortunate to be so near success, and yet to miss it! But the veil which hid the fate of La Perouse and his companions was not destined to be removed for a long time yet.

[6]Eighth month of the Republican calendar, from 18th April to 20th May.

After surveying the northern extremities of Santa Cruz, without any result so far as the object of his expedition was concerned, D'Entrecasteaux directed his course to De Surville's Land of the Arsacides. He reconnoitred the northern coast, and thence reached the shores of Lousiade, which La Perouse had announced his intention of visiting when he left Salomon Island, and surveyed Cape Deliverance. Bougainville was wrong in supposing that this cape belonged to New Guinea; it is the extreme point of an island, called Rossel after one of the officers who has given an account of the expedition.

After coasting along a series of low and rocky islands, which were named after the principal officers, the vessels reached Cape William, on the coast of New Guinea. They then directed their course to Dampier's Strait. After sailing along the northern coast of New Britain, several small and mountainous islands, hitherto unknown, were discovered. Upon the 17th of July a small island in the neighbourhood of the Anchorite Islands was sighted.

D'Entrecasteaux had long been suffering from dysentery and scurvy, and was in extreme danger. Following the advice of his officers, he decided to take leave of the *Espérance*, and endeavoured to reach Waihoun more quickly. Upon the 20th of July he sunk under long and protracted sufferings. After a stay at Waihoun and Bouro Islands, at which latter place the President overwhelmed the French with civilities, and where Bougainville was still remembered by the natives, the expedition left, under command of D'Auribeau. He also unfortunately fell ill, and the command was transferred to Rossel, under whose orders the vessels passed first Boutong, and then Saleyer Straits, and reached Sourabaya upon the 19th of October.

Sad news here awaited the members of the expedition. Louis XVI. had been beheaded. France was at war with Holland and all the European powers. Although both the *Recherche* and the *Espérance* needed many repairs, and the health of the crews needed repose, D'Auribeau was about to start for Mauritius, when he was detained by the Dutch governor. Fearing that the news from Europe, affecting as it did the various members of the expedition so differently, might lead to disaffection in his colony, he subjected his "prisoners", as he called the French, to most humiliating conditions, which they could not escape. Irritation and hatred were rampant, when it occurred to D'Auribeau to unfurl the white flag. However, the greater part of the officers and men of science, amongst them Billardière, obstinately refused to respect the condi-

View of the Island of Bouron.

tions imposed; and being arrested by order of the Dutch authorities, were distributed throughout the different ports of the colony.

After the death of D'Auribeau, which occurred upon the 21st of Aug., 1794, Rossel became head of the expedition. He undertook to convey all documents of every kind collected during the voyage to France; but being taken prisoner by an English frigate, he was deprived of his property, in defiance of justice; and when France obtained the objects of natural history, of which she had been robbed – the expression is not too strong when we recall the instructions given by the French government with regard to Captain Cook's expedition – they were in so bad a condition that they had lost much of their value. Thus ended this unfortunate expedition. Although its principal object had not been attained, it had at least resulted in some geographical discoveries; it had completed or rectified those made by preceding navigators; and to it, especially to the exertions of La Billardière, are due the acquisition of an immense number of facts in natural history.

## III.

Captain Marchand's voyage – The Marquesas – Discovery of Nouka-Hiva – Manners and customs of the inhabitants – Revolution Islands – The coast of America and Tchinkitané Port – Cox Strait – Stay at the Sandwich Islands – Macao – Disappointment – Return to France – Discoveries made by Bass and Flinders upon the Australian coast – Captain Baudin's expedition – Endracht and De Witt Islands – Stay at Timor – Survey of Van Diemen's Land – Separation between the *Géographe* and the *Naturaliste* – Stay at Port Jackson – Convicts – Agricultural wealth of New South Wales – Return of the *Naturaliste* to France – Cruise of the *Géographe* and of the *Casuarina* to the Islands of Nuyts, Edels, Endracht, and De Witt – Second stay at Timor – Return to France.

Etienne Marchand, a captain in the merchant service, returning to France from Bengal in 1788, met with the English Captain Portlock in the roadstead of St. Helena. Their conversation naturally fell upon commerce, and the value of various articles of trade. Like a sensible man, Marchand allowed his companion to talk, and only put in a few words himself now and again, and thus drew from Portlock the interesting information that furs, and more especially otter skins, which could be obtained for a mere trifle upon the eastern coast of North America, realized an enormous price in China; whilst at the same time a cargo brought from the Celestial Empire would return a large profit in Europe.

Upon arriving in France, Marchand communicated what he had learned to his ship-owners, MM. Baux of Marseilles, and they at once resolved to act upon the knowledge he had obtained. Navigation in the Pacific Ocean required a ship of special strength and excellence. MM. Baux ordered the construction of a vessel of 300 tons' burden, plated with copper, and provided with every necessary for defence in case of attack, and for repairs in the event of accident, and also with everything likely to promote trade and to ensure the health of the crews during a voyage of three or four years.

Two captains, MM. Masse and Prosper Chanal, were associated with Marchand in the command of the expedition, and the rest of the party consisted of three lieutenants, two surgeons, three volunteers, and a crew of thirty-nine seamen. Four cannon, two howitzers, four swivel guns, with the needful ammunition, &c, formed the equipment.

Although the vessel was only to reach Cape Horn at the beginning of winter, the *Solide* left Marseilles upon the 14th of December, 1790. After a short stay at Praya, Cape Verde Islands, Marchand proceeded to Staten Island, which he reached upon the 1st of April, 1791. He then doubled Tierra del Fuego, and entered the Pacific. His intention was to proceed immediately to the northwestern coast of America, but at the beginning of May the water on board was already so tainted that he required a fresh supply.

Under these circumstances, the captain decided to reach the Marquesas Islands of Mendoza which are situated in S. lat. 6° and near 141° west of the Paris meridian.

"The situation of these islands," says Fleurien, who published an interesting account of this voyage, "was the more suitable for his purpose, because with a view to escaping the calms often met with in too easterly a course, he had resolved to cross the line at 142° west longitude.

This group of islands had been discovered in 1595 by Mendoza, and visited by Cook in 1774. Magdalena Island, the most southerly of the group, was reached upon the 12th of June.

The captain, and his associate Chanal, had calculated with such precision, that the *Solide* anchored off the Mendoza Islands, after a cruise of seventy-three days from the time of leaving Staten Island, without having noticed any land whatever. Constant astronomical observations alone ensured the safety of the vessel in a sea where the currents were unequal, and it was quite impossible to regulate the course of the ship by any ordinary calculations.

Marchand made for San Pedro, which lay on the west. He soon recognized Dominica, Santa Cristina, and Hood Island, the most northerly of the group, and finally anchored in Madre-de-Dios Bay, where he was enthusiastically welcomed by the natives, crying "Tayo, Tayo".

Finding it impossible to obtain the number of pigs he required at this port, the captain decided upon visiting the remaining bays of Santa Cristina Island, which he found better populated, more fertile, and more picturesque than that of Madre-de-Dios.

The stay of the English in the Marquesas Islands had been too short to allow of accurate observations of the manners and customs of the inhabitants. We will therefore make a few extracts from the description given by Etienne Marchand.

"These natives are tall, strong, and active. Their complexion is clear brown, but many differ little in this respect from the lower orders in Europe. The climate renders clothing unnecessary, but they tattoo their entire bodies so regularly (each arm and leg, for example, exactly like its fellow), that the effect is by no means bad. The way of arranging the hair varies, and fashion is as despotic in the Marquesas as in other countries. Some wear necklaces of red beads, others a string of small pieces of light wood. Although both men and women have their ears pierced, ear-rings are not usually worn. But a young native girl has been seen strutting about wearing as a neck ornament the rusty iron shaving-dish which she had stolen from the ship's barber, whilst a man was equally proud of sporting the ramrod of Captain Marchand's gun, which he had placed in the orifice of his ear, letting part of it hang down."

Cook affirms that these islanders, like the Tahitans, were acquainted with "Kaba". Certain it is that they called the brandy, which was offered them on the *Solide*, by the name of the pepper-plant. It appeared that they did not indulge to excess in this liquor, for none of them were ever seen in a state of drunkenness.

The English did not mention in their account of the natives an act of civility, which Captain Chanal thought worthy of special record. It consisted in offering to a friend a piece of food which had been already chewed, that he might have no trouble but that of

swallowing it. We may easily imagine that the French in spite of their appreciation of the good-will conveyed in this action, were little likely to avail themselves of it.

To Marchand we owe also the curious observation that their huts are raised upon flat stones, and that the stilts which they use indicate that Santa Cristina is subject to inundations. In the exhibition at the Trocadero, one of these stilts, extremely well made and carved, was exhibited; and M. Hamy, whose thorough knowledge of everything relating to Oceania is well known, has written an essay upon this singular object.

Beyond the usual occupations of fishing, the construction of their weapons, pirogues, and domestic implements, the natives of Santa Cristina pass their time in singing, dancing, and amusing themselves. The common expression of "killing the time" seems to have been invented to mark the uselessness of the actions which make up their lives.

During the earlier days of the stay in Madre-de-Dios Bay, Marchand had observed something which led him to the discovery of a group of islands hitherto unknown to the older navigators or to Cook. Upon a clear evening, at sunset, he noticed a spot upon the horizon, which had the appearance of a lofty peak. As this appeared several nights in succession, he concluded that it was land, and finding it not mentioned upon any of the charts, it seemed probable that it was some unknown island.

Marchand determined to satisfy himself upon this point, and leaving Santa Cristina upon the 20th of June, he had the satisfaction of discovering a group of small islands in the north-west, which were situated in 7° south latitude. He gave his own name to the most important of them. The natives were evidently of the same race as that which peopled the Marquesas. Shortly afterwards several other islands were discovered; including Baux Island, which is identical with Nouka-Hiva, the Deux Frères, and Masse and Chanal Islands. This group, since united by geographers to that of the Marquesas, received the name of Revolution Islands.

The course was then directed to the American coast. It was too late in the season to attempt to reach William's Sound or Cook's River, on the sixth parallel. Marchand accordingly resolved upon making for Engano Cape and entering the Norfolk Bay of Dixon, which is identical with the Guadaloupe Bay of the Spaniards.

Upon the 7th of August Engano Cape was sighted, and after five days of calm anchor was cast in Guadaloupe Bay. There had not

been a single case of scurvy on board, after 242 days' navigation, ten of which only were passed in port, at Praya and Madre-de-Dios, and after traversing some 5,800 leagues of sea. This was certainly a wonderful fact, due to the provision of the ship-owners, who had spared nothing that could conduce to the health of the crews, and also to the care with which the captains had observed the sanitary measures commended to them by experience.

During his stay in this port, which the natives called Tchinkitané, Marchand bought a number of otter skins, one hundred of which were of the very first quality.

The natives are ugly, stunted, but well proportioned. They have round, flat faces, small, sunken, bleared eyes, and prominent cheek-bones, which do not add to their beauty.

It is difficult to define the colour of their skins, so carefully is it disguised under a thick coating of grease, and the black and red substances which they rub in. Their hair is coarse, thick, and bushy, covered with ochre, down, and all the filth accumulated by time and neglect, and adds not a little to their unprepossessing appearance.

The women, though not so black as the men, are even more ugly. They are short and thick-set; their feet turn inwards, and their incredibly filthy habits make them repulsive. The coquetry which is innate in the female mind, induces them to add to their natural charms by the use of a labial ornament, as ugly as it is inconvenient, of which we have already spoken in our account of Captain Cook's stay in these waters.

By means of an incision just below the lower lip, they make an opening parallel to that of the mouth, into which they insert an iron or wooden skewer, and from time to time they gradually increase the size of the instrument, in accordance with advancing age.

Finally, they introduce a piece of wood, made for the purpose, of the size and shape of the bowl of an ordinary table-spoon. This ornament, weighing upon the projecting part, naturally forces down the lower lip upon the chin, and develops the beauty of a large, gaping mouth, in shape not unlike an oven, revealing a row of dirty, yellow teeth. This bowl is removable at pleasure, and when it is absent the opening in the lower lip presents the appearance of a second mouth, which is little smaller than the natural one, and in some cases has been known to be three inches in length.

The *Solide* left Tchinkitané upon the 21st of August, and steered to the south-east, in the hope of coming upon Queen Charlotte's Islands, which had been discovered in 1786 by La Perouse. These

islands extend over a distance of nearly seventy leagues. Upon the 23rd, Etienne Marchand sighted Manteau Bay (Dixon's Cloak Bay), which was carefully surveyed by Captain Chaual.

Next day the vessels entered Cox Strait, and began to trade with the Indians for furs.

The navigators were immensely astonished at seeing two enormous paintings, evidently of great age, and some gigantic sculptures, which, although not bearing the very smallest comparison to the *chef-d'œuvres* of Greece, testified none the less to artistic tastes little to be expected from the miserable population.

The lands which form Cox Strait and Bay are low and covered with firs. The soil, composed of the remains of plants and broken rocks, does not appear to have much depth, and the productions are similar to those of Tchinkitané.

The population may be estimated at 400. Not unlike Europeans in height and figure, they are less hideous than the Tchinkitaneans.

This stay in Cloak Bay was not as productive of trade in furs as Marchand had expected, and he therefore decided to send an expedition under Captain Chanal to the more southerly islands. The object of the expedition was the survey of the regions which had hitherto been unvisited. Dixon was the only navigator who had crossed these waters, and none of his crew had landed. It is therefore not astonishing that many of his assertions were either rectified or denied after this more careful exploration.

After sighting Nootka Sound, Berkley Bay was reached, but just as the *Solide* was about to enter it, a three-masted ship was seen approaching the harbour from the south, which was precisely what Marchand had intended doing. This decided the French navigator to proceed immediately to the coast of China, and dispose of his merchandize before the vessel he now saw should have time to reach it and compete with him.

The best route to follow was that of the Sandwich Islands, and upon the 5th of October, the heights of Mauna Loa, and Mauna-Koa were made out by the French. They seemed quite free from snow, which was contrary to the description given of them by Captain King.

So soon as Owhyhee Island was in sight, Marchand wisely decided to conduct all his trade on board. He obtained pigs, fowls, cocoa-nuts, bananas, and various fruits from this island, and was delighted at finding amongst them pumpkins and water-melons, no doubt from the seeds sown by Captain Cook.

Four days were passed in trade, then the route to China was resumed, and in due course Tinian Island, one of the Mariannas, was sighted.

Commodore Anson's glowing description of this island will be recalled. Byron, as we have already mentioned, was quite astonished at the different aspect it presented to him. But the fact is, some fifty years earlier Tinian was flourishing and counted thirty thousand inhabitants, and the victorious Spaniards had since introduced an epidemic which had decimated the population, whilst the miserable survivors had been torn from their country and sent to Guaham as slaves.

Marchand did not land at Tinian – which according to the accounts of every navigator who had visited it since Byron, had relapsed into barbarism – but made for the southern extremity of Formosa.

Reaching Macao upon the 28th of November, he heard news which disconcerted him. The Chinese Government had just passed a law prohibiting the introduction of furs into the ports of the empire under most severe penalties. Was this the result of some unknown clause in a secret treaty with Russia, or was it due to the cupidity and avarice of a few mandarins? In either case it was impossible to infringe the law.

Marchand wrote to MM. Baux's agents in Canton; but the same prohibition held good in that town also, and it was useless to think of reaching Whampoa, where he would have had to pay duty, amounting to at least six thousand piastres.

The only course open to Marchand was to go to Mauritius, and thence return to Marseilles. It is unnecessary to describe the return voyage, which was accomplished without any unusual incidents.

What were the scientific results of this expedition? Nothing to speak of, from a geographical point of view. They may be enumerated as follows: – The discovery of that portion of the Marquesas Islands which had escaped the notice of Captain Cook and his predecessors, a more thorough examination of the country, and the manners and customs of the natives of Santa Cristina in the same group, of Tchinkitané and Cloak Bays, and of Queen Charlotte's Islands off the American coast. Small as these results might appear for an official expedition, they were not unsatisfactory for a vessel equipped by private enterprise; moreover, Captain Marchand and his colleagues had turned new discoveries to such good account, and studied the narratives of earlier voyagers so carefully, that they carried out the plan of their expedition more precisely than many experienced navigators might have clone. And, in their turn, they rendered valuable assistance to their successors by the accuracy of their charts and drawings.

Circumstances were to prove less favourable for the publication of an account of a scientific expedition undertaken some years later, under the auspices of the French Government, having for its object the survey of the Australian coast. Although the results of the voyage made by Nicolas Baudin were most abundant, they seem up to this date to have been little recognized, and scientific dictionaries and biographies say as little as possible of his expedition.

From the time of Tasman's discovery of the western coast of New Holland, much had been done towards exploring this immense continent. Cook had carefully surveyed the eastern coast, discovering Endeavour Strait, and had urged upon his government the great advantages which would accrue from the founding of a colony in Botany Bay. In 1788, Philip, with his band of convicts, had laid the foundation of Port Jackson and of English power in this fifth continent of the world. In 1795 and 1796, Flinders, a midshipman, and Surgeon Bass, with a small vessel called the *Tom Thumb*, had explored twenty miles of the River George, and made a careful survey of a long stretch of coast.

In 1797, Bass discovered a large harbour, which he named Western Port on account of its situation.

"His provisions were now exhausted," says Desborough Coolley, "and in spite of his earnest wish to make an accurate and minute survey of his new discoveries, he was obliged to retrace his steps. He was only provided with provisions for six weeks; still, by aid of fish and sea-birds, which he obtained in abundance, he succeeded in extending his voyage for another five weeks, although he had taken on board two convicts, whom he had picked up. This voyage of six hundred miles in an open boat, is one of the most remarkable on record. It was not undertaken from necessity, but with the view to exploring unknown and dangerous shores."

In 1798, Bass, accompanied by Flinders, discovered the strait which now bears his name, and which divides Tasmania from New Holland, and in a schooner of some twenty-five tons' burden, he made the tour of Van Diemen's land. These brave adventurers collected facts, and made observations of the rivers and ports of this country which were of great use in the future colonization of the continent. Bass and Jackson were both enthusiastically received at Port Jackson.

Upon his return to England, Flinders received command of the *Investigator*, with the rank of naval lieutenant. This vessel was especially equipped for a voyage of discovery upon the Australian coast. The south and north-western shores, the Gulf of Carpentaria, and Torres Straits, were to be explored.

Public attention in France had been attracted to New Holland by the narratives published by Cook and D'Entrecasteaux. This wonderful continent, with its strange unknown animals, and forests of gigantic eucalyptus, alternating with barren plains producing nothing but prickly plants, was long to present all but invincible obstacles to the explorer.

The French Institute was the mouthpiece of popular opinion, in demanding from the government the organization of an expedition to the southern continent. As a result of their representations, twenty-four scientific men were selected to participate in the voyage.

No previous expedition had been so fortunate in the number of scientific men attached to the staff. Astronomers, geographers, mineralogists, botanists, zoologists, draughtsmen, and gardeners, all mustered four or five strong. Foremost amongst them we may mention, Leschenaut de Latour, François Péron, and Borg de Saint Vincent. Officers and sailors had been carefully selected.

Among the first were François-André Baudin, Peureux de Mélay, Hyacinthe de Bougainville, Charles Baudin, Emmanuel Hamelen, Pierre Milius, Mangin, Duval d'Ailly, Henri de Freycinet, all of whom in after-life rose to be admirals or vice-admirals; Le Bas Sante-Croix, Pierre Gillaume Gicquel, Jacques-Philippe Montgéry, Jacques de Saint Cricq, Louis de Freycinet, all future naval captains.

The narrative says, "The plans for the expedition were such as to guarantee its success, and the attainment of the results so eagerly desired. All the experiences of preceding navigators, in the latitudes through which we were to pass, all that theories and reasoning could suggest, had been called into requisition. Most accurate calculations of the variable winds, monsoons, and currents had been made, and the misfortunes which overtook us were in every case due to our deviation from our valuable instructions."

A third vessel of lesser draught was equipped at Mauritius. The navigators were then to proceed to Van Diemen's Land, D'Entrecasteaux, Bass, and Banks Straits, and thence, having determined the situation of the Hunter Islands, to pass behind St. Peter and St. Francis Islands, and survey the country behind them, in the hope of finding the strait supposed to be connected with the Gulf of Carpentaria and to divide New Holland into two parts.

This survey accomplished, Leuvin, Edels, and Eadracht Islands were next to be visited, Swan River to be followed as far as possible, and a survey taken of Rottnest Island and the coast near it. From thence the expedition was to proceed to Shark Bay, to determine various points in De Witt Land, and, leaving the coast at North West Cape, to go to Timor, in the Moluccas, for a well-earned rest.

After allowing sufficient time for the crews to recover from their fatigue, the coast of New Guinea was to be surveyed, with the view to ascertaining whether it was broken up into islands by various straits, the further portion of Gulf of Carpentaria was to be explored, various districts in Arnheim Land were to be recon-noitred, and from thence the expedition was to proceed to Mauritius, on its way to Europe.

A more splendid programme was impossible, and it was clearly traceable to the able mind which had laid down the route taken by La Perouse and D'Entrecasteaux. If the expedition were skilfully conducted the results could not fail to be considerable.

The *Géographe*, a corvette of thirty guns, and the *Naturaliste*, a large transport ship, were equipped at Havre for the expedition.

Nothing had been forgotten, the provisions were abundant and of good quality; each vessel was provided with all kinds of scientific instruments by the best makers, a library of the most trust-worthy authorities, passports couched in the most flattering terms and signed by every government in Europe, and unlimited credit in all the towns of Asia and Africa. In short, every possible measure was taken to ensure the success of this important expedition.

Upon the 19th of October, 1800, the two vessels left Havre amidst the acclamations of an immense multitude. A short stay was made at Port Santa Cruz in Teneriffe, and thence they proceeded without stopping to Mauritius, where several officers were left who were too ill to proceed when the expedition set sail upon the 25th of April, 1801.

This was not an encouraging beginning, and discontent was rife when it was ascertained that the allowance of fresh bread was to be limited to half a pound weekly, and that the usual ration of wine was to be replaced by three-sixths of a bottle of the inferior tafia of Mauritius, whilst biscuits and salt meats were to be the staple food. This ill-advised economy resulted in the illnesses of the crew, and the discontent of many of the scientific staff.

The length of the voyage from France to Mauritius, and the long stay in that island, had consumed much valuable time, and the favourable season was on the wane. Baudin, fearing to attempt to reach Van Diemen's Land, decided to commence his exploration upon the north-west coast of New Holland. He forgot that he would thus maintain a southerly course, so that his advance would coincide with that of the season.

The coast of New Holland was discovered upon the 27th of May. It was low, barren, and sandy. Geography Bay, Naturalist Cape, Depuch Creek, and Piquet Point, were successively sighted and named. In the last-named spot the naturalists landed, and reaped a rich harvest of plants and shells.

Meantime, however, the violence of the waves carried away the two vessels, and twenty-five of the crew were forced to spend several days on shore, unable to obtain any but brackish water. They could not succeed in killing any sort of game, and their only nourishment was a species of samphire, containing a quantity of carbonate of soda and acid juice.

A sloop which had been driven on shore by the force of the waves had to be abandoned, together with guns, sabres, cartridges, cables, tackle, and many other valuable articles.

"But the worst part of this last misfortune," says the narrative, "was the loss of Vasse, of Dieppe, one of the most able of the crew of the *Naturaliste*. Swept away by the waves three times in his efforts to re-embark, he was finally swallowed up without the possibility of assistance being rendered to him, or even the fact of his death being ascertained – so violent were the waves, and so dark the night!"

The foul weather continued, the wind blew in hurricanes, fine rain fell uninterruptedly, and the *Naturaliste* was lost to view in a thick fog which prevailed until Timor was reached.

Upon reaching Rottnest Island – which he had named as a place of rendezvous to Captain Hamilton in case of separation – Baudin, to the surprise of every one, gave orders to make for Shark's Bay, upon the coast of Endracht Island.

The coast of this part of New Holland is a succession of low and almost level sandy barren lands, with grey or reddish soil, intercepted here and there by slight ravines. The coast is almost perpendicular, and is protected by inaccessible reefs; it well deserves the name of "the iron coast", which was bestowed upon it by the able hydrographer, Boullanger.

Native hut in Endracht Land
(Facsimile of early engraving.)

From Dirk Hartog Island (where Endracht Land commences), Doore Islands, Bernier Islands (where troops of kangaroos were met with), and Dampier roadstead, were successively sighted, as far as Shark's Bay, which was thoroughly explored.

Upon leaving Endracht Land, which offers no attractions, De Witt Land – extending from the North West Cape to Arnheim Land, over ten degrees of latitude and fifteen of longitude – was thoroughly surveyed. Much the same incidents and dangers were met with by the explorers as they successively named Hermit and Forester islands, the latter with volcanic soil. The Basseterre, in Geography channel – low lands, which were avoided with difficulty – with Bedont and Lacepede Islands, Capes Borda and Mollien, Champagny d'Arcole, Freycinet, Lucas, and other islands, were seen and named.

"Amidst these numberless islands," says the narrative, "there was little to please the navigators. The sun shines unprotected by any clouds, and, except during the nocturnal storms, there is no movement even of the water. Man appears to have fled from this ungrateful soil, for no trace of his presence is to be seen."

It is difficult for the traveller, who turns in despair from the inhospitable islands of this forsaken coast, where dangers of every sort assail him, and no provisions are to be had, to reflect that this barren country adjoins groups of Asiatic islands upon which nature has lavished her treasures and delights with a liberal hand.

The discovery of the Buonaparte Archipelago completed the survey of this miserable region. It is situated between 13° 15' S. lat, and 123° 30' long. W. of Paris.

"The wretched food upon which we had lived since we left Mauritius had tried the strongest constitutions. The ravages of scurvy had been severely felt, our store of water was very low, and there was no possibility of replenishing it in this miserable region. The time approached for the return of the monsoon, and its accompanying storms must be avoided on this coast; above all, we must procure a boat to enable us to rejoin the *Naturaliste*."

Moved by all these considerations, the captain decided to direct his course to Timor Island, and he anchored there upon the 22nd of August, in the roadstead of Coupang.

It is unnecessary to enter into details of the reception accorded to the navigators. Hospitality and kindness are ever valuable to the recipients, but there is a sameness in an account of them which is wearisome to the reader. We need only dwell upon the sore need of rest for the suffering crew: ten of those who landed were in the

King of the Island of Timor.
(Facsimile of early engraving.)

worst stage of scurvy, and many others had the swollen and inflamed gums which precede the attack of this scourge of seamen.

Unfortunately, although the scurvy yielded to the remedies applied, it was succeeded by dysentery, which in a few days laid low eighteen men.

At length, upon the 21st of September, the *Naturaliste* appeared. Her captain had patiently awaited the arrival of the *Géographe* in Shark's Bay, that being the rendezvous appointed by Baudin, but which he had failed to keep. The officers availed themselves of this stay thoroughly to survey the shores of Rottnest Island, and to explore the Swan River, and Albrolhos or Houtman Rocks.

Two Dutch inscriptions, scratched upon tin plates, had been discovered by Captain Hamelin upon Dirk Hartog Island. One recorded the passage, upon the 25th of October, 1616, of the ship *Eendraght*, from Amsterdam; and the other, the stay of the *Geelwinck* in this port in 1697, under command of Captain Vlaming.

"The result of the examinations made by the officers of the *Naturaliste* was as follows: – The so-called, Shark's Bay extends from Cape Cuvier on the north, to Freycinet Gulf; the eastern coast is all part of the mainland; and the western consists of the islet of Koks, Bernier, Doore, and Dirk Hartog Islands, and a small portion of the mainland. The peninsula of Péron occupies the centre of this extensive bay, and to the east and west are the harbours of Hamelin and Henri Freycinet."

Unfortunately even the sickness among their unfortunate crews did but restore temporary concord between Captain Baudin and his staff. He himself had been attacked by a fever, and for a few hours it was supposed that he was dead.

Upon his recovery eight days later, however, he did not hesitate to place one of his officers, M. Picquet, ensign, under arrest. All the members of his staff disapproved of this action, and offered repeatedly many flattering tokens of their esteem and regard to the disgraced officer. As M. Picquet was made lieutenant upon his return to France, it would appear that he was not in fault.

Captain Baudin had deviated from the instructions given him by the Institute. He now proceeded to Van Diemen's Land, leaving Timor upon the 13th of November, 1801. The French found themselves in sight of the southern coast of this island exactly two months later; the ravages of disease continued on board, and the number of victims was considerable.

The two ships at length reached D'Entrecasteaux Strait, which

The Swan River.
(Facsimile of early engraving.)

had escaped the notice of Tasman, Furneaux, Cook, Marion, Hunter and Bligh, and the discovery of which was the result of a mistake, which might have had dangerous consequences. The vessels had anchored in this spot for the sake of obtaining water, and several boats were sent in search of it.

"At half-past nine," says Péron, "we were at the mouth of Swan River. This spot appeared to me to exceed in beauty and picturesque effect anything that I had hitherto met with. Seven mountain ranges rise one above the other, forming the background of the harbour; whilst on the right and left lofty hills shut it in, and present the appearance of a number of rounded capes and romantic creeks. Vegetation is most luxuriant, the shores abound in hardy trees, growing so densely that it is almost impossible to penetrate into the forest. Flocks of paroquets and cockatoos, of most brilliant plumage, hover above them, while the blue-ringed tomtits sport beneath their branches. The sea was almost calm, and scarcely ruffled by the passage of the innumerable black swans continuously passing to or fro."

All who went in search of a watering-place were not equally pleased with their reception by the natives.

Captain Hamelin, in company with MM. Leschenant and Petit, and several officers and sailors, had encountered some natives, to whom he offered various presents. As they were about to re-embark the French were assailed by a shower of stones, one of which wounded Captain Hamelin severely. The natives brandished their assegais, and made many threatening gestures, but could not provoke the strangers to retaliate by a single shot – a most rare example of moderation and humanity!

"The geographical observations made by Admiral D'Entrecasteaux in Van Diemen's Land are so wonderfully correct," says the narrative, "that it would be scarcely possible to imagine anything more perfect of their kind. Their principal author, M. Beautemps-Beaupré has indeed fully merited the esteem of his fellow countrymen and the gratitude of all navigators. In every case where investigation was possible, this skilful engineer made sure of every point. His survey of the strait of D'Entrecasteaux, and the numberless bays and channels comprised in it, was especially thorough. Unfortunately his explorations did not extend to that portion of Van Diemen's Land which lies north-east of the strait, and which was only superficially examined by the French boats."

It was to this portion of the coast that the hydrographers more particularly directed their attention, in the hope that by adding the results of their observations to that of their fellow-countrymen they might gain a thorough knowledge of the coast. This undertaking, which was to complete the results of D'Entrecasteaux's exertions, detained the navigators until the 6th of February. The details and incidents of such exploration are always alike, and offer little to interest the general reader. For this reason we shall not dwell upon them, in spite of their importance, except when they contain anecdotes of interest.

The *Naturaliste* and *Géographe* next proceeded to the exploration of Banks' and Bass's straits.

Upon the morning of the 6th of March we coasted the islets of Taillefer and Schouten Island, at a good distance. Towards midday we found ourselves opposite Forester's Cape, and our skilful geographer, M. Boullanger, embarked in the long-boat, commanded by M. Maurouard, to survey the coast. The ship was to follow a route parallel with that of the boat, of which it was never to lose sight for a moment; but M. Boullanger had scarcely been gone a quarter of an hour when Capt. Baudin, without any apparent reason, tacked round and gained the more open sea. The boat was lost to sight, and the coast was not neared again until night was approaching. A strong breeze had arisen, which, increasing every moment, added to the uncertainty of our movements. Night fell, and the coast upon which we had abandoned our unhappy comrades was hidden from our sight. The three following days were vainly spent in the endeavour to find the missing boats."

This calm narration would appear to veil strong indignation against Captain Baudin.

What can have been his motive for forsaking his sailors and two of his ablest officers? This is a problem which the most attentive perusal of Péron's narrative fails to elucidate.

To enter the straits of Banks and Bass was to tread in the footsteps of the latter, and of Flinders, who had made these waters the special field of their discoveries; but when, upon the 29th of March, 1802, the *Géographe* commenced coasting the south-western shore of New Holland, one portion of it only was known – that which extends from Cape Leuwin to St. Peter and St. Francis Islands. The land stretching from the eastern boundary of Nuytsland to Port Western had never yet been trodden by an European foot. All the importance of this cruise is apparent when we reflect that it was undertaken to decide whether New Holland consisted of one island only, and whether any large rivers flowed in to the sea from it.

Latreille Island, Mount Tabor Cape, Cape Folard, Descartes Bay, Bouffler Cape, Estaing Bay, Rivoli Bay, Mongo Cape, were all successively sighted and named. An extraordinary take of dolphins had delighted the crew, when a sail was seen upon the horizon. It was of course supposed that it was the *Naturaliste*, from which the *Géographe* had been separated by violent storms since the night of the 7-8 March. As the vessel was making rapid way, she was soon abreast of the *Géographe*. She carried the English colours. It was the *Investigator*, under command of Captain Flinders, eight months from Europe, sent for the completion of the survey of New Holland. Flinders had been engaged for three months in the exploration of the coast. He, too, had suffered from storms and tempest in Bass's Strait; during one of the latter he had lost a boat, containing eight men and his chief officer.

The *Géographe* visited in succession Cape Crêtet, the Peninsula of Fleurien (which is about twenty miles in extent), the Gulf of St. Vincent (so called by Flinders), Kangaroo Island, Althorp Islands, Spencer Gulf – upon the western coast of which is Port Lincoln, the finest and safest harbour in New Holland – and the islands of St. Francis and St. Peter. Certainly Captain Baudin, in order to render this hydrographical survey complete, should have followed out his instructions, and penetrated beyond St. Peter and St. Francis Islands. The weather, however, was too unpropitious, and this exploration was reserved for a future expedition.

Scurvy meantime made fearful ravages amongst the adventurers. More than half the crew were incapable of service. Two only of the helmsmen were in a fit condition for duty. How could anything else be expected in a vessel which was not provided with either wine or brandy, but was provisioned only with fœtid water, biscuits infested with maggots, and putrid meats, the mere smell of which was injurious?

Winter, too, had set in in the southern hemisphere, and the crews were in sore need of rest. The nearest harbour was Port Jackson, and the shortest passage thither was by Bass's Strait. Baudin, who, always appears to have disliked following a beaten track, thought differently, and gave orders for doubling the southern extremity of Van Diemen's Land.

Upon the 20th of May anchor was cast in Adventure Bay. The sick who could be moved were carried on shore, where water was

A sail was seen on the horizon.

plentiful. But the stormy waters were no longer passable; a thick fog prevailed, and only the sound of the waves breaking upon the shore saved the vessels from running aground. The number of sick increased. The ocean claimed a fresh victim each succeeding day. Upon the 4th of June there were only six men equal to their work, and the tempest increased in fury, yet the *Géographe* escaped destruction once more.

Upon the 17th of June a vessel was signalled, and from her captain the navigators learned that the *Naturaliste*, after waiting vainly for her consort at Port Jackson, had gone in search of her – that the abandoned boat had been rescued by an English vessel, and the crew had been received upon the *Naturaliste*.

The *Géographe* was awaited with eager impatience at Port Jackson, where help of every kind was prepared for her.

The *Géographe* was for three days within reach of Port Jackson, and yet unable to enter the harbour, for want of able-bodied seamen to work her. An English sloop, with a pilot, and the necessary men for working the vessel, was, however, sent to the rescue.

The entrance to Port Jackson is only two miles in width, but it widens until it forms a large harbour containing water enough for the largest ships, and space enough to accommodate all comers in perfect safety. A thousand ships of the line might easily anchor there, according to Commodore Philips' report.

"Towards the centre of this magnificent port, and upon its southern coast, the town of Sydney is situated. Built upon two adjacent hills, and watered by a small river which runs through it, this rising town presents a pleasant and picturesque appearance.

'The eye is at once struck by the fortifications, and the hospital, which is large enough to contain two or three hundred sick, and was brought from England in pieces by Commodore Philips. Immense warehouses, for the reception of the cargoes of the largest vessels, are built upon the shore. Ships of all kinds were being constructed in the yards from the wood of the country."

With a sentiment of respect, which almost amounts to veneration, the sloop in which M. Bass made the discovery of the strait which separates Tasmania from New Holland is preserved. Snuffboxes made of the wood of her keel are valued as relics by their possessors; and the governor of the fort could think of no more acceptable present for Captain Baudin than a piece of the wood of this famous vessel, mounted in silver, upon which the chief details of the discovery of Bass's Straits were engraved. Equally worthy of

The sick were carried on shore.

View of Sydney.
(Facsimile of early engraving.)

admiration were the prison (capable of lodging two hundred prisoners), the wine and provision warehouses, the exercising ground (overlooked by the governor's house), the barracks, observatory, and the English church, of which the foundations were at this time but just laid.

"The great change in the conduct and condition of the convicts was not less interesting.

"We found new cause for surprise in the population of the colony. A more worthy subject for the reflection of a philosopher or statesman never existed – no brighter example of the influence of social institutions can be imagined – than that afforded on the distant shores of which we are speaking. Here are to be found the formidable ruffians who in a civilized country were the terror of their government. Transported to these foreign shores, ejected from European society, and placed from their first arrival between the certainty of punishment on the one hand and the hope of a better fate in store for them upon the other, surrounded by a surveillance as benevolent as it is active, they are absolutely forced to relinquish their anti-social habits.

"The majority, after expiating their crimes by hard labour, receive the rank of citizenship. Interested themselves in the maintenance of order and justice, for the sake of the preservation of such property as they have accumulated, many of them having become husbands and fathers, the closest of all ties bind them to their present situation.

"The same revolution, brought about by the same means, takes place in the lives of the women and wretched girls. By degrees accustomed to more correct principles of conduct, they in time become the mothers of hard-working, and honest families."

The welcome accorded to the French at Port Jackson was in the highest degree satisfactory. Every possible facility for the prosecution of their researches was afforded to the naturalists, whilst the military authorities and private inhabitants vied with each other in offering provisions and help of every kind.

Many were the successful excursions in the neighbourhood, and the naturalists delighted in examining the famous vineyards of Rose Hill, to which the finest plants from the Cape, the Canary Islands, Madeira, Xeres, and Bordeaux had teen transported.

When questioned, the vine-dressers said the plants sprout more vigorously here than anywhere else, but the first breath of wind from the north-west is enough to destroy everything; buds, flowers, and leaves alike withering beneath its scorching heat.

Somewhat later, the culture of the vine, transported to a more favourable locality, increased greatly; and although it has as yet not attained to any remarkable growth, furnishes a wine which is pleasant to the taste and very alcoholic.

The Blue Mountains, which for a long time bounded European research, are thirty miles beyond Sydney. Lieutenant Dawes and Captain Tench Paterson – who explored Hawkesbury River, the Nile of New Holland – Hacking, Bass, and Barraillier, had alike failed to scale them.

Already, the thinning of the trees in the neighbouring forests, and the excellence of the grass, had rendered New South Wales an excellent pasturage. Cattle and sheep had been largely imported.

"They multiplied so quickly, that in State pastures alone there were no less than 1800 head of cattle within a short time of our stay at Port Jackson; of these 514 were bulls, 121 oxen, and 1165 cows. The increase and growth of these animals was so rapid, that in less than eleven months the number of oxen and cows had reached from 1,856 to 2,450, which would be at the rate of increase per annum of 650 head, or one third of the entire number.

"Carrying this calculation on at the same rate for a period of thirty years, or even reducing the increase by one half, it is clear that New South Wales would be teeming throughout its length and breadth with cattle.

"Sheep farming has had even greater success. The increase of flocks upon these distant shores is so prolific that Captain MacArthur, one of the richest landowners of New South Wales, does not hesitate to assert, in a pamphlet published for that purpose, that in twenty years New Holland alone will be able to supply England with all the wool which is now imported from neighbouring countries, and the price of which amounts yearly to 1,800,000*l*. sterling."

We know now how very little exaggeration there was in these calculations, although at that time they appeared most wonderful. It is interesting to read of the growth of this industry, and the impression produced by it, in its earlier stages, upon the French navigators.

The crew had many of them recovered their health, but the number of able sailors was still so small that it was necessary to send the *Naturaliste* back to France, after selecting the most healthy of the crew. She was replaced by a vessel of thirty tons burden, called the *Casuarina*, the command of which was entrusted to Louis de

Freycinet. The slight build and low draught of this vessel made it valuable for coasting purposes.

The *Naturaliste*, says Péron, with the records of the expedition, and the results of the observations made during the two voyages, also took away with it "more than 40,000 animals of different kinds, collected from the various countries which had been visited during the two years". Thirty-two huge cases contained these collections, certainly the richest ever brought together in Europe, which when exhibited in the house occupied by myself and M. Bellefin, excited the admiration of all the English visitors, especially of the celebrated naturalist, Paterson.

The *Géographe* and the *Casuarina* left Port Jackson upon the 18th of November, 1802. On this new trip the explorers surveyed King Island, Hunter Island, and the north-western portion of Van Diemen's Land, thus completing the geography of the coast of this huge island. From the 27th of December, 1802, till the 15th of February, 1803, Captain Baudin was engaged in reconnoitring the Kangaroo Islands, upon the south-western coast of Australia, with the two gulfs opposite to them.

"It was indeed strange," says Péron, "to observe the monotonous and sterile character of the different portions of New Holland – the greater on account of its contrast to that of the neighbouring countries. On the north-west we had been charmed by the fertile islands of the Timor Archipelago, with their lofty mountains, rivers, streams, and forests. Yet scarcely forty-eight hours had passed since we left the desert shores of De Witt Land. Again, on the south, the wonderful vegetation and smiling slopes of Van Diemen's Land had excited our admiration, and yet more recently we had been delighted with the verdure and fertility of King Island.

"The scene changes; we reach the shore of New Holland, and are once more face to face with the desolation, the description of which must already have wearied the reader as much as it surprised the philosopher and oppressed the explorer."

The engineers who accompanied the *Casuarina* for the survey of Spencer Gulf, and the peninsula which divides it from the Gulf of St. Vincent, were obliged to abridge the prosecution of their discoveries in Lincoln Port, and content themselves with the thorough survey which enabled them to decide positively that no great river discharges itself into the ocean in this region. The time for their return to Kangaroo Island had arrived. But in spite of their conviction that if they delayed they would be left behind, they did not hasten their movements sufficiently, and upon reaching the rendezvous found that the captain of the *Géographe* had already started, without concerning himself in the least about the *Casuarina*, although her stock of provisions was very inadequate.

Baudin decided to continue the exploration of the coast and the survey of St. Francis Archipelago alone – a most important undertaking, as no navigator had examined its islands separately since its first discovery by Peter Nuyts in 1627.

Flinders had really just made this exploration; but Baudin was not aware of this, and fancied himself the first European who had entered these waters since their discovery.

When the *Géographe* reached King George's Harbour upon the 6th of February, the *Casuarina* had already arrived there, but in such a damaged condition that her captain had been obliged to run her aground.

King George's Sound, discovered in 1791 by Vancouver, is of great importance, as being the only point throughout an extent of coast equal to the distance between Paris and St. Petersburg where it is possible to rely upon obtaining sweet water at all seasons of the year.

In spite of its advantages in this respect, the surrounding country is very barren. M. Boullanger in his "Journal" says, "The aspect of the country inland at this point is perfectly horrible; even birds are scarce: it is a silent desert."

In one of the recesses of this bay, known as Oyster Harbour, a naturalist, named M. Faure, discovered a large river, named after the French, the mouth of which was as wide as the Seine at Paris. He undertook to ascend it, and thus penetrated as far as possible into the interior of the country. About two leagues from the entrance of the river his further progress was arrested by two embankments, solidly constructed of stones, connected with a small island, and forming an impassable obstacle.

This barrier was pierced by several openings, most of them above the low tide level, and much wider upon the side facing the sea than upon the other.

By these openings the fish which entered the river at high tide could easily pass through, but could not return, and were consequently imprisoned in a sort of reservoir, where the natives could catch them at their leisure.

M. Faure found no less than five of these erections in the space of less than the third of a mile – a most singular proof of the ingenuity of the barbarous natives of the country, who in other respects appear upon the level of brutes.

In King George's Harbour one of the officers attached to the *Géographe*, named M. Ransonnet, more fortunate than Vancouver and D'Entrecasteaux, had an interview with the natives. This was the first time a European had been able to approach them.

M. Ransonnet says, "We had scarcely appeared when eight natives, who, upon our first appearance on their coast, had vainly called to us by cries and gestures, appeared suddenly together. After awhile three of them, who were no doubt women, went away again. The remaining five, first throwing their assegais to a distance, to convince us, probably, of their pacific intentions, assisted us in landing. At my suggestion, the sailors offered them various presents, which they received with an air of satisfaction, but without enthusiasm. Whether from apathy, or as a mark of confidence, they returned the presents to us with a pleased expression; and upon our once more presenting them with the same things, they left them upon the ground or surrounding rocks.

"They were accompanied by many large and handsome dogs. I did all I could to induce them to part with one. I offered them all I had, but their refusal was persistent. They probably employed them in hunting the kangaroo, which, with the fish that I had seen them pierce with their assegais, formed their staple food. They drank some coffee, and ate some salt beef and biscuits, but refused the bacon we offered, and left it behind them upon the stones without touching it.

"These natives are tall, thin, and very active. They have long hair, black eyebrows, short flat noses, sunken eyes, large mouths, with projecting lips, and fine and very white teeth. The inside of their mouths seemed as black as the outside of their bodies.

"The three who appeared the oldest among them, and who might have been from forty to fifty years of age, had large black beards. Their teeth appeared to have been filed, and the cartilage of the nose pierced. Their hair was trimmed, and curled naturally.

"The other two, whose ages we took to be from sixteen to eighteen, were not tatooed at all. Their long hair was gathered into a chignon, powdered with red dust, similar to that which the elder ones had rubbed over their bodies.

"They were all naked, and wore no ornament, excepting a large waistband, composed of a number of small fringed strips of kangaroo skin. They talked volubly, and sang in snatches, but always in the same key, and accompanied their song with the same gestures. In spite of the friendly feeling which continued to exist between us, they never allowed us to approach the spot where the other natives, probably their wives, were hidden."

After a stay of twelve days in King George's Harbour, the explorers again put to sea. They rectified and completed the maps drawn by D'Entrecasteaux and Vancouver of Lecon, Edel, and Endrant Lands, which were in turn visited and surveyed, between the 7th and the 26th of March. Thence Baudin proceeded to De Witt Land, which was almost unknown when he visited it the first time. He hoped to succeed better than De Witt, Vianen, Dampier, and St. Allouarn, who had all been unsuccessful in their efforts to explore it; but the breakers, reefs, and sandbanks, rendered navigation extremely perilous.

A new source of danger shortly afterwards arose, in the singular illusion of the mirage. "The effect," says the narrative, "was to make the *Géographe* appear to be surrounded by reefs, although at the time she was a full league away from them, and every one on board the *Casuarina* imagined her to be in the most imminent danger. Only when it became too exaggerated to be real was the magic of the illusion dispelled."

Upon the 3rd of May the two vessels once more cast anchor in Coupang Port, Timor Island. One month later, after re-victualling, Captain Baudin set sail for De Witt Land, where he now hoped to find the winds favourable for an advance to the east. From thence he proceeded to Mauritius, where he died upon the 16th of September, 1803. It appears probable that the precarious state of his health had some influence upon his conduct of this expedition, and possibly his staff would have had less reason to complain of him had he been in full possession of all his faculties. This, however, is a question for psychologists to decide.

The *Géographe* entered Lorient roadstead upon the 23rd of March, and three days later the vast collection of natural curiosities was landed.

The narrative says, "Besides an immense number of cases, containing minerals, dried plants, fish, reptiles, and zoophytes, preserved in brandy, stuffed or dissected quadrupeds and birds, we had seventy large cases filled with vegetables in their natural state, comprising nearly two hundred species of useful plants, and about six hundred varieties of seeds. In addition to all this, at least a hundred living animals."

Water-carrier at Timor.
(Facsimile of early engraving.)

We cannot better complete our account of the results of this expedition than by giving an extract from the report laid before the Government by the Institute, relating more particularly to the zoological collection made by MM. Péron and Lesueur.

"It comprises more than 100,000 specimens of large and small animals. Many important new species are already recognized, and there still remain, according to the statement made by the professor at the museum, upwards of 2500 to be classified."

When we reflect that Cook's second voyage, the most successful undertaken up to this period, had produced only 250 specimens that the united voyages of Carteret, Wallis, Furneaux, Meares, and even Vancouver, had not accumulated so many, and when we admit that the same statement applies to all succeeding French expeditions, it is evident that MM. Péron and Lesueur introduced more new animals to Europe than all other modern travellers put together.

Moreover, the geographical and hydrographical results were considerable. The English Government has always refused to acknowledge them, and Desborough Cooley, in his "History of Voyages", subordinates Baudin's discoveries to those of Flinders. It was even suggested that Flinders was detained prisoner at Mauritius for six years and a half, in order to allow French authors time to consult his maps, and arrange the details of their voyages accordingly. This accusation is too absurd to need refutation.

The two navigators, French and English, have each fairly earned a place in the history of the discovery of the Australian coasts, and it is unnecessary to praise one at the expense of the other.

In the preface to the second edition of his "Voyage de la Corvette *Australis*", which was revised and corrected by Louis de Freycinet, Péron has given each his due meed of praise; and to his able work we refer all readers who are interested in the question.

# CHAPTER II.

## AFRICAN EXPLORERS.

Shaw in Algeria and Tunis – Horneman in Fezzan – Adanson at Senegal – Houghton in Senegambia – Mungo Park and his two voyages to the Djoliba, or Niger – Sego – Timbuctoo – Sparrman and Le Vaillant at the Cape, at Natal, and in the Interior – Lacerda in Mozambique, and at Cazembé – Bruce in Abyssinia – Sources of the Blue Nile – Tzana Lake – Browne's journey in Darfur.

An Englishman named Thomas Shaw, a chaplain in Algeria, had profited by his twelve years' stay in Barbary to gather together a rich collection of natural curiosities, medals, inscriptions, and various objects of interest. Although he himself never visited the southern portion of Algeria, he availed himself of the facts he was able to obtain from well-informed travellers, who imparted to him a mass of information concerning the little known and scarcely visited country. He published a book in two large quarto volumes, which embraced the whole of ancient Numidia.

It was rather the work of a learned man than the account of a traveller, and it must be admitted that the learning is occasionally ill-directed. But in spite of its shortcomings as a geographical history, it had a large value at the time of its publication, and no one could have been better situated than Shaw for collecting such an enormous mass of material.

The following extract may give an idea of the style of the work: –

"The chief manufacture of the Kabyles and Arabs is the making 'hykes', as they call their blankets. The women alone are employed in this work; like Andromache and Penelope of old, they do not use the shuttle, but weave every thread of the wool with their fingers. The usual size of a hyke is six yards long and five or six feet broad, serving the Kabyle and Arab as a complete dress during the day, and as a covering for the bed at night. It is a loose but troublesome garment, as it is often disarranged and slips down, so that the person who wears it is every moment obliged to tuck it up and rearrange it. This shows the great use there is of a girdle whenever men are in active employment, and explains the force of the Scripture injunction *of having our loins girded*. The method of wearing this garment, with the use it is at other times put to as bed-covering, makes it probable that it is similar to if not identical with the *peplus* of the ancients. It is likewise probable that the loose garment flung over the shoulder, the *toga* of the Romans, was of this kind, as the drapery of statues is arranged very much in the same manner as the Arab hyke.

It is unnecessary to linger over this work, which has little interest for us. We shall do better to turn our attention to the journey of Frederic Conrad Horneman to Fezzan.

This young German offered his services to the African Society of London, and, having satisfied the authorities of his knowledge of medicine and acquaintance with the Arabic language, he was engaged, and furnished with letters of introduction, safe-conducts, and unlimited credit.

Leaving London in July, 1797, he went first to Paris. Lalande introduced him to the Institute, and presented him with his "Mémoire sur l'Afrique", and Broussonet gave him an introduction to a Turk from whom he obtained letters of recommendation to certain Cairo merchants who carried on business in the interior of Africa.

During his stay at Cairo, Horneman devoted himself to perfecting his knowledge of Arabic, and studying the manners and customs of the natives. We must not omit to mention that the traveller had been presented by Monge and Berthollet to Napoleon Buonaparte, who was then in command of the French forces in Egypt. From him he received a cordial welcome, and Buonaparte placed all the resources of the country at his service.

As the safer method of travelling, Horneman resolved to disguise himself as a Mohammedan merchant. He quickly learned a few prayers, and adopted a style of dress likely to impose upon unsuspecting people. He then started, accompanied by a fellow-countryman named Joseph Frendenburg, who had been a Mussulman for more than twelve years, had already made three pilgrimages to Mecca, and was perfectly familiar with the various Turkish and Arabic dialects. He was to act as Horneman's interpreter.

On the 5th of September, 1798, the traveller left Cairo with a caravan, and visited the famous oasis of Jupiter Ammon or Siwah, situated in the desert on the east of Egypt. It is a small independent

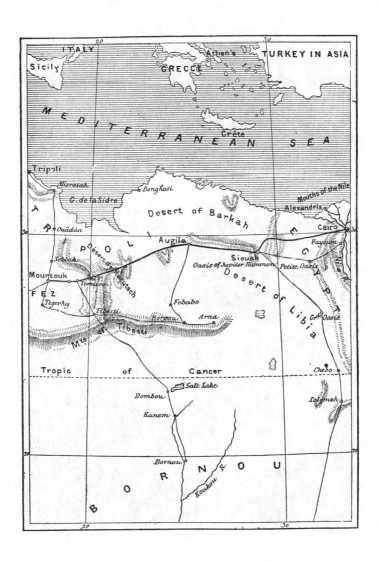

"He received a cordial welcome."

state, which acknowledges the Sultan, but is exempt from paying tribute. The town of Siwah is surrounded by several villages, at distances of a mile or two. It is built upon a rock in which the inhabitants have hollowed recesses for their dwellings. The streets are so narrow and intricate that a stranger cannot possibly find his way among them.

This oasis is of considerable extent. The most fertile portion comprises a well-watered valley, about fifty miles in circumference, which is productive of corn and edible vegetables. Dates of an excellent flavour are its most valuable export.

Horneman was anxious to explore some ruins which he had noticed, for he could obtain little information from the natives. But every time he penetrated to any distance in the ruins, he was followed by a number of the inhabitants, who prevented him from examining anything in detail. One of the Arabs said to him, "You must still be a Christian at heart, or you would not so often visit the works of the infidels."

This remark put a speedy end to Horneman's further explorations. As far as his superficial examination enabled him to judge, it was really the oasis of Ammon, and the ruins appeared to him to be of Egyptian origin.

The immense number of catacombs in the neighbourhood of the town, especially on the hill overlooking it, indicate a dense population in ancient times. The traveller endeavoured vainly to obtain a perfect head from one of these burial-places. Amongst the skulls he procured, he found no certain proof that they had been filled with resin. He met with many fragments of clothing, but they were all in such a state of decay that it was impossible to decide upon their origin or use.

After a stay of eight days in this place, Horneman crossed the mountains which surrounded the oasis of Siwah, and directed his steps towards Schiatah. So far no misfortune had interrupted his progress. But at Schiatah he was denounced as a Christian and a spy. Horneman cleverly saved his life by boldly reading out a passage in the Koran which he had in his possession. "Unfortunately, his interpreter, expecting that his baggage would be searched, had burned the collection of fragments of mummies, the botanical specimens, the journal containing the account of the journey, and all the books. This loss was quite irreparable."

A little further on, the caravan reached Augila, a town mentioned by Herodotus, who places it some ten days' journey from the oasis of Ammon. This accords with the testimony given by Horneman, who reached it in nine days' forced march. At Augila a number of merchants from Bengasi, Merote, and Mokamba had joined the caravan, amounting altogether to no less than a hundred and twenty persons. After a long journey over a sandy desert, the caravan entered a country interspersed with hills and ravines, where they found trees and grass at intervals. This was the desert of Harutsch. It was necessary to cross it in order to reach Temissa, a town of little note, built upon a hill, and surrounded by a high wall. At Zuila the Fezzan country was entered. The usual ceremonies, with interminable compliments and congratulations, were repeated at the entrance to every town. The Arabs appear to lay great stress upon these salutations, little trustworthy as they are, and travellers constantly express surprise at their frequent recurrence.

Upon the 17th of November, the caravan halted at Murzuk, the capital of Fezzan. It was the end of the journey. Horneman says that the greatest length of the cultivated portion of Fezzan is about three hundred miles from north to south, but to this must be added the mountainous region of Harutsch on the east, and the various deserts north and west. The climate is never pleasant; in summer the heat is terrible, and when the wind blows from the south, it is all but insupportable, even to the natives, and in winter the north wind is so cold that they are obliged to have recourse to fires.

The produce of the country consists principally of dates and vegetables. Murzuk is the chief market; there are collected the products of Cairo, Bengazi, Tripoli, Ghâdames, Ghât, and the Soudan. Among the articles of commerce are male and female slaves, ostrich feathers, skins of wild beasts, and gold-dust or nuggets. Bornu produces copper; Cairo silks, calicoes, woollen garments, imitation coral, bracelets, and indian manufactures. Fire-arms, sabres, and knives are imported by the merchants of Tripoli and Ghâdames.

The Fezzan country is ruled by a sultan descended from the scherifs, whose power is limitless, but who, nevertheless, pays a tribute of four thousand dollars to the Bey of Tripoli. Horneman, without giving the grounds of his calculation, informs us that the population amounts to seventy-five thousand inhabitants, all of whom profess Mohammedanism.

Horneman's narrative gives a few more details of the manners and customs of the people. He ends his report to the African Society by saying that he proposes visiting Fezzan again in the hope of obtaining new facts.

We learn, further, that Frendenburg, Horneman's faithful associate, died at Murzuk. Attacked by a violent fever, Horneman was forced to remain much longer than he desired in that town. While still only partially recovered, he went to Tripoli for change and rest, hoping there to meet with Europeans. Upon the 1st of December, 1799, he returned to Murzuk, and left it finally with a caravan upon the 7th of April, 1800. He was irresistibly attracted towards Bornu, and perished in that country, which was to claim so many victims.

During the eighteenth century, Africa was literally besieged by travellers. Explorers endeavoured to penetrate into it from every side. More than one succeeded in reaching the interior, only to meet with repulse or death. The discovery of the secrets of this mysterious continent was reserved for our own age, when the unexpected fertility of its resources has astonished the civilized world.

The facts relating to the coast of Senegal needed confirmation, but the French superiority was no longer undisputed. The English, with their earnest and enterprising character, were convinced of its importance in the development of their commerce, and determined upon its exploration. But before proceeding to the narrative of the adventures of Major Houghton and Mungo Park, we will devote a small space to the record of the work done by the French naturalist, Michel Adanson.

Devoted from early youth to the study of natural history, Adanson wished to become famous by the discovery of new species. It was hopeless to dream of obtaining them in Europe, and, in spite of opposition, Adanson selected Senegal as the field of his labours. He says, in a manuscript letter, that he chose it because it was the most difficult to explore of all European settlements, and, being the hottest, and most unhealthy, and most dangerous, was the least known by naturalists. Certainly a choice founded upon such reasoning gave proof of rare courage and ambition.

It is true that Adanson was by no means the first naturalist to encounter similar dangers, but he was the first to undertake them, with so much enthusiasm, at his own cost, and without hope of reward. Upon his return, he had not sufficient money to pay for the publication of his account of the discoveries he had made.

Embarking upon the 3rd of March, 1749, on board the *Chevalier Marin*, commanded by D'Apres de Mannevillette, he touched at Santa Cruz, Teneriffe, and disembarked at the mouth of the Senegal, which he took to be the Niger of ancient geographers.

During nearly five years he was engaged in exploring the colony in every direction, visiting in turn Podor, Portudal, Albreda, and the mouth of the Gambia. With unceasing perseverance, he collected a rich harvest of facts in the animal, vegetable, and mineral kingdoms.

To him is due the first exact account of a gigantic tree called the Baobab, which is often called Adansonia after him; of the habits of the grasshoppers, which form the chief food of certain wild tribes; of the white ants, and the dwellings they construct; and of a certain kind of oyster, which attach themselves to trees at the mouth of the Gambia. He says, –

"The natives have not the difficulty one might anticipate in catching them; they simply cut off the bough to which they cling. They often cluster to the number of over two hundred on one branch, and if there are several branches, they form a bunch of oysters such as a man could scarcely carry."

In spite of the interest of these and similar discoveries, there are few new facts for the geographer to glean. A few words about the Yolofs and Mandingoes comprise all there is to learn. If we followed Adanson throughout his explorations, we should gain little fresh information.

The same cannot be said of the expedition of which we are about to give some account. Major Houghton, captain in the 69th regiment, and English Governor of the Fort of Goree, had been familiar from his youth, part of which was passed with the English Embassy in Morocco, with the manners and customs of the Moors and the negroes of Senegambia. In 1790, he proposed to the African Society to explore the course of the Niger, penetrate as far as Timbuctoo and Houssa, and return by way of the Sahara. The carrying out of this bold plan met with but one obstacle, but that was almost sufficient to upset it.

Houghton left England upon the 16th of October, 1790, and anchored in Jillifree harbour, at the mouth of the Gambia, upon the 10th of November. Well received by the King of Barra, he followed the course of the Gambia to a distance of three hundred leagues, traversed the remainder of Senegambia, and reached Gonda Konda in Yanvi.

Walknaer, in his "History of Voyages", says, "He purchased a negro, a horse, and five asses, and prepared to proceed with the merchandise which was to pay his expenses to Mendana, the capital of the little kingdom of Woolli. Fortunately his slight knowledge of the Mandingo language enabled him to understand a negress

The Baobab.

who was speaking of a plot against him. The merchants trading on the river, imagining commerce to be his sole object, and fearing that he might compete with them, had determined upon his death.

"In order to avoid the threatened danger, he thought it wise to deviate from the usual route, and, accordingly, crossed the river with his asses, and reached the northern shore in the kingdom of Cantor."

Houghton then crossed the river a second time, and entered the kingdom of Woolli. He at once sent a messenger to the king, bearing presents, and asking for protection. He was cordially received, and the traveller was welcomed to Mendana, the capital, which he describes as an important town, situated in the midst of a fertile country, in which many herds of cattle graze.

Houghton was justified in anticipating a successful issue to his voyage; everything appeared to pressage it, when an event occurred which was the first blow to his hopes. A hut next that in which he slept took fire, and the whole town was soon in flames. His interpreter, who had made several attempts to rob him, seized this opportunity, and fled with a horse and three asses.

Still the King of Woolli continued his protection of the traveller, and loaded him with presents, precious not on account of their value, but as signs of the good-will which they demonstrated. This friend of the Europeans was named Djata. Humane, intelligent, and good-hearted, he wished the English to establish a factory in his kingdom.

Houghton, in a letter to his wife, says, –

"Captain Littleton, during a stay of four years here, has amassed a considerable fortune. He possesses several ships which trade up and down the river. At any time one can obtain, for the merest trifle, gold, ivory, wax, and slaves. Poultry, sheep, eggs, butter, milk, honey, and fish are extremely abundant, and for ten pounds sterling a large family might be maintained in luxury. The soil is dry, the air very healthy; and the King of Woolli told me that no white man had ever died at Fataconda."

Houghton then followed the Falemé river as far as Cacullo, which in D'Anville's map is called Cacoulon, and whilst in Bambouk gleaned a few facts about the Djoliba river, which runs through the interior of the Soudan. The direction of this river he ascertained to be southward as far as Djeneh, then west by east to Timbuctoo – facts which were later confirmed by Mungo Park. The traveller was cordially received by the King of Bambouk, who provided him with a guide to Timbuctoo, and with cowries to pay his expenses during the journey. It was hoped that Houghton would reach the Niger without accident, when a note, written in pencil and half effaced, reached Dr. Laidley. It was dated from Simbing, and stated that the traveller had been robbed of his baggage, but that he was prosecuting his journey to Timbuctoo. This was followed by accounts from various sources, which gave rise to a suspicion that Houghton had been assassinated in Bambara. This fate was uncertain until it was discovered by Mungo Park.

Walknaer says, –

"Simbing, where Houghton wrote the last words ever received from him, is a little walled town on the frontier of the kingdom of Ludamar. Here he was abandoned by his negro servants, who were unwilling to accompany him to the country of the Moors. Still he continued his route, and, after surmounting many obstacles, he advanced to the north, and endeavoured to cross the kingdom of Ludamar. Finally he reached Yaouri, and made the acquaintance of several merchants, on their way to sell salt at Tischet, a town situated near the marshes of the great desert, and six days' journey north of Yaouri. Then, by bribing the merchants with a gun and a little tobacco, he persuaded them to conduct him to Tischet. All this would lead us to suppose that the Moors deceived him, either as to the route he should have followed, or as to the state of the country between Yaouri and Timbuctoo.

"After two days' march, Houghton, finding himself deceived, wished to return to Yaouri. The Moors robbed him of all he possessed, and fled. He was forced to reach Yaouri on foot. Did he die of hunger, or was he assassinated by the Moors? This has never been rightly determined, but the spot where he perished was pointed out to Mungo Park."

The loss of Houghton's journals, containing the observations made during his journey, deprived science of the result of all his fatigue and devotion. To ascertain what he accomplished, one must have recourse to the *Proceedings of the African Society*. At this time Mungo Park, a young Scotch surgeon, who had just returned from a voyage to the East Indies on board the *Worcester*, learnt that the African Society were anxious to find an explorer willing to penetrate to the interior of the country watered by the Gambia. Mungo Park, who had long wished to acquaint himself with the productions of the country, and the manners and customs of the inhabitants, offered his services. He was not deterred by the apprehension that his predecessor, Houghton, had probably perished.

Portrait of Mungo Park.
(Facsimile of early engraving.)

At once accepted by the Society, Mungo Park hastened his preparations, and left Portsmouth upon the 22nd of May, 1795. He was furnished with introductions to Dr. Laidley, and a credit of two hundred pounds sterling. Landing at Jillifree, at the mouth of the Gambia, in the kingdom of Barra, and following the river, he reached Pisania, an English factory belonging to Dr. Laidley. He directed his attention first to acquiring a knowledge of the Mandingo language, which was most generally used, and in collecting the facts most likely to be useful in the execution of his plans.

His stay here enabled him to obtain more accurate information than his predecessors with regard to the Feloups, the Yolofs, the Foulahs, and the Mandingoes. The Feloups are morose, quarrelsome, and vindictive, but faithful and courageous. The Yolofs are a powerful and warlike nation, with very black skins. Except in colour and speech, they resemble the Mandingoes, who are gentle and sociable. Tall and well-made, their women are, comparatively speaking, pretty. Lastly, the Foulahs, who are the lightest in colour, seem much attached to a pastoral and agricultural life. The greater part of these populations are Mohammedans, and practise polygamy.

Upon the 2nd of December, Mungo Park, accompanied by two negro interpreters, and with a small quantity of baggage, started for the interior. He first reached the small kingdom of Woolli, the capital of which, Medina, comprises a thousand houses. He then proceeded to Kolor, a considerable town, and, after two days' march across a desert, entered the kingdom of Bondou. The natives are Foulahs, professing the Mohammedan religion; they carry on a brisk trade in ivory, when they are not engaged in agriculture.

The traveller soon reached the Falemé river, the bed of which, near its source in the mountains of Dalaba, is very auriferous. He was received by the king at Fataconda, the capital of Bondou, and had great difficulty in convincing him that he travelled from curiosity. His interview with the wives of the monarch is thus described. Mungo Park says, –

"I had scarcely entered the court, when I was surrounded by the entire seraglio. Some begged me for physic, some for amber, and all were most desirous of trying the great African specific of *blood-letting*. They are ten or twelve in number, most of them young and handsome, wearing on their heads ornaments of gold or pieces of amber. They rallied me a good deal upon different subjects, particularly upon the whiteness of my skin and the length of my nose. They insisted that both were artificial. The first, they said, was produced, when I was an infant, by dipping me in milk, and they insisted that my nose had been pinched every day till it had acquired its present unsightly and unnatural conformation."

Leaving Bondou by the north, Mungo Park entered Kajaaga, called by the French Galam. The climate of this picturesque country, watered by the Senegal, is far healthier than that of districts nearer the coast. The natives call themselves Serawoollis, and are called Seracolets by the French. The colour of their skin is jet black, and in this respect they are scarcely distinguishable from the Yolofs.

Mungo Park says, "The Serawoollis are habitually a trading people. They formerly carried on a great commerce with the French in gold-dust and slaves, and still often supply the British factories on the Gambia with slaves. They are famous for the skill and honesty with which they do business."

At Joag, Mungo Park was relieved of half his property by the envoys of the king, under pretence of making him pay for the right to pass through his kingdom. Fortunately for him, the nephew of Demba-Jego-Jalla, King of Kasson, who was about to return to his country, took him under his protection. They reached Gongadi, where there are extensive date plantations, together, and thence proceeded to Samia, on the shores of the Senegal, on the frontiers of Kasson.

The first town met with in this kingdom was that of Tiesie, which was reached by Mungo Park on the 31st of December. Well received by the natives, who sold him the provisions he needed at a reasonable price, the traveller was subjected by the brother and nephew of the king to endless indignities.

Leaving this town upon the 10th of January, 1796, Mungo Park reached Kouniakari, the capital of Kasson – a fertile, rich, and well-populated country, which can place forty thousand men under arms. The king, full of kindly feeling for the traveller, wished him to remain in his kingdom as long as the wars between Kasson and Kajaaga lasted. It was more than probable that the countries of Kaarta and Bambara, which Mungo Park wished to visit, would be drawn into it. The advice of the king to remain was prudent, and Park had soon reason enough to regret not having followed it.

But, impatient to reach the interior, the traveller would not listen, and entered the level and sandy plains of Kaarta. He met crowds of natives on the journey who were flying to Kasson to

Natives of Senegal.

escape the horrors of war. But even this did not deter him; he continued his journey until he reached the capital of Kaarta, which is situated in a fertile and open plain.

He was kindly received by the king, Daisy Kourabari, who endeavoured to dissuade him from entering Bambara, and, finding all his arguments useless, advised him to avoid passing through the midst of the fray, by entering the kingdom of Ludamar, inhabited by Moors. From thence he could proceed to Bambara.

During his journey Mungo Park noticed negroes who fed principally upon a sort of bread made from the berries of the lotus, which tasted not unlike gingerbread. This plant, *rhamnus lotus*, is indigenous in Senegambia, Nigritia, and Tunis.

"So," says Mungo Park, "there can be little doubt of this fruit being the lotus mentioned by Pliny as the food of the Lybian Lotophagi. I have tasted lotus bread, and think that an army may very easily have been fed with it, as is said by Pliny to have been done in Lybia. The taste of the bread is so sweet and agreeable, that the soldiers would not be likely to complain of it."

On the 22nd February, Mungo Park reached Jarra, a considerable town, with houses built of stone, inhabited by negroes from the south who had placed themselves under the protection of the Moors, to whom they paid considerable tribute. From Ali, King of Ludamar, the traveller obtained permission to travel in safety through his dominions. But, in spite of this safe-conduct, Park was almost entirely despoiled by the fanatical Moors of Djeneh. At Sampaka and Dalli, large towns, and at Samea, a small village pleasantly situated, he was so cordially welcomed that he already saw himself in fancy arrived in the interior of Africa, when a troop of soldiers appeared, who led him to Benown, the camp of King Ali.

"Ali," says Mungo Park, "was sitting upon a black morocco cushion, clipping a few hairs on his upper lip – a female attendant holding a looking-glass before him. He was an old man of Arab race, with a long white beard, and he looked sullen and angry. He surveyed me with attention, and inquired of the Moors if I could speak Arabic. Being answered in the negative, he appeared surprised, and continued silent. The surrounding attendants, and especially ladies, were much more inquisitive. They asked a thousand questions, inspected every part of my apparel, searched my pockets, and obliged me to unbutton my waistcoat to display the whiteness of my skin. They even counted my toes and fingers, as if they doubted whether I was in truth a human being."

An unprotected stranger, a Christian, and accounted a spy, Mungo Park was a victim to the insolence, ferocity, and fanaticism of the Moors. He was spared neither insults, outrages, nor blows. They attempted to make a barber of him, but his awkwardness in cutting the hairy face of the king's son exempted him from this degrading occupation. During his captivity he collected many particulars regarding Timbuctoo which is so difficult of access to Europeans, and was the bourne of all early African explorers.

"Houssa," a scherif told him, "is the largest town I have ever seen. Walet is larger than Timbuctoo, but as it is farther from the Niger, and its principal trade is in salt, few strangers are met there. From Benown to Walet is a distance of six days' journey. No important town is passed between the two, and the traveller depends for sustenance upon the milk procurable from Arabs, whose flocks and herds graze about the wells and springs. The road leads for two days through a sandy desert, where not a drop of water is to be had."

It takes eleven days to go from Walet to Timbuctoo, but water is not so scarce on this journey, which is generally made upon oxen. At Timbuctoo there are a number of Jews who speak Arabic, and use the same forms of prayer as the Moors.

The events of the war decided Ali to proceed to Jarra. Mungo Park, who had succeeded in making friends with the sultan's favourite, Fatima, obtained permission to accompany the king. The traveller hoped, by nearing the scene of action, to manage to escape. As it happened, the King of Kaarta, Daisy Kourabari, soon after marched against the town of Jarra. The larger number of inhabitants fled, and Mungo Park did the same.

He soon found means to get away, but his interpreter refused to accompany him. He was forced to start for Bambara alone, and destitute of resources.

The first town he came to was Wawra, which properly belongs to Kaarta, but was then paying tribute to Mansong, King of Bambara. Mungo Park says, –

"Upon the morning of the 7th of July, as I was about to depart, my landlord, with a great deal of diffidence, begged me to give him a lock of my hair. He had been told, he said, that white men's hair made a *saphic* (talisman) that would give the possessor all the knowledge of the white man. I had never before heard of so simple a mode of education, but I at once complied with the request; and my landlord's thirst for learning was so great that he cut and pulled at my hair till he had cropped one side of my head pretty closely,

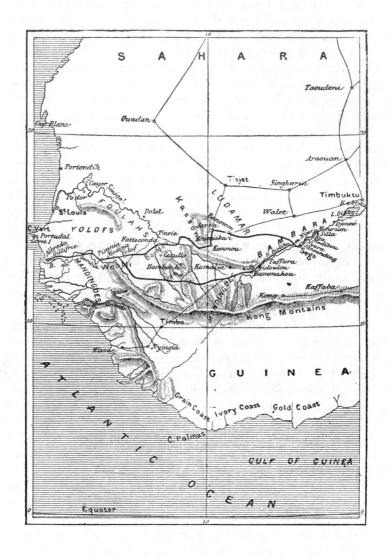

*ankatod* (good for nothing), *jankra lemen* (a regular plague), which expressions I thought applied to myself. As the pit had very much the appearance of a grave, I thought it prudent to mount my horse, and was about to decamp when the slave, who had gone before to the village, returned with the corpse of a boy about nine or ten years of age, quite naked. The negro carried the body by an arm and leg, and threw it into the pit with a savage indifference such as I had never seen. As he covered the body with earth, the Dooty kept repeating, *naphula attemata* (money lost), whence I concluded the boy had been his slave."

Mungo Park left Koulikorro where he had obtained food by writing saphics or talismans for the natives, upon the 21st of August, and reached Bammmakoa, where a large salt-market is held. From an eminence near the town he perceived a high range in the kingdom of Kong, whose ruler had a more numerous army than the King of Bambara.

Once more robbed by brigands of all he possessed, the unfortunate traveller found himself, in the rainy season, alone in a vast desert, five leagues from the nearest European settlement, and for the moment gave way to despair. But his courage soon revived; and reaching the town of Sibidoulou, his horse and clothes, which had been stolen from him by Foulah robbers, were restored to him by the *mansa*, or chief Kamalia, or Karfa Taura advised him to await the cessation of the rainy season, and then to proceed to Gambia with a caravan of slaves. Worn out, destitute, attacked by fever, which for five months kept him prostrate, Mungo Park had no choice but to remain in this place.

Upon the 19th of April the caravan set out. We can readily imagine the joy experienced by Mungo Park when all was ready. Crossing the desert of Jallonka, and passing first the principal branch of the Senegal river, and then the Falemé, the caravan finally reached the shores of the Gambia, and on the 12th of June, 1797, Mungo Park once more arrived at Pisania, where he was warmly welcomed by Dr. Laidley, who had despaired of ever seeing him again.

The traveller returned to England upon the 22nd of September. So great was the impatience with which an account of his discoveries, certainly the most important in this part of Africa, was awaited, that the African Society allowed him to publish for his own profit an abridged account of his adventures.

He had collected more facts as to the geography, manners, and

and would have done the same with the other had I not signified my disapprobation, assuring him that I wished to reserve some of this precious material for a future occasion."

First Gallon and then Mourja, a large town, famous for its trade in salt, were passed, after fatigues and incredible privations. Upon nearing Sego, Mungo Park at last perceived the Djoliba. "Looking forward," he says, "I saw, with infinite pleasure, the great object of my mission – the long-sought-for, majestic Niger, glittering in the morning sun, as broad as the Thames at Westminster, and flowing slowly to the eastward. I hastened to the brink, and, having drunk of the water, lifted up my fervent thanks in prayer to the Great Ruler of all things for having thus far crowned my endeavours with success.

"The fact of the Niger flowing towards the east did not, however, excite my surprise; for, although I had left Europe in great hesitation on this subject, and rather believed it ran in the contrary direction, I had made frequent inquiries during my progress, and had received from negroes of different nations such clear and decisive assurances that its course *was towards the rising sun* as scarce left any doubt in my mind, more especially as I knew that Major Houghton had collected similar information in a similar manner.

"Sego, the capital of Bambara, at which I had now arrived, consists, properly speaking, of four distinct towns; two on the northern bank of the river, called Sego Korro and Sego Boo, and two on the southern bank, called Sego Sou Korro and Sego See Korro. They are all surrounded with high mud walls; the houses are built of clay, of a square form, with flat roofs; some of them have two storeys, and many of them are whitewashed. Besides these buildings, Moorish mosques are seen in every quarter, and the streets, though narrow, are broad enough for every practical purpose in a country where wheel carriages are unknown. From the best information I could obtain, I have reason to believe that Sego contains altogether about thirty thousand inhabitants. The king of Bambara resides permanently at Sego See Korro; he employs a great many slaves in conveying people over the river; and the money they take, though the fare is only ten cowries for each person, furnishes a considerable revenue to the king in the course of a year."

By advice of the Moors, the king refused to receive the traveller, and forbade him to remain in his capital, where he could not have protected him from ill-treatment. However, to divest his refusal of all appearance of ill-will, he sent him a bag containing 5,000 cowries, of the value of about a pound sterling, to buy provisions.

The messenger sent by the king was to serve as guide as far as Sansanding. Protest and anger were alike impossible; Mungo Park could do nothing but follow the orders sent. Before reaching Sansanding, he was present at the harvest of vegetable butter, which is the produce of a tree called Shea.

"These trees," says the narrative, "grow in great abundance all over this part of Bambara. They are not planted by the natives, but are found growing naturally in the woods; and, in clearing land for cultivation, every tree is cut down but the shea. The tree itself very much resembles the American oak; the fruit – from the kernel of which, after it has been dried in the sun, the butter is prepared by boiling in water – has somewhat the appearance of a Spanish olive. The kernel is imbedded in a sweet pulp, under a thin green rind, and the butter produced from it, besides the advantage of keeping a whole year without salt, is whiter, firmer, and, to my palate, of a richer flavour than the best butter I ever tasted from cows' milk. It is a chief article of the inland commerce of these districts."

Sansanding, a town containing from eight to ten thousand inhabitants, is a market-place much frequented by the Moors, who bring glass-ware from the Mediterranean forts, which they exchange for gold-dust and cotton. Mungo Park was not able to remain at this place, for the importunities of the natives and the pernicious insinuations of the Moors warned him to continue his route. His horse was so worn out by fatigue and privation that he felt obliged to embark on the river Djoliba or Niger.

At Mourzan, a fishing village upon the northern bank of the river, everything combined to induce Park to relinquish his enterprise. The further he advanced to the eastward down the river, the more he placed himself in the power of the Moors. The rainy season had commenced and it would soon be impossible to travel otherwise than by boat. Mungo Park was now so poor that he could not even hire a boat; he was forced to rely upon public charity.

To advance further under these circumstances was not only to risk his life, but to place the results of all his fatigues and efforts in jeopardy. To return to Gambia was scarcely less perilous; to do so he must traverse hundreds of miles on foot through hostile countries. Still the hope of returning home might sustain his courage.

"Before leaving Silla," says the traveller, "I thought it incumbent on me to collect from the Moorish and negro traders all the information I could concerning the further course of the Niger eastward, and the situation and extent of the kingdoms in its neighbourhood.

"Two days' journey eastward of Silla is the town of Djenneh, which is situated on a small island in the river, and is said to contain as many inhabitants as Sego itself, or any other town in Bambara. At a distance of two days' more, the river widens and forms a considerable lake, called Dibby (or the dark lake), concerning the extent of which, all I could learn was that, in crossing it from east to west, the canoes lose sight of land for one whole day. From this lake the water issues in many different streams, which finally become two branches, one flowing to the north-east, the other to the east; but these branches join at Kabra, which is one day's journey to the south of Timbuctoo, and is the port or shipping-place of that city. The tract of land between the two streams is called Timbala, and is inhabited by negroes. The whole distance by land from Djenneh to Timbuctoo is twelve days' journey. North-east of Masena is the kingdom of Timbuctoo, the great object of European research, the capital of the kingdom being one of the principal marts for the extensive commerce which the Moors carry on with the negroes. The hope of acquiring wealth in this pursuit, and zeal for propagating their religion, have filled this extensive city with Moors. The king himself and all the chief officers of his court are Moors, and are said to be more intolerant and severe in their principles than any other of the Moorish tribes in this part of Africa."

Mungo Park was then forced to retrace his steps, and that through a country devastated by inundation and heavy rains. He passed through Mourzan, Kea, and Modibon, where he regained his horse; Nyara, Sansanding, Samea, and Sai, which is surrounded by a deep moat, and protected by high walls with square towers; Jabbéa, a large town, from which he perceived high mountain ranges, and Taffara, where he was received with little hospitality.

At the village of Souha, Park begged a handful of grain of a "dooty", who answered that he had nothing to give away.

"Whilst I was examining the face of this inhospitable old man, and endeavouring to find out the cause of the sullen discontent which was visible in his eye, he called to a slave who was working in the corn-field at a little distance, and ordered him to bring his spade with him. The Dooty then told him to dig a hole in the ground, pointing to a spot at no great distance. The slave with his spade began to dig in the earth, and the Dooty, who appeared to be a man of very fretful disposition, kept muttering to himself until the pit was almost finished, when he repeatedly pronounced the word

customs of the country than all preceding travellers; he had determined the position of the sources of the Senegal and Gambia, and
surveyed the course of the Niger or Djoliba – which he proved to
run eastwards, whilst the Gambia flowed to the west.

Thus a point, which up to this time had been disputed by geographers, was definitely settled. It was no longer possible to
confound the three rivers, as the French geographer Delisle had
done, in 1707, when he represented the Niger as running eastward
from Bornu, and flowing into the river Senegal on the west. He
himself, however, had admitted and corrected this error, in his later
maps of 1722 and 1727, no doubt on account of the facts ascertained by André Brue, governor of Senegal.

Houghton, indeed, had learned much from the natives of the
course of the Niger through the Mandingo country, and of the relative positions of Sego, Djennéh, and Timbuctoo; but it was
reserved for Mungo Park to fix positively, from personal knowledge, the position of the two first-named towns, and to furnish
circumstantial details of the country, and the tribes who inhabit it.

Public opinion was unanimous as to the importance of the great
traveller's exploration, and keenly appreciative of the courage,
skill, and honesty exhibited by him.

A short time later, the English government offered Mungo Park
the conduct of an expedition to the interior of Australia; but he
refused it.

In 1804, however, the African Society determined to complete
the survey of the Niger, and proposed to Mungo Park the command
of a new expedition for its exploration. This time the great traveller
did not refuse, and upon the 30th of January 1805, he left England.
Two months later he landed at Goree.

He was accompanied by his brother-in-law, Anderson, a surgeon,
by George Scott, a draughtsman, and by thirty-five artillery-men.
He was authorized to enrol as many soldiers as he liked in his service, and was provided with a credit of five hundred pounds.

"These resources," says Walknaer, "so vast in comparison with
those furnished by the African Society, were, to our thinking, partly
the cause of his loss. The rapacious demands of the African kings
grew in proportion to the riches they supposed our traveller to possess; and the effort to meet the enormous drain made upon him,
was in great part the cause of the catastrophe which brought the
expedition to an end."

Four carpenters, one officer and thirty-five artillery-men, and a

Mandingo merchant named Isaac, who was to act as guide, with the leaders of the expedition already mentioned, composed an imposing caravan. Mungo Park left Cayee upon the 27th of April, 1805, and reached Pisania the next day. From this place, ten years earlier, he had started upon his first exploration. Taking an easterly direction, he followed his former route as far as Bambaku, upon the shores of the Niger. When he arrived at this place, the number of Europeans was already reduced to six soldiers and a carpenter; the remainder had succumbed to fatigue, or the fevers incidental to the inundations. The exactions of the various petty chiefs through whose domains the expedition passed had considerably diminished the stock of merchandise.

Mungo Park was now guilty of an act of grave imprudence. Remarking that trade was very active at Sansanding, a town containing eleven thousand inhabitants, and that beads, indigo, antimony, rings, bracelets, and other articles not likely to be spoiled in the transit to England, were freely exhibited for sale, "he opened," says Walknaer, "a large shop, which he stocked with European merchandise, for sale wholesale and retail; and probably the large profits he made excited the envy of the merchants. The natives of Djenneh, the Moors, and merchants of Sansanding, joined with those of Sego in offering, in the presence of Modibinne, to give the King of Mansong a larger and more valuable quantity of merchandise than he had received from the English traveller, if he would seize his baggage, and then kill him, or send him out of Bambarra. But in spite of his knowledge of this fact, Mungo Park still kept his shop open, and he received as the proceeds of one single day's business, 25,756 pieces of money, or cowries."

Upon the 28th of October Anderson expired, after four months' illness, and Mungo Park found himself once more alone in the heart of Africa. The King of Mansong had accorded him permission to build a boat, which would enable him to explore the Niger. Naming his craft the *Djoliba*, he fixed upon the 16th of November for his departure.

Here his journal ends, with details on the riverside populations, and on the geography of the countries he was the first to discover. This journal, when it reached Europe, was published, imperfect as it was, as soon as the sad fact was realized that the writer had perished in the waters of the Djoliba. It contained in reality no new discovery, but it was recognized as useful to geographical science. Mungo Park had determined the astronomical position of the more important towns, and thereby furnished material for a map of Senegambia. The perfecting of this map was entrusted to Arrowsmith, who stated in an advertisement, that, finding wide dif ferences between the positions of the towns as shown in the journal by each day's travel and that furnished by the astronomical observations, it was impossible to reconcile them; but that, in accordance with the latter, he had been obliged to place the route followed by Mungo Park in his first voyage farther north.

It was reserved for the Frenchman Walknaer to discover a curious discrepancy in Mungo Park's journal. This was a singular error upon the part of the traveller, which neither the English editor nor the French translator (whose work was badly performed) had discovered. Mungo Park in his diary records events as happening upon the 31st of April. As every one knows that that month has only thirty days, it followed that during the course of his journey the traveller had made a mistake of a whole day, reckoning in his calculations from the evening instead of the morning. Hence important rectifications were necessary in Arrowsmith's map; but none the less, when once Mungo Park's error is recognized, it is evident that to him we owe the first faithful map of Senegambia.

Although the facts that reached the English Government allowed no room for doubt as to the fate of the traveller, a rumour that white men had been seen in the interior of Africa induced the Governor of Senegal to fit out an expedition. The command was entrusted to the negro merchant Isaac, Mungo Park's guide, who had faithfully delivered the traveller's journal to the English authorities. We need not linger over the account of this expedition, but merely relate that which concerns the last days of Mungo Park.

At Sansanding, Isaac encountered Amadi Fatouma, the native who was with Park on the *Djoliba* when he perished, and from him he obtained the following recital: –

"We embarked at Sansanding, and in two days reached Silla, the spot where Mungo Park completed his first journey.

"After two days' navigation we reached Djenneh. In passing Dibby, three boats, filled with negroes armed with lances and arrows, but without fire-arms, approached us. We had passed successively Racbara and Timbuctoo, when we were pursued by these boats, which we repulsed with difficulty, and only after killing several natives. At Gourounia we were attacked by seven boats, but succeeded in repulsing them. Constant skirmishes ensued, with heavy loss to the blacks, until we reached Kaffo, where we remained for a day. We then proceeded down the river as far as Carmusse, and anchored off Gournou. Next day we perceived a Moorish detachment, who allowed us to pass.

"We then entered the country of Houssa. Next day we reached Yaori, and sent Amadi Fatouma into the town, with presents for the chief and to purchase food. The negro, before accepting the presents, enquired if the white traveller intended to revisit his country. Mungo Park, to whom the question was reported, replied that he should never return."

It is supposed that these words brought about his death. The negro chief, once convinced that he should not see Mungo Park again, determined to keep the presents intended for his king.

Meantime, Amadi Fatouma reached the king's residence, at some distance from the river. The prince, warned of the presence of the white men, sent an army next day to the small village of Boussa, on the river side. When the *Djoliba* appeared it was assailed by a shower of stones and arrows. Park threw his baggage into the river, and jumped in with his companions. All perished.

Thus miserably died the first Englishman who had navigated the Djoliba and visited Timbuctoo. Many efforts were made in the same direction, but almost all were destined to fail.

At the end of the eighteenth century, two of Linnæus's best pupils explored the south of Africa in the interests of natural history. Sparrman undertook to search for animals, and Thunberg for plants. The account of Sparrman's expedition, which, as we have said, was interrupted by his voyage in Oceania, after Cook's expedition, was the first to appear. It was translated into French by Le Tourneur. In his preface, which is still allowed to stand, Le Tourneur deplored the loss of the learned explorer, who he said had died during a voyage to the Gold Coast. Just as the work was published, Sparrman reappeared, to the great astonishment of Le Tourneur.

Sparrman had reached Africa upon the 30th of April, 1772, and landed at the Cape of Good Hope. At this time the town was only two miles across each way, including the gardens and plantations adjoining it on one side. The streets were wide, planted with oaks, and the houses were white, or, to Sparrman's surprise, painted green.

His object in visiting the Cape was to act as tutor to the children of a M. Kerste; but upon his arrival in Cape Town, he found that his employer was absent at his winter residence in False Bay. When the spring came round, Sparrman accompanied Kerste to Alphen, a property which he possessed near Constance. The naturalist availed himself of the opportunity to make many excursions in the neighbourhood, and attempt the somewhat dangerous ascent of the Table Mountain. By these means he became acquainted with the manners and customs of the Boers, and their treatment of their slaves. The violence of the latter was so great that the inhabitants of the town were obliged to sleep with locked doors, and provided with firearms close at hand.

Nearly all over the colony a rough hospitality ensured a certain welcome for the traveller. Sparrman relates several curious experiences of his own.

"I arrived one evening," he says, "at the dwelling of a farmer named Van der Spooei, a widower, born in Africa, and father of the proprietor of the Red Constance, or the Old Constance.

"Making believe not to see me approach, he remained stationary in the entry of his house. As I approached him, he offered his hand, still without attempting to come forward, and said, 'Good day! You are welcome! How are you? *Who* are you? A glass of wine perhaps? or a pipe? Will you partake of something?' I answered his questions laconically, and accepted his offers in the same style as they were offered. His daughter, a well-made girl of some fourteen or fifteen years of age, brought in dinner, which consisted of a fine breast of lamb, stewed with carrots. The meal over, she offered me tea so pleasantly that I was quite puzzled whether to admire the dinner or my charming hostess the most. Both father and daughter showed the greatest kindness and good will. I spoke to my host several times, in hopes of breaking his silence; but his replies were brief; and I observed that he only once commenced a conversation himself, when he pressed me to remain over night in his house. I bid him farewell, deeply impressed with his hospitality."

Sparrman undertook several similar expeditions, among others, one to Hout Bay and Paarl, in which he had frequent occasion to notice the exaggerations to be met with in the narrative of Kolbe, his predecessor.

He intended to continue his explorations during the winter, and projected a journey into the interior, when the fine season should return. When the frigates commanded by Captain Cook, the *Resolution* and *Adventure*, arrived at the Cape, Forster invited the young Swedish naturalist to accompany him; and Sparrman was thus enabled to visit New Zealand, Van Diemen's Land, New

Holland, Otaheite, Tierra del Fuego, the Antarctic Regions, and New Georgia, before his return to the Cape, where he landed on the 22nd of March, 1775.

His first care upon his return was to organize his expedition to the interior; and in order to add to his available resources he practised medicine and surgery during the winter. A cargo of corn, medicine, knives, tinder-boxes, and spirits for the preservation of specimens was collected, and packed in an immense waggon, drawn by five yoke of oxen.

Sparrman says, –

"The conductor of this cart needs dexterity, not only in his management of the animals, but in the use of the whip of African drivers. These instruments are about fifteen feet long, with a thong of the same or greater length, and a tongue of white leather almost three feet long. The driver holds this formidable instrument in both hands, and from his seat in front of the waggon can reach the foremost oxen with it. He distributes his cuts unceasingly, well understanding how and where to distribute them in such a manner that the hide of the animals feels the whip."

Sparrman was to accompany the waggon on horseback, and was accompanied by a young colonist, named Immelman, who wished to penetrate into the interior for recreation. They started upon the 25th of July, 1775. After passing Rent River, scaling the Hottentot Holland Kloof, and crossing the Palmite, they entered a desert country, interspersed with plains, mountains, and valleys, without water, but frequented by antelopes of various kinds, with zebras and ostriches.

Sparrman soon reached the warm mineral baths at the foot of the Zwartberg, which, at that time, were much frequented, the company having built a house near the mountains. At this point the explorer was joined by young Immelman, and together they started for Zwellendam, which they reached upon the 2nd of September. We will give a few of the facts they collected about the inhabitants.

The Hottentots are as tall as Europeans, their hands and feet are small, and their colour a brownish yellow. They have not the thick lips of the Kaffirs and natives of Mozambique. Their hair is black and woolly, curly, but not thick. They rub the entire body with fat and soot. A Hottentot who paints himself looks less naked, and more complete, so to say, than one who only rubs himself with grease. Hence, the saying, "A Hottentot without paint is like a shoe without blacking".

A Hottentot.
(Facsimile of early engraving.)

These natives usually wear a cloak called karos, made of sheep's skin, with the wool turned inwards. The women arrange it with a long point, which forms a sort of hood, in which they place their children. Both men and women wear leather rings upon their arms and legs – a custom, which gave rise to the fable that this race rolled puddings round their limbs, to feed on from time to time. They also wear copper and iron rings, but these ornaments are less common.

The kraal, or Hottentot village, is a collection of huts in a circle, all very similar, and of the shape of beehives. The doors, which are in the centre, are so low that they can only be entered on the knees. The hearth is in the middle of the hut, and the roof has no hole for the escape of the smoke.

The Hottentots must not be confounded with the Bushmen. The latter live only for hunting and robbery; their skill in throwing poisoned arrows, their courage, and the wildness of their lives, render them invincible.

At Zwellendam, Sparrman saw the quagga, a species of horse, like a zebra in shape, but with shorter ears.

The explorer next visited Mossel Bay, a harbour little used, as it is too much exposed to the westwinds; and thence he proceeded to the country of the Houtniquas, or, as Burchell's map calls them, the Antiniquas. This woody country appeared fertile, and the colonists established there are prosperous. Sparrman met with most of the quadrupeds of Africa in this district, such as elephants, leopards, lions, tiger cats, hyenas, monkeys, hares, antelopes, and gazelles.

We will not attempt to follow Sparrman to all the small settlements he visited. An enumeration of the streams, kraals, or villages he passed would convey no information to the reader. Rather let us gather from his narratives a few curious and novel details concerning two creatures which he describes, the sheep of the Cape, and the "honey-guide".

"When a sheep is to be killed," he says, "the very leanest of the flock is selected. It would be impossible to use the others for food. Their tails are of a triangular shape, and are often a foot and a half long, and occasionally six inches thick in the upper part. One of these tails will weigh eight or twelve pounds, and they consist principally of delicate fat, which some persons eat with bread instead of butter. It is used in the preparation of food, and sometimes to make candles."

After describing the two-horned rhinoceros, hitherto unknown, the gnu – an animal in form something between the horse and the

A Bosjeman.
(Facsimile of early engraving.)

ox – the gazelle, the baboon, and the hippopotamus, the habits of which were previously imperfectly known, Sparrman describes a curious bird, of great service to the natives, which he calls the honey-guide.

"This bird," he says, "is remarkable neither in size nor colour. At first sight it would be taken for a common sparrow, but it is a little larger than that bird, of a somewhat lighter colour, with a small yellow spot on each shoulder, and dashes of white in the wings and tail.

"In its own interests, this bird leads the natives to the bees' nests, for it is very fond of honey, and it knows that whenever a nest is destroyed, a little honey will be spilled, or left behind, as a recompense for its services.

"It seems to grow hungry in the morning and evening. In any case, it is then that it leaves its nest, and by its piercing cries attracts the attention of the Hottentots or the colonists. The cries are almost always answered by the appearance of natives or settlers, when the bird, repeating its call unceasingly, slowly flies from place to place towards the spot where the bees have made their home. Arrived at the nest, whether it be in the cleft of a rock, in a hollow tree, or in some underground cavity, the guide hovers about it for a few seconds, and then perches hard by, and remains a silent, and hidden spectator of the pillage, in which he hopes subsequently to have his share. Of this phenomenon I have myself twice been a witness."

On the 12th of April, 1776, on his way back to the Cape, Sparrman heard that a large lake, the only one in the colony, had been discovered to the north of the Schneuwberg district. A little later, the traveller got back to the Cape, and embarked for Europe with the numerous natural history collections he had made.

About the same time, between 1772-1775, Thunberg, the Swede, whom Sparrman had met at the Cape, made three successive journeys in the interior of Africa. They were not, any more than Sparrman's, actual journeys of discovery; and we owe the acquisition of no new geographical fact to Thunberg. He did but make a vast number of interesting observations on the birds of the Cape, and he also ascertained a few interesting details respecting the various races of the interior, which turned out to be far more fertile than was at first supposed.

Thunberg was followed in the same latitudes by an English officer, Lieutenant William Paterson, whose chief aim was to collect plants and other objects of natural history. He penetrated a little farther north than the Orange River, and into Kaffraria a good deal further east than Fish River. To him we owe the first notice of the giraffe; and his narrative is rich in important observations on the natural history, structure, and inhabitants of the country.

It is a curious fact that the Europeans attracted to South Africa by zeal for geographical discovery, were far less numerous than those whose motive was love of natural history. We have already mentioned Sparrman, Thunberg, and Paterson. To this list we must now add the name of the ornithologist Le Vaillant.

Born at Paramaribo, in Dutch Guiana, of French parents, who traded in birds, Le Vaillant visited Europe with them as a mere child, and traversed Holland, Germany, Lorraine, and the Vosges, on his way to Paris. It will readily be understood that this wandering life awoke in him a taste for travelling; and his passion for birds, early excited by the examination of private and public collections, made him eager to enrich science by descriptions and drawings of unknown species.

Now what country would afford the richest ornithological harvest? The districts near the Cape had been explored by botanists, and by a scientific man who had made quadrupeds his chief study; but no one had as yet traversed them to collect birds.

Le Vaillant arrived at the Cape on the 29th of March, 1781, after the loss of his vessel in an explosion, with nothing but the clothes he wore, ten ducats, and his gun.

Others would have been disheartened, but Le Vaillant did not despair of extricating himself from his painful position. Confident in his skill with the gun and the bow, in his strength and agility, as well as in his skill in preparing the skins of animals, and in stuffing birds so that their plumage should retain all its origin gloss, the naturalist had soon opened relations with the wealthiest collectors of the Cape.

One of these, an official named Boers, provided Le Vaillant with every requisite for a successful journey, including carts, oxen, provisions, objects for barter, and horses. Even servants and guides were appointed, free of cost, to the explorer. The kind of researches to which Le Vaillant intended to devote himself influenced his mode of travelling. Instead of seeking frequented and beaten tracks, he tried to avoid them, and to penetrate into districts neglected by Europeans, hoping in them to meet with birds unknown to science. As a result he may be said always to have taken nature by surprise, coming into contact with natives whose manners had not yet been modified by intercourse with whites; so that the information he gives us brings savage life, as it really is, more vividly before us than anything told us by his predecessors or successors. The only mistake made by Le Vaillant was the entrusting of the translation of his notes to a young man who modified them to suit his own notions. Far from taking the scrupulous care to be exact which distinguishes modern editors, he exaggerated facts; and, dwelling too much on the personal qualities of the traveller, he gave to the narrative of the journey a boastful tone very prejudicial to it.

After three months' stay at the Cape and in its neighbourhood, Le Vaillant started, on the 18th December, 1781, for a first journey eastwards, and in Kaffraria. His equipment this time consisted of thirty oxen – ten for each of his two waggons, and ten as reserve – three horses, nine dogs, and five Hottentots.

Le Vaillant first crossed the Dutch districts already explored by Sparrman, where he met with vast herds of zebras, antelopes, and ostriches, arriving in due course at Zwellendam, where he bought some oxen, a cart, and, a cock – the last serving as an alarm-clock throughout the journey. Another animal was also of great use to him. This was a monkey he had tamed, and promoted to the post, alike useful and honourable, of taster – no one being allowed to touch any fruit or root unknown to the Hottentots till Master Rees had given his verdict upon it.

Rees was also employed as a sentinel; and his senses, sharpened by use and the struggle for life, exceeded in delicacy those of the most subtle Redskin. He it was who warned the dogs of the approach of danger. If a snake approached, or a troop of monkeys were disporting themselves in a neighbouring thicket, Rees' terror and his shrieks quickly revealed the presence of a disturbing element.

From Zwellendam, which he left on the 12th January, 1782, Le Vaillant made his way eastwards, at some little distance from the sea. He pitched his camp on the banks of the Columbia (Duywen Hock) river and made many very successful hunting excursions in a district rich in game, finally reaching Mossel Bay, where the howls of innumerable hyenas frightened the oxen.

A little farther on he entered the country of the Houtniquas, a Hottentot name signifying men filled with honey. Here not a step could be taken without coming upon swarms of bees. Flowers sprang up beneath the feet of the travellers; the air was heavy with their perfume; their varied colours lent such enchantment to the scene that some of the servants would have liked to halt. Le Vaillant however hastened to press on. The whole of this district, down to

Till Master Rees had given his verdict.

the sea, is occupied by colonists, who breed cattle, make butter, cultivate timber, and collect honey, sending their merchandise to the Cape for sale.

A little beyond the last post of the company, Le Vaillant, having entered a district peopled by thousands of "turacos", and other rare birds, pitched his hunting camp; but his plans were terribly upset by the continuous fall of heavy rains, the result of which was to reduce the travellers to great straits for want of food.

After many a sudden change of fortune and many hunting adventures, an account of which would be very amusing, though beyond the scope of our narrative, Le Vaillant reached Mossel Bay. Here, with what delight we can easily imagine, he found letters from France awaiting him. One excursion after another was now made in various directions, until Kaffraria was entered. It was difficult to open relations with its people who sedulously avoided the whites, having suffered the loss of many men and much cattle at their hands. Moreover the Tamboukis had taken advantage of their critical position to invade Kaffraria and commit numerous depredations, whilst the Bosjemans hunted them down unmercifully. Without fire-arms, and attacked on so many sides at once, the Kaffirs were driven to hiding themselves, and were retiring northwards.

As matters stood it was, useless to attempt to penetrate into the mountainous districts of Kaffraria, and Le Vaillant retraced his steps. He then visited the Schneuwberg mountains, the Karroo desert and the shores of the Buffalo River, returning to the Cape on the 2nd April, 1783.

The results of this long campaign were important. Le Vaillant obtained some decided information about the Gonaquas, a numerous race which must not be confounded with the Hottentots properly so called, but are probably the offspring of their inter-marriage with the Kaffirs. With regard to the Hottentots themselves, the information collected by Le Vaillant agrees on almost every point with that obtained by Sparrman.

"The Kaffirs seen by Le Vaillant," says Walknaer, "were most of them taller than either the Hottentots or the Gonaquas. They have neither the retiring jaws nor prominent cheek bones which are so repulsive in the Hottentots, but are less noticeable in the Gonaquas, neither have they the broad flat faces and thick lips of their neighbours the negroes of Mozambique. Their faces, on the contrary, are round, their noses fairly prominent, and their teeth the whitest and most regular of any people in the world. Their complexion is of a clear dark brown; and, but for this one characteristic, says Le Vaillant, any Kaffir woman would be considered very pretty, even beside a European."

During Le Vaillant's sixteen months of absence, the aspect of the Cape had completely changed. When the traveller left he admired the modest bearing of the Dutch women; on his return he found them thinking only of amusement and dress. Ostrich feathers were so much in vogue that they had to be imported from Europe and Asia. All those brought by our traveller were quickly bought up. The birds which he had sent to the colony on every possible opportunity now amounted to one thousand and twenty-four specimens; and Mr. Boers' house, where they were kept, was converted into a regular natural history museum.

Le Vaillant's journey had been so successful that he could not but wish to begin another. Although his friend Boers had returned to Europe, he was able, with the aid of the many other friends he had made, to collect the materials for a fresh trip. On the 15th June, 1783, he started at the head of a caravan numbering nineteen persons. He also took thirteen dogs, one he- and two she-goats, three cows, thirty-six draught and fourteen reserve oxen, with two for carrying the baggage of the Hottentot servants.

We shall not, of course, follow the traveller in his hunting excursions; all we need to know is that he succeeded in making a collection of marvellous birds, that he introduced the first giraffe to Europe, and that he traversed the whole of the vast space between the tropic of Capricorn on the west and the 14th meridian on the east. He returned to the Cape in 1784, he embarked for Europe, and arrived at Paris early in January, 1785.

The first native people met with by Le Vaillant in his second voyage were the Little Namaquas, a race but very little known, and who soon died out – the more readily that they occupied a barren country, subject to constant attacks from the Bosjemans. Although of fair height, they are inferior in appearance to the Kaffirs and Namaquas, to whose customs theirs bear a great resemblance.

The Caminouquas, or Comeinacquas, of whom Le Vaillant gives many particulars, exceed them in height. He says, –

"They appear taller even than the Gonaquas, although possibly they are not so in reality; but the illusion is sustained by their small bones, delicate and emaciated appearance, and slender limbs. The long mantle of light material which hangs from the shoulder to the ground adds to their height. They look like drawn out men. Lighter

A Kaffir woman.
(Facsimile of early engraving.)

in colour than the Cape natives, they have better features than the other Hottentot tribes, owing to the fact that their noses are less flat and their cheek bones less prominent."

Of all the races visited by Le Vaillant, the most peculiar and most ancient was that of the Houzonanas, a tribe which had not been met with by any other northern traveller; but they appear identical with the Bechuanas, although the part of the country assigned to them does not coincide with that which they are known to have occupied for many years.

"The Houzonanas," says the narrative, "are small in stature, the tallest being scarcely five feet four in height. These small beings are perfectly proportioned, and are surprisingly strong and active. They have an imposing air of boldness. Le Vaillant considers them the best endowed mentally, and the strongest physically, of all the savage races he had met with. In face they resemble the Hottentots, but they have rounder chins, and they are far less black. They have curly hair, so short that Le Vaillant at first imagined it to be shaven."

One striking peculiarity of the Houzonanas is a large mass of flesh upon the back of the women, which forms a natural saddle, and oscillates strangely with every movement of the body. Le Vaillant describes a woman whom he saw with her child about three years old, who was perched upon his feet behind her like a footman behind a cabriolet.

We will pass over the traveller's description of the appearance and customs of these various races, many of which are now extinct, or incorporated in some more powerful tribe. Although by no means the least curious portion of his narrative, the details are so exaggerated that we prefer to omit them.

Upon the eastern coast of Africa, a Portuguese traveller, named Fransisco José de Lacerda y Almeida, left Mozambique in 1797, to explore the interior. The account of this expedition to a place which has only lately been revisited, would be of great interest; but unfortunately, so far as we know, his journal has not been published. His name is often quoted by geographers, and they appear to know what countries he visited; but in France, at least, no lengthened notice of this geographer exists which would furnish the details of his exploration. A very few words will convey all that we have been able to collect of the history of a man who made most important discoveries, and whose name has most unfairly been forgotten.

Lacerda, the date and place of whose birth are unknown, was an engineer, and he was professionally engaged in settling the boundary of the frontier between the Spanish and Portuguese possessions in South America. Whilst thus employed, he collected a mass of interesting particulars of the province of Mato Grosso, which are given in the *Rivesta trimensal do Brazil*. We cannot tell what circumstances led him, after this successful expedition, to the Portuguese possessions in Africa; nor is it easy to imagine his motive for crossing South Africa from the eastern shore to the kingdom of Loanda. It is however certain that he left the well-known town of Teté in 1797, in command of an important caravan bound for the States of Cazembé.

This country was governed by a king as renowned for his benevolence and humanity as for his bravery. He inhabited a town called Lunda, which was two miles in extent, and situated upon the eastern shore of the lake called Mofo. It would have been interesting to compare these localities with those that we know of in the same parallels to-day; but the lack of details obliges us to desist, merely observing that the word Lunda was well-known to Portuguese travellers. As regards Cazembé, there is no longer any question as to its position.

Well received by the king, Lacerda remained some twelve days with him, and then proceeded upon his journey. Unfortunately, when a day or two's march from Lunda he succumbed to fatigue and the unhealthiness of the climate.

The native king collected the traveller's notes and journals, and ordered them to be sent with his remains to Mozambique. But unfortunately the caravan entrusted with these precious memorials was attacked, and the remains of the unfortunate Lacerda were left in the heart of Africa. His notes were brought to Europe by a nephew, who had accompanied the expedition.

We now come to the account of the expeditions undertaken in the east of Africa, foremost amongst which is that of the well-known traveller Bruce. A Scotchman by birth, like so many other African explorers, James Bruce was brought up for the bar; but the sedentary nature of his occupation had little charm for him, and he embraced an opportunity of entering commercial life. His wife died a few years after their marriage, and Bruce started for Spain, where he employed his leisure in studying Arabic monuments. He wished to publish a detailed account of those in the Escorial, but the Spanish Government refused him the necessary permission.

Returning to England, Bruce began to study Eastern languages,

Portrait of James Bruce.
(Facsimile of early engraving.)

and more especially the Ethiopian, which at that time was known only through the imperfect works of Ludolf. One day Lord Halifax half jestingly proposed to him an exploration of the sources of the Nile. Bruce entered enthusiastically into the subject, and set to work to realize it. He overcame every objection, conquered every difficulty, and in June, 1768, left England for the shores of the Mediterranean. Bruce visited some of the islands of the Archipelago, Syria, and Egypt. Leaving Djedda he proceeded to Mecca, Lobheia, and arrived at Massowah upon the 19th September, 1769. He had taken care to obtain a firman from the Sultan, and also letters from the Bey of Cairo, and the Sheriff of Mecca. This was fortunate, for the Nawab, or governor did all in his power to prevent his entering Abyssinia, and endeavoured to make him pay heavily with presents. Abyssinia had been explored by Portuguese missionaries, thanks to whose zeal some information about the country had been obtained, although far less accurate in detail than that which we owe to Bruce. Although his veracity has often been questioned, succeeding travellers have confirmed his assertions.

From Massowah to Adowa the road rises gradually, and passes over the mountains which separate Tigré from the shores of the Red Sea.

Adowa was not originally the capital of Tigré. A manufacture of a coarse cotton cloth which circulates as current money in Abyssinia was established there. The soil in the neighbourhood is deep enough for the cultivation of corn.

"In these districts," says Bruce, "there are three harvests a year. The first seeds are sown in July and August, when the rain flows abundantly. In the same season they sow 'tocusso', 'teff', and barley. About the 20th of November they reap the first barley, then the wheat, and last of all the 'teff'. In some of these they sow immediately upon the same ground without any manure, barley, which they reap in February, and then often sow 'teff', but more frequently a kind of vetch or pea, called Shimbra; these are cut down before the first rains, which are in April; yet with all the advantages of a triple harvest, which requires neither manure nor any expensive processes, the farmer in Abyssinia is always very poor."

At Fremona, not far from Adowa, are the ruins of a Jesuit convent, resembling rather a fort than the abode of men of peace. Two days' journey further on, one comes to the ruins of Axum, the ancient capital of Abyssinia. "In one square," says Bruce, "which I apprehend to have been the centre of the town, there are forty obelisks, none of which have any hieroglyphics on them. The two first have fallen down, but a third a little smaller than them is still standing. They are all hewn from one block of granite, and on the top of that which is standing there is a *patera*, exceedingly well engraved in the Greek style.

"After passing the convent of Abba Pantaleon, called in Abyssinia Mantillas, and the small obelisk on a rock above, we follow a path cut in a mountain of very red marble, having on the left a marble wall forming a parapet about five feet high. At intervals solid pedestals rise from this wall, bearing every token of having served to support colossal statues of Sirius, the barking Anubis, or the Dog star. One hundred and thirty-three of these pedestals with the marks just mentioned are still in their places, but only two figures of the dog were recognizable when I was there; these, however, though much mutilated, were evidently Egyptian.

"There are also pedestals supporting the figures of the Sphinx. Two magnificent flights of steps, several hundred feet long, all of granite, exceedingly well finished, and still in their places, are the only remains of a magnificent temple. In an angle of this platform where the temple stood, is the present small church of Axum. This church is a mean, small building, very ill kept and full of pigeons' dung." It was near Axum that Bruce saw three soldiers cut from a living cow a steak for their midday meal.

In his account of their method of cutting the steak Bruce says, "The skin which had covered the flesh that was cut away was left intact, and was fastened to the corresponding part by little wooden skewers serving as pins. Whether they put anything between the skin and the wounded flesh I do not know, but they soon covered the wound with mud. They then forced the animal to rise, and drove it on before them, to furnish them, no doubt, with another meal when they should join their companions in the evening."

From Tigré, Bruce passed into the province of Siré, which derives its name from its capital, a town considerably larger than Axum, but constantly a prey to putrid fevers. Near it flows the Takazzé, the ancient Siris, with its poisonous waters bordered by majestic trees.

In the province of Samen, situated amongst the unhealthy and broiling Waldubba Mountains, and where many monks had retired to pray and do penance, Bruce stayed only long enough to rest his beasts of burden, for the country was not only haunted by lions and hyenas, and infested by large black ants, which destroyed part of his baggage, but also torn with civil war; so that foreigners were anything but safe. This made him most anxious to reach Gondar, but when he arrived typhoid fever was raging fiercely. His knowledge of medicine was very useful to him, and procured him a situation under the governor, which was most advantageous to him, as it rendered him free to scour the country in all directions, at the head of a body of soldiers. By these means he acquired a mass of valuable information upon the government, manners, and customs of the country, and the chief events of its history, which combined to make his work the most important hitherto published about Abyssinia.

It was in the course of one of these excursions that Bruce discovered the sources of the Blue Nile, which he took to be the true Nile. Arrived at the church of St. Michael, at Geesh, where the river is only four paces wide, and some four inches deep, Bruce became convinced that its sources must be in the neighbourhood, although his guide assured him that he must cross a mountain before he found them. The traveller was not to be deceived.

" 'Come! come!' " said Bruce, " 'no more words. It is already late; lead me to Geesh and the sources of the Nile, and show me the mountain that separates us from it.' He then made me go round to the south of the church, and coming out of the grove of cedars surrounding it, 'This is the mountain,' he said, looking maliciously up into my face, 'that when you were on the other side of it, was between you and the fountains of the Nile; there is no other. Look at that green hillock in the centre of that marsh.

It is there that the two fountains of the Nile are to be found. Geesh is at the top of the rock, where you see those very green trees. If you go to the fountains, pull off your shoes as you did the other day, for these people are all Pagans, and they believe in nothing that you believe, but only in the Nile, to which they pray every day as if it were God, as you perhaps invoke it yourself.' I took off my shoes, and rushed down the hill towards the little green island, which was about two hundred yards distant. The whole of the side of the hill was carpeted with flowers, the large roots of which protruded above the surface of the ground; and as I was looking down, and noticing that the skin was peeling off the bulbs, I had two very severe falls before I reached the edge of the marsh; but at last I approached the island with its green sod. It was in the form of an altar, and apparently of artificial construction. I was in rapture as I gazed upon the principal fountain which rises in the midle of it. It is easier to imagine than to describe what I felt at that moment, standing opposite the sources which had baffled the genius and courage of the most celebrated men for three thousand years."

Bruce's narrative contains many other curious observations, but we must now pass on to his account of Lake Tzana.

"Lake Tzana," according to his narrative, "is by far the largest sheet of water known in these regions. Its extent, however, has been greatly exaggerated. Its greatest breadth from Dingleber to Lamgue, i.e. from east to west, is thirty-five miles, but it decreases greatly at each end, and in some parts is not above ten miles broad. Its greatest length is forty-nine miles from north to south, measured from Bab-Baha to a point a trifle to the S.W.¼W. of the spot where the Nile, after flowing through the lake with an ever perceptible current, bends towards Dara in the Allata territory. In the dry season, from October to March, the lake decreases greatly; but when the rains have swollen the rivers, which unite at this place like the spokes of a wheel at the nave, the lake rises, and overflows a portion of the plain. If the Abyssinians, great liars at all times, are to be believed, there are forty-five islands in Lake Tzana; but this number may be safely reduced to eleven. The largest is named Dek, Daka, or Daga; the next in size are Halimoon, on the Gondar side of the lake, Briguida, on the Gorgora side, and Galila, beyond Briguida. All these islands were formerly used as prisons for Abyssinian chieftains, or as retreats by such as were dissatisfied at court, or wished to secure their valuables in troubled times."

And now having visited Abyssinia with Bruce, let us return to the north.

Some light was now being thrown upon the ancient civilization of Egypt. The archaeological expedition of Pococke, Norden, Niebuhr, Volney, and Savary had been published in succession, and the Egyptian Society was at work upon the publication of its large and magnificent work. The number of travellers increased daily, and amongst others W.G. Browne determined to visit the land of the Pharoahs.

From his work we learn much alike of the monuments and ruins which make this country so interesting, and of the customs of its inhabitants. The portion of the work relating to Darfur is entirely new, no Europeans having previously explored it. Browne attained a high place among travellers by his discovery that the Bahr-el-Abiad is the true Nile, and because he endeavoured not indeed to discover its source, that he could scarcely hope to do, but to ascertain its latitude and course.

Arriving in Egypt upon the 10th of January, 1792, Browne set out upon his first expedition to Siwâh, and discovered, as Horneman did later, the oasis of Jupiter Ammon. He had little more opportunity than his successor for exploring the catacombs and ruins, where he saw many skulls and human remains.

"The ruins of Siwâh," he says, "resembled too much those of Upper Egypt to leave any doubt that the buildings to which they belonged were built by the same race of men. The figures of Isis and Anubis are easily recognizable on them, and the proportions of their architectural works, though smaller, are the same as those of the Egyptian temples.

"The rocks I noticed in the neighbourhood of Siwâh were of the sandstone formation, bearing no relation whatever to the stones of these ruins; so that I should think that the materials for these buildings cannot have been obtained on the spot. The people of Siwâh have preserved no credible traditions respecting these objects. They merely imagined them to contain treasures, and to be frequented by demons."

After leaving Siwâh, Browne made various excursions in Egypt, and then settled in Cairo, where he studied Arabic. He left this town upon the 10th of September, 1792, and visited in succession Kaw, Achmin, Gergeh, Dendera, Kazr, Thebes, Assoûan, Kosseir, Memphis, Suez, and Mount Sinai; then wishing to enter Abyssinia, but convinced that he could not do so by way of Massowah, he left Assiût for Darfur, with a Soudan caravan, in May, 1793. The caravan halted upon its way to Darfur at the different towns of Ainé, Dizeh, Charyeh, Bulak, Scheb, Selinceh, Leghéa and Ber-el-Malha.

Being taken ill at Soueini, Browne was detained there, and only reached El-Fascher after a long delay. Here his annoyances and the exactions levied recommenced, and he could not succeed in obtaining an interview with the Sultan. He was forced to spend the winter at Cobbeh, awaiting his restoration to health, which only took place in the summer of 1791. This time of forced inaction was not, however, wasted by the traveller; he acquainted himself with the manners and dialects of Darfur. Upon the return of summer, Browne repaired to El-Fascher, and recommenced his applications for admittance to the Sultan. They were attended with the same unsuccessful results, until a crowning act of injustice at length procured for him the interview he had so long solicited in vain.

"I found the monarch seated on his throne."

"I found," he says, "the monarch Abd-el-Raschman seated on his throne under a lofty wooden canopy, of Syrian and Indian stuffs indiscriminately mixed. The floor in front of the throne was spread with small Turkey carpets. The meleks (officers of the court) were seated at some little distance off on the right and left, and behind them stood a line of guards, wearing caps ornamented in front with a small copper plate and a black ostrich feather. Each bore a spear in his right hand, and a shield of hippopotamus-hide on the left arm. Their only clothing was a cotton shirt, of the manufacture of the country. Behind the throne were fourteen or fifteen eunuchs, clothed in rich stuffs of various kinds and all manner of colours. The space in front was filled with petitioners and spectators, to the number of more than fifteen hundred. A kind of hired eulogist stood on the monarch's left hand, crying out at the top of his voice during the whole ceremony, 'See the buffalo, the son of a buffalo, the powerful Sultan Abd-el-Raschman El-rashid. May God protect thy life, O master, may God assist thee and render thee victorious.' "

The Sultan promised justice to Browne, and put the matter into the hands of the meleks, but he only obtained restitution of a sixth of that of which he had been robbed.

The traveller had merely entered Darfur to cross it. He found it would be no easy task to leave it, and that in any case he must give up the idea of prosecuting his exploration; he says, –

"On the 11th of December, 1795, (after a delay of three months) I accompanied the chatib (one of the principal officers of the country) to the monarch's presence. I shortly stated what I required, and the chatib seconded me, though not with the zeal that I might have wished. To my demand for permission to travel no answer was returned, and the iniquitous despot, who had received from me no less than the value of about 750 piastres in goods, condescended to give me twenty meagre oxen, worth about 120 piastres. The state of my purse would not permit me to refuse even this mean return, and I bade adieu to El-Fascher as I hoped for ever."

Browne was not able to leave Darfur till the spring of 1796, when he joined the caravan which was about to return to Egypt.

The town of Cobbeh, although not the resort of the merchants, must be considered the capital of Darfur. It is more than two miles in length, but is extremely narrow, each house stands in a field surrounded by a palisade, and between each there is a plot of fallow land.

The plain in which the town is situated runs W.S.W., to a distance of some twenty miles. Almost all the inhabitants are merchants, who trade with Egypt. Their number may be estimated at six thousand, the larger proportion being slaves. The entire population of Darfur cannot exceed two hundred thousand, but Browne only arrived at this calculation by estimating the number of recruits raised for the war with Kordofan.

"The inhabitants of Darfur," says the narrative, "are of various races. Some, chiefly fakeers or priests and traders, come from the west, and there are a good many Arabs, none of whom are permanent residents. They are of various tribes; the greater number lead a wandering life on the frontiers, where they pasture their camels, oxen, and horses. They are not in such complete dependence on the Sultan as always to contribute to his forces in war; or to pay him tribute in time of peace."

After the Arabs come the people, of Zeghawa, which once formed a distinct kingdom, whose chief could put a thousand horsemen in the field. The Zeghawas speak a different dialect from the people of Für. We must also include the people of Bego or Dageou, who are now subject to Darfur, but are the issue of a tribe which formerly ruled the country.

The natives of Darfur are inured to hunger and thirst, but they indulge freely in an intoxicating liquor called *Bouzza* or *Merissé*. Thieving, lying, and dishonesty, with their accompanying vices, prevail largely among them.

"In buying and selling the parent glories in deceiving the son, the son the parent, and atrocious frauds are committed in the name of God and of the Prophet.

"Polygamy, which it is well known is tolerated by their religion, is indulged in to excess by the people of Darfur. When Sultan Teraub went to war with Korodofan, he took in his retinue five hundred women, leaving as many in his palace. This may at first sight seem ridiculous, but it must be remembered that these women had to grind corn, draw water, dress food, and perform all the domestic work for a large number of people, so that there was plenty for them to do."

Browne's narrative contains many medical observations of interest, and gives valuable advice as to the mode of travelling in Africa, with particulars of the animals, fish, metals, and plants of Darfur. We do not give them here, because they do not contain anything of special interest for us.

# CHAPTER III.

## ASIA AND ITS INHABITANTS.

Witzen's account of Tartary – China as described by the Jesuits and Father Du Halde – Macartney in China – Stay at Chu-Sang – Arrival at Nankin – Negotiations – Reception of the Embassy by the Emperor – Fêtes and ceremonies at Zhe Hol – Return to Pekin and Europe – Volney – Choiseul Gouffier – Le Chevalier in Troas – Olivier in Persia – A semi-Asiatic country – Pallas's account of Russia.

At the end of the seventeenth century, a traveller named Nicolas Witzen had explored eastern and northern Tartary, and in 1692 published a curious narrative of his journey. This work, which was in Dutch, and was not translated into any other European language, did not win for its author the recognition he deserved. A second edition, illustrated with engravings which were meritorious rather from their fidelity to nature than their artistic merit, was issued in 1705, and in 1785 the remaining copies of this issue were collected, and appeared under a new title. But it attracted little notice, as by this time further, and more curious particulars had been obtained.

From the day that the Jesuits first entered the Celestial Empire, they had collected every possible fact with regard to the customs of this immense country, which previous to their stay there had been known only through the extravagant tales of Marco Polo. Although China is the country of stagnation, and customs and fashion always remain much the same in it, the many events which had taken place made it desirable to obtain more exact particulars of a nation with whom Europeans might possibly enter into advantageous friendly relations.

The Jesuits published the result of these investigations in the rare work entitled "Lettres Edifiantes", which was revised and supplemented by a zealous member of their order, Father Du Halde. It would be useless to attempt any reproduction of this immense work, for which a volume would be required, and it is the less necessary as at this day we have fuller and more complete details of the country than are to be found even in the learned father's book. To the Jesuits also belong the merit of many important astronomical observations, facts concerning natural history, and the compilation of maps, which were till quite lately authorities on remote districts of the country consulted with advantages.

Towards the end of the eighteenth century, Abbé Grosier, of the order of St. Louis du Louvre, published in an abridged form, a new description of China and Tartary. He made use of the work of his predecessor, Du Halde, and at the same time rectified and added to it. After an account of the fifteen provinces of China and Tartary, with the tributary States, such as Corea, Tonking, Cochin China, and Thibet, the author devotes several chapters to the population and natural history of China, whilst he reviews the government, religion, manners, literature, science, and art of the Chinese.

Towards the end of the eighteenth century, the English Government, being desirous of entering into commercial relations with China, sent an Envoy-extraordinary to that country named George Macartney.

This diplomatist had already visited the courts of Europe and Russia, had been governor of the English Antilles and Madras, and Governor-General of India.

He had acquired in the course of his travels in such varied climates, and amid such diverse peoples, a profound knowledge of human nature. His narrative of his voyages is rich in facts and observations calculated to give Europeans a true idea of the Chinese character.

Personal accounts of travel are always more interesting than anonymous ones.

Although the great *I* is generally hateful, it is not so in travels, where the assertion *I* have been there, *I* have done such or such a thing, carries weight, and gives interest to the narrative.

Macartney and his suite sailed in a squadron consisting of three vessels, the *Lion*, the *Hindustan* and the *Jackal*, which left Portsmouth on the 26th September, 1792.

After a few necessary delays at Rio-de-Janeiro, St. Paul and Amsterdam Islands, where some seal-hunters were seen, at Batavia, and Bantam, in Java, and at Poulo Condere, the vessels cast anchor off Turon (Han San) in Cochin China, a vast harbour, of which only a very bad chart was then in existence.

The arrival of the English was at first a cause of uneasiness to the

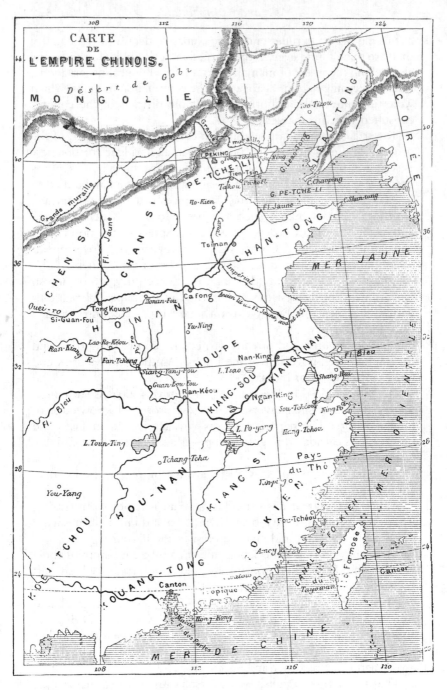

Gravé par E. Morieu 23. r. de Brea Paris.

natives of Cochin China. But when they were once informed of the motives which had brought the English to their country, they sent an ambassador of high rank on board with presents for Macartney, who was shortly afterwards invited to a banquet at the governor's, followed by a dramatic entertainment. During the short stay many notes were taken of the manners and customs of the people, unfortunately too hurriedly to admit of accuracy.

As soon as the sick had recovered and fresh provisions had been obtained the vessels set sail. A short stay was made at the Ladrone Islands, and the squadron then entered the Strait of Formosa, where it encountered stormy weather, and took refuge in Chusan Harbour. During this stay the map of this archipelago was rectified and an opportunity was taken to visit Tinghai, where the English excited as much curiosity as they felt themselves at the sight of the many things which were new to them.

Many of the facts which surprised them are familiar to us, the appearance of the houses, the markets and dress of the Chinese, the small feet of the women, and many other particulars to which we need not refer. We will only allude to the account of the method employed by them in cultivating dwarf trees.

"This stunted vegetation," says Macartney, "seems to be highly appreciated in China, for specimens of it are found in all the larger houses. It is an art peculiar to the Chinese, and the gardeners skill consists in knowing how to produce it. Independently of the satisfaction of triumphing over a difficulty, he has the advantage of introducing into rooms plants whose natural size would have precluded such a possibility.

"The following is the method employed in China for the production of dwarfed trees. The trunk of a tree of which it is desired to obtain a dwarfed specimen, is covered as nearly as possible where it separates into branches with clay or mould, over which is placed a linen or cotton covering constantly kept damp. This mould is sometimes left on for a whole year, and throughout that time the wood it covers throws out tender, root-like fibres. Then the portions of the trunk from which issue these fibres, with the branch immediately above them, are carefully separated from the tree and placed in fresh mould, where the shoots soon develop into real roots, whilst the branch forms the stem of a plant which is in a manner metamorphosed. This operation neither destroys nor alters the productive faculties of the branch which is separated from the parent tree. When it bears fruit or flowers it does so as plentifully as when it was upon the original stem. The extremities of the branches intended to be dwarfed are always pulled off, which precludes the possibility of their growing tall, and forces them to throw out shoots and lateral branches. These shoots are tied with wire, and assume the form the gardener chooses. When it is desired to give an aged appearance to the tree, it is constantly moistened with theriaca or treacle, which attracts to it, multitudes of ants, who not content with devouring the sweetmeat, attack the bark of the tree, and eat it away in such a manner as to produce the desired effect."

Upon leaving Chusan, the squadron entered the Yellow Sea, never before navigated by an European vessel. The river Hoang-Ho flows into it, and it is from the immense quantity of yellow mud brought down by it in its long and tortuous course that the sea derives its name.

The English vessels cast anchor in Ten-chou-Fou Bay, and thence entered the gulf of Pekin, and halted outside the bar of Pei-Ho. There being only three or four feet of water on this bar at low tide, the vessels could not cross it.

The mandarins appointed by the government to receive the English ambassador, arrived shortly after, bringing numerous presents; whilst the gifts intended for the emperor were placed in junks, and Macartney went on board a yacht which had been prepared for him.

The first town reached was Takoo, where Macartney received a visit from the viceroy of the province and the principal mandarin. Both were men of venerable and dignified aspect, polite and attentive, and entirely free from obsequiousness.

"It has been rightly said," remarks Macartney, "that a people are as they are made, and the English had continual proof of this truth in the effect produced upon the Chinese character by the fear of the iron power that ruled them. Apart from this fear they were cheerful and confiding, but in the presence of their rulers they appeared most timid and embarrassed."

In ascending the Pei-Ho towards Pekin, the course was retarded by the many windings of the river. The country through which they passed was highly cultivated, with houses and villages at intervals upon the banks of the river or inland, alternating with cemeteries and pyramids of bags of salt, producing a charming and ever varying landscape. When night approached, lanterns of every hue, fastened to the masts and rigging of the yachts, produced the fantastic effect of many-coloured lights.

Chinese magic-lantern.
(Facsimile of early engraving.)

Tieng Tsing signifies "heavenly spot", and the town owes this name to its agreeable climate and clear blue sky, and the fertility of its neighbourhood. In this place, the ambassador was received by the viceroy and a legate sent by the emperor. From them Macartney learned that the emperor was at his summer palace in Tartary, and that the anniversary of his birthday was to be celebrated there upon the 13th of September. The ambassador and his suite were therefore to go up by water as far as Tong Schou, about a dozen miles from Pekin, and thence proceed by land to Zhe Hol, where the emperor awaited them. The presents might be sent on afterwards. Although the first intimation was pleasant, the latter was singularly disagreeable to Macartney, for the presents consisted for the most part of delicate instruments, which had been taken to pieces for safety and packed separately. The legate would not consent to their being left where they would be free from danger of being disturbed. Macartney was obliged to obtain the intervention of the viceroy for the protection of these proofs of the genius and knowledge of Europe.

The cortège reached Tien Tsing, a town which appeared as long as London, and contained not less than seven hundred thousand inhabitants. A vast crowd assembled on the banks of the river to see the English pass, and the river swarmed with junks teeming with natives.

The houses in this city are built of blue with a few red bricks, some are two storeys high, but that is unusual. Here the English saw the employment of those carriages with sails which had long been considered fabulous. They consist of two barrows made of bamboo, with one large wheel between them.

When there is not sufficient wind to propel the carriage, says the narrative, it is drawn by one man, while another pushes behind and keeps it steady. When the wind is favourable, the sail, which is a mat attached to two sticks placed upon either side of the carriage, renders the help of the man in front unnecessary.

The banks of the Pei-Ho are in many parts protected by breastworks of granite, to arrest inundation, and here and there dikes, also of granite, provided with a sluice, by means of which water is conveyed to the fields below. The country, although well cultivated was often devastated by famines, following upon inundations, or resulting from the ravages of locusts.

Thus far, the cortège had been sailing through the immense alluvial plain of Pe-tche-Li. Not until the fourth day after leaving Tien

Tsing was the blue outline of mountains perceived on the horizon. Pekin was now in sight; and on the 6th of August, 1793, the yachts anchored within two miles of the capital, and half a mile from Tong-Chow-Fow.

In order to leave the presents which could not be taken to Zhe Hol, at the palace, called "The garden of eternal spring", it was necessary to land. The inhabitants of Tong-Chow-Fow, who were already greatly excited by the appearance of the English, were still more amazed at the first sight of a negro servant. His skin, his jet black colour, his woolly hair, and all the distinguishing marks of his race, were absolutely novel in this part of China. The people could not remember seeing anything at all like him before. Some of them even doubted if he could be a human being at all, and the children cried out in fear that it was a black devil. But his good humour soon reconciled them to his appearance, and they became accustomed to look upon him without fear or displeasure.

The English were especially surprised at seeing upon a wall the sketch of a lunar eclipse which was to take place in a few days. They ascertained among other facts, that silver is an article of commerce with the Chinese, for they have no coined money, but use ingots bearing only a sign, indicative of their weight. The English were struck with the extraordinary resemblance between the religious ceremonies of Fo and those of the Christians.

Macartney states, that certain authors maintain that the apostle Thomas visited China; while the Missionary Tremore contends, that this is merely a fiction palmed upon the Jesuits by the devil himself.

Ninety small carriages, forty-four wheelbarrows, more than two hundred horses, and over three thousand men, were employed in the transport of the presents of the British government to the emperor. Macartney and three of his suite accompanied the convoy in palanquins. An enormous crowd followed them. The English ambassador was greeted at the gates of Pekin by volleys of artillery. Once beyond the fortifications, he found himself in a wide unpaved street, with houses on either side, one or two storeys high. Across the street extended a wooden triumphal arch in three partitions, each with a lofty and highly decorated roof.

The embassy afforded ample material for the tales which at this time filled the imagination of the people. It was declared that the presents brought for the emperor consisted of everything that was rare in other countries and unknown in China. It was gravely asserted that among the animals, there was an elephant not larger than a monkey, but as fierce as a lion, and a cock which was fed upon coal. Everything which came from England was supposed to differ from anything hitherto seen in Pekin, and to possess the very opposite qualities to those usual to it.

The wall of the imperial palace was at once recognized by its yellow colour. Through the gate were seen artificial hills, lakes and rivers with small islets, and fantastic buildings amidst the trees.

At the end of a street terminating at the northern wall of the city, was a vast edifice of considerable height, which contained an enormous bell. The English explored the town in various directions, and on the whole were not favourably impressed. They concluded that a Chinaman visiting London, with its bridges and innumerable ships, its squares and monuments, would carry away a better idea of the importance of the capital of Great Britain than they could do of Pekin.

Upon their arrival at the palace, where the presents for the emperor were to be displayed, the governor discussed with Macartney the best way to arrange and display them. They were finally placed in a large and well-decorated hall, which at the time contained nothing but a throne and a few vases of old china.

It is unnecessary to enter upon the interminable negotiations which arose out of the resolve of the Chinese, that Macartney should prostrate himself before the emperor; which humiliating proposition they had prepared for by the inscription placed upon the yachts and carriages of the embassy, "Ambassador bringing tribute from England".

It is in Pekin that the field is situated which the emperor, in accordance with ancient custom, sows every spring. Here, too, is to be found the "Temple of the Earth", to which the sovereign resorts at the summer solstice, to acknowledge the astral power which lightens the world, and to give thanks for its beneficent influence.

Pekin is merely the seat of the Imperial government in China, and has neither shipping, manufactures, nor trade.

Macartney computes the number of inhabitants at three millions. The one-storeyed houses in the town appear insufficient for so large a population, but a single house accommodates three generations. This density of the population is the result of the early ages at which marriages are contracted. These hasty unions are often brought about from prudential motives by the Chinese, the children, and especially the sons, being responsible for the care of their parents.

Emperor of China.
(Facsimile of early engraving.)

The embassy left Pekin on the 2nd of September, 1793, Macartney, travelling in a post-chaise, probably the first carriage of the kind which ever entered Tartary.

As the distance from Pekin increased, the road ascended and the soil became more sandy, and contained less and less clay and black earth. Shortly afterwards, vast plains, planted with tobacco, were crossed. Macartney imagines tobacco to be indigenous, and not imported from America, and thinks that the habit of smoking was spontaneous in Asia.

The English soon noticed that as the soil became more and more barren, the population decreased. At the same time the Tartar element became larger and larger, and the difference between the manners of the Chinese and their conquerors was less marked.

Upon the fifth day of the journey, the far-famed Great Wall was seen.

"The first glance at this fortified wall," says Macartney, "is enough to give an impression of an enterprise of surprising grandeur. It ascends the highest mountains to their very loftiest peaks, it goes down into the deepest valleys, crossing rivers on sustaining arches, and with its breadth often doubled and trebled to increase its strength, whilst at intervals of about a hundred paces rise towers or strong bastions. It is difficult to understand how the materials for this wall were brought to and used in places apparently inaccessible, and it is impossible sufficiently to admire the skill brought to bear upon the task. One of the loftiest mountains over which the wall passes has been ascertained to be no less than 5,225 feet high.

"This fortification – for the simple word 'wall' gives no just idea of the wonderful structure – is said, to be 1,500 miles long, but it is not quite finished. The fifteen hundred miles was the extent of the frontier which separates colonized China from the various Tartar tribes. Such barriers as these would not suffice in modern times for nations at war.

"Many of the lesser works in the interior of this grand rampart have yielded to the effect of time, and fallen into ruins; others have been repaired; but the principal wall appears throughout to have been built with such care and skill as never to have needed repairs. It has now been preserved more than two thousand years, and appears as little susceptible of injury as the rocks which nature herself has planted between China and Tartary."

Beyond the wall nature seems to proclaim the entrance into a

The great wall of China.

new country; the temperature is colder, the roads are more rugged, and the mountains are less wooded. The number of sufferers from goitre in the Tartar valleys is very considerable, and, according to the estimate given by Dr. Gillan, physician to the embassy, comprises a sixth of the population. The portion of Tartary in which this malady rages is not unlike many of the cantons of Switzerland and Savoy.

The valley of Zhe Hol, where the emperor possesses a summer palace and garden, was at length reached. This residence is called "The abode of pleasant freshness", and the park surrounding it is named the "Garden of innumerable trees". The embassy was received with military honours, amid an immense crowd of people, many of whom were dressed in yellow. These were inferior lamas or monks of the order of Fo, to which the emperor also belonged.

The disputes as to prostration before the emperor begun in Pekin were continued here. At last Tchien Lung consented to content himself with the respectful salutation with which English nobles are accustomed to greet their own sovereign. The reception accordingly took place, with every imaginable pomp and ceremony.

The narrative says, –

"Shortly after daybreak the sound of many instruments, and the confused voices of distant crowds, announced the approach of the emperor. He soon appeared, issuing from behind a high mountain, bordered with trees, as if from a sacred grove, and preceded by a number of men who proclaimed his virtues and power in loud voices. He was seated in a chair carried by sixteen men; his guards, the officers of his household, standard and umbrella bearers, and musicians accompanied him. He was clothed in a robe of sombre-coloured silk, and wore a velvet cap, very similar in shape to that of Scotch mountaineers. A large pearl was conspicuous on his forehead, and was the only jewel or ornament he wore."

Upon entering the tent, the emperor mounted the steps of the throne, which he alone is allowed to ascend. The first minister, Ho Choo-Tang, and two of the chief officers of his household, remained near, and never addressed him but in a kneeling position. When the princes of royal blood, the tributary princes, and state officers, were in their places, the president of the customs conducted Macartney within a foot of the left-hand side of the throne, which in the Chinese court is considered the place of honour. The ambassador was accompanied by the minister plenipotentiary, and followed by his page and interpreter.

Chinese Prime Minister.
(Facsimile of early engraving.)

Macartney, in accordance with the instructions given him by the president, raised above his head the magnificent square golden box studded with diamonds which contained the King of England's letter to the emperor. Then mounting the few steps leading to the throne, he bowed the knee, and, with a short prefatory compliment, presented the box to his Imperial Majesty. The Chinese monarch received it graciously, and said, as he placed it on one side, "that he experienced much satisfaction at the token of esteem and friendship offered by his Britannic Majesty in sending to him an embassy with a letter and rich gifts; that, for his part, he had the like friendly greetings towards the King of Great Britain, and he hoped the same harmony would always continue between their respective subjects."

After a few moments of private conversation with the ambassador, the emperor presented gifts to him and to the minister plenopotentiary. They were then conducted to cushions, in front of which were tables covered with a number of vessels containing meat and fruits. The emperor also partook of these, and continued to overwhelm the ambassadors with expressions of regard and esteem which had a great effect in raising the English in the estimation of the Chinese public. Macartney and his suite were later invited to visit the gardens of Zhe Hol. During their walk in the grounds, the English met the emperor, who stopped to receive their respectful salutations, and order his first minister, who was looked upon as little less than a vice-emperor, and several other grandees to accompany them.

The Chinese conducted the English over a portion of the grounds laid out as pleasure-gardens, which formed only a small portion of the vast enclosure. The rest is sacred to the use of the women of the imperial family, and was as rigorously closed to the Chinese ministers as to the English embassy.

Macartney was then led through a fertile valley, in which there were many trees, chiefly willows of enormous size. Grass grows abundantly between the trees, and its luxuriance is not diminished by cattle or interfered with by mowing. Arriving upon the shores of an irregular lake, of vast extent, the whole party embarked in yachts, and proceeded to a bridge which is thrown across the narrowest part of the lake, and beyond which it appeared to stretch away indefinitely.

Upon the 17th of September Macartney and his suite were present at a ceremony which took place upon the anniversary of the emperor's birthday. Upon the morrow and following days splendid fêtes succeeded each other, Tchien Lung participating in them with great zest. Dancers on the tight-rope, tumblers, conjurors (of unrivalled skill), and wrestlers, performed in succession. The natives of various portions of the empire appeared in their distinctive costumes and exhibited the different productions of their provinces. Music and dancing were succeeded by fireworks, which were very effective, although they were let off in daylight.

The narrative says, –

"Several of the designs were novel to the English. One of them I will describe. A large box was raised to a great height, and the bottom being removed as if by accident, an immense number of paper lamps fell from it. When they left the box they were all neatly folded; but in filling they opened by degrees and sprung one out of the other. Each then assumed a regular form, and suddenly a beautifully coloured light appeared. The Chinese seemed to understand the art of shaping the fireworks at their fancy. On either side of the large boxes were smaller ones, which opened in a similar manner, letting fall burning torches, of different shapes, as brilliant as burnished copper, and flashing like lightning at each movement of the wind. The display ended with the eruption of an artificial volcano."

It is the usual custom for the Emperor of China to conclude his birthday festivities by hunting in the forests of Tartary; but in the present case advancing age rendered that diversion unwise, and his Majesty decided to return to Pekin, the English embassy being invited to precede him thither.

Macartney, however, felt that it was time to terminate his mission. In the first place, it was not customary for ambassadors to reside long at the Chinese court; and in the second, the fact that the Chinese emperor, defrayed the expenses of the embassy naturally induced him to curtail his stay. In a short time he received from Tchien Lung the reply to the letter of the King of England, and the presents intended for the English monarch, as well as a number for the members of his suite. This Macartney rightly interpreted as his *congé*!

The English went back to Tong Chou Fou by way of the imperial canal. Upon this trip they saw the famous bird "Leutzé", fishing for its master. It is a species of cormorant, and is so well trained that it is unnecessary to place either a cord or ring round its neck to prevent it from swallowing any of its prey.

The famous bird Leutzé.

"Upon every boat or raft there are ten or twelve of these birds, ready to plunge the instant they receive a sign from their masters. It is curious to see them catch enormous fish, and carry them in their beaks.

Macartney mentions a singular manner of catching wild ducks and other water-birds. Empty jars and calabashes are allowed to float upon the water for several days, until the birds are accustomed to the sight of them. A man then enters the water, places one of the jars upon his head, and advancing gently, seizes the feet of any bird which allows him to come near enough: he rapidly immerses it in the water to choke it, and then noiselessly continues his search until his bag is full.

The embassy visited Canton and Macao, and thence returned to England. We need not dwell upon the return voyage.

We must now consider that portion of Asia which may be called the interior. The first traveller to be noticed is Volney.

Every one knows, by repute at least, his book on Ruins; but his account of his adventures in Egypt and Syria far surpasses it. There is nothing exaggerated in the latter; it is written in a quiet, precise manner, and is one of the most instructive of books. The members of the Egyptian Expedition refer to it as containing exact statements as to climate, the productions of the soil, and the manners of the inhabitants.

Volney prepared himself most carefully for the journey, which was a great undertaking for him. He determined to leave nothing to chance, and upon reaching Syria he realized that he could not possibly acquire the knowledge of the country he desired unless he first made himself acquainted with the language of the people. He therefore retired to the monastery of Mar-Hannd, in Libiya, and devoted himself to the study of Arabic.

Later on, in order to learn something of the life led by the wandering tribes of the Arabian desert, he joined company with a sheik, and accustomed himself to the use of a lance, and to live on horseback, thus qualifying himself to accompany the tribes in their excursions. Under their protection he visited the ruins of Palmyra and Baalbec, cities of the dead, known to us only by name.

"His style of writing," says La Beuve, "is free from exaggeration, and marked by singular exactness and propriety. When, for example, he wishes to illustrate the quality of the Egyptian soil, and in what respect it differs from that of Africa, he speaks of 'this black, light, greasy earth', which is brought up and deposited by the

Nile. When he wishes to describe the warm winds of the desert, with their dry heat, he compares them 'to the impression which one receives upon opening a fierce oven to take out the bread'; according to his description, speaking of the fitful winds, he says they are not merely laden with fog, but gritty and powdery, and in reality full of fine dust, which penetrates everything; and of the sun, he says it 'presents to view but an obscured disk'."

If such an expression may be used in speaking of a rigid statement of facts, Volney attained to true beauty of expression – to an actual physical beauty, so to speak, recalling the touch of Hippocrates in his "De Aere, Aquis et Locis". Although no geographical discoveries can be imputed to him, we must none the less recognize in him one of the first travellers who had a true conception of the importance of their task. His aim was always to give a true impression of the places he visited; and this in itself was no small merit, at a time when other explorers did not hesitate to enliven their narratives with imaginary details, with no recognition whatever of their true responsibility.

The Abbé Barthélemy, who in 1788 was to publish his "Voyage du jeune Anacharsis", was already exercising a good deal of influence on public taste, by his popularity in society and position as a man of science, and drawing special attention to Greece and the neighbouring countries. It was evidently whilst attending his lessons that De Choiseul imbibed his love for history and archæology.

Nominated ambassador at Constantinople, De Choiseul determined to profit by the leisure he enjoyed in travelling as an artist and archæologist through the Greece of Homer and Herodotus. Such a journey was the very thing to complete the education of the young ambassador, who was only twenty-four years of age, and if he knew himself, could not be said to have any acquaintance with the ways of the world.

Sensible of his shortcomings, he surrounded himself with learned and scientific men, amongst them the Abbé Barthélemy, the Greek scholar, Ansse de Villoison, the poet Delille, the sculptor Fauvel, and the painter Cassas. In fact, in his "Picturesque History of Greece" he himself merely plays the *rôle* of Mæcenas.

M. de Choiseul Gouffier engaged as private secretary a professor, the Abbé Jean-Baptiste Le Chevalier, who spoke Greek fluently. The latter, after a journey to London, where M. de Choiseul's business detained him long enough for him to learn English, went to Italy, and was detained at Venice by severe illness for seven months. After this he joined M. de Choiseul Gouffier at Constantinople.

Le Chevalier occupied himself principally with the site of Troy. Well versed in the Iliad, he sought for, and believed he identified, the various localities mentioned in the Homeric poem.

His able geographical and historical book at once provoked plentiful criticism. Upon the one side learned men, such as Bryant, declared the discoveries made by Choiseul to be illusory, or the reason that Troy, and, as a matter of course, the Ten Years Siege, existed only in the imagination of the Greek poet; whilst others, and principally the English portion of his critics, adopted his conclusions. The whole question was almost forgotten, when the discoveries made quite recently by Schliemann, reopened the discussion.

Guillaume-Antoine Olivier, who traversed the greater portion of the Western hemisphere, at the end of the last century, had a strange career. Employed by Berthier de Sauvigny to translate a statistical paper on Paris, he lost his patron and the payment for his labours in the first outburst of the Revolution. Wishing to employ his talent for natural history away from Paris, he was nominated, by the minister Roland, to a mission to the distant and little-known portions of the Ottoman Empire. A naturalist, named Bruguère, was associated with him.

The two friends left Paris at the end of 1792, and were delayed for four months at Versailles, until a suitable ship was found for them.

They only reached Constantinople at the end of the following May, carrying letters relating to their mission to M. de Semonville. But this ambassador had been recalled, and his successor, M. de Sainte Croix had heard nothing of their undertaking. What was the best thing to do whilst awaiting the reply to the inquiries sent to Paris by M. de Sainte Croix?

The two friends could not remain inactive. They therefore decided to visit the shores of Asia Minor, and some islands in the Egyptian Archipelago.

The French minister had excellent reasons for not supplying them with much money, and their own resources being limited, they were unable to do more than make a flying visit to these interesting countries.

Upon their return to Constantinople they found a new ambassador, named Verninac, who had received instructions to send them to Persia, where they were to endeavour to awaken the sympathy of the government for France, and to induce it to declare war against Russia.

At this time the most deplorable anarchy reigned in Persia. Usurpers succeeded each other upon the throne, to the great detriment of the welfare of the inhabitants. War was going on in Khorassan at the time that Olivier and Bruguère arrived. An opportunity occurred for them to join the shah in country as yet unvisited by any European; but unfortunately Bruguère was in such bad health that they were not only forced to lose the chance, but were detained for four months in an obscure village buried amongst the mountains.

In September, 1796, Mehemet returned to Teheran. His first act was to order a hundred Russian sailors whom he had taken prisoners on the Caspian Sea, to be put to death, and their limbs to be nailed outside his palace walls – a disgusting trophy worthy of the butcher tyrant.

The following year Mehemet Ali was assassinated, and his nephew Fehtah-Ali Shah, succeeded him, after a short struggle.

It was difficult for Olivier to discharge his mission with this constant change of reigning sovereigns. He was forced to renew his negotiations with each succeeding prince. Finally, the travellers, realizing the impossibility of obtaining anything definite under such circumstances, returned to Europe, and left the question of alliance between France and Persia to a more favourable season. They stopped upon their homeward journey at Bagdad, Ispahan, Aleppo, Cyprus, and Constantinople.

Although this journey had been fruitless as regarded diplomacy, and had contributed no new discovery to geography, Cuvier, in his eulogy of Olivier, assures us that, so far as natural history was concerned, much had been achieved. This may be the better credited, as Olivier was elected to the Institute as the successor to Daubenton.

Cuvier, in academic style, says that the narrative of the voyage published, in three quarto volumes, was warmly received by the public.

"It has been said," he continues, "that it might have been of greater interest if the censor had not eliminated certain portions; but allusions were found throughout the whole volume, which were inadmissible, as it does not do to say all we know, especially of Thamas Kouli Khan.

"M. Olivier had no greater regard for his assertions than for his fortune; he quietly omitted all that he was told to leave out, and restricted himself to a quiet and simple account of what he had seen."

A journey from Persia to Russia is not difficult; and was less so in the eighteenth century than to-day. As a matter of fact, Russia only became an European power in the days of Peter the Great. Until the reign of that monarch she had been in every particular – manners, customs, and inhabitants – Asiatic. With Peter the Great and Catherine II., however, commerce revived, high roads were made, the navy was created, and the various tribes became united into one nation.

The empire was vast from the first, and, conquest has added to its extent. Peter the Great ordered the compilation of charts, sent expeditions round the coast to collect particulars as to the climate, productions, and races of the different provinces of his empire; and at length he sent Behring upon the voyage which resulted in the discovery of the straits bearing his name.

The example of the great emperor was followed by his successor, Catherine II. She attracted learned men to her court, and corresponded with the savants of the whole world. She succeeded in impressing the nations with a favourable idea of her subjects. Interest and curiosity were awakened, and the eyes of Western Europe were fixed upon Russia. It became recognized that a great nation was arising, and many doubts were entertained as to the result upon European interests. Prussia had already changed the balance of power in Europe, by her victories under Frederick II.; Russia possessed resources of her own, not only in men, but in silver and riches of every kind – still unknown or untested.

Thus it came to pass that publications concerning that country possessed an attraction for politicians, and those interested in the welfare of their country, as well as for the scientific men to whom descriptions of manners and customs foreign to their experience were always welcome.

No work had hitherto excelled that of the naturalist Pallas, which was translated into French between 1788-1793. It was a narrative of a journey across several provinces of the Russian empire. The success of this publication was well deserved.

Peter Simon Pallas was a German naturalist, who had been summoned to St. Petersburg by Catherine II. in 1668, and elected by her a member of the Academy of Sciences. She understood the art of

enlisting him in her service by her favours. Pallas, in acknowledgment of them, published his account of fossil remains in Siberia.
England and France had just sent expeditions to observe the transit
of Venus. Russia, not to be behindhand, despatched a party of
learned men, of whom Pallas was one, to Siberia.

Seven astronomers and geometers, five naturalists, and a large
number of pupils, made up the party, which was thoroughly to
explore the whole of the vast territory.

For six whole years Pallas devoted himself to the successive
explorations of Orenburg upon the Jaik, the rendezvous of the
nomad tribes who wander upon the shores of the Caspian Sea;
Gouriel, which is situated upon the borders of the great lake which
is now drying up; the Ural Mountains, with their numberless iron-
mines; Tobolsk, the capital of Siberia; the province of Koliwan,
upon the northern slopes of the Atlas; Krasnojarsk, upon the
Jenissei; and the immense lake of Bakali, and Daouria, on the frontiers of China. He also visited Astrakan; the Caucasus, with its
varied and interesting inhabitants; and finally, he explored the Don,
returning to St. Petersburg on the 30th of July, 1774.

It may well be believed that Pallas was no ordinary traveller. He
was not merely a naturalist; he was interested in everything that
affects humanity; geography, history, politics, commerce, religion,
science, art, all occupied his attention; and it is impossible to read
his narrative without admiring his enlightened patriotism, or
without recognizing the penetration of the sovereign who understood the art of securing his services.

When his narrative was once arranged, written, and published,
Pallas had no idea of contenting himself with the laurels he had
gained. Work was his recreation, and he found occupation in
assisting in the compilation of a map of Russia.

His natural inclinations led him to the study of botany, and by
his works upon that subject he obtained a distinctive place among
Russian naturalists.

One of his later undertakings was a description of Southern
Russia, a physical and topographical account of the province of
Taurius – a work which, originally published in French, was after-
wards translated into English and German.

Delighted with this country, which he had visited in 1793-94, he
desired to settle there. The empress bestowed some of the crown
lands upon him, and he transported his family to Simpheropol.

Pallas profited by the opportunilty to undertake a new journey in the northern provinces of the empire, the Steppes of the Volga, and the countries which border the Caspian Sea as far as the Caucasus. He then explored the Crimea. He had seen parts of the country twenty years before, and he now found great changes. Although he complains of the devastation of the forests, he commends the increase of agricultural districts, and the centres of industries which had been created. The Crimea is known to be considerably improved since that time – it is impossible to foresee what it may yet become.

Enthusiastic though he was at first in his admiration of this province, Pallas was exposed to every kind of treachery on the part of the Tartars. His wife died in the Crimea; and finally, disgusted with the country and its inhabitants, he returned to Breton to end his days. He died there on the 8th of September, 1811.

He left two important works, from which naturalists, geographers, statesmen, and merchants, were able to gather much trustworthy information upon countries then but little known, and the commodities and resources of which were destined to have a large influence over European markets.

# CHAPTER IV.

## THE TWO AMERICAS.

The western coast of America – Juan de Fuca and De Fonte – The three voyages of Behring and Tschirikow – Exploration of the straits of De Fuca – Survey of the Archipelago of New Georgia and of part of the American coast – Exploration of the interior of America – Samuel Hearn – Discovery of the Coppermine River – Mackenzie, and the river named after him – Fraser River – South America – Survey of the Amazon by Condamine – Journey of Humboldt and Bonpland – Teneriffe – The Guachero cavern – The "Llaños" – The Electric eels – The Amazon, Negro, and Orinoco rivers – The earth-eaters – Results of the journey – Humboldt's second journey – The "Volcanitos", or little volcanoes – The cascade at Tequendama – The bridge of Jcononzo – Crossing the Quindin on men's backs – Pinto and Pinchincha – Ascent of Chimborazo – The Andes – Lima – The transit of Mercury – Exploration of Mexico – Puebla and Cofre de Perote – Return to Europe.

We have more than once had occasion to speak of expeditions for the survey of the coasts of America. We have told of the attempts of Fernando Cortes and of the voyages and explorations of Drake, Cook, La Perouse, and Marchand. It will be well now to go back for a time, and with Fleurieu sum up the series of voyages along the western coast of America, to the close of the eighteenth century.

In 1537, Cortes with Francisco de Ulloa, discovered the huge peninsula of California, and sailed over the greater part of the long and narrow strait now known as the Vermilion Sea.

He was succeeded by Vasquez Coronado and Francisco Alarcon, who – the former by sea, and the latter by land – devoted themselves to seeking the channel which was erroneously supposed to connect the Atlantic and Pacific. They did not, however, penetrate beyond 36° N. lat.

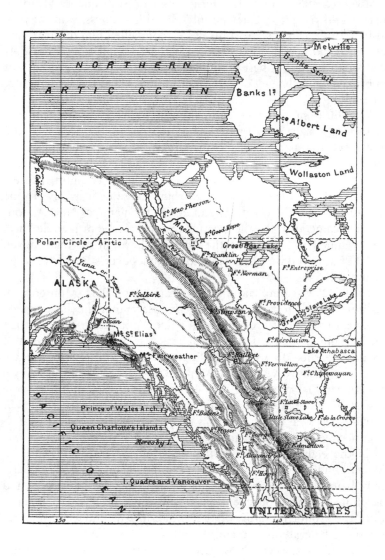

Two years later, in 1542, the Portuguese Rodrique de Cabrillo, reached 44° N. lat., where the intense cold, sickness, want of provisions, and the bad state of his vessel, compelled him to turn back. He made no actual discovery, but he ascertained that, from Port Natividad to the furthest point reached by him, the coast-line was unbroken. The channel of communication seemed to recede before all explorers.

The little success met with appears to have discouraged the Spaniards, for at this time they retired from the ranks of the explorers. It was an Englishman, Drake, who, after having sailed along the western coast as far as the Straits of Magellan, and devastated the Spanish possessions, reached the forty-eighth degree, explored the whole coast, and, returning the same way, gave to the vast districts included within ten degrees the name of New Albion.

Next came, in 1592, the greatly fabulous voyage of Juan de Fuca, who claimed to have found the long-sought Strait of Anian, when he had but found the channel dividing Vancouver's Island from the mainland.

In 1602 Viscaino laid the foundations of Port Monterey in California, and forty years later took place that much contested voyage of Admiral De Fuente, or De Fonte according as one reckons him a Spaniard or a Portuguese, which has been the text of so many learned discussions and ingenious suppositions. To him we owe the discovery of the Archipelago of St. Lazarus above Vancouver's Island; but all that he says about the lakes and large towns he claims to have visited must be relegated to the realms of romance, as well as his assertion that he discovered a communication between the two oceans.

In the eighteenth century the assertions of travellers were no longer blindly accepted. They were examined and sifted, those parts only being believed which accorded with the well-authenticated accounts of others. Buache, Delisle, and above all Fleurieu, inaugurated the prolific literature of historical criticism, and we have every reason to be grateful to them.

The Russians, as we know, had greatly extended the field of their knowledge, and there was every reason to suppose that their hunters and Cossacks would soon reach America, if, as was then believed, the two continents were connected in the north. But from such unprofessional travellers no trustworthy scientific details could be expected.

A few years before his death the Emperor Peter I. drew up, with

Port Monterey.
(Facsimile of early engraving.)

his own hands, a plan of an expedition, with instructions to its members, which he had long had in view for ascertaining whether Asia and America are united, or separated by a strait.

The arsenal and forts of Kamschatka being unable to supply the necessary men, stores, &c., captains, sailors, equipment, and provisions, had to be imported from Europe.

Vitus Behring, a Dane, and Alexis Tschirikow, a Russian, who had both given many a proof of skill and knowledge, were appointed to the command of the expedition, which consisted of two vessels built at Kamschatka. They were not ready to put to sea until July 20th, 1720. Steering north-east along the coast of Asia, of which he never for a moment lost sight, Behring discovered, on the 15th August, in 67° 18' N. lat. a cape beyond which the coast stretched away westwards.

In this first voyage Behring did not apparently see the coast of America, though he probably passed through the strait to which posterity has given his name. The fabulous strait of Anian gave place to Behring Straits. A second voyage made by the same explorers the following year was without results.

Not until June 4th, 1741, were Behring and Tschirikow in a position to start again. This time they meant to bear to the east after reaching 50° N. lat. till they should come to the coast of America; but the two vessels were separated in a gale of wind on the 28th August, and were unable to find each other again throughout the trip. On the 18th July Behring discerned the American continent in 58° 28' N. lat. and the succeeding days were devoted to the survey of the vast bay between Capes St. Elias and St. Hermogenes.

Behring spent the whole of August in sailing about the islands known as the Schumagin archipelago, off the peninsula of Alaska; and, after a struggle, lasting until the 24th September, with contrary winds, he sighted the most southerly cape of the peninsula, and discovered part of the Aleutian group.

Exhausted by long illness, however, the explorer was now no longer able to direct the course of his vessel, and could not prevent her from running aground on the little island bearing his name. There, on the 8th December, 1741, this brave man and skilful explorer perished miserably.

The remnant of his crew who survived the fatigues and privations of winter in this desolate spot, succeeded in making a large sloop of the remains of the vessel, in which they returned to Kamschatka.

Meanwhile Tschirikow, after waiting for his superior officer until the 25th June, made land between 55° 56' N. lat., where he lost two boats with their crews, without being able to find out what had become of them. Unable after this catastrophe to open communication with the natives, he went back to Kamschatka.

The way was now open, and adventurers, merchants, and naval officers eagerly rushed in, directing their efforts carefully to the Aleutian Islands and the peninsula of Alaska.

The expeditions sent out by the English, and the progress made by the Russians, had, however, aroused the jealousy and anxiety of the Spanish, who feared lest their rivals should establish themselves in a country nominally belonging to Spain, though she owned not a single colony in it.

The Viceroy of Mexico now remembered the discovery of an excellent port by Viscaino, and resolved to found a "presidio" there. Two expeditions started simultaneously, the one by land, under Don Gaspar de Partola, the other by sea, consisting of two packets, the *San Carlos* and *San Antonio*, and after a year's search found again the harbour of Monterey, alluded to by Viscaino.

After this expedition the Spanish continued the exploration of the Californian coast. The most celebrated voyages were those of Don Juan de Ayala and of La Bodega, which took place in 1775, and resulted in the discovery of Cape Engano and Guadalupe Bay. Next to these rank the expeditions of Arteaga and Maurelle.

We have already related what was done by Cook, La Perouse, and Marchand, so we can pass on to say a few words on the expeditions of Vancouver. This officer, who had accompanied Cook on his second and third voyage, was naturally appointed to the command of the expedition sent out by the English government with a view to settling the disputes with the Spanish government as to Nootka Sound.

George Vancouver was commissioned to obtain from the Spanish authorities the formal cession of this great harbour, of such vast importance to the fur trade. He was then to survey, the whole of the north-west coast, from 30° N. lat. to Cook's River in 61° N. lat. Lastly, he was to give special attention to the Straits of De Fuca and the bay explored in 1749 by the *Washington*.

The two vessels, the *Discovery* of 340 tons, and the *Chatham* of 135 – the latter under the command of Captain Broughton – left Falmouth on the 1st of April, 1791. After touching at Teneriffe, Simon Bay, and the Cape of Good Hope, Vancouver steered southwards, sighted St. Paul's Island, and sailed towards New Holland, between the routes taken by Dampier and Marion; and through latitudes which had not yet been traversed. On the 27th September was sighted part of the coast of New Holland, ending in abrupt and precipitous cliffs, to which the name of Cape Chatham was given. As many of his crew were down with dysentery, Vancouver decided to anchor in the first harbour he came to, to get water, wood, and above all provisions, of which he stood sorely in need. Port George III. was the first reached, where ducks, curlews, swans, fish, and oysters abounded; but no communication could be opened with the natives, although a recently abandoned village of some twenty huts was seen.

We need not follow Vancouver in his cruise along the south-west coast of Holland, as we shall learn nothing new from it.

On the 28th November Van Diemen's Land was doubled, and on the 2nd December the coast of New Zealand was reached and anchor cast by the two vessels in Dusky Bay. Here Vancouver completed the survey left unfinished by Cook. A gale soon separated the *Discovery* from the *Chatham*, which was found again in Matavai Bay, Tahiti. During the voyage there from Dusky Bay, Vancouver discovered some rocky islands, which he called the Snares, and a large island named Oparra, whilst Captain Broughton had discovered Chatham Island, on the east of New Zealand. The incidents of the stay at Tahiti resemble those of Cook's story too close for repetition.

On the 24th January the two vessels started for the Sandwich Islands, and stopped for a short time off Owyhee, Waohoo, and Ottoway. Since the murder of Cook many changes had taken place in this archipelago. English and American vessels now sometimes visited it to take whales, or trade in furs, and their captains had given the natives a taste for brandy and fire-arms. Quarrels between the petty chiefs had become more frequent, the most complete anarchy prevailed everywhere, and the number of inhabitants was already greatly diminished.

On the 17th March, 1792, Vancouver left the Sandwich Islands and steered for America, of which he soon sighted the part called by Drake New Albion. Here he almost immediately met Captain Grey, who was supposed to have penetrated, in the *Washington*, into De Fuca Strait, and discovered a vast sea. Grey at once disavowed the discoveries with which he was so generously credited explaining that he had only sailed fifty miles up the Strait, which

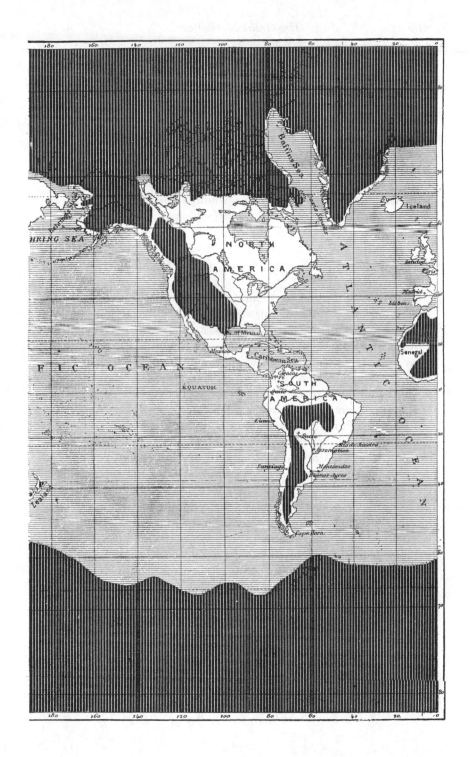

runs from east to west till it reaches a spot where, according to some natives, it veers to the north and disappears.

Vancouver in his turn entered De Fuca Strait, and recognized Discovery Port, Admiralty Entry, Birch Bay, Desolation Sound, Johnston Strait, and Broughton Archipelago. Before reaching the northern extremity of this long arm of the sea, he met two small Spanish vessels under the command of Quadra. The two captains compared notes, and gave their names to the chief island of the large group known collectively as New Georgia.

Vancouver next visited Nootka Sound and the Columbia River, whence he sailed to San Francisco, off which he anchored. It will be understood that it is impossible to follow the details of the minute survey of the vast stretch of coast, between Cape Mendoçino and Port Conclusion, in N. lat. 56° 37', which required no less than three successive trips.

"Now," says the great navigator, "that we have achieved the chief aim of the king in ordering this voyage, I flatter myself that our very detailed survey of the north-west coast of America will dispel all doubts, and do away with all erroneous opinions as to a north-west passage; surely no one will now believe in there being a communication between the North Pacific and the interior of the American continent in the part traversed by us."

Leaving Nootka, to survey the coast of South America before returning to Europe, Vancouver touched at the Small Cocoa-Nut Island – which, as we have already observed, little deserves its name – cast anchor off Valparaiso, doubled Cape Horn, took in water at St. Helena, and re-entered the Thames on the 12th of September, 1795.

The fatigue incidental to this long expedition had so undermined the health of the explorer that he died in May, 1798, leaving the account of his voyage to be finished by his brother.

Throughout the arduous survey, occupying four years, of 900 miles of coast, the *Discovery* and *Chatham* lost but two men. It will be seen from this how apt a pupil of Cook the great navigator was; and we do not know whether most to admire in Vancouver his care for his sailors and humanity to the natives, or the wonderful nautical skill he displayed in this dangerous cruise.

While explorers thus succeeded each other on the western coast of America, colonists were not idle inland. Already established on the borders of the Atlantic, where a series of states had been founded from Florida to Canada, the white men were now rapidly forcing their way westwards. Trappers, and *coureurs des bois*, as the French hunters were called, had discovered vast tracts of land suitable for cultivation, and many English squatters had already taken root, not, however, without numerous conflicts with the original owners of the soil, whom they daily tried to drive into the interior. Emigrants were soon attracted in large numbers by the fertility of a virgin soil, and the more liberal constitution of the various states.

Their number increased to such an extent, that at the end of the seventeenth century the heirs of Lord Baltimore estimated the produce of the sale of their lands at three thousand pounds; and in the middle of the following century, 1750, the successors of William Penn also made a profit ten times as great as the original price of their property. Yet emigration was even then not sufficiently rapid, and convicts were introduced. Maryland numbered 1,981 in 1750. Many scandalous abuses also resulted from the compulsory signing by new comers of agreements they did not understand.

Although the lands bought of the Indians were far from being all occupied, the English colonists continued to push their way inland, at the risk of encounters with the legitimate owners of the soil.

In the north the Hudson's Bay Company, holding a monopoly of the fur trade, were always on the look-out for new hunting-grounds, for those originally explored were soon exhausted. Their trappers made their way far into the western wilds, and gained valuable information from the Indians whom they pressed into their service, and taught to get drunk. By this means the existence of a river flowing northwards, past some copper-mines, from which some natives brought fine specimens to Fort Prince of Wales, was ascertained. The company at once, i.e. in 1769, decided to send out an expedition, to the command of which they appointed Samuel Hearn.

For a journey to the Arctic regions, where provisions are difficult to obtain and the cold is intense, a few well-seasoned men are required, who can endure the fatigue of an arduous march over snow, and bear up against hunger. Hearn took with him only two whites, and a few Indians on whom he could depend.

In spite of the great skill of the guides, who knew the country, and were familiar with the habits of the game it contained, provisions soon failed. Two hundred miles from Fort Prince of Wales the Indians abandoned Hearn and his two companions, who were obliged to retrace their steps.

The chief of the expedition, however, was a rough sailor, accustomed to privations, so he was not discouraged. If he had failed the first time, that was no reason why a second attempt should not succeed.

In March, 1770, Hearn started again to try and cross the unknown districts. This time he was alone with five Indians, for he had noticed that the inability of the whites to endure fatigue excited the contempt of the natives. He had penetrated 500 miles when the severity of the weather compelled him to wait for a less severe temperature. He had had a terrible experience. At one time to have, indeed, more game than can be eaten; but more often to have no food whatever, and be compelled for a week at a time to gnaw old leather, pick bones which had been thrown aside, or to seek, often in vain, for a few berries on the trees; and lastly, to endure fearful cold – such is the life of an explorer in these Arctic regions.

Hearn started once more in April, wandered about the woods until August, and had arranged to spend the winter with an Indian tribe which had received him well, when an accident which deprived him of his quadrant compelled him to continue his journey.

Privations, miseries, and disappointments, had not quenched the ardour of Hearn's indomitable spirit. He started again on the 7th December, and penetrating westwards below the 60th parallel N. lat. he came to a river. Here he built a canoe, and went in it down the stream, which flowed into an innumerable series of large and small lakes. Finally, on the 13th July, 1771, he reached the Coppermine River. The Indians with him now declared that they had been for some weeks in the country of the Esquimaux, and that they meant to massacre all they should meet of that hated race.

An encounter very soon took place.

"Coming," says Hearn, "upon a party of Esquimaux asleep in their tents, the Indians fell upon them suddenly, and I was compelled to witness the massacre of the poor creatures."

Of twenty individuals, not one escaped the sanguinary rage of the Indians; and they put to death with indescribable tortures an old woman who had in the first instance eluded them.

"After this horrible carnage," says Hearn, "we sat down on the grass, and made a good dinner off fresh salmon."

Here the river widened considerably. Had Hearn arrived at its mouth? The water was still quite sweet. There were, however, signs of a tide on the shores, and a number of seals were disporting themselves in the water. A quantity of whale blubber was found in the tents of the Esquimaux. Everything in fact combined to prove that the sea was near. Hearn seized his telescope, and saw stretching before him a huge sheet of water, dotted with islands. There was no longer any doubt; it was the sea!

On the 30th June, Hearn got back to the English posts, after an absence of no less than a year and five months.

The company recognized the immense service just rendered by Hearn, by appointing him Governor of Fort Prince of Wales. During his expedition to Hudson's Bay, La Perouse visited this post, and there found the journal of Samuel Hearn's expedition. The French navigator returned it, on condition that he would publish it. We do not know why its appearance in accordance with the promise given by the English traveller to the French sailor was delayed until 1795.

Not until the close of the eighteenth century did the immense chain of lakes, rivers, and portages become known, which, emanating from Lake Superior, receive all the waters flowing from the Rocky Mountains, and divert them to the Arctic Ocean. It was to the brothers Frobisher, fur traders, and to a Mr. Pond, who reached Athabasca, that their discovery is partially due.

Thanks to their efforts, travelling in these parts became less difficult. One explorer succeeded another, posts were established, and the country was opened to all comers. Soon after a rumour was spread of the discovery of a large river flowing in a north-westerly direction.

It was Alexander Mackenzie who gave his name to it. Starting on the 3rd June, 1789, from Fort Chippewyan, on the southern shores of the Lake of the Hills, accompanied by a few Canadians, and several Indians who had been with Samuel Hearn, he reached 67° 45' N. lat., where he heard that the sea was not far off on the east, but that he was even nearer to it on the west. It was evident that he was quite close to the north-western extremity of America.

On the 12th July, Mackenzie reached a large sheet of shallow water covered with ice, which he could not believe to be the sea, though no land could be seen on the horizon. It was, however, the Northern Ocean, as he became assured when he saw the water rising, although the wind was not violent. The tide was coming in! The traveller then gained an island at a little distance from the shore, from which he saw several whales gambolling in the water.

Mackenzie's first view of the North Pacific Ocean.

He therefore named the island, which is situated in N. lat. 69° 11', Whale Island. On the 12th September the expedition safely returned to Fort Chippewyan.

Three years later Mackenzie, whose thirst for discovery was unslaked, ascended Peace River, which rises in the Rocky Mountains. In 1793, after forcing his way across this rugged chain, he made out on the other side the Tacoutche-Tesse River, which flows in a south-westerly direction. In the midst of dangers and privations more easily imagined than described, Mackenzie descended this river to its mouth, below Prince of Wales Islands. There, he wrote with a mixture of grease and vermilion, the following laconic but eloquent inscription on a wall of rock: "Alexander Mackenzie, come from Canada overland, July 22nd, 1793." On the 24th August he re-entered Fort Chippewyan.

In South America no scientific expedition took place during the first half of the eighteenth century. We have now only to speak of Condamine. We have already told of his discoveries in America, explaining how when the work was done he had allowed Bouguer to return to Europe, and left Jussieu to continue the collection of unknown plants and animals which was to enrich science, whilst he himself went down the Amazon to its Mouth.

"Condamine," says Maury in his "Histoire de l'Académie des Sciences", "may be called the Humboldt of the eighteenth century. An intellectual and scientific man, he gave proof in this memorable expedition of an heroic devotion to the progress of knowledge. The funds granted to him by the king for his expedition were not sufficient; he added 100,000 livres from his private purse; and the fatigue and suffering he underwent led to the loss of his ears and legs. The victim of his enthusiasm for science, on his return home he met with nothing but ridicule and sarcasm from a public who could not understand a martyr who aimed at winning anything but Heaven. In him was recognized, not the indefatigable explorer who had braved so many dangers, but the infirm and deaf M. de Condamine, who always held his ear-trumpet in his hand. Content, however, with the recognition of his fellow-savants, to which Buffon gave such eloquent expression in his reply to the address at his reception at the French Academy, Condamine consoled himself by composing songs; and maintained until his death, which was hastened by all he had undergone, the zeal for information on all subjects, even torture, which led him to question the executioner on the scaffold of Damiens."

Few travellers before Condamine had had an opportunity of penetrating into Brazil. The learned explorer hoped, therefore, to render his journey useful by making a map of the course of the river, and putting down all his observations on the singular costumes worn by the natives of that little frequented country.

After Orellana, whose adventurous trip we have related, Pedro de Ursua was sent in 1559 by the Viceroy of Peru to seek for Lake Parima and the El Dorado. He was murdered by a rebel soldier, who committed all manner of outrages on his way down the river, and finished his course by being abandoned on Trinity Island.

Efforts of this kind did not throw much light on the course of the river. The Portuguese were more fortunate. In 1636 and 1637 Pedro Texeira with forty-seven canoes, and a large number of Spaniards and Indians, followed the Amazon as far as the junction of its tributary the Napo, and then ascended, first it, and afterwards the Coca, to within thirty miles of Quito, which he reached with a few men.

The map drawn up by Sanson after this trip, and as a matter of course copied by all geographers, was extremely defective, and until 1717 there was no other. At that time the copy of a map drawn up by Father Fritz, a German missionary, came out in Vol. xii. of the "Lettres Édifiantes", a valuable publication, containing a multitude of interesting historical and geographical facts. In this map it was shown that the Napo is not the true source of the Amazon, and that the latter, under the name of the Marañon, issues from Lake Guanuco, thirty leagues east of Lima. The lower portion of the course of the river was badly drawn, as Father Fritz was too ill when he went down it to observe closely.

Leaving Tarqui, five leagues from Cuenca, on the 11th May, 1743, Condamine passed Zaruma, a town once famous for its goldmines, and having crossed several rivers on the hanging bridges, which look like huge hammocks slung from one side to the other, reached Loxa, four degrees from the line, and 400 fathoms lower than Quito. Here he noticed a remarkable difference of temperature, and found the mountains to be mere hills compared with those of Quito.

Between Loxa and Jaen de Bracamoros the last buttresses of the Andes are crossed. In this district rain falls every day throughout the year, so that a long stay cannot be made there. The whole country has declined greatly from its former prosperity. Loyola, Valladolid, Jaen, and the greater number of the Peruvian towns at

Portrait of Condamine.
(Facsimile of early engraving.)

a distance from the sea, and the main road between Carthagena and Lima, were in Condamine's time little more than hamlets. Yet forests of cocoa-nut trees grow all around Jaen, the natives thinking no more of them than they do of the gold dust brought down by their rivers.

Condamine embarked on the Chincipe, wider here than the Seine at Paris, and went down it as far as its junction with the Marañon, beyond which the latter river becomes navigable, although its course is broken by a number of falls and rapids, and in many places narrows till it is but twenty fathoms wide. The most celebrated of these narrows is the *pongo*, or gate, of Manseriche, in the heart of the Cordillera, where the Amazon has hewn for itself a bed only fifty-five fathoms wide, with all but perpendicalar sides. Condamine, attended only by a single negro, met with an almost unparalleled adventure on a raft in this pongo.

"The stream," he says, "the height of which had diminished twenty-five feet in thirty-six hours, continued to decrease in volume. In the middle of the night, part of a large branch of a tree caught between the woodwork of my boat, penetrating further and further as the latter sunk with the water, so that if I had not been awake and on guard at the time, I should have found myself hanging from a tree, on my raft. The least of the evils threatening me would have been the loss of my journals and note-books, the fruit of eight years of work. Fortunately, I eventually found means to free my raft, and float it again."

In the midst of the woods near the ruined town of Santiago, where Condamine arrived on the 10th July, lived the Xibaro Indians, who had been for a century in revolt against the Spaniards, who tried to free them to labour in the gold-mines.

Beyond the pongo of Manseriche a new world was entered, a perfect ocean of fresh water – a labyrinth of lakes and rivers, and channels, set in an impenetrable forest. Although he had lived in the open air for more than seven years, Condamine was struck dumb by this novel spectacle of water and trees only with nothing else besides. Leaving Borja on the 14th July, the traveller soon passed the mouth of the Morona, which comes down from the volcano of Sangay, the ashes from which are sometimes flung beyond Guayaquil. He next passed the three mouths of the Pastaca, a river at this time so much swollen that the width of no one of its mouths could be estimated.

On the 19th of the same month Condamine reached Laguna,

Celebrated narrows of Manseriche.
(Facsimile of early engraving.)

where Pedro Maldonado, governor of the province of Esmeraldas, who had come down the Pastaca, had been waiting for him for six weeks. At this time Laguna was a large community, of some thousand Indians capable of bearing arms, who recognized the authority of the missionaries of the different tribes.

"In making a map of the course of the Amazon," says Condamine, "I provided myself with a resource against the *ennui* of a quiet voyage with nothing to break the monotony of the scenery, though that scenery was new to me. My attention was continually on the strain as, compass and watch in hand, I noted the deflexions in the course of the river, the time occupied in passing from one bend to another, the variations in the breadth of its bed and in that of the mouths of its tributaries, the angle formed by the latter at the confluence, the position and size of the islands, and above all the rate of the current and that of the canoe. Now on land and now in the canoe, employing various modes of measurement, which it would be superfluous to explain here, every instant was occupied. I often sounded, and measured geometrically the breadth of the river and that of its tributaries. I took the height of the sun at the meridian every day, and I noted its amplitude at its rising and setting, wherever I went."

On the 25th July, after having passed the Tigre River, Condamine came to a new mission station, that of a tribe called Yameos, recently rescued from the woods by the Fathers. Their language is difficult to learn, and their mode of pronouncing it extraordinary. Some of their words are nine or ten syllables long, and yet they can only count up to three. They use a kind of peashooter with great skill, firing from it small arrows tipped with a poison which causes instantaneous death.

The following day the explorer passed the mouth of the Ucayale, one of the most important of the tributaries of the Marañon, and which might even be its source. Beyond it the main stream widens sensibly.

Condamine reached on the 27th the mission station of the Omaguas, formerly a powerful nation, whose dwelling extended along the banks of the Amazon for a distance of 200 leagues below the Napo. Originally strangers in the land, they are supposed to have come down some river rising in Granada, and to have fled from the Spanish yoke. The word Omagua means flat head in Peruvian, and these people have the singular custom of

Omagua Indians.

squeezing the foreheads of new-born babies between two flat pieces of wood, to make them, as they say, resemble the full moon. They also use two curious plants, the floripondio and the curupa, which makes them drunk for twenty-four hours, and causes very wonderful dreams. So that opium and hatchich have their counterparts in Peru.

Cinchona, ipecacuanha, simaruba, sarsaparilla, guaiacum, cocoa, and vanilla grow on the banks of the Marañon, as does also a kind of india-rubber, of which the natives make bottles, boots, and syringes, which, according to Condamine, require no piston. They are of the shape of hollow pears, and are pierced at the end with a little hole, into which a pipe is fitted. This contrivance is much used by the Omaguas; and when a fête is given, the host, as a matter of politeness, always presents one to each of his guests, who use them before any ceremonial banquet.

Changing boats at San Joaquin, Condamine arrived at the mouth of Napo in time to witness, during the night of the 31st July or the 1st August, the emersion of the first satellite of Jupiter, so that he was able to determine exactly the latitude and longitude of the spot – a valuable observation, from which all other positions on the journey could be calculated.

Pevas, which was reached the next day, is the last of the Spanish missions on the Marañon. The Indians collected there were neither all of the same race nor all converts to Christianity. They still wore bone ornaments in the nostrils and the lips, and had their cheeks riddled with holes, in which were fixed the feathers of birds of every colour.

St. Paul is the first Portuguese mission. There the river is no less than 900 fathoms wide, and often rises in violent storms. The traveller was agreeably surprised to find the Indian women possessed of pet birds, locks, iron keys, needles, looking-glasses, and other European utensils, procured at Para in exchange for cocoa. The native canoes are much more convenient than those used by the Indians of the Spanish possessions. They are in fact regular little brigantines, sixty feet long by seven wide, manned by forty oarsmen.

Between St. Paul and Coari several large and beautiful rivers flow into the Amazon. On the south the Yutay, Yuruca, Tefé, and Coari; on the north the Putumayo and Yupura. On the shores of the last-named river lives a cannibal race. Here Texeira set up a barrier, on the 26th June, 1639, which was to mark the frontier between the district in which the Brazilian and Peruvian languages respectively were to be used in dealing with the Indians.

Purus River and the Rio Negro, connecting the Orinoco with the Amazon, the banks dotted with Portuguese missions under the direction of the monks of Mount Carmel, were successively surveyed. The first reliable information on the important geographical fact of the communication between the two great rivers, is to be found in the works of Condamine, and his sagacious comments on the journeys of the missionaries who preceded him. It was in these latitudes that the golden lake of Parimé and the fabulous town of Manoa del Dorado are said to have been situated. Here, too, lived the Manaos Indians, who so long resisted the Portuguese.

Now were passed successively the mouth of the Madera River – so called on account of the quantity of timber which drifts down from it, the port of Pauxis – beyond which the Marañon takes the name of the Amazon, and where the tide begins to be felt, although the sea is more than 200 miles distant – and the fortress of Topayos, at the mouth of a river coming down from the mines of Brazil, on the borders of which live the Tupinambas.

Not until September did the mountains come in sight on the north – quite a novel spectacle, since for two months Condamine had not seen a single hill. They were the first buttresses of the Guiana chain.

On the 6th September, opposite Fort Paru, Condamine left the Amazon, and passed by a natural canal to the Xingu River, called by Father D'Acunha the Paramaribo. The port of Curupa was then reached, and lastly Para, a large town, with regular streets and houses of rough or hewn stone. To complete his map, the explorer was obliged to visit the mouth of the Amazon, where he embarked for Cayenne, arriving there on the 20th February, 1774.

This long voyage had the most important results. For the first time the course of the Amazon had been laid down in a thoroughly scientific manner, and the connexion between it and the Orinoco ascertained. Moreover Condamine had collected a vast number of interesting observations on natural history, physical geography, astronomy, and the new science of anthropology, then in its earliest infancy.

We have now to relate the travels of a man who recognized, better than any one else had done, the connexion between geography and the other physical sciences. We allude to Alexander von

Portrait of Alex. de Humboldt.
(Facsimile of early engraving.)

Humboldt. To him is due the credit of having opened to travellers this fertile source of knowledge.

Born at Berlin, in 1759, Humboldt's earliest studies were carried on under Campe, the well-known editor of many volumes of travels. Endowed with a great taste for botany, Humboldt made friends at the university of Göttingen with Forster the younger, who had just made the tour of the world with Captain Cook. This friendship, and the enthusiastic accounts given of his adventures by Forster, probably did much to rouse in Humboldt a longing to travel. He took the lead in the study of geology, botany, chemistry, and animal magnetism; and to perfect himself in the various sciences, he visited England, Holland, Italy, and Switzerland. In 1797, after the death of his mother, who objected to his leaving Europe, he went to Paris, where he became acquainted with Aimé Bonpland, a young botanist, with whom he at once agreed to go on several exploring expeditions.

It had been arranged that Humboldt should accompany Captain Baudin, but the delay in the starting of his expedition exhausted the young enthusiast's patience, and he went to Marseilles with the intention of joining the French army in Egypt. For two whole months he waited for the sailing of the frigate which was to take him; and, weary of inaction, he went to Spain with his friend Bonpland, in the hope of obtaining permission to visit the Spanish possessions in America.

This was no easy matter, but Humboldt was a man of rare perseverance. He was thoroughly well-informed, he had first-rate introductions, and he was, moreover, already becoming known. In spite, therefore, of the extreme reluctance of the government, he was at last authorized to explore the Spanish colonies, and take any astronomical or geodesic observations he chose.

The two friends left Corunna on the 5th June, 1799, and reached the Canaries thirteen days later. Of course, as naturalists they were in duty bound not to land at Teneriffe without ascending the Peak.

"Scarcely any naturalist," says Humboldt in a letter to La Metterie, "who, like myself, has passed through to the Indies, has had time to do more than go to the foot of this colossal volcano, and admire the delightful gardens of Orotava. Fortunately for me our frigate, the *Pizarro*, stopped for six days. I examined in detail the layers of which the peak of Teyde is composed. We slept in the moonlight at a height of 1,200 fathoms. At two o'clock in the morning we started for the summit, where we arrived at eight o'clock, in spite of the violent wind, the great heat of the ground, which burnt our boots, and the intense cold of the atmosphere. I will tell you nothing about the magnificent view, which included the volcanic islands of Lancerote, Canaria, and Gomera, at our feet; the desert, twenty leagues square, strewn with pumice-stone and lava, and without insects or birds, separating us from thickets of laurel-trees and heaths; or of the vineyards studded with palms, banana, and dragon-trees, the roots of which are washed by the waves. We went into the very crater itself. It is not more than forty or sixty feet deep. The summit is 1,904 fathoms above the sea-level as estimated by Borda in a very careful geometric measurement. . . . The crater of the Peak – that is to say, of the summit – has been inactive for several centuries, lava flowing from the sides only. The crater, however, provides an enormous quantity of sulphur and sulphate of iron."

In July, Humboldt and Bonpland arrived at Cumana, in that part of America known as Terra Firma. Here they spent some weeks in examining the traces left by the great earthquake of 1797. They then determined the position of Cumana, which was placed a degree and a half too far north on all the maps – an error due to the fact of the current bearing to the north near La Trinidad, having deceived all travellers. In December, 1799, Humboldt wrote from Caracas to the astronomer, Lalande: –

"I have just completed an intensely interesting journey in the interior of Paria, in the Cordillera, of Cocolar, Tumeri, and Guiri. I had two or three mules loaded with instruments, dried plants, &c. We penetrated to the Capuchin mission, which had never been visited by any naturalist. We discovered a great number of new plants, chiefly varieties of palms; and we are about to start for the Orinoco, and propose pushing on from it perhaps to San Carlos on the Rio Negro, beyond the equator. We have dried more than 1,600 plants, and described more than 500 birds, picked up numberless shells and insects, and I have made some fifty drawings. I think that is pretty well in four months, considering the broiling heat of this zone."

During this first trip Humboldt visited the Chayma and Guarauno Missions. He also climbed to the summit of the Tumiriquiri, and went down into the Guacharo cavern, the entrance to which, framed as it is with the most luxuriant vegetation, is truly magnificent. From it issues a considerable river, and its dim recesses echo to the gloomy notes of birds. It is the Acheron of the Chayma Indians for, according to their mythology and that of the natives of Orinoco, the souls of the dead go to this cavern. To go down into the Guacharo signifies in their language to die.

The Indians go into the Guacharo cavern once a year, in the middle of summer, and destroy the greater number of the nests in it with long poles. At this time many thousands of birds die a violent death, and the old inhabitants of the cave hover above the heads of the Indians with piercing cries, as if they would defend their broods.

The young birds which fall to the ground are opened on the spot. Their peritoneum is covered with a thick layer of fat, extending from the abdomen to the anus, and forming a kind of cushion between the legs. At the time called at Caripe the oil harvest, the Indians build themselves huts of palm leaves outside the cavern, and then light fires of brushwood, over which they hang clay pots filled with the fat of the young birds recently killed. This fat, known under the name of the Guacharo oil or butter, is half-liquid, transparent, without smell, and so pure that it can be kept a year without turning rancid.

Humboldt continues: "We passed fifteen days in the Caripe valley, situated at a height of 952 Castilian varas above the sea-level, and inhabited by naked Indians. We saw some black monkeys with red beards. We had the satisfaction of being treated with the greatest kindness by the Capuchin monks and the missionaries living amongst these semi-barbarous people."

From the Caripe valley the two travellers went back to Cumana by way of the Santa Maria Mountains and the Catuaro missions, and on the 21st November they arrived – having come by sea – at Caracas, a town situated in the midst of a valley rich in cocoa, cotton, and coffee, yet with a European climate.

Humboldt turned his stay at Caracas to account by studying the light of the stars of the southern hemisphere, for he had noticed that several, notably the Altar, the Feet of the Centaur, and others, seemed to have changed since the time of La Caille.

At the same time he put his collections in order, despatching part of them to Europe, and most thoroughly examined some rocks, with a view to ascertaining of what materials the earth's crust was here composed.

After having explored the neighbourhood of Caracas, and ascended the Silla, which although close to the town, had never

Humboldt's route.

been scaled by any native, Humboldt and Bonpland went to Valencia, along the shores of a lake called Tacarigua by the Indians, and exceeding in size that of Neufchâtel in Switzerland. Nothing could give any idea of the richness and variety of the vegetation. But the interest of the lake consists not only in its picturesque and romantic beauty; the gradual decrease in the volume of its waters attracted the attention of Humboldt, who attributed it to the reckless cutting down of the forests in its neighbourhood, resulting in the exhaustion of its sources.

Near this lake Humboldt received proof of the truth of the accounts he had heard of an extraordinary tree, the palo de la vaca, or cow-tree, which yields a balsamic and very nutritive milk, drawn off from incisions made in the bark.

The most arduous part of the trip began at Porto Caballo, at the entrance to the llanos, or perfectly flat plains stretching between the hills of the coast and the Orinoco valley.

"I am not sure," says Humboldt, "that the first sight of the llanos is not as surprising as that of the Andes."

Nothing in fact could be more striking than this sea of grass, from which whirls of dust rise up continually, although not a breath of wind is felt at Calabozo, in the centre of this vast plain. Humboldt first tested the power of the gymnotus, or electric eel, large numbers of which are met with in all the tributaries of the Orinoco. The Indians, who were afraid of exposing themselves to the electric discharge of these singular creatures, proposed sending some horses into the marsh containing them.

"The extraordinary noise made by the shoes of the horses," says Humboldt, "made the eels come out of the ooze and prepare for battle. The yellowish livid gymnoti, resembling serpents, swam on the top of the water, and squeezed themselves under the bodies of the quadrupeds which had disturbed them. The struggle which ensued between animals so differently constituted presented a very striking spectacle. The Indians, armed with harpoons and long canes, surrounded the pond on every side, and even climbed into the trees, the branches of which stretched horizontally over the water. Their wild cries, as they brandished their long sticks, prevented the horses from running away and getting back to the shores of the pond; whilst the eels, driven mad by the noise, defended themselves by repeated discharges from their electric batteries. For a long time they appeared victorious, and some horses succumbed to the violence of the repeated shocks which they received upon their vital organs from every side. They were stunned, and sank beneath the water.

"Others, panting for breath, with manes erect, and wild eyes full of the keenest suffering, tried to fly from the scene, but the merciless Indians drove them back into the water. A very few, who succeeded in eluding the vigilance of the guards, regained the bank, stumbling at every step, and lay down upon the sand, exhausted with fatigue, every limb paralyzed from the electric shocks received from the eels.

"I never remember receiving a more terrible shock from a Leyden jar than I did from a gymnotus on which I accidentally trod just after it came out of the water."

The astronomic position of Calabozo having been determined, Humboldt and Bonpland resumed their journey to the Orinoco. The Uriticu, with its numerous and ferocious crocodiles, and the Apure, one of the tributaries of the Orinoco, the banks of which are covered with a luxuriant vegetation such as is only met with in the tropics, were successively crossed or descended.

The latter stream is flanked on either side by thick hedges, with openings here and there, through which boars, tigers, and other wild animals, made their way to quench their thirst. When the shades of night shut in the forest, so silent by day, it resounds with the cries of birds and the howling or roaring of beasts of prey, vying with each other as to which shall make the most noise.

While the Uriticu is inhabited by fierce crocodiles, the Apure is the home of a small fish called the "carabito", which attacks bathers with great fury, often biting out large pieces of flesh. It is only four or five inches long, but more formidable than the largest crocodile, and the waters it frequents are carefully avoided by the Indians, in spite of their fondness for bathing, and the relief it affords them, persecuted as they are by ants and mosquitos.

Our travellers went down the Orinoco as far as the Temi, which is connected by a short portage with the Cano-Pimichino, a tributary of the Rio Negro.

The banks of the Temi, and the adjacent forests, are often inundated, and then the Indians make waterways, two or three feet wide, between the trees. Nothing could be more quaint or imposing than floating amongst the gigantic growths, beneath their green foliage. Sometimes, three or four hundred leagues inland, the traveller comes upon a troop of fresh-water dolphins, spouting up

Gigantic vegetation on the banks of the Temi.

water and compressed air in the manner which has gained for them the name of blowers.

It took four days to transport the canoes from the Tenir to the Cano-Pimichino, as a path had to be cleared with axes.

The Pimichino flows into the Rio-Negro, which is in its turn a tributary of the Amazon.

Humboldt and Bonpland went down the Rio-Negro as far as San Carlos, and then up the Casiquiaro, an important branch of the Orinoco, which connects it with the Rio-Negro. The shores of the Casiquiaro are inhabited by the Ydapaminores, who live entirely on smoked ants.

Lastly, the travellers went up the Orinoco nearly to its source, at the foot of the Duida volcano, where their further progress was stopped by the hostility of the Guaharibos and the Guaica Indians, who were skilful marksmen with the bow and arrow. Here was discovered the famous El Dorado lake, with its floating islets of talc.

Thus was finally solved the problem of the junction of the Orinoco and the Marañon, which takes place on the borders of the Spanish and Portuguese territories, two degrees above the equator.

The two travellers then floated with the current down the Orinoco, traversing by this means five hundred leagues in twenty-five days, after which they halted for three weeks at Angostura, to tide over the time of the great heat, when fever is prevalent, regaining Cumana in October, 1800.

"My health," says Humboldt, "was proof against the fatigue of a journey of more than 1300 leagues, but my poor comrade Bonpland, was, immediately on his return, seized with fever and sickness, which nearly proved fatal. A constitution of exceptional vigour is necessary to enable a traveller to bear the fatigue, privations, and interruptions of every kind with which he has to contend in these unhealthy districts, with impunity. We were constantly surrounded by voracious tigers and crocodiles, stung by venomous mosquitoes and ants, with no food for three months but water, bananas, fish, and tapioca, now crossing the territory of the earth eating Otomaques, now wandering through the desolate regions below the equator, where not a human creature is seen for 130 leagues. Few indeed are those who survive such perils and such exertions, fewer still are those who, having surmounted them, have sufficient courage and strength to encounter them a second time."

We have seen what an important geographical discovery

rewarded the perseverance of the explorers who had completed the examination of the whole of the district north of the Amazon, between Popayan and the mountains of French Guiana. The results obtained in other branches of science were no less novel and important.

Humboldt had discovered that there exists amongst the Indians of the Upper Orinoco and the Rio Negro a race with extremely fair complexions, differing entirely from the natives of the coast. He also noticed the curious tribe of the Otomaques.

"These people," he says "who disfigure their bodies with hideous paintings, eat nothing but loam for some three months, when the height of the Orinico cuts them off from the turtles which form their ordinary food. Some monks say they mix earth with the fat of crocodiles' tails, but this is a very false assertion. We saw provisions made of unadulterated earth, prepared only by slow, roasting and moistening with water."

Amongst the most curious of the discoveries made by Humboldt, we must mention that of the "curare", the virulent poison which he saw manufactured by the Catarapeni and Maquiritare Indians, and a specimen of which he sent to the Institute with the "dapiche", a variety of Indian rubber hitherto unknown, being the gum which exudes spontaneously from the roots of the trees known as "jacio" and "cucurma", and dries underground.

Humboldt concluded his first journey by the exploration of the southern districts of San Domingo and Jamaica, and by a short stay in Cuba, where he and his companions made several experiments with a view to facilitating the making of sugar, surveyed the coast of the island, and took some astronomical observations.

These occupations were interrupted by the news of the starting of Captain Baudin, who, it was said, was to double Cape Horn and examine the coasts of Chili and Peru. Humboldt, who had promised to join the expedition, at once left Cuba, and crossed South America, arriving on the coast of Peru in time, as he thought, to receive the French navigator. Although Humboldt had throughout his long journey worked with a view to timing his arrival in the Peruvian capital to meet Baudin, it was only when he reached Quito that he ascertained that the new expedition was making for the Pacific by way of the Cape of Good Hope.

In May, 1801, Humboldt, still accompanied by the faithful

Bonpland, embarked at Cartagena, whence he proposed going first
to Santa Fé de Bogota, and then to the lofty plains of Quito. To
avoid the great heat the travellers spent some time at the pretty village of Turbaco, situated on the heights overlooking the coast,
where they made the necessary preparations for their journey. In
one of their excursions in the neighbourhood they visited a very
strange region, of which their Indian guides had often spoken under
the name of *Volcanitos*.

This is a volcanic district, set in a forest of palms, and of the tree
called "tola", about two miles to the east of Turbaco. According to
a legend, the country was at one time one vast collection of burning
mountains, but the fire was quenched by a saint, who merely
poured a few drops of holy water upon it.

In the centre of an extensive plain Humboldt came upon some
twenty cones of greyish clay, about twenty-five feet high, the
mouths of which were full of water. As the travellers approached a
hollow sound was heard, succeeded in a few minutes by the escape
of a great quantity of gas. According to the Indians these phenomena had recurred for many years.

Humboldt noticed that the gas which issues from these small
volcanoes was a far purer azote than could then be obtained by
chemical laboratories.

Santa Fé is situated in a valley 8,600 feet above the sea-level.
Shut in on every side by lofty mountains, this valley appears to have
been formerly a large lake. The Rio-Bogota which receives all the
waters of the valley, has forced a passage for itself near the
Tequendama farm, on the south-west of Santa-Fé, beyond which it
leaves the plain by a narrow channel and flows into the Magdalena
basin. As a natural consequence, were this passage blocked, the
whole plain of Bogota would be inundated and the ancient lake
restored. There exists amongst the Indians a legend similar to that
connected with Roland's Pass in the Pyrenees, telling how one of
their heroes split open the rocks and drained dry the valley of
Bogota, after which, content with his exploit, he retired to the
sacred town of Eraca, where he did penance for 2,000 years,
inflicting upon himself the greatest torture.

The cataract of Tequendama, although not the largest in the
world, yet affords a very beautiful sight. When swollen by the addition of all the waters of the valley, the river, a little above the Falls,
is 175 feet wide, but on entering the defile which appears to have
been made by an earthquake, it is not more than forty feet in

breadth. The abyss into which it flings itself, is no less than 600 feet deep. Above this vast precipice constantly rises a dense cloud of foam, which, falling again almost immediately, is said to contribute greatly to the fertility of the valley.

Nothing could be more striking than the contrast between the valley of the Rio Bogota and that of the Magdalena: the one with the climate and productions of Europe, the corn, the oaks and other trees of our native land; the other with palms, sugar-canes, and all the growths of the tropics.

One of the most interesting of the natural curiosities met with by our travellers on the trip, was the bridge of Jcononzo, which they crossed in September, 1801. At the bottom of one of the contracted ravines, known as "cañons", peculiar to the Andes, a little stream, the Rio Suma Paz, has forced for itself a narrow channel. To cross this river would be impossible, had not nature herself provided two bridges, one above the other, which are justly considered marvels of the country.

Three blocks of rock detached from one of the mountains by the earthquake which produced this mighty fissure, have so fallen as to balance each other and form a natural arch, to which access is obtained by a path along the precipice. In the centre of this bridge there is an opening through which the traveller may gaze down into the infinite depth of the abyss, at the bottom of which rolls the torrent, its terrible roar mingled with the incessant screaming of thousands of birds. Sixty feet above this bridge is a second, fifty feet long by forty wide, and not more than eight feet thick in the middle. To serve as a parapet, the natives have made a slender balustrade of reeds along the edges of this second bridge, from which the traveller can obtain a fine view of the magnificent scene beneath him.

The heavy rain and bad roads made the journey to Quito very exhausting, but for all that Humboldt and Bonpland only halted there for an absolutely necessary rest, quickly pressing on for the Magdalena valley, and the magnificent forests clothing the sides of the Trinidiu in the Central Andes.

This mountain is considered one of the most difficult to cross in the whole chain. Even when the weather is favourable, twelve days, at least, are necessary for traversing the forests, in which not a human creature is seen and no food can be obtained. The highest point is 1,200 feet above the sea-level, and the path leading up to it is in many parts only one foot wide. The traveller is generally carried, bound to a chair in a sitting posture, on the back of a native, as a porter carries a trunk.

"We preferred to go on foot," says Humboldt in a letter to his brother, "and the weather being very fine we were only seventeen days in these solitudes, where not a trace is to be seen of any inhabitant. The night is passed in temporary huts made of the leaves of the heliconia, brought on purpose. On the western slopes of the Andes marshes have to be crossed, into which one sinks up to the knees, and the weather having changed when we reached them, it rained in torrents for the last few days. Our boots rotted on our feet, and we reached Carthago with naked and bleeding feet, but enriched with a fine collection of new plants.

"From Carthago we went to Popayan by way of Buga, crossing the fine Cauca valley, and skirting along the mountain of Choca, with the platina-mines for which it is famous.

"We spent October, 1801, at Popayan, whence we made excursions to the basaltic mountains of Julusuito and the craters of the Puracé volcano, which discharge hydro-sulphuric steam and porphyritic granite with a terrible noise.

"The greatest difficulties were met with in going from Popayan to Quito. We had to pass the Pasto Paramos, and that in the rainy season, which had now set in. A 'paramo' in the Andes is a district some 1,700 or 2,000 fathoms high, where vegetation ceases, and the cold is piercing.

"We went from Popayan to Almager and thence to Pasto, at the foot of a terrible volcano, by way of the fearful precipices forming the ascent to the summit of the Cordillera, thus avoiding the heat of the Patia valley, where one night will often bring on the fever known as the *Calentura de Patia*, lasting three or four months.

The province of Pasto consists entirely of a frozen plateau almost too lofty for any vegetation to thrive on it, surrounded by volcanoes and sulphur-mines from which spiral columns of smoke are perpetually issuing. The inhabitants have no food but batatas, and when they run short they are obliged to live upon a little tree called "achupalla", for which they have to contend with the bear of the Andes. After being wet through night and day for two months, and being all but drowned in a sudden flood, accompanied by an earthquake near the town of Jbarra, Humboldt and Bonpland arrived on the 6th January, 1801, at Quito, where they were received in cordial and princely style by the Marquis of Selva-Alegre.

Quito is a fine town, but the intense cold and the barren mountains surrounding it make it a gloomy place to stay in. Since the great earthquake of the 4th February, 1797, the temperature has considerably decreased, and Bouguer, who registered it at an average of from 15° to 16° would be surprised to find it varying from 4° to 10° Reaumur. Cotopaxi and Pinchincha, Antisana and Illinaza, the various craters of one subterranean fire, were all examined by the travellers, a fortnight being devoted to each.

Humboldt twice reached the edge of the Pinchincha crater, never before seen except by Condamine.

"I made my first trip," he says, "accompanied only by an Indian. Condamine had approached the crater by the lower part of its edge which was covered with snow, and in this first attempt I followed his example. But we nearly perished. The Indian sank to the breast in a crevasse, and we found to our horror that we were walking on a bridge of frozen snow, for a little in advance of us there were some holes through which we could see the light. Without knowing it we were in fact on the vaults belonging to the crater itself. Startled, but not discouraged, I changed my plan. From the outer rim of the crater, flung as it were upon the abyss, rise three peaks, three rocks, which are not covered with snow, because the steam from the volcano prevents the water from freezing. I climbed upon one of these rocks and on the top of it found a stone attached on one side only to the rock and undermined beneath, so as to protrude like a balcony over the precipice. This stone was but about twelve feet long by six broad, and is terribly shaken by the frequent earthquakes, of which we counted eighteen in less than thirty minutes. To examine the depths of the crater thoroughly we lay on our faces, and I do not think imagination could conceive anything drearier, more gloomy, or more awful than what we saw. The crater consists of a circular hole nearly a league in circumference, the jagged edges of which are surrounded by snow. The interior is of pitchy blackness, but so vast is the gulf that the summits of several mountains situated in it can be made out at a depth of some 300 fathoms, so only fancy where their bases must be!

"I have no doubt that the bottom of the crater must be on a level with the town of Quito. Condamine found this volcano extinct and covered with snow, but we had to take the bad news to the inhabitants of the capital, that the neighbouring burning mountain is really active."

Humboldt ascended the volcano of Antisana to a height of 2,773 fathoms, but could go no further, as the cold was so intense that the blood started from the lips, eyes, and gums of the travellers. It was impossible to reach the crater of Cotopaxi.

On the 9th June, 1802, Humboldt, accompanied by Bonpland, started from Quito to examine Chimborazo and Tungurunga. The peak of the latter fell in during the earthquake of 1797, and Humboldt found its height to be but 2,531 fathoms, whilst in Condamine's time it was 2,620 fathoms.

From Quito the travellers went to the Amazon by way of Lactacunga, Ambato and Rio-Bamba situated in the province laid waste by the earthquake of 1797, when 40,000 inhabitants were swallowed up by water and mud. Going down the Andes, Humboldt and his companions had an opportunity of admiring the remains of the Yega road, leading from Cusco to Assuay, and known as the Inca's road. It was built entirely of hewn stones, and was very straight. It might have been taken for one of the best Roman roads. In the same neighbourhood are the ruins of a palace of the Inca, Fupayupangi, described by Condamine in the minutes of the Berlin Academy.

After a stay of ten days at Cuença, Humboldt entered the province of Jaen, surveyed the Marañon as far as the Rio Napo, and with the aid of the astronomical observations he was able to make, supplemented Condamine's map. On the 23rd October, 1802, Humboldt entered Lima, where he successfully observed the transit of Mercury.

After spending a month in that capital he started for Guayaquil, whence he went by sea to Acapulco in Spanish America.

The vast number of notes collected by Humboldt during the year he spent in Mexico, and which led to the publication of his Essay on Spanish America, would, after what we have said of his previous proceedings, be enough to prove, if proof were needed, what a passion he had for knowledge, how indomitable was his energy and how immense his power of work.

At one and the same time he was studying the antiquities and the history of Mexico, the character, customs, and language of its people, and taking observations in natural history, physical geography, chemistry, astronomy, and topography.

The Tasco, Moran, and Guanajuato mines, which yield a profit of several million piastres per annum, first attracted the attention of Humboldt, who had early studied geology. He then examined the

Jerullo volcano, which, although situated in the centre of an
immense plain thirty-six leagues from the sea, and more than forty
from any volcano, discharged earth on the 29th September, 1759,
and formed a mountain of cinders and clay 1,700 feet high.

In Mexico the travellers were able to obtain everything necessary
to the arrangement of the immense collections they had accumulated, to classify and compare the observations each had taken, and
to prepare their geographical map for publication.

Finally, in January, 1804, they left Acapulco to examine the
eastern slopes of the Cordilleras, and to take the dimensions of the
two lofty Puebla volcanoes.

"Popocatepetl," says Desborough Cooley, "is always active,
although nothing but smoke and ashes have issued from its crater
for centuries. It is not only 2,000 feet higher than the loftiest mountains of Europe, but is also the loftiest mountain in Spanish
America." In spite of the great quantity of snow which had recently
fallen, Humboldt accomplished the ascent of the Cofre, 1300 feet
higher than the peak of Teneriffe, obtaining from its summit, an
extensive and varied view, embracing the Puebla plain and the
eastern slopes of the Mexican Cordilleras, clothed with thick forests
of "liquidambar", tree-ferns and sensitive plants. The travellers
were able to make out the port of Vera Cruz, the castle of San Juan
d'Ulloa and the sea-shore.

This mountain owes its name of Cofre to a naked rock of pyra-
midal form which rises like a tower from its summit at a height of
500 feet.

After this last trip Humboldt went down to Vera Cruz, and
having fortunately escaped the yellow fever then decimating the
population, he set sail for Cuba, where he had left the greater part
of his collection, going thence to Philadelphia. There he remained
a few weeks to make a cursory study of the political constitution of
the United States, returning to Europe in August, 1804.

The results of Humboldt's travels were such, that he may be
justly called the discoverer of Equinoctial America, which before
his time had been explored without becoming really known,
while many of its innumerable riches were absolutely ignored. It
must be fully acknowledged that no traveller ever before did so
much as Humboldt for physical geography and its kindred sciences. He was the very ideal of a traveller, and the world is
indebted to him for important generalizations concerning magnetism and climate; whose results are plainly seen in the

isothermal lines of modern maps. The writings of Humboldt mark an era in the science of geography, and have led to many further researches.

### END OF THE GREAT NAVIGATORS OF THE EIGHTEENTH CENTURY.

ML                                    5/02